The Economics of Small Island Tourism

THE FONDAZIONE ENI ENRICO MATTEI (FEEM) SERIES ON ECONOMICS, THE ENVIRONMENT AND SUSTAINABLE DEVELOPMENT

Series Editor: Carlo Carraro, *University of Venice, Venice and Research Director, Fondazione Eni Enrico Mattei (FEEM), Milan, Italy*

Editorial Board

The Fondazione Eni Enrico Mattei (FEEM) was established in 1989 as a non-profit, non-partisan research institution. It carries out high-profile research in the fields of economic development, energy and the environment, thanks to an international network of researchers who contribute to disseminate knowledge through seminars, congresses and publications. The main objective of the Fondazione is to foster interactions among academic, industrial and public policy spheres in an effort to find solutions to environmental problems. Over the years it has thus become a major European institution for research on sustainable development and the privileged interlocutor of a number of leading national and international policy institutions.

The Fondazione Eni Enrico Mattei (FEEM) Series on Economics, the Environment and Sustainable Development publishes leading-edge research findings providing an authoritative and up-to-date source of information in all aspects of sustainable development. FEEM research outputs are the results of a sound and acknowledged co-operation between its internal staff and a worldwide network of outstanding researchers and practitioners. A Scientific Advisory Board of distinguished academics ensures the quality of the publications.

This series serves as an outlet for the main results of FEEM's research programmes in the areas of economics, energy and the environment.

Titles in the series include:

Valuing Complex Natural Resource Systems
The Case of the Lagoon of Venice
Edited by Anna Alberini, Paolo Rosato and Margherita Turvani

Tourism and Sustainable Economic Development
Macroeconomic Models and Empirical Methods
Edited by Rinaldo Brau, Alessandro Lanza and Stefano Usai

The Economics of Small Island Tourism
International Demand and Country Risk Analysis
Riaz Shareef, Suhejla Hoti and Michael McAleer

The Economics of
Small Island Tourism

International Demand and Country Risk Analysis

Riaz Shareef
Edith Cowan University, Australia

Suhejla Hoti
University of Western Australia

Michael McAleer
University of Western Australia

THE FONDAZIONE ENI ENRICO MATTEI (FEEM) SERIES ON
ECONOMICS, THE ENVIRONMENT AND SUSTAINABLE
DEVELOPMENT

Edward Elgar
Cheltenham, UK • Northampton, MA, USA

Published by
Edward Elgar Publishing Limited
The Lypiatts
15 Lansdown Road
Cheltenham
Glos GL50 2JA
UK

Edward Elgar Publishing, Inc.
William Pratt House
9 Dewey Court
Northampton
Massachusetts 01060
USA

A catalogue record for this book
is available from the British Library

Library of Congress Control Number: 2008927960

ISBN 978 1 84720 649 7

Printed and bound in Great Britain by MPG Books Ltd, Bodmin, Cornwall

Contents

Foreword

Matteo Manera

This monograph analyses the conditional volatility in two data series, specifically the monthly international tourist arrivals to seven Small Island Tourism Economies (SITEs), namely Barbados, Cyprus, Dominica, Fiji, Maldives, Malta and Seychelles, and the monthly risk returns for six separate SITEs, namely the Bahamas, Cyprus, Dominican Republic, Haiti, Jamaica, and Malta. These two series exhibit distinct seasonal patterns and positive trends. Moreover, the conditional volatilities have increased rapidly for extended periods, and stabilised thereafter. Most importantly, there have been increasing variations in monthly international tourist arrivals and country risk returns in SITEs for extended periods, with subsequently dampened variations. Such fluctuating variations over time are interpreted as the conditional volatility in tourist arrivals and risk returns, respectively, and can be modelled using modern financial econometric time series techniques.

The authors have identified several reasons why it is crucial to model and forecast the uncertainty or volatility in international tourist arrivals. First, governments as well as tour operators need to examine the underlying uncertainty that is intrinsic to the total numbers, as well as in the growth rate, of monthly international tourist arrivals, and country risk ratings and risk returns. Second, in the literature it is widely believed that the forecast confidence intervals are time varying. Therefore, more accurate confidence intervals can be obtained by modelling the conditional variance of the errors. Finally, if the heteroscedasticity in the errors is examined carefully and is dealt with accurately, more efficient estimators for the parameters in the conditional mean can be obtained.

Fluctuating variations, or conditional volatility, in international monthly tourist arrivals and country risk returns are typically associated with unanticipated events. There are time-varying effects related to SITEs, such as natural disasters, ethnic conflicts, crime, the threat of terrorism and business cycles in tourist source countries, among many others, which cause variations in monthly international tourist arrivals and country risk returns. Owing to the nature of these events, recovery from variations in monthly international tourist arrivals and risk returns from unanticipated events may take longer for some countries than for others. These time-varying effects may not necessarily exist within SITEs, but may be intrinsic to the tourist source countries as well as other external factors, such as oil prices which affect risk returns.

This monograph shows how the generalised autoregressive conditional heteroskedasticity (GARCH) model can be used to measure the conditional volatility in monthly international tourist arrivals and country risk returns to seven SITEs. It is, for example, possible to measure the extent to which the 1991 Gulf War influenced variations in monthly international tourist arrivals and risk returns in Cyprus, and to what extent the *coups d'état* of 1987 and 2000 affected subsequent monthly international tourist arrivals to Fiji.

An awareness of the conditional volatility inherent in monthly international tourist arrivals, risk returns and techniques for modelling such volatility are vital for a critical analysis of SITEs, which depend heavily on earnings from tourism for their macroeconomic stability. The information that can be ascertained from these models about the volatility in monthly international tourist arrivals and risk returns is crucial for policy-makers, as such information would enable them to instigate policies regarding income, bilateral exchange rates, employment, government revenue, and so forth. Such information is also crucial for decision makers in the private sector, as it would enable them to alter their operations according to fluctuations in volatility.

Chapter 2 evaluates the common characteristics which impinge on SITEs and the implications of sustainable economic prosperity. These economies are relatively small in size and have small populations. They are all islands surrounded by very delicate ecosystems, and have an overwhelming reliance on international tourism for economic development. In analysing the common attributes of these economies, the main attributes which form the acronym SITE are examined in detail. Moreover, their geographical location, economic features, social indicators, political attributes, vulnerability and numerous other important characteristics are analysed in view of their implications for the economic well-being of these isolated locations.

In Chapter 4 the main economic activities and their prominence in the economic well-being of SITEs are examined. Based on the available data, the compositions of international tourists who visit six of these SITEs are analysed. The principal tourist source countries are from the G7 and the trends in tourism earnings in SITEs coincide with the economic cycles of these tourism source countries. Additionally, new and emerging source countries appear as globalisation and democratisation continue at current rates. The break-up of the former Soviet Union created new and relatively wealthy economies, which have also become new tourism sources to some SITEs.

The GARCH model is well established in the financial economics and econometrics literature. After the initial development by Engle (1982), extensive theoretical developments regarding the structural and statistical properties of the model have evolved (for derivations of the regularity conditions and asymptotic properties of a wide variety of univariate and multivariate GARCH models see, for example, Ling and McAleer (2002a, b; 2003a, b) and McAleer (2005)). Wide-ranging applications of GARCH models include economic and financial time series data, such as share prices and returns, stock market indexes and returns, and intellectual property (especially patents), among others. Such widespread analysis has led to the GARCH model being at the forefront of estimating volatility in economic and financial time series.

This monograph introduces the concept of conditional volatility and uses the GARCH model to analyse monthly international tourist arrivals and country risk returns in SITEs. Moreover, GARCH is applied to model monthly international tourist arrivals and risk returns in SITEs, which rely overwhelmingly on tourism as a primary source of export revenue. Such research would be expected to make a significant contribution to the existing tourism research literature, as tourism research on the volatility of monthly international tourist arrivals would appear to be very limited.

Chapter 3 reviews 53 published empirical studies on tourism demand analysis between 1989 and 2003. The purpose of this survey is to analyse the empirical literature on tourism demand pertaining to small island tourism economies, of which there have only been ten such published papers. As a result, the aim of the chapter is also to introduce recent developments in the empirical literature on international tourism demand and to evaluate the significance of the modelling process in leading journals in tourism, applied economics and forecasting, since 1995. There is evidence from this review that there is a dearth of applications of conditional volatility models in tourism research.

The GARCH model is appealing because both the conditional mean, which is used to capture the trends and growth rates in international tourism arrivals, and the conditional variance, which is used to capture deviations from the mean monthly international tourist arrivals, can be estimated simultaneously. Consequently, the parameter estimates of both the conditional mean and the conditional variance can be obtained jointly for purposes of statistical inference.

In Chapter 5, an extensive review of the theoretical developments and structural properties in the GARCH literature, and the implications of constant conditional correlations of the standardised shocks of the conditional variance for tourism planning and promotion, are addressed.

In Chapter 6 the uncertainty in monthly international tourist arrivals from the eight major tourist source countries to the Maldives is modelled. Maldives is probably the only SITE which relies entirely on tourism for the economic well-being of the nation. Tourism accounts for a substantial proportion of foreign exchange earnings, which enables importation of consumer as well as capital goods for economic development. Moreover, tourism provides a significant share of government revenue, and therefore is a key determinant of development expenditure. Tourism also provides employment for a considerable proportion of the workforce in SITEs where there is abundant low-skilled labour. Risk ratings and risk returns of six SITEs, namely the Bahamas, Cyprus, Dominican Republic, Haiti, Jamaica and Malta, are considered in Chapter 7, these being the only SITEs for which monthly International Country Risk Guide (ICRG) risk ratings and risk returns are available.

The main contributions of this monograph are as follows. First, the importance of conditional volatility in monthly international tourist arrivals and country risk returns is examined and modelled, and the macroeconomic implications for SITEs are appraised. The main reason for this examination is because, if heteroscedasticity exists in the data generating process, there are numerous ramifications for tourism and country risk analysis. If heteroscedasticity exists, then it should be explicitly accommodated in order to address a variety of issues, such as uncertainty surrounding tourist arrivals and country risk ratings. Second, the conditional volatilities are estimated, and an economic interpretation from the estimated results is provided. In achieving these two objectives, the monograph presents an extensive assessment of the important characteristics and the impact of tourism in small island economies in relation to their gross domestic product, balance of payments, employment, and foreign direct investment, among other factors. The monograph also critically examines the literature on empirical tourism demand and country risk analysis, and introduces and applies conditional volatility models to tourism demand and country risk.

An important aspect to be examined empirically is the effects of positive and negative shocks in monthly international tourism arrivals and risk returns, which may have different effects on the volatility in these two data generating processes. For this reason, two popular univariate models of conditional volatility, namely the Generalised Autoregressive Conditional Heteroscedasticity (GARCH) model of Engle (1982) and Bollerslev (1986), and the asymmetric GJR model of Glosten, Jagannathan and Runkle (1992), are estimated and compared.

In Chapter 8, the important issues that are addressed in this monograph and the major findings of this research are summarised. The monograph concludes with a discussion of some issues that are likely to be useful for further research.

REFERENCES

Bollerslev, T. (1986), 'Generalised autoregressive conditional heteroscedasticity', *Journal of Econometrics*, **31**, 307–327.

Engle, R.F. (1982), 'Autoregressive conditional heteroscedasticity with estimates of the variance of United Kingdom inflation', *Econometrica*, **50**, 987–1007.

Glosten, L., R. Jagannathan and D. Runkle (1992), 'On the relation between the expected value and volatility of nominal excess return on stocks', *Journal of Finance*, **46**, 1779–801.

Ling, S. and M. McAleer (2002a), 'Necessary and sufficient moment conditions for the GARCH(r,s) and asymmetric power GARCH(r,s) models', *Econometric Theory*, **18**, 722–9.

Ling, S. and M. McAleer (2002b), 'Stationarity and the existence of moments of a family of GARCH processes', *Journal of Econometrics*, **106**, 109–17.

Ling, S. and M. McAleer (2003a), 'Asymptotic theory for a vector ARMA-GARCH model', *Econometric Theory*, **19**, 278–308.

Ling, S. and M. McAleer (2003b), 'On adaptive estimation in non-stationary ARMA models with GARCH errors', *Annals of Statistics*, **31**, 642–74.

McAleer, M. (2005), 'Automated inference and learning in modeling financial volatility', *Econometric Theory*, **21**(1), 232–61.

Acknowledgements

In preparing this monograph, we have greatly benefited from the generous comments and constructive suggestions of Felix Chan, Carmelo León, Christine Lim, Andreu Sansó and Les Oxley. We would also like to thank participants at a number of seminars and conferences for helpful comments and suggestions.

We are grateful to the World Tourism Organization and Ministry of Tourism of Maldives for providing international tourist arrivals data.

The first author wishes to acknowledge the financial support of Mr Mohamed Umar Maniku, M. Rukkara, Malé 20-06, Republic of Maldives, while the second and third authors are thankful for the financial support of the Australian Research Council.

Riaz Shareef
Suhejla Hoti
Michael McAleer

List of Abbreviations

ABC/OAG	Accredited Business Communicator/Official Airline Guide
ACFs	Autocorrelation Coefficients
ADF	Augmented Dickey-Fuller
ADLM	Autoregressive Distributed Lag Model
AGOA	Africa Growth and Opportunity Act
AIC	Akaike Information Criterion
AIDS	Acquired Immunodeficiency Syndrome
AIDS	Almost Ideal Demand System
ARCH	Autoregressive Conditional Heteroscedasticity
ARIMA	Autoregressive Integrated Moving Average
ARMA	Autoregressive Moving Average
ARMA-AGARCH	ARMA-Asymmetric GARCH
ASEAN	Association of South East Asian Nations
BBC	British Broadcasting Corporation
BHHH	Berndt, Hall, Hall and Hausman
B-J	Box and Jenkins (1976)
CARICOM	Caribbean Community and Common Market
CBI	Caribbean Basin Initiative
CCC	Constant Conditional Correlation
CET	Common External Tariff
CRDW	Cointegrating Regression Durbin Watson
CUSUM	Cumulative Sum
DCC	Dynamic Conditional Correlation
DC	District of Columbia
DW	Durbin-Watson
ECCB	Eastern Caribbean Central Bank
ECCU	Eastern Caribbean Currency Union
ECM	Error Correction Model
ECONBASE	Economics Database
EconData DX	Economics Data Time Series Database Data Explorer
ECONLIT	Economics Literature Database
ECTEL	Eastern Caribbean Telecommunications
EFTA	European Free Trade Area

EU	European Union
FDI	Foreign Direct Investment
FEEM	Fondazione Eni Enrico Mattei
FNM	Free National Movement
G7	Group of Seven
GARCH	Generalised Autoregressive Conditional Heteroscedasticity
GDP	Gross Domestic Product
GJR	Glosten, Jagannathan and Runkle
GNP	Gross National Product
GSM	General Structural Model
HIV	Human Immunodeficiency Virus
ICRG	International Country Risk Guide
ICT	Information and Communications Technologies
IFS	International Financial Statistics
IMF	International Monetary Fund
ITRs	International Tourism Receipts
J-B	Jarque-Bera (1971)
LDC	Least Developed Country
LISREL	Linear Structural Relations
LM	Lagrange-Multiplier
M2	Broad Money
MABSE	Mean Absolute Sum of Squared Errors
MAD	Mean Absolute Deviation
MAPE	Mean Absolute Percentage Error
MES	Minimum Efficient Scale
NAFTA	North American Free Trade Association
ODA	Official Development Assistance
OECD	Organisation of Economic Cooperation and Development
OECS	Organization of Eastern Caribbean States
OLS	Ordinary Least Squares
PACFs	Partial Autocorrelation Coefficients
PP	Phillips-Perron
PPMCC	Pearson Product Moment Correlation Coefficient
QMLE	Quasi-Maximum Likelihood Estimators
RMSE	Root Mean Square Error
RMSPE	Root Mean Square Percentage Error
SBC	Schwarz's Bayesian Criterion
SIDS	Small Island Developing States
SITE	Small Island Tourism Economy
SNA	System of National Accounts

STMA	Seychelles Tourism Marketing Authority
STSMs	Structural Time Series Models
SURE	Seemingly Unrelated Regression Model
TPI	Tourism Price Index
UNDP	United Nations Development Programme
USD	United States Dollars
VAR	Vector Autoregressive
VAT	Value Added Tax
WDI	World Development Indicators
WTO	World Tourism Organisation

1. Introduction

Volatility in monthly international tourist arrivals is defined as the squared deviation from the mean monthly international tourist arrivals. Consequently, volatility is directly related to the (possibly time-varying) standard deviation, which is a common measure of risk in finance. The conditional volatility in two data series are analysed in the monograph, specifically monthly international tourist arrivals to seven Small Island Tourism Economies (SITEs), namely Barbados, Cyprus, Dominica, Fiji, Maldives, Malta and Seychelles, and monthly country risk returns for six separate SITEs, namely the Bahamas, Cyprus, Dominican Republic, Haiti, Jamaica, and Malta.

Monthly international tourist arrivals and country risk returns exhibit distinct seasonal patterns and positive trends. Moreover, they have increased rapidly for extended periods, and stabilised thereafter. Most importantly, there have been increasing variations in monthly international tourist arrivals and country risk returns in SITEs for extended periods, with subsequently dampened variations. Such fluctuating variations over time are interpreted as the conditional volatility in tourist arrivals and risk returns, respectively, and can be modelled using modern financial econometric time series techniques.

There are several reasons why we need to model and forecast the uncertainty or volatility in international tourist arrivals. First, governments as well as tour operators need to examine the underlying uncertainty that is intrinsic to the total numbers, as well as in the growth rate, of monthly international tourist arrivals, and country risk ratings and risk returns. Second, in the literature it is widely believed that the forecast confidence intervals are time varying. Therefore, more accurate confidence intervals can be obtained by modelling the conditional variance of the errors. Finally, if the heteroscedasticity in the errors is examined carefully and is dealt with accurately, more efficient estimators for the parameters in the conditional mean can be obtained.

This monograph models the conditional volatility of the logarithm of monthly international tourist arrivals and the growth rate of monthly international tourist arrivals in a univariate as well as multivariate framework for seven SITEs. The sample periods for these seven SITEs are as follows: Barbados, January 1973 to December 2002 (Barbados Tourism Authority); Cyprus, January 1976 to December 2002 (Cyprus Tourism Organization and

Statistics Service of Cyprus); Dominica, January 1990 to December 2001 (Central Statistical Office); Fiji, January 1968 to December 2002 (Fiji Islands Bureau of Statistics); Maldives, January 1986 to June 2003 (Ministry of Tourism); Malta, January 1968 to February 2004 (National Statistics Office) and Seychelles, January 1971 to May 2003 (Ministry of Information Technology and Communication). In the case of Cyprus, monthly tourist arrivals data were not available for 1995, so the mean monthly tourist arrivals for 1993, 1994, 1996 and 1997 were used to construct the data for 1995 in estimating the trends and volatilities in international tourist arrivals.

The monograph also models the conditional volatility of the numbers, logarithms, annual difference, and the log-difference of monthly international tourist arrivals to the Maldives from its eight major tourist source countries, namely Italy, Germany, UK, Japan, France, Switzerland, Austria and the Netherlands, from January 1994 to December 2003 (Ministry of Tourism). The monograph also models the conditional volatility of country risk returns (log-difference of the country risk ratings) for six SITEs. The monthly International Country Risk Guide (ICRG) data for the Bahamas and Cyprus are available from December 1984 to May 2002, Dominican Republic, Haiti and Jamaica from January 1984 to May 2002, and Malta from April 1986 to May 2002.

In this monograph, the GARCH family of models, particularly the symmetric GARCH(1,1) and asymmetric GJR(1,1) models to be explained below, in both the univariate and multivariate frameworks, are estimated to examine the features of conditional volatility in monthly international tourism arrivals in seven SITEs.

This monograph is about addressing the importance of conditional volatility (or uncertainty) in monthly international tourist arrivals and country risk indicators. Conditional volatility is examined and the macroeconomic implications for SITEs are appraised. There exists heteroscedasticty in monthly international tourist arrivals and country risk ratings and there are considerable ramifications for SITEs. Hence, heteroscedasticty is explicitly accommodated to address a variety of issues, such as uncertainty surrounding tourist arrivals and country risk ratings. Second, the conditional volatilities are estimated, and an economic interpretation from the estimated results is provided. In achieving these two objectives, the monograph presents an extensive assessment of the important characteristics and the impact of tourism in small island economies in relation to their gross domestic product, balance of payments, employment, and foreign direct investment, among other factors. An important feature of the monograph is that it is an entirely new area of research on Small Island Tourism Economies.

2. Salient Features of Small Island Tourism Economies[1]

2.1 INTRODUCTION

Empirical analysis in tourism demand has typically been based on the consumer theory of demand, one of the foundations of microeconomics. Supply and demand of international tourism as a good or service can be viewed as international trade, and the consumption of international tourism requires the crossing of borders. However, application of international trade theory to analyse international tourism demand may not be feasible because most international trade theories are based on relative factor endowments.

In international tourism demand analysis, it is not possible to compute factor endowments. However, it is possible to measure the worth of a tourist attraction by counting the number of people who visit, or money spent while visiting, an attraction. The theoretical elegance is obscured when the worth of a tourist attraction in a cross sectional setting is to be analysed. Hence, it is conceivable to place tourist attractions or destinations with similar attributes in an analytical framework. Small Island Tourism Economies (SITEs) are an example of a tourist destination.

This chapter evaluates the common characteristics which impinge on SITEs and the implications of sustainable economic prosperity. These economies are relatively small in size and have small populations. They are all islands surrounded by very delicate ecosystems, and have an overwhelming reliance on international tourism for economic development. In analysing the common attributes of these economies, the main attributes which form the acronym SITE are examined in detail. Moreover, their geographical location, economic features, social indicators, political attributes, vulnerability and numerous other important characteristics are analysed in view of their implications for the economic well-being of these isolated locations.

In Section 2.2, the principal attributes of SITEs, namely their (relatively) small size, island nature, and reliance on tourism receipts, are examined. This analysis will be followed by examining the implications of being small in Section 2.3. Such implications are the geographical features, fragility of the environment, high volatility of real GDP growth, the narrow productive base, international trade, lack of access to international capital markets, poverty prevalence, institutional set-up, economic vulnerability, and the distinct political characteristics of SITEs. Finally, in Section 2.4 conclusions are drawn and some new directions for further research are presented.

2.2   SMALL ISLAND TOURISM ECONOMIES

In the existing literature on Small States, Small Island States, and Small Island Developing States (SIDS), several attempts have been made to conceptualise the size of an economy. However, there has been little agreement as to the definition of what constitutes a small economy. While taking the extant literature into account, to achieve the aims and objectives of this research, it is necessary to appreciate the notion of size. The aim of this section is to formulate a coherent and economically meaningful explanation of the size of an economy, and to examine the implications of being a SITE. In order to draw policy prescriptions, it is important to formulate a meaningful definition of size.

A SITE is best defined by examining its three main properties, which are its (relatively) small size, its nature as an island and its reliance on tourism receipts. These three aspects of SITEs will now be discussed.

2.3   SMALL SIZE

The world economy is highly integrated and every economy tries to influence the competitiveness of their exports through contraction and expansion of international trade. At the same time, they also try to attract imports at the most competitive prices. These two procedures are simultaneously implemented in the management of the macroeconomy, affecting the trade account and the balance of payments. Most economies do not seem to accomplish this unilaterally. Some countries achieve this by being members of an economic cooperation group, such as the European Union, NAFTA, and ASEAN. In reality, all developing countries are price takers, and the small economies are a small subset of developing economies. Small economies do not have any control over the prices of their imports and exports. In fact, they are price takers because their volume of trade is much smaller with respect to their markets, as well as with other trading partners. In this respect, analysing the size of an economy can be difficult. Armstrong and Read (2000) argue that the above explanation tends to focus on the inclusion of larger countries and the exclusion of smaller economies. For example, they argue that countries like Australia and Canada are regarded as small in spite of their relative geographic largeness.

Size is a relative rather than an absolute concept. In the literature on small economies, size deals with quantifiable variables, where population, GDP, and land area are most widely used. Streeten (1993) states that setting criteria does not always lead to the same result, but we know a small economy when we see it, and the simplest measure of size is population. Furthermore, according to Streeten (1993), Hong Kong exports more manufactured products than India, and has a large enough impact on clothing markets in advanced countries to be subjected to import controls. Hong Kong would, therefore, be considered as large and India as small. India has an estimated population of more than one billion, around four times larger than the USA, but has a national income the size of The Netherlands, which has a population of 16 million.

The level of population has been employed as the sole determinant of an economy's size. Armstrong and Read (2000) claim that population figures are often used because they are convenient and provide information about the size of the domestic market and the local labour force. The most well-known example in conceptualising the size of economy is in Kuznets (1960), where a country with a population of 10 million or less is regarded as small. According to the World Bank's World Development Indicators 2002, there are 130 world economies with populations of less than 10 million, so these can be regarded as small. The British Commonwealth uses a threshold of 1.5 million. The British Commonwealth is an organisation formed by the former British colonies under the auspices of the United Kingdom of Great Britain and Northern Ireland to promote technical cooperation and advance economic and social development. Furthermore, in the literature on economic growth, it is well established that population has a strong relationship between land area and GDP. As such, implementing population as a criterion to determine the size of an economy can possibly assist in explaining the economic, social and political deficiencies that are intrinsic to SITEs.

In the literature on small economies, it is difficult to substantiate why a particular population ceiling is used, and there have been variations in the level of thresholds, which also seem to be chosen arbitrarily. In determining the choice of countries for this monograph, neither a population nor a GDP threshold is used. SITEs such as the Dominican Republic, Haiti, Jamaica, and Mauritius have populations above one million and yet share numerous features of being small. Undesirable outcomes are inevitable when a population, GDP or a land-area threshold is chosen because countries can overshoot it but still feature 'smallness'.

The SITEs chosen in this analysis are: Antigua and Barbuda, Bahamas, Barbados, Comoros, Cyprus, Dominica, Dominican Republic, Fiji, Grenada,

Haiti, Jamaica, Maldives, Malta, Mauritius, Samoa, Seychelles, St Kitts and Nevis, St Lucia, St Vincent and the Grenadines, and Vanuatu. Where otherwise specified, the data presented here are taken from the World Development Indicators (WDI) 2002 CD-ROM, published by the World Bank. In making this choice, a certain population or a GDP threshold has not been used because this would not be convenient. The choice is based on the availability of data, the island nature of the economies, and with tourism earnings being 15 per cent or higher as a percentage of total export earnings. In the chosen SITEs, Dominican Republic, Haiti, Jamaica and Mauritius have populations above one million, yet share numerous features of being small. It is important to note that unfavourable results are inevitable if a single economic criterion, such as population, GDP or land area, is used. There is a variety of countries that overshoot a chosen benchmark level of a selected criterion, but still feature 'smallness'.

The per capita GDP (in constant 1995 US Dollars) in these countries also ranges widely. The World Bank definition of a low income country is where the per capita GDP is USD765 or less, lower-middle income country is with a per capita GDP of between USD756 to USD2995, upper-middle income country is with a per capita GDP of between USD2996 to 9265 and a higher income country has per capita GDP above USD9266. There are two low income SITEs, namely Comoros and Haiti, and three high income SITEs, which are The Bahamas, Cyprus and Malta. The remaining countries are either low or high middle income SITEs. The SITEs are in four geographic regions of the world, with eleven in the Caribbean Sea, three in the Pacific Ocean, four in the Indian Ocean and two in the Mediterranean Sea.

For a preliminary assessment of 'smallness' without implementing a threshold, the populations of the 20 SITEs are examined with particular reference to the end of the sample period, which is 2000 (see Table 2.1). The populations of the 20 SITEs show that they are home to more than 24 million people, consisting of less than 1 per cent of the total population of all the developing countries combined. They range in size from micro-economies such as St Kitts and Nevis with only 41 000 people, to mini-economies like Antigua and Barbuda, Dominica, Grenada, and Seychelles, with populations of between 50 000 and 100 000. Furthermore, The Bahamas, Barbados, Maldives, Malta, Samoa, St Lucia, St Vincent and the Grenadines, and Vanuatu have populations of between 100 000 and 500 000. This is the population range into which most SITEs fall. Cyprus and Fiji have populations of between 500 000 and one million. The remaining four SITEs are Dominican Republic, Haiti, Jamaica and Mauritius, each with populations of more than one million.

In a ground-breaking contribution to the subject of small states, Armstrong and Read (1995) best explain the size of an economy by using the concept of sub-optimality in a macroeconomic framework. The principle behind the concept is the incorporation of the interaction between production and trade, while a necessary condition of minimum efficient scale (MES) is upheld for the economy. The MES is the level of output of goods and services at which production is feasible. In small economies particularly, the level of GDP is determined by the MES, the shape of the average cost curve below the MES, and transport costs. This approach to conceptualise size is appropriate and provides a more precise understanding of the implications of being small.

Table 2.1   Common Measures of Size

SITE	Mean 1980–2000		2000		WDI Income Group	Area (Km^2)
	Pop.*	GDP**	Pop.	GDP		
Antigua	0.0639	6 637	0.0680	9 138	Up-Mid	440
Bahamas	0.2553	13 064	0.3030	13 928	High	10 010
Barbados	0.2584	7 051	0.2670	8 282	Up-Mid	430
Comoros	0.4372	528	0.5580	436	Low	2 230
Cyprus	0.6869	9 974	0.7570	14 063	High	9 240
Dominica^a	0.0730	3 371	0.0730	3 371	Up-Mid	750
Dom. Rep.	7.0580	1 507	8.3730	2 062	Low-Mid	48 380
Fiji	0.7317	2 346	0.8119	2 395	Low-Mid	18 270
Grenada	0.0928	2 639	0.0980	3 832	Up-Mid	340
Haiti	6.5378	463	7.9590	367	Low	27 560
Jamaica	2.4001	1 720	2.6330	1 785	Low-Mid	10 830
Maldives	0.2142	1 318	0.2760	1 933	Low-Mid	300
Malta	0.3661	7 035	0.3900	10 223	High	320
Mauritius	1.0689	2 943	1.1861	4 429	Up-Mid	2 030
Samoa	0.1612	1 213	0.1700	1 440	Low-Mid	2 830
Seychelles	0.0714	5 925	0.0812	7 000	Up-Mid	450
St Kitts	0.0423	4 489	0.0410	6 830	Up-Mid	360
St Lucia	0.1349	3 086	0.1560	3 968	Up-Mid	610
St Vincent	0.1067	2 057	0.1150	2 771	Low-Mid	390
Vanuatu	0.1504	1 245	0.1970	1 177	Low-Mid	12 190

Notes:
* For Dominica, data on population are only available for 2000.
** Population is denoted as Pop. (in millions).
^{a} GDP refers to GDP per capita.

Source: World Development Indicators (WDI) of World Bank (2002).

2.4   ISLAND ECONOMIES

Dommen (1980, p. 932) argued that 'not all free-standing land masses are islands' and 'an island is not a piece of land completely surrounded by water'. This had been established through comparing and matching economic, social and political indicators, and not due to the geological nature of land formations of the countries chosen. However, the SITEs examined here are sovereign island economies because of their geological nature. They are all archipelagic, have risen from the ocean through volcanic activity, and lie along the weaker parts of the earth's crust. Tourists typically reach these countries by air, while freight is usually carried by sea.

These island economies have the world's most delicate ecosystems and are consistently threatened by natural disasters and the effects of environmental damage. According to Briguglio (1995), all islands are insular but are not situated in remote areas of the globe. Generally, insularity and remoteness lead to transport and communications problems. In this regard, Armstrong and Read (2002, p. 438) reiterate that 'both internal and external communication and trade may be very costly and have implications for their internal political and social cohesiveness as well as competitiveness'. Most of these SITEs are in regions frequently affected by unfavourable climatic conditions, which typically affect the entire population and economy.

2.5   RELIANCE ON TOURISM

Tourism plays a dominant role in the economic well-being of SITEs, with tourism earnings accounting for a significant proportion of the value added in their national product. The fundamental aim of tourism development in SITEs is to increase foreign exchange earnings to finance imports. As seen in Figure 2.1, these SITEs have an overwhelming reliance on tourism, which accounts for the highest proportion in export earnings. On average, earnings from tourism accounts for 39 per cent of total export earnings among the 20 SITEs, a considerably large proportion in comparison to other countries. In economic planning, tourism has a predominant emphasis in SITEs where the climate is well suited for tourism development and the islands are strategically located.

A large proportion of tourism earnings is almost instantaneously spent to finance imports to sustain the tourism industry. As indicated in Commonwealth Secretariat/World Bank Joint Task Force on Small States (2000), tourism-related imports are comprised mostly of non-indigenous goods. Meat and dairy products are heavily imported in the Caribbean, while imports of construction material for building tourism-related facilities are more prominent in the Maldives. Labour is also imported for employment in

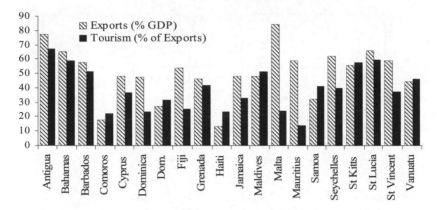

Source: World Development Indicators (WDI) of World Bank (2002).

Figure 2.1   Export Earnings as a Percentage of GDP and International Tourism Receipts (ITRs) as a Percentage of Export Earnings in 20 SITEs

tourism, resulting in substantial foreign exchange outflows. Figure 2.2 shows that across many of the 20 SITEs, International Tourism Receipts (ITRs) have been the principal engine of sustainable economic growth.

In SITEs, tourism facilities are mostly enclave developments, and the effects of these facilities on the domestic economy are sometimes limited. Tourism requires careful planning in order to maintain sustainability and to limit environmental damage. While tourism has contributed to economic development in many SITEs, it needs to be managed responsibly in order to secure the country's long-term sustainability.

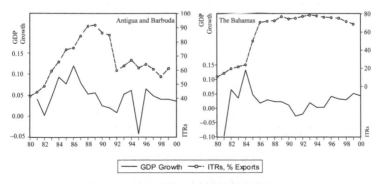

Source: World Development Indicators (WDI) of World Bank (2002).

Figure 2.2   International Tourism Receipts (ITRs) and Real GDP Growth in SITEs

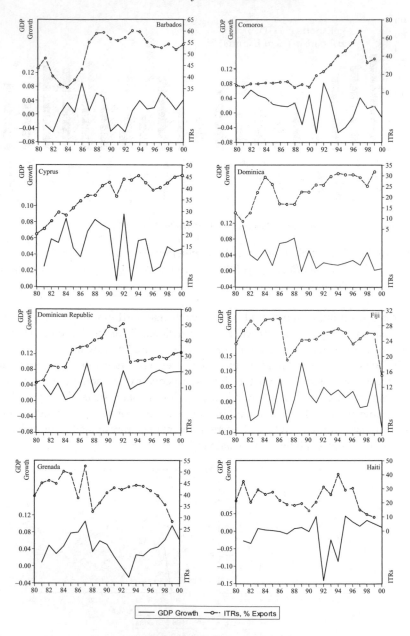

Source: World Development Indicators (WDI) of World Bank (2002).

Figure 2.2   International Tourism Receipts (ITRs) and Real GDP Growth in SITEs (continued)

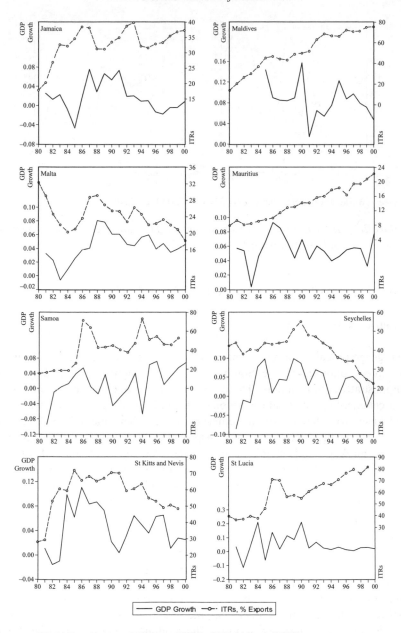

Source: World Development Indicators (WDI) of World Bank (2002).

*Figure 2.2   International Tourism Receipts (ITRs) and Real GDP Growth in
SITEs (continued)*

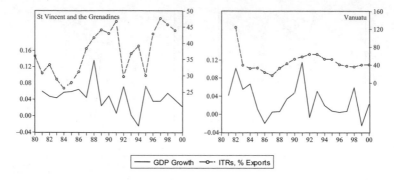

Source: World Development Indicators (WDI) of World Bank (2002).

Figure 2.2   International Tourism Receipts (ITRs) and Real GDP Growth in SITEs (continued)

2.6   THE IMPLICATIONS OF BEING A SITE

Geographical Features

The geographical locations of many SITEs (see Table 2.2), and particularly the three countries in the South Pacific, have significant economic and administrative implications. These countries are quite far from major trade and commerce centres and it becomes difficult to offset any disadvantages that arise from having small domestic markets. The main impediment to commerce is the higher cost of transportation between the SITEs to their export markets and suppliers of inputs. As most of the SITEs are archipelagos in the Pacific and Indian oceans and the Caribbean Sea, it is virtually impossible to successfully institute a reliable small domestic market. The ocean between the outer atolls makes the settlements difficult to navigate, and SITEs do not have efficient and reliable transport network to support a robust commercial distribution network.

The volume of cargo to import into SITEs is relatively small, and SITEs tend to pay higher unit costs of transportation because of the limited quantities required. The higher cost of transportation between SITEs and their overseas markets makes exports uncompetitive and imports more expensive. Hence, there is a considerable loss in export earnings as well as a loss in domestic consumer surplus. The Commonwealth Secretariat/World Bank (2000) study gives an indicator of transport costs determined by using a ratio of insurance and freight debits to merchandise imports. It has been demonstrated that SITEs are heavily represented among countries facing the

Table 2.2　Geographical Location, Climate and Natural Resources in SITEs

SITE	Location	Climate	Natural resources
1. Antigua and Barbuda	In the Caribbean, islands between the Caribbean Sea and the North Atlantic Ocean, east-southeast of Puerto Rico.	Tropical marine; little seasonal temperature variation.	Negligible; pleasant climate fosters tourism.
2. The Bahamas	Caribbean, chain of islands in the North Atlantic Ocean, southeast of Florida.	Tropical marine; moderated by warm waters of Gulf Stream.	Salt, aragonite, timber, arable land and pleasant climate fosters tourism.
3. Barbados	Caribbean, island between the Caribbean Sea and the North Atlantic Ocean, northeast of Venezuela.	Tropical; rainy season (June to October).	Petroleum, fish, natural gas and pleasant climate fosters tourism.
4. Comoros	Southern Africa, group of islands in the Mozambique Channel, about two-thirds of the way between northern Madagascar and northern Mozambique.	Tropical marine; rainy season (November to May).	Negligible; pleasant climate fosters tourism.
5. Cyprus	Middle East, island in the Mediterranean Sea, south of Turkey.	Temperate, Mediterranean with hot, dry summers and cool winters.	Copper, pyrites, asbestos, gypsum, timber, salt, marble, clay earth pigment and pleasant climate fosters tourism.
6. Dominica	Caribbean, island between the Caribbean Sea and the North Atlantic Ocean, about half-way from Puerto Rico to Trinidad and Tobago.	Tropical; moderated by northeast trade winds; heavy rainfall.	Timber, hydropower, arable land and pleasant climate fosters tourism.
7. Dominican Republic	Caribbean, eastern two-thirds of the island of Hispaniola, between the Caribbean Sea and the North Atlantic Ocean, east of Haiti.	Tropical maritime; little seasonal temperature variation; seasonal variation in rainfall.	Nickel, bauxite, gold, silver and pleasant climate fosters tourism.
8. Fiji	Oceania, island group in the South Pacific Ocean, about two-thirds from Hawaii to New Zealand.	Tropical marine; only slight seasonal temperature variation.	Timber, fish, gold, copper, offshore oil potential, hydropower and pleasant climate fosters tourism.
9. Grenada	Caribbean, island between the Caribbean Sea and Atlantic Ocean, north of Trinidad and Tobago.	Tropical; tempered by northeast trade winds.	Timber, tropical fruit, deepwater harbours and pleasant climate fosters tourism.

Table 2.2   Geographical Location, Climate and Natural Resources in SITEs (continued)

SITE	Location	Climate	Natural resources
10. Haiti	Caribbean, western one-third of the island of Hispaniola, between the Caribbean Sea and the North Atlantic Ocean, west of the Dominican Republic.	Tropical; semi-arid where mountains in east cut off trade winds.	Bauxite, copper, calcium carbonate, gold, marble, hydropower and pleasant climate fosters tourism.
11. Jamaica	Caribbean, island in the Caribbean Sea, south of Cuba	Tropical; hot, humid; temperate interior.	Bauxite, gypsum, limestone and pleasant climate fosters tourism.
12. Maldives	Southern Asia, group of atolls in the Indian Ocean, south-southwest of India.	Tropical; hot, humid; dry, northeast monsoon (November to March); rainy, southwest monsoon (June to August).	Fish and pleasant climate fosters tourism.
13. Malta	Southern Europe, islands in the Mediterranean Sea, south of Sicily (Italy).	Mediterranean with mild, rainy winters and hot, dry summers.	Limestone, salt, arable land and pleasant climate fosters tourism.
14. Mauritius	Southern Africa, island in the Indian Ocean, east of Madagascar.	Tropical, modified by southeast trade winds; warm, dry winter (May to November); hot, wet, humid summer (November to May).	Arable land, fish and pleasant climate fosters tourism.
15. Samoa	Oceania, group of islands in the South Pacific Ocean, about half-way from Hawaii to New Zealand.	Tropical; rainy season (October to March), dry season (May to October).	Hardwood forests, fish, hydropower and pleasant climate fosters tourism.
16. Seychelles	Eastern Africa, group of islands in the Indian Ocean, northeast of Madagascar.	Tropical marine; humid; cooler season during southeast monsoon (late May to September); warmer season during northwest monsoon (March to May).	Fish, copra, cinnamon trees and pleasant climate fosters tourism.
17. St Kitts and Nevis	Caribbean, islands in the Caribbean Sea, about one-third from Puerto Rico to Trinidad and Tobago.	Tropical tempered by constant sea breezes; little seasonal temperature variation; rainy season (May to November).	Arable land and pleasant climate fosters tourism.

Table 2.2   Geographical Location, Climate and Natural Resources in SITEs (continued)

SITE	Location	Climate	Natural resources
18. St Lucia	Caribbean, island between the Caribbean Sea and North Atlantic Ocean, north of Trinidad and Tobago.	Tropical, moderated by northeast trade winds; dry season from January to April, rainy season from May to August.	Forests, sandy beaches, minerals (pumice), mineral springs, geothermal potential and pleasant climate fosters tourism.
19. St Vincent and the Grenadines	Caribbean, islands in the Caribbean Sea, north of Trinidad and Tobago.	Tropical; little seasonal temperature variation; rainy season (May to November).	Hydropower, cropland and pleasant climate fosters tourism.
20. Vanuatu	Oceania, group of islands in the South Pacific Ocean, about three-quarters of the way from Hawaii to Australia.	Tropical; moderated by southeast trade winds.	Manganese, hardwood forests, fish and pleasant climate fosters tourism.

Source: CIA World Fact Book (2002).

highest costs. The ratios given for the respective countries are as follows: Kiribati 26, Solomon Islands 20, Trinidad and Tobago 18, and Seychelles 18. These numbers are significantly higher than the median value of 14 per cent for all developing countries combined. The economies of scale achieved through large-scale production disappear due to the higher transport costs. As a result, there is no incentive to improve efficiency or promote innovative methods of production.

Fragility of the Environment

Most of the SITEs are situated in regions where there is a high occurrence of cyclones, floods, hurricanes, drought, volcanic activity and other natural calamities. The persistent incidence of such natural disasters results in severe economic disruption through infrastructure damage, cessation of production and export losses. Owing to the catastrophic nature of many of these disruptions, extensive income and development opportunities are regularly forgone, while the entire physical environment, population and economy are considerably affected. The very existence of these small islands is threatened. In 2000, the United Nations Disaster Relief Organization estimated that the impact on the 25 most disaster-prone countries entailed costs of between 28 per cent and 1200 per cent of their annual GDP. In Vanuatu, a series of cyclones in 1989 devastated the entire economy to the extent of twice the size of their GDP.

SITEs can also suffer from other kinds of disasters experienced by larger developing countries. Some SITEs have a high incidence of HIV/AIDS, particularly in Haiti. The population estimates for Haiti given in Table 2.1 explicitly accommodate the effects of excess mortality due to AIDS, which has resulted in lower life expectancy, higher infant mortality and death rates, lower population and growth rates, and changes in the distribution of population by age and sex than would otherwise be expected. Such disasters could well have a disproportionate impact in small communities with already limited capacity.

The worldwide development that has occurred over the second half of the 20th century has posed major global environmental concerns for SITEs. This is due to the fragility of some ecosystems, especially when they are surrounded by delicate coral reefs, a prominent feature of SITEs. Over the last 20 years, changes in climatic conditions around the world suggest that that there is an increase in the probability and severity of natural calamities. As a consequence of the increase in the emissions of greenhouse gases, it has been suggested that there will be widespread global warming, and the subsequent rise in sea levels would increase by around one metre over the next 100 years. This would result in the complete extinction of SITEs like the Maldives. Additionally, other SITEs would experience widespread soil erosion, which could result in the disappearance of some of the world's most popular beaches.

High Volatility of Real GDP Growth

The square of the deviation from the mean of a GDP growth rate is known as the volatility of GDP growth. In SITEs, the volatility of the GDP growth rate tends to be very high. The real GDP growth rate and its volatility are given in Figure 2.3. In a study by the Commonwealth Secretariat (2000), the standard deviation of annual real per capita GDP growth is about 25 per cent higher in small states compared with larger developing countries.

In this monograph, the number of observations varies among SITEs according to the availability of data. Eleven SITEs have data from 1977–2000, five SITEs have data from 1978–2000, and the four remaining SITEs have data from 1979–2000, 1980–2000, 1981–2000 and 1985–2000. The lowest mean volatility of real GDP growth rate recorded was 8.1 for Malta, while the highest mean volatility was for 56.9 for St Lucia. The highest individual volatility figure recorded was 555.1 for Dominica.

According to the Commonwealth Secretariat/World Bank (2000), the high volatility in the GDP growth rate recorded among SITEs is due to three main

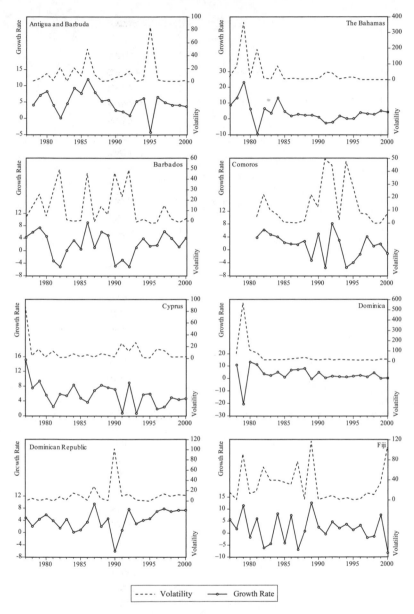

Source: World Development Indicators (WDI) of World Bank (2002).

Figure 2.3 Mean and Volatility of Real GDP Growth Rates

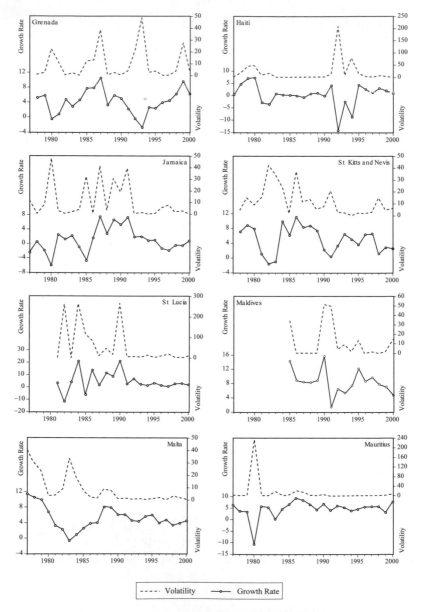

Source: World Development Indicators (WDI) of World Bank (2002).

Figure 2.3   Mean and Volatility of Real GDP Growth Rates (continued)

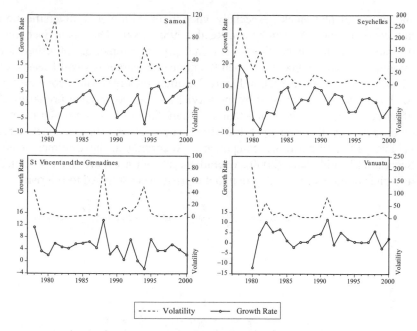

Source: World Development Indicators (WDI) of World Bank (2002).

Figure 2.3 Mean and Volatility of Real GDP Growth Rates (continued)

reasons. SITEs are very open to the influence of the rest-of-the-world markets due to the high dependability of imports and exports, and are more susceptible to changes in the rest-of-the-world market conditions. Moreover, SITEs have a small range of uncompetitive exports and limited options to avoid losses. Finally, SITEs are prone to natural disasters, which affect every activity within the economy.

The prominence of these factors varies significantly among SITEs because, in poorer countries, specialisation in production and trade is highly prevalent. For example, the Maldives' sole economic activities are fisheries and tourism. In contrast, SITEs like Cyprus and Seychelles are both highly diversified economies with greater participation in international trade, which increases their hedging capacity towards any adverse shocks in world markets.

The Narrow Productive Base

The most prominent feature in SITEs is their limited production base and small domestic markets. Many of these SITEs are relatively undiversified in their production of exports, which makes them vulnerable to external economic and environmental shocks, especially when there is little or no diversification in their economies (Armstrong and Read, 1998a, 2000). There is no incentive or motivation for diversification of industry or promotion of efficiency through domestic competition when the domestic market is small because of its small population. As seen in Figure 2.4, the structures of the economies in SITEs are heavily dominated by the services sector comprising primarily of offshore financial services and tourism. Manufacturing is composed mainly of garments, with some light industries, such as assembly of machinery, vehicle parts and hardware components. According to the Commonwealth Secretariat/World Bank (2000), overall merchandise exports have declined over the period under investigation, but tourism has continued to flourish.

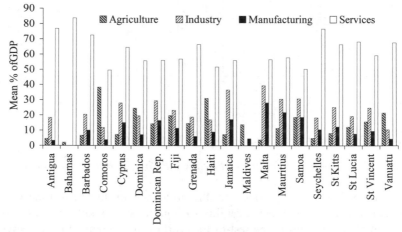

Source: World Development Indicators (WDI) of World Bank (2002).

Figure 2.4   Structure of the Economy of 20 SITEs

Although SITEs have made considerable headway in terms of economic development, they have also managed to achieve higher per capita incomes and exceptionally high economic growth records. This is mainly due to SITEs having larger per capita natural resource abundance, particularly for the development of tourism. Therefore, the intrinsic economic shortcomings of being small are offset by the high natural resource abundance. Furthermore, social indicators in SITEs tend to be higher compared with larger developing countries (see Table 2.3). They tend to have higher formal education attainment, better health care facilities and access to safe drinking water, as well as other advantages, which are a clear reflection of sound domestic social policies.

Since the failure of import substitution strategies and efforts to promote infant industries for economic development in the LDCs in the 1970s and

Table 2.3   Selected Health Indicators of 20 SITEs

SITE	Health				Education				
	Life expectancy at birth, total (years)	Improved sanitation facilities (% of population with access)	Improved water source (% of pop. with access)	Health expenditure, total (% of GDP) (1998)	Illiteracy rate, adult total (% of people ages 15 and above)	School enrolment, pre-primary (% gross)	School enrolment, primary (% gross)	School enrolment, secondary (% gross)	School enrolment, tertiary (% gross)
1 Antigua and Barbuda	75	96	91	2	5	11	93	87	25
2 Bahamas[a]	69	93	96	4	.	.	.	.	.
3 Barbados	75	100	100	7	.	77	87	105	31
4 Comoros[b]	61	98	96	4	44	2	76	25	1
5 Cyprus[c]	78	100	100	5	3	51	83	83	20
6 Dominica	76	.	.	6	.	.	.	.	.
7 Dominican Republic	67	71	79	5	16	34	133	66	23
8 Fiji[a]	69	43	47	4	7	17	112	70	14
9 Grenada	72	97	94	5	.	.	.	.	.
10 Haiti[a]	53	28	46	4	50	63	152	29	1
11 Jamaica	75	84	71	6	13	83	98	90	9
12 Maldives[a]	68	56	100	8	3	.	.	59	.
13 Malta[d]	78	100	100	7	8	101	107	92	31
14 Mauritius	72	99	100	3	15	100	108	71	7
15 Samoa[e]	69	99	99	6	20	59	102	73	5
16 Seychelles	72	.	.	.	.	.	.	.	.
17 St Kitts and Nevis	71	96	98	6	.	.	.	.	.
18 St Lucia	71	.	98	4	.	.	.	.	.
19 St Vincent and the Grenadines	73	96	93	6	.	.	.	.	.
20 Vanuatu	68	100	88	.	.	.	.	.	.

Notes:
a   Secondary School Enrolments for The Bahamas, Fiji, Haiti and Maldives are 1997 figures.
b   Health Expenditure figure for Comoros is 1997.
c   Health Expenditure figure for Cyprus is 1993.
d   Health Expenditure figure for Malta is 1991.
e   Health Expenditure figure for Samoa is 1999.

Source: World Development Indicators of World Bank (2002).

1980s, emphasis has been diverted towards export promotion in line with the rapid economic development of the East Asian Tiger economies, including South Korea, Singapore, Taiwan, Hong Kong, Malaysia and Thailand. Consequently, development of tourism, which is an invisible export, has given greater impetus to advance development strategies. This aspect is clearly evident from Figure 2.2, as expansion in tourism industries in SITEs has increased real GDP growth.

The fundamental aim of tourism development is to increase foreign exchange earnings in order to finance imports in countries where there is a unique tourism resource endowment. This concept is especially applicable to those island economies which are strategically located, and where the climate is well suited for sustainable tourism development. The SITEs analysed in this monograph depend highly on tourism for economic development. The rapid expansion of tourism is associated with adverse macroeconomic consequences, such as consistent growth in imports. This means the large proportion of what is being earned through tourism leaves the economy, almost instantaneously, in order to pay for imports.

According to the Commonwealth Secretariat/World Bank (2000), imports for most SITEs are mainly comprised of non-indigenous goods. Meat and dairy products feature heavily in the Caribbean, while countries such as Maldives mainly import construction material for tourism-related facilities. Maldives also imports labour from neighbouring countries like Sri Lanka, India and Bangladesh, which results in the significant outflow of foreign exchange. In SITEs, tourism facilities are mostly enclave developments, so their impact on the domestic economy can sometimes be very limited. Tourism is an industry where careful planning is required so that it can be developed with the intention of sustaining it for the long term by minimising environmental damage.

In most SITEs, diversification of economic activity is virtually non-existent. Manufacturing income has been transferred towards services sectors, such as tourism and offshore banking services. Those SITEs which continue to manufacture have been faced with unfavourable market prices in traditional crops. One striking feature among most of these SITEs is that when one principal economic activity declines, another dominant activity takes over. However, in Seychelles, extensive diversification has taken place in the aftermath of the Iranian Revolution of 1979, and the economy has grown increasingly prosperous.

International Trade

As illustrated in Figure 2.5, the proportion of trade to GDP is relatively higher among SITEs. The limited productive base in SITEs results in limited

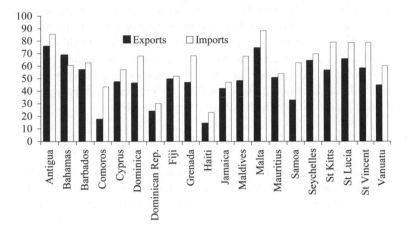

Source: World Development Indicators (WDI) of World Bank (2002).

Figure 2.5   Trade as a Proportion of GDP

range of goods and services produced. However, they consume a broader range of goods and services through international trade.

The advantages of international trade to these smaller populations is that they are able to obtain a greater variety of goods at relatively lower prices than if they were confined to domestically produced goods. Similarly, producers in SITEs can sell their produce to the world market (provided that they have appropriate market access), where they can earn more than by producing solely for the domestic demand. The need and incidence of participating in international markets gives SITEs greater access to new ideas, information and the ability to exploit greater opportunities for higher returns.

Being a trading partner in international markets means that SITEs hold a much greater stake as they are bound by international trading rules, regulations and various arrangements like any other trading partner, although they have a smaller proportion of world trade. Inside bigger markets, SITEs do not necessarily receive preferential treatment, although former British colonies receive preferential treatment for certain produce, such as banana exports. Therefore, the terms of trade of SITEs do not exhibit a higher statistically significant volatility than their larger counterparts. Economic activities in SITEs are highly dependent on international trade, which means that even a minor disturbance in world markets can have a major impact on a SITE's terms of trade. This will have adverse balance of payments consequences. Subsequently, a temporary halt to income receipts will eventuate until the problem is resolved. A good example would be the events of 11 September, 2001, which resulted in a significant decline in foreign exchange earnings through tourism for most SITEs.

SITEs tend to rely heavily on their import tariff receipts to finance development expenditure. Due to the scale of their openness to trade, this is a cost effective and convenient revenue option. Trade liberalisation measures will result in a reduction in revenue and will subsequently increase government debt. As a result, adverse macroeconomic consequences would be unavoidable because, in most SITEs, government budget accounts for nearly one-half of GDP, which will affect real growth.

Access to International Capital Markets

Capital markets in SITEs are not developed, so they need to have access to international capital markets in order to hedge against adverse external shocks and the profound volatility of GDP growth. There is a need for consistent inflow of foreign capital in SITEs because there is a direct benefit from foreign direct investment. It is a common feature among SITEs that they depend heavily on official development assistance, particularly from former colonists, to finance development expenditures. They have limited access to commercial borrowing because they are perceived to suffer from frequent natural disasters, as well as other high risk factors. SITEs have been particularly affected by the declining trends in aid, as the flow of Official Development Assistance (ODA) fell dramatically during the 1990s. Due to changing global circumstances, such as the collapse of the Soviet Union, ODA was diverted from the least developed countries towards former Soviet allies. As seen in Figure 2.6, SITEs have experienced a decline in per capita aid of around USD145 in 1990 to less than USD100 in 2000.

Even though SITEs have relatively lower levels of indebtedness, they have difficulty in borrowing in international capital markets because they are considered risky entities. The cost of obtaining important information and country risk issues are the major impediments to borrowing. Taking this into account, the integration of SITEs into international financial capital markets is relatively difficult.

Foreign Direct Investment (FDI) not only brings financial capital, but also the benefits of exposure to foreign competition and new ideas. FDI plays the important role of linking the more isolated SITEs to the developed world. Entrepreneurship from the outside world is an important source of knowledge and expertise in creating efficiency and improving management control in the private sector by bringing in state-of-the-art technology while increasing market opportunities. In Maldives, a Danish firm introduced frontier tourist arrival transfers to resorts by sea planes. This has created a new dimension to tourism in Maldives because tourists can now have a unique aerial view of the islands while transit to their actual destination. Figure 2.6 shows SITEs had received substantial inflows of FDI in the late 1990s. Total flows of FDI

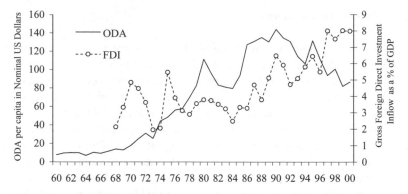

Source: World Development Indicators (WDI) of World Bank (2002).

Figure 2.6   Official Development Assistance and Foreign Direct Investment Flows

to SITEs averaged about USD2.1 billion annually during 1996–2000, which was around 15 per cent above the official development assistance and aid flows, but with a very different distribution among the regions and countries. Nearly 80 per cent of the FDI received by SITEs went to just seven countries.

Poverty Prevalence

Many SITEs continue to suffer from chronic poverty, despite the fact that some of them have been able to achieve relatively high per capita GDP. As shown in Table 2.3, most SITEs have reasonably better social indicators. It is generally accepted that with the increase in per capita real income, poverty should decline. However, poverty continues to be an unabated challenge in SITEs. There is no published data on poverty indicators on SITEs but according to the Commonwealth Secretariat/World Bank (2000), there are number of SITEs that have higher poverty rates than their per capita incomes. From anecdotal evidence, the above observation can be substantiated since SITEs are island archipelagos whose inhabitants are dispersed across some vast areas. Almost all economic activity is confined to the capital, while the dispersed communities remain poor. The income disparity between urban and rural sectors is so great due to the uneven distribution of income. The hardship for inhabitants of SITEs can be further aggravated due to environmental damage, income volatility, and so forth. As the poor are unable to cope with unanticipated shocks to their incomes, inequality within the economy increases over time.

Institutional Arrangements

Like all other economies around the world, SITEs are sovereign countries and must provide public services. The public sector plays a prominent role in the development process of these economies. The private sectors in SITEs are smaller, with the importance of size being that it significantly determines the ability for firms to survive and compete in the global environment.

In most SITEs, provision of public services is expensive and inefficient because they incur considerable internal transport costs. These countries are island archipelagos and are spread across a vast area of ocean. The physical infrastructure has to be imported, so that the provision of necessary services takes on an extra burden. It is not feasible to provide countrywide education at all levels, as most available training facilities are intended to prepare generalists. Therefore, many who are qualified are sent abroad for specialised training. The disadvantage of sending qualified local personnel to study abroad is that those who go may choose to stay abroad as they could receive higher remuneration and a better quality of life than that offered in SITEs. Most SITEs do not have the potential to provide the necessary technical and human support, and must be provided with support from abroad to sustain their training and education of their people.

The public sector is the largest employer in SITEs, and the public sector wage bill takes a substantial proportion of the government budget. This runs the budget in deficit in most of these countries, leaving a smaller share for development expenditures. It is a common characteristic among SITEs that important public servants have multiple portfolios, which sees one person responsible for a wide range of sectors. Therefore, corruption is a widespread phenomenon in SITEs. This results in a lack of transparency and abuse of power, while increasing the burden on general administration. There are substantial benefits of efficiency if one individual is capable of doing multiple jobs. However, in SITEs, if such a person leaves the job, there is significant loss in capacity. SITEs depend largely on international financial aid for development, and due to constrained institutional capacity, they are unable to represent themselves in international financial and trade negotiations. The outcome from these negotiations is important to SITEs if they choose to be part of the international community, and can profoundly affect any progress in economic development.

The biggest disadvantage of being small is that SITEs cannot exploit economies of large-scale operations (Armstrong and Read, 1998b). The private business in these economies is not well known, and therefore they have difficulty in attracting business. The local entrepreneurs in SITEs do not possess sufficient funds to influence business from overseas through marketing or for research and development. It is not an easy task to use existing resources and skills in these economies to develop new products to be sold abroad.

Local markets in SITEs operate in oligopolistic competition. Due to the nature of the institutional framework, regulation of markets is too challenging, especially when the trader himself is the regulator. It is essential that private sector institutions are developed and established in SITEs to increase the distribution of income. This will further increase the need for local skilled personnel to be trained to generate innovation and increase investment.

Economic Vulnerability

Considering the difficult circumstances experienced by SITE economies, it is perfectly conceivable that they are relatively vulnerable to economic, environmental and international relations shocks. Vulnerability means exposure to exogenous shocks over which the affected country has little or no control, and relatively low resilience to withstand and recover from these shocks. Small states are less likely to be resilient to these shocks, particularly given the narrow economic structures and limited resources (Armstrong and Read, 2002).

The Commonwealth has compiled a vulnerability index that measures small countries according to quantifiable components of exposure and resilience to external shocks. This analysis confirms that SITEs are considerably more vulnerable than other developing countries. There are three main components in this index, namely the degree of economic diversification based on the UNCTAD diversification index, the degree of export dependence, and the incidence of natural disasters.

The 20 SITEs examined in this chapter appear in the Commonwealth ranking of a sample of 111 developing countries. Table 2.4 is a summary of the analysis taken from the Commonwealth Vulnerability Index and is given for the SITEs analysed in this monograph. These 20 SITEs are the most vulnerable according to the Commonwealth Study. Of the 28 most highly vulnerable countries in the world, 12 SITEs, namely Antigua and Barbuda, The Bahamas, Dominica, Fiji, Grenada, Maldives, Samoa, Seychelles, St Kitts and Nevis, St Lucia, St Vincent and the Grenadines, and Vanuatu, are included. Six of the 20 SITEs, namely Barbados, Comoros, Haiti, Jamaica, Malta and Mauritius, were categorised as Higher Medium Vulnerability. Cyprus was considered as Lower Medium, while the Dominican Republic was excluded as it is not in the British Commonwealth.

Table 2.4   SITEs According to the Commonwealth Vulnerability Index

High Vulnerability	Higher Medium Vulnerability	Lower Medium Vulnerability	SITEs not in the British Commonwealth
Antigua and Barbuda	Barbados	Cyprus	Dominican Republic
The Bahamas	Comoros	·	·
Dominica	Haiti	·	·
Fiji	Jamaica	·	·
Grenada	Malta	·	·
Maldives	Mauritius	·	·
Samoa	·	·	·
Seychelles	·	·	·
St Kitts and Nevis	·	·	·
St Lucia	·	·	·
St Vincent and the Grenadines	·	·	·
Vanuatu	·	·	·

Source: Commonwealth Secretariat/World Bank (2000).

Political Features of SITEs

The SITEs examined in this monograph were colonised and their ownership has changed between Britain and France. The most significant political attributes of the 20 SITEs analysed in this chapter are given in Table 2.5. Comoros and Haiti were French colonies, while the Dominican Republic was a Haitian colony. The remaining 17 are former British colonies, which gained independence in the latter half of the 20th century, and all are now part of the British Commonwealth. Haiti has the longest history of independence, having gained it from France in 1804.

Since independence, most SITEs have had constitutional rule to date, but there have been exceptions. In Cyprus, constitutional rule was adopted in 1960, and negotiations to create the basis for a new or revised constitution to govern the island and to improve relations with the Greeks and Turkish Cypriots have been held intermittently. In 1975, Turkish Cypriots created their own constitution and governing bodies called the 'Turkish Federated State of Cyprus', which was later renamed the 'Turkish Republic of Northern Cyprus' in 1983. A new constitution for the Turkish Cypriot area was passed by referendum on 5 May 1985. Negotiations are currently being held to unify Cyprus.

Table 2.5   Colonial History and Political Attributes of SITEs

SITE	Colonised by	Independence Day	Constitution Adopted	Government Type
Antigua and Barbuda	UK	1-Nov-1981	1-Nov-1981	Constitutional Monarchy
The Bahamas	UK	10-Jul-1973	10-Jul-1973	Constitutional Parliamentary Democracy
Barbados	UK	30-Nov-1966	30-Nov-1966	Parliamentary Democracy
Comoros	France	6-Jul-1975	12-Dec-2001	Republic
Cyprus[1]	UK	16-Aug-1960	16-Aug-1960	Republic
Dominica	UK	3-Nov-1978	3-Nov-1978	Republic
Dominican Republic	Haiti	27-Feb-1844	28-Nov-1966	Representative Democracy
Fiji	UK	10-Oct-1970	10-Oct-1970	Republic
Grenada	UK	7-Feb-1974	19-Dec-1973	Constitutional Monarchy
Haiti	France	1-Jan-1804	Mar-1987	Elected Government
Jamaica	UK	6-Aug-1962	6-Aug-1962	Constitutional Parliamentary Democracy
Maldives[2]	UK	26-Jul-1965	1-Jan-1998	Republic
Malta	UK	21-Sep-1964	13-Dec-1974	Republic
Mauritius	UK	12-Mar-1968	12-Mar-1968; amended 12-Mar-1992	Parliamentary Democracy
Samoa[3]	UK	1-Jan-1962	1-Jan-1962	Constitutional Monarchy under Native Chief
Seychelles	UK	29-Jun-1976	18-Jun-1993	Republic
St Kitts and Nevis	UK	19-Sep-1983	19-Sep-1983	Constitutional Monarchy with Westminster-style Parliament
St Lucia	UK	22-Feb-1979	22-Feb-1979	Westminster-style Parliamentary Democracy
St Vincent and the Grenadines	UK	27-Oct-1979	27-Oct-1979	Parliamentary Democracy; Independent State within the Commonwealth
Vanuatu	France/UK	30-Jul-1980	30-Jul-1980	Republic

Notes:
1. Turkish Cyprus claimed self-rule on 13 February 1975.
2. Maldives was a British Protectorate.
3. Independence was gained from a New Zealand-administered UN trusteeship.

Source: CIA World Fact Book (2000).

In Fiji, a constitution was adopted in October 1970, but suspended in October 1987. A new constitution was proposed in September 1988 and promulgated in July 1990, but was amended in July 1997 to allow non-ethnic

Fijians a greater say in government and to make multi-party government mandatory. This was enforced in July 1998. The May 1999 election was the first test of this amendment to the constitution, introducing (not racially prescribed) open voting for the first time at the national level.

The constitution was first approved in Haiti in March 1987, suspended in June 1988, and subsequently in March 1989, most articles were reinstated. In October 1991, the government claimed to be observing the constitution, which finally returned to constitutional rule in October 1994.

Historically, small economies have been politically and strategically vulnerable. During the colonial era, political and strategic vulnerability of small economies was totally under the control of larger economic powers like Britain, France and Spain. Small states have traditionally been considered as strategic military outposts, and the same perception prevails today. In the present political climate, this type of vulnerability has been referred to as a relationship between small states and their larger neighbours, including global powers. This is due to limited strategic options being available to small island states, as well as their vulnerability to external political pressures. For example, with regard to the SITEs analysed in this monograph, those in the Caribbean are highly influenced by the USA, although they are former British colonies, those in the Indian Ocean are influenced heavily by India, while those in the Pacific are affected by Australian Government policy. Cyprus and Malta are considerably vulnerable to Greece and Italy, respectively. Armstrong and Read (2002) state that the main concern of the strategic vulnerability literature is the ability of small states to establish, maintain and enforce their territorial sovereignty with regard to larger states.

In this context, a prominent example would be when the USA invaded the island of Grenada under the Reagan administration. The US invasion of Grenada and the toppling of its Marxist government can be seen as part of a greater regional conflict. This conflict involved the USA and its Central American and Caribbean allies on one side, and Fidel Castro's Cuba, the Sandinista government of Nicaragua, and various Marxist guerrilla armies on the other. Ronald Reagan and his administration were concerned that the Grenadian Marxist government of Prime Minister Maurice Bishop was allowing Cuba to gain undue influence in Grenada, specifically by constructing a military-grade airport with Cuban military engineers.

On 13 October, 1983, the Grenadian Army, controlled by former Deputy Prime Minister Bernard Coard, seized power in a bloody coup. The severity of the violence, coupled with Coard's hard-line Marxism, caused deep concern among neighbouring Caribbean nations, as well as in Washington, DC. Moreover, the presence of nearly 1000 American medical students in Grenada caused added concern. However, along with concern came opportunity. With President Reagan's worldwide efforts to confront what he viewed as the threat by the Soviet Union and other Communist countries (such as Cuba), the turmoil in the Caribbean provided a timely excuse to eliminate a Marxist government and embarrass Fidel Castro. It should also be noted that on 23 October, 1983, American foreign policy and pride suffered a terrible attack when a Muslim suicide bomber destroyed the Marine barracks in Beirut, killing 240 US Marines. A successful campaign in Grenada would prove helpful in alleviating the pain of that setback.

In spite of the protection given under international law, small states have greater difficulty in exercising their sovereignty, especially when they are island archipelagos with 200-mile Exclusive Economic Zones. For surveillance of these large areas of the sea, a formidable investment in airborne equipment is required, which these small economies simply cannot afford.

2.7 CONCLUSION

The most important characteristics of SITEs have been examined, while taking account of the implications for economic development. The common size measures given in Table 2.1 clearly show that the most prominent feature of these economies is that they are small. SITEs are well known for having a limited productive base and small domestic markets. Many of these SITEs are necessarily and relatively undiversified in their production of exports. SITEs face difficulties when they need to respond to any changing external circumstances because there is a capacity constraint in the private sector. In order to tackle this problem, SITEs have to rely considerably on international trade and FDI. This is beneficial in terms of gaining access to international competition and to new ideas.

SITEs do not have developed capital markets domestically, and so they need to gain access to international capital markets to hedge against adverse external shocks and the profound volatility of GDP growth. SITEs are considered risky entities, making it increasingly costly and difficult for them to gain access to private international capital markets.

In drawing up an exhaustive list of the common characteristics of these SITEs, one has to take into account the fact that there is ample diversity among SITEs. For instance, if one compares the stage of development of Mauritius with any of the South Pacific SITEs, there is considerable variation among them, although these SITEs have similar difficulties in gaining access to markets for their exports. Therefore, when policy advice is delivered to one SITE, a general set of policies cannot be prescribed for all SITEs. Instead, the specific domestic and regional circumstances should be taken into account as each SITE is unique.

The efforts of SITEs to exploit economies of scale and to diversify their productive base within their small domestic markets does not necessarily imply that these SITEs have smaller per capita GDP, or an exceptionally poor record on economic growth. SITEs may be better off relative to larger developing countries because of their per capita natural resource abundance, with the best example being the development of tourism. In this regard, the disadvantage of being small is offset by the higher per capita natural resource abundance. In SITEs, social indicators tend to be higher relative to larger developing countries, and tend to have attained providing quality social services which reflect policy effectiveness.

Being former colonies of some of the G7 countries, the most noticeable advantage for these economies has been in the post-colonial era, where they benefited from relatively high inflows of official development assistance. These were mostly in the form of grants-in-kind, where SITEs did not have any obligation to repay funding. This inflow of aid has been relatively high in per capita terms, and has been skewed primarily towards the advancement of social infrastructure, such as schools and hospitals. This inflow of official assistance also explains their economic development records.

The diseconomies of scale in the provision of public services in SITEs have resulted in the public sector playing a major role in a large proportion of their economic activities and in the provision of social services. In order to address the issue of overcoming their inherent scale limitations and indivisibility, SITEs rely heavily on international trade in goods and services and openness to FDI, which can be considered one of their major strengths.

In comparing the economic well-being of SITEs with larger developing countries, there are substantially qualitative differences in the per capita incomes and economic growth rates between SITEs and other relatively large developing countries. One possible explanation for this outcome is that SITEs have relatively large natural resource abundance, which fosters tourism and offsets the inherent disadvantages of being small.

NOTE

1. Parts of Sections 2.2, 2.3 and 2.4 of this chapter were presented at the Biennial International Congress of the Modelling and Simulation Society of Australia and New Zealand, Townsville, Australia, 14–17 July, 2003, International Conference on Tourism and Sustainable Development Macro and Micro Issues, jointly organized by the Centre for North–South Economic Research, University of Cagliari, Fondazione Eni Enrico Mattei (FEEM) and the World Bank, Sardinia, Italy, September, 2003, and the PhD Conference on Economics and Business, University of Western Australia, Perth, Australia, November 2003.

REFERENCES

Armstrong, H.W. and R. Read (1995), 'Western European micro-states and autonomous regions: The advantages of size and sovereignty', *World Development*, **23**(7), 1229–45.

Armstrong, H.W. and R. Read (1998a), 'Trade and growth in small states: The impact of global trade liberalisation', *World Economy*, **21**(4), 563–85.

Armstrong, H.W. and R. Read (1998b), 'Trade, competition and market structure in small states: The role of contestability', *Bank of Valletta Review*, **18**, 1–18.

Armstrong, H.W. and R. Read (2000), 'Comparing the economic performance of dependent territories and sovereign micro-states', *Economic Development & Cultural Change*, **48**(2), 285–306.

Armstrong, H.W. and R. Read (2002), 'The phantom of liberty? Economic growth and the vulnerability of small states', *Journal of International Development*, **14**(3), 435–58.

Briguglio, L. (1995), 'Small island developing states and their economic vulnerabilities', *World Development*, **23**(9), 1615–32.

Central Intelligence Agency (2002), *World Factbook*.

Commonwealth Secretariat/World Bank Joint Task Force on Small States (2000), 'Small states: Meeting challenges in the global economy', available at http://www.thecommonwealth.org [last accessed: July 2007].

Dommen, E. (1980), 'Some distinguishing characteristics of island states', World *Development*, **8**, 931–43.

Kuznets, S. (1960), 'Economic growth of small nations', in E.A.G. Robinson (ed.), *The Economic Consequences of the Size of Nations*, London: Macmillan, pp. 14–32.

Streeten, P. (1993), 'The special problems of small countries', *World Development*, **21**, 197–202.

World Bank (2002), *World Development Indicators*, CD-ROM.

3. A Survey of Empirical Analysis in Tourism Demand

3.1 INTRODUCTION

Tourism forms part of international trade and is considered to be an invisible export. Therefore, a natural starting point for analysing tourism demand would be to consult the international trade literature. Among many different kinds of international trade, the most closely linked to this analysis would be trade in financial services. In 1999, the trade in services accounted for nearly 20 per cent of the value of all international trade, but there has been little research conducted on this topic. The next strand of literature is research in empirical tourism, on which a large proportion of this monograph is focused.

The international trade literature exposes aspects that make it unattractive for incorporating international tourism. The most extensively used theory in international trade is the Heckscher-Ohlin theory, which explains that international trade flows are mainly based on relative factor endowments. This theory can only be applied when factors of production can be sensibly approximated by, for instance, capital and labour. In tourism, the most important factors of production are unique and virtually impossible to quantify. For example, how is it possible to measure the worth of the Taj Mahal, in Agra, India, a natural wonder such as the Grand Canyon in Colorado, USA, the Niagara Falls in Canada and the USA, the undersea world of the Maldives in the Indian Ocean, and the Great Barrier Reef in Australia, all of which are among countless significant international tourist attractions? In this regard, one can argue that it is not theoretically appealing to explain international tourist flows in a cross-sectional manner. Therefore, if one can collect tourist destinations of similar characteristics, it would be conceivable to place them in a collective analytical framework.

One such collective framework would be SITEs, on which this monograph is focused. In the international tourism research literature, the popularity of a destination is ascertained by comparing the number of tourists who visit a particular destination or the earnings made at a particular destination. A destination can be very popular but it may only be able to carry a certain number of tourists. If the rate of growth of the carrying capacity in tourist destinations does not grow with the rate of growth of the number of travellers around the world, then the substitutability of tourist destinations would increase and the measure of popularity of a tourist destination may be flawed.

The most interesting and fascinating aspect of research in international tourism flows is the investigation of the effects of different variables that vary over time, a notable example being the ethnic conflict in Sri Lanka which began in 1983. Sri Lanka is one of the world's most exotic countries due to its climatic and geological features, along with its rich Buddhist heritage. Additionally, some interesting time-varying influences in popular tourist destinations relating to international tourism include the crime rate in the Caribbean countries, political unrest such as the *coups d'état* of 1987 and 2000 in Fiji, the political situation in Cyprus, the ever-growing threat of global terrorism, such as the events of 11 September, 2001, and so forth. These aspects are usually overlooked in standard trade models.

Empirical research in international tourism is vast. There is a multitude of areas of research within tourism itself. One such area is alternative tourism, which stresses the issues relating to the search for new possibilities to attract tourists within a particular destination, with the intention of sustaining tourism. Research has taken place in assessing attitudes and perceptions of residents on the impact of tourism development on community life. Moreover, the changes to community life and aspirations due to the introduction of tourism have been analysed. Over the last twenty years, tourism development has become an important economic development phenomenon in terms of increasing foreign exchange earnings and employment, particularly in small island economies. The volume of empirical research in relation to assessing the economic impact of tourism is relatively low. The qualitative analysis of tourism development has been directed towards identifying the possibilities of increased economic impacts due to alternative types of sustainable and unsustainable tourism development.

Ecotourism is a popular and developing area of research. Ecotourism is based on nature and culture that is ecologically sustainable, and supports the well-being of local communities. This type of tourism appeals to visitors who want contact with nature, local communities and indigenous cultures and is targeted towards travellers with special interests who are searching for unique and authentic experiences. Ecotourism takes into account the impacts of the tourist industry upon the environmental, social, cultural and economic fabrics of the local community, while conducting its activities in harmony with nature.

Tourism is a labour-intensive industry and requires a relatively large number of semi-skilled and unskilled workers, so much so that employment in tourism is a growing area of research. There are numerous other areas of research in tourism, such as environmental and sustainable tourism, health and tourism, image and tourism, morphology of tourist resorts, planning and policy in tourism, resort life cycle, corporate tourism, society culture and tourism, the roles of tour operators, island economies (destinations) and tourism, and seasonality in tourism.

The complex consumer behaviour of international tourism poses many challenges to the marketing strategist, as well as to the policy maker, on the implications of international tourism earnings. The tourism product is a composite of a wide variety of goods and services, and is considered an invisible export where the purchase of the product involves foreign currency transactions. Additionally, the consumer has to be transported across borders to complete the transaction and the consumption cycle. Based on a theoretical rationale, international tourism demand is generally perceived to be influenced primarily by the income of the tourists in the tourist generating country, and relative prices between the tourist source and destination countries. The relative price is further divided into a relative cost-of-living component and a relative transportation-cost-to-destination component. Moreover, there are other potential influencing factors, such as preferences and tastes.

This chapter analyses the econometric techniques applied in estimating and forecasting international tourism demand. An accurate view of the forecasts of tourist arrivals is particularly important for policy makers, hoteliers, airlines and various other ancillary service providers of the tourism industry. At the macroeconomic level, earnings from tourism play an important role for every country, particularly for SITEs, which are heavily reliant on tourism earnings in generating national income. A greater understanding of the relationship between tourism earnings and their constituent determinants has important policy implications for the key economic indicators in SITEs, such as the real GDP growth rate, bilateral exchange rates, inflation rate and foreign currency reserves.

There have been many research studies in international tourism demand over the last three decades. These studies primarily involve empirical estimation of elasticities of demand of the independent variables with respect to international tourism, as well as forecasting international tourist arrivals. The most widely used measurements of international tourism are the number of international tourist arrivals at a particular destination, expenditures of international tourists at the destination, and earnings from international tourism as a percentage of GDP. On a few occasions, there have been attempts to analyse the findings of these studies in a comprehensive manner to expose the underlying relationships that bind the basic ideas and significance of the empirical results. The most notable examples of such recent studies are, in chronological order: Crouch (1994a, b), Witt and Witt (1995), Ong (1995), Crouch (1996) and Lim (1997a, b, c). In the review that is presented in this chapter, every attempt is made to minimise any overlap with the survey papers mentioned above.

According to Crouch (1994a), most studies have emphasised the macroeconomic implications of tourism, while determining the future outlook of tourism demand among one or more destinations. Crouch (1994a, p. 41) stated that 'Microeconomic studies of individual or household tourism behaviour are rare', while Crouch (1994b, p. 21) concluded that 'the wide variety of the results that narratives review of the research cannot adequately reveal the underlying nature of the relationships between the demand for international tourism and its determinants'. Consequently, Crouch (1996) undertakes a meta-analysis, which employs more scientific procedures to integrate the research findings, so that some generalisations can be made about the variations among the research findings. Moreover, Lim (1997a) asserts that there has been a lack of diagnostic tests in tourism demand models, so that inferences based on the empirical findings of such models have to be treated with caution.

3.2 RESEARCH PUBLICATIONS IN INTERNATIONAL TOURISM DEMAND ANALYSIS

In this chapter, 53 empirical papers in tourism research published between 1989 and 2003 are evaluated. The purpose of this survey is to evaluate the empirical literature on tourism demand pertaining to SITEs. The search was undertaken using the ECONLIT, ECONBASE and Business Source Elite databases, which located only 10 published journal articles on small islands economies from 1989 to December 2003. As a result, the objective of this survey has been modified to introduce recent developments in the empirical literature on international tourism demand and to evaluate the significance of the modelling process in the leading journals in tourism, applied economics and forecasting, since 1995. The year 1995 was chosen as a cut-off point to minimise any overlap with the previously published research surveys, most of which have already incorporated the papers published prior to 1995.

Three papers published prior to 1995, which were based on Barbados, namely Carey (1989, 1991, 1992), are included in this review because they have significant relevance to the monograph. At the end of this chapter, the principal attributes of the papers that are analysed are given in Appendices 3.1 and 3.2. The papers surveyed are as follows: Akis (1998), Burger et al. (2001), Carey (1989, 1991, 1992), Chan et al. (1999), Cho (2003), Chu (1998), Daniel and Ramos (2002), De Mello et al. (2002), Dharmaratne (1995), Divisekera (2003), Downward (2003), Garcia-Ferrer and Queralt (1997), Garín-Muñoz and Amaral (2000), Goh and Law (2002), González and Moral (1995, 1996), Greenidge (2001), Hui and Yuen (1998, 2002), Jensen (1998), Kim and Song (1998), Kulendran (1996), Kulendran and King (1997), Kulendran and Wilson (2000), Kulendran and Witt (2001, 2003),

Lanza et al. (2003), Lathiras and Siriopoulos (1998), Ledesma-Rodriguez and Navarro-Ibanez (2001), Lee et al. (1996), Lim and McAleer (1999, 2001a, 2001b, 2002), Morley (1998), Narayan (2003a, b), Papatheodorou (1999), Payne and Merva (2002), Qu and Lam (1997), Romilly et al. (1998), Song et al. (2000, 2003), Sorensen (1999), Turner et al. (1998), Turner and Witt (2001), Venegas and Croes (2000), Vogt and Wittayakorn (1998), Webber (2001), Wong (1997), and Yoon and Shafer (1996).

In the empirical literature on examining international tourism demand, most papers are found in publications that serve both academic and non-academic practitioners. The most prominent of these journals are the leading three, namely *Annals of Tourism Research*, *Tourism Management* and *Journal of Travel Research*, as well as *Tourism Analysis* and *Tourism Economics*. The 53 papers reviewed in this chapter were published in tourism, economics, and travel journals, and are illustrated in alphabetical order in Table 3.1. Empirical analyses of tourism demand feature in Annals of Tourism Research and Tourism Economics, which have also included a substantial number of applied econometrics papers in international tourism demand.

Table 3.1　　Journals that Publish Research on International Tourism Demand

Journal	Frequency
Annals of Tourism Research	11
Applied Economics	5
Atlantic Economic Journal	1
International Journal of Forecasting	4
International Journal of Tourism Research	3
Journal of Travel Research	2
Mathematics and Computers in Simulation	1
Pacific Economic Bulletin	1
Pacific Tourism Review	1
Service Industries Journal	1
Social and Economic Studies	1
Tourism Analysis	2
Tourism Economics	11
Tourism Management	8
World Development	1
Total	53

In this review, publications in *Annals of Tourism Research* and *Tourism Economics* have the highest frequency of occurrence, with 11 papers each, or approximately 40 percent of all the papers combined. These two journals are followed closely by *Tourism Management*, which publishes a number of papers related to various aspects of international tourism demand, and has a relatively large proportion of eight of 53 papers, or roughly 15 per cent of the total papers surveyed. *Applied Economics* has five papers, *International Journal of Forecasting* has four papers, *International Journal of Tourism Research* has three papers, and *Journal of Travel Research* and *Tourism Analysis* each has two of the surveyed papers. There are seven journals, each of which has published one paper analysed in the survey.

The years of publication for each of the 53 papers presented in this survey are given in Table 3.2. Apart from three papers, all were published from 1995 to 2003. In 1998, ten papers appeared; the largest number of papers published in any one year. During the period 1995–2003, there have been seven papers published on empirical analyses of tourism demand in small island tourism economies. This is a relatively small number of publications in14 years, with

Table 3.2   Year of Publication of Research on International Tourism
            Demand

Year of Publication	Frequency
1989*	1
1990	0
1991*	1
1992*	1
1993	0
1994	0
1995*	2
1996*	4
1997	4
1998	10
1999*	4
2000**	5
2001*	8
2002*	6
2003	5
Total	*53*

Note: * (**) denotes one (two) publication(s) on small economies.

an effective rate of publication being one paper in every two years. Based on this number, one may conclude that the extant literature on empirical analyses of tourism demand for small island economies is still somewhat limited.

3.3   ECONOMIC HYPOTHESIS ANALYSED

The international tourism demand literature is primarily involved with identifying the elements which determine tourism demand. Such elements are called tourism demand determinants. The second strand of empirical investigation entails quantitative analysis, which is concerned with measuring the extent to which the identified determinants affect the demand for tourism. The first step in the traditional procedure in the empirical evaluation of tourism demand is to develop hypotheses that are well founded on the microeconomic theory of demand. All of the 53 papers analysed have dealt with these strands of tourism demand analysis.

Table 3.3 illustrates the different types of hypotheses analysed in the international tourism demand literature, and the frequency with which they have been examined. The most frequently analysed hypothesis was the determinant of tourism demand. Just over one-half, or 27 of 53 papers, analysed the determinants of tourism demand. The theory of tourism demand states that consumers maximise utility from the consumption of a tourism product which depends on their income (as reflected in the level of national income in the tourist source country), price of tourism product (own price), and the cost of purchasing the tourism product from competitor destinations (price of substitutes). According to demand theory, assuming that the price of tourism good remains unchanged, if there is a positive change in the level of

Table 3.3   Economic Hypotheses Tested in International Tourism Demand

Economic Hypothesis Tested	Frequency
Determinants of Tourism Demand	27
Time Series Behaviour of Tourism Demand and Forecasting	12
Tourism Demand and Cointegration	6
Tourism Demand and Seasonality	4
Optimal Hotel Capacity	2
Specialisation in Tourism and the long-run implications	1
Impact of Environmental Change and Tourist Arrivals	1
Total	*53*

income of tourists, the demand for tourism around the world would increase. Suppose the price of tourism within the tropics increases but the price of tourism in the temperate zone remain unchanged. Assuming that income has not changed, tourism demand within the tropics will decline and will increase in the temperate zone. Such behaviour of tourists would only occur if tourism within the tropics and the temperate zone are perfect substitutes. Such hypotheses have been examined in the international tourism literature.

Time series behaviour of tourism demand and forecasting is examined in 23 per cent, or 12 of the 53 papers. Time series behaviour in tourism demand includes lagged dependent variables, moving averages of an appropriate order, and no explanatory variables in an autoregressive model. In this case, the hypothesis examines to what extent habit persistence exists in tourism demand and how the non-deterministic component in tourism demand in previous periods influence the current period tourism demand. This is based on the Box-Jenkins (1976) methodology of Autoregressive Moving Average (ARMA) representation. The ARMA representation has been implemented in 12 papers to obtain post-sample forecasts in tourism demand.

It is also well founded that most variables that affect tourism demand often vary with time, which means that they may be non-stationary. When variables are non-stationary, regression analysis tends to produce apparently significant t-ratios and exceptionally high R^2, but the inferences will be spurious. Engle and Granger (1987) show that, when one or more variables are non-stationary, this does not necessarily mean that they are actually related. In fact, regressions based on such variables are spurious. Furthermore, they explain that variables such as tourist arrivals, their income, price of the tourist good, and prices of substitutes belong to the same system of behaviour. In such a structure, there should be a force that keeps them together over a long period of time. This is called a cointegrating relationship. In the international tourism literature, the issue of spurious regression and cointegration has received little attention until recently. In the 53 papers, only six papers have analysed the hypothesis that there is a cointegrating relationship among the tourism demand determinants.

Seasonality is a phenomenon of tourism demand and can be observed in high frequency data such as weekly, monthly or quarterly data. Despite the existence of seasonality in tourism demand, only four of the 53 papers have investigated it. Two papers, namely Carey (1989, 1991), analysed the hypothesis of determining optimal hotel capacity and its associated components in Barbados, Lanza et al. (2003) analysed the hypothesis of specialisation in tourism and the long-term implications for 13 OECD countries, and Chan et al. (1999) examined the sudden environmental change and implications for tourist arrivals in Singapore.

3.4   ANALYSIS OF EMPIRICAL STUDIES

In this section, empirical issues are assessed with respect to the 53 papers. This assessment is based on the Descriptions of Models given in Appendix 3.1, and the Analysis of Models in Appendix 3.2. The Descriptions of Analysis constitute discussion of empirical issues such as sample data, functional form, dependent variables, and independent variables. Under Analysis of Models, the topics outlined are recognition of omitted variables, model specification, methods of estimation, descriptive statistics, diagnostic testing, and empirical implications of the findings.

Descriptions of Models

This section deals with the empirical issues relating to data sources, which further explores the various frequencies in data, sample sizes and the different types of data used. This will be followed by an identification of the various tourist destinations and source countries addressed in the 53 papers. Moreover, the functional form of tourism demand models, and the dependent and independent variables included in tourism demand models, are examined.

Data sources
There are many sources in which tourism data are available. The primary source of tourism data is the World Tourism Organisation (WTO) Yearbook of Tourism Statistics. It publishes figures on international tourist arrivals and receipts from tourism disaggregated by country of origin for all WTO member countries on an annual basis. On request, they provide electronic data free of charge. For some descriptive analysis in this monograph, WTO data are used. The International Financial Statistics (IFS) of the International Monetary Fund (IMF) publishes macroeconomic data for its member countries on a monthly basis, which is widely used in tourism demand analysis. Independent international journals and other commercial publications disseminate data on trends and travel patterns of tourists around the world. Comprehensive data on variables, such as tourist bed nights and duration of stay, are obtainable from the national tourism organisations in destination countries. Information on economic variables pertaining to a particular destination or an origin country, such as personal disposable income, consumers' expenditure, tourist expenditures and population size, are generally published in the statistical publications of national statistical bureaux of the respective countries.

Depending on the analysis undertaken, data are usually sourced from more than one entity. Various authors frequently used data from multiple sources within one analysis. For univariate analysis, data from a single source seem sufficient, whereas for multivariate analysis, data from more than one source are necessary. An important qualification is the quality of tourism data used. A large proportion of tourism demand analysis is based on aggregated data for an extended period, which may not accurately reflect the individual tourist's behaviour. Furthermore, the data used are subject to errors of measurement, which may be carried forward into the modelling process.

The principal sources of data that are used in the 53 papers are outlined in Table 3.4. There are statistical bureaux established at the national level in most countries around the world. Of the 53 papers, nearly half as many papers used data obtained from national statistical bureaux. Since tourism has become such a lucrative industry around the world, countries have established their own national tourism authorities, with the mandate for research and development in and promotion of their tourism industries. These organisations are responsible for analysing trends in emerging tourist source countries, as well as formulating strategies to tap into new markets. Data from such authorities were used in 14 papers.

Most multivariate models in tourism demand require economic variables, such as income and price. The IMF/IFS publishes monthly, quarterly and

Table 3.4   Data Sources in Tourism Demand Analysis

Data Sources	Frequency
National Statistical Bureaux	25
National Tourism Authority	14
IMF/IFS	12
WTO	11
ABC/OAG World Airways Guide	10
Central Bank Publications	9
OECD Publications	9
Government Ministries	4
EconData DX Database	3
Survey Data	3
Commercial Bank Publications	2
Non-governmental Organisations	2
Privately-owned Travel Publications	2
Regional Agency Data	2
World Economic Outlook	2
Wold Bank World Tables	1
Single Source	*37*
Multiple Sources	*16*

annual data for the four main macroeconomic national accounts, the real, fiscal, monetary and external, of its sovereign member nations. The usefulness of this data source is reflected in the 12 of 53 papers. The WTO is regarded as the principal source of tourism data because it is the only organisation which provides data for a large pool of countries, which are also its members. Although reliable data are obtainable for over 140 countries and territories from around the world, the WTO can only provide annual data. This is a drawback because tourism demand entails a high level of autoregression and seasonality. Such important features can only be captured using monthly or quarterly data. In spite of this shortcoming, 11 papers used annual data from the WTO.

Transport costs between destination and tourist source countries are an important exogenous variable in the analysis of tourism demand. The ABC/OAG World Airways Guide was known to be the main publisher of airfare data. However, to the best of our knowledge they have discontinued their publication. During the sample period, 10 of 53 papers used the airfares published in the ABC/OAG World Airways Guide as a proxy for transportation costs.

Central banks often publish disaggregated data of what is being published in the IMF/IFS, and such data were used in nine papers. There are nine papers which are based on OECD countries and they used data published by the OECD. Survey data are collected by means of a questionnaire or an interview, but are consequently costly and difficult to compile. The success of survey data depends on how the questionnaire is designed and the response rate of the random sample chosen. Hence, an analysis based on survey data will provide a partial account of the properties of the population surveyed. Since survey data are based on an hypothesis where the questionnaire is customised, a favourable response rate on a survey will produce valuable results.

In the 53 papers, Downward (2003) and Yoon and Shafer (1996) were the only papers that were based on survey data. In four papers, data provided by government ministries were used, while data from the EconData DX Database were used in three papers. Data from regional agencies in destination countries, non-governmental organisations, privately-owned travel publications, commercial bank publications, and *World Economic Outlook* published by the IMF, appeared on two occasions. Finally, 16 of 53 papers used data from a single source, which is inclusive of the three surveys mentioned above, while 27 studies used data from multiple sources.

Characteristics of data
A classification of the type of data used, their sampling frequencies and the frequency of occurrence are reported in Table 3.5. Over 90 per cent of the

Table 3.5   Sampling Frequency of International Tourism Data

Type of Data	Sampling Frequency	Frequency
Time Series Data	Annual	20
	Quarterly	14
	Monthly	13
		47
Pooled Data	Annual	4
	Daily	2
		6
Survey Data		2
	Total	*55*

Note: Chan et al. (1999) and Goh and Law (2002) used two samples.

papers reviewed based their econometric modelling on time series data, of which 20 papers used annual data, 14 used quarterly data, 13 used monthly data, and one paper used weekly data. Since tourism demand is highly seasonal and there is strong habit persistence, analyses based on annual data will not capture these two prominent features of tourism demand.

Time series cross-section (or pooled) data were used in only seven papers. The pooled data technique reduces the problem of collinearity and improves the efficiency of estimates. In situations where samples are small, by pooling data we can achieve greater degrees of freedom. Such data better represent the adjustment dynamics by identifying and estimating the effects not detected in studies using solely cross-section or pure time series data. Panel data techniques allow the construction and comparison of models that take into account the existence of more complex behaviour.

Nevertheless, there are some limitations in the application of panel data due to the way in which the data base may be structured, and information may be distorted by measurement errors and the length of the time series.

The sample sizes used in the 53 papers are classified into arbitrarily set frequency bands, and are given in Table 3.6. There are two papers, Chan et al. (1999) and Goh and Law (2002), which use two samples. The former uses two samples of the same number of observations, while the latter uses two samples of different sizes.

In the international tourism literature, questions regarding the robustness of the model to structural change in the data, due perhaps to business cycles or other random shocks which affect world wide travel or regional travel, have not been adequately addressed. An exception is De Mello et al. (2002),

Table 3.6   Sample Sizes Used in International Tourism Demand

Number of Observations Used	Frequency
0–25	9
26–50	17
51–75	11
76–100	3
101–150	2
151–200	5
201–300	3
301–400	2
401–500	·
501 and above	3
Total	*55*

Note: Chan et al. (1999) and Goh and Law (2002) used two samples.

who sub-divide the sample and conduct separate analyses to assess the responsiveness of UK per capital real tourism expenditure in the two separate samples. They found that there was a structural break in UK per capital real tourism expenditure to Spain and Portugal during the periods 1969–1979 and 1980–1997. One of the important events which contributed to the structural breaks was Spain's membership in the European Free Trade Area (EFTA) in 1980. Furthermore, the negotiations for Spain's and Portugal's EU membership, which began in mid-1979 and 1978, respectively, resulted in the beginning of a partnership from an era of isolation.

In 68 per cent, or 36 papers of 53, small samples were commonly used, where such a sample is arbitrarily defined as one with fewer than 75 observations. The most frequently occurring sample range was between 26 and 50 observations, and is used in more than one-third of the cases, or in 17 of 53 papers. This is followed by 11 papers which use samples between 51 and 75 observations. In nine instances, fewer than 25 observations were used. Samples above 100 observations account for a under one-third, or 17 of 53 papers.

It is generally held that the appropriate sample size is determined by the type of analysis that is being undertaken, especially by the specification and estimation method used for a given model. For linear regression models using ordinary least squares, the reported sample sizes may be adequate where the data are stationary. However, samples of fewer than 100 observations may be viewed as insufficient for the specification, estimation and evaluation of a wide variety of ARIMA models.

International tourism markets and destinations. Table 3.7 identifies the particular tourism source countries analysed in the 53 papers and the frequency with which they are modelled. In precisely one-half of the papers, arrivals from the UK were included in the analysis. Historically, tourists from the UK are known to have travelled widely as the UK is strategically located to reach most destinations internationally. London's Heathrow Airport, widely regarded as the world's busiest, can boast of handling more than 30 million passengers per year, and flights to almost anywhere in the world are available daily. The UK is also host to a number of well-known tour operators such as Kuoni, known for selling tourist packages, particularly for destinations within the tropics.

Twenty of the 53 papers include an analysis of arrivals from the USA, the world's richest country. American tourists are mostly known to choose domestic tourism due to the vast tourism industry in the USA, particularly Hawaii. Caribbean destinations are also popular with US tourists, due to their proximity to the US State of Florida. However, in the recent past, US tourists have been known to travel to remote destinations of the world, such as Fiji in the Pacific Ocean and to destinations in the Indian Ocean. It is not clear whether US travellers to remote destinations travel directly from the USA because priority in data maintenance of tourist head counts is based on nationality and not country of residence. Nevertheless, most US tourists who

Table 3.7   Tourism Source Countries

Tourism Source	Frequency	Tourism Source	Frequency
UK	26	Malaysia	4
USA	22	Italy	3
Japan	15	Norway	3
Germany	11	Spain	2
New Zealand	9	Switzerland	2
Australia	8	China	2
France	7	Philippines	2
Netherlands	6	Belgium	1
Singapore	5	Thailand	1
Korea	4	CARICOM	1
Taiwan	4	Finland	1
Sweden	4	India	1
Canada	4	Greece	1
Hong Kong	4		

travel to the Maldives in the Indian Ocean are US expatriates working in the Middle East.

Data from Japanese tourist arrivals are analysed on 15 occasions, recording the third highest market examined. Due to the emergence of Japan as the world's second largest economy in the 1980s, Japanese tourists travel to almost all tourist destinations around the world, from tropical to heritage destinations. Moreover, in Nozawa (1992), it is stated that the Japanese government introduced a new policy aimed at nearly doubling the amount of Japanese overseas travel from 5.5 million trips in 1986 to 10 million trips by 1990.

German tourists are keen on tropical tourism, cultural tourism, and ecotourism, among others. In the 53 papers, Germany records the fourth highest tourist source countries examined.

Although New Zealand and Australia are quite isolated from the rest of the world, assessment of tourism demand from these two countries appeared on nine and eight occasions, respectively, in the 53 studies.

French tourists normally choose their tropical holidays in Martinique and Guadeloupe in the Caribbean, and in Tahiti and New Caledonia in the Pacific because these are overseas departments of France. French tourist demand was analysed on seven occasions, which is the seventh highest frequency. This is a surprising result since France is one of the G7 countries and the French are perceived to travel internationally like their G7 counterparts. Source countries which appeared less than six times are given in Table 3.7.

In most papers, specifically in 48 of the 53 reviewed, tourism demand is analysed as inbound, such that demand for tourism is examined from the destination's perspective. Demand for tourism analysed as outbound is usually examined from the tourist-generating countries' perspective. In the survey, five papers specifically define tourism demand as outbound, of which four papers are for UK international tourist departures and one is for Australian international tourist departures. The remaining 47 papers analyse tourism demand as inbound. Overall, we can conclude that tourism demand, in general, is analysed as inbound tourism demand.

There are altogether 43 destinations analysed which appeared on 92 occasions in the 53 papers. Several papers have included multiple destinations, which will be explained in detail below. Australia recorded the most frequently analysed destination with 12 occurrences. Although one of the world's most desired destinations, Australia's remoteness has a substantial bearing on travel costs. The availability of large high frequency data sets for international tourists arriving in Australia gives substantial scope for empirical analysis of the tourism industry. Spain records the second highest frequency. Spain is the world's second most popular tourism destination in terms of both the number of tourist arrivals and the volume of tourism receipts (WTO, Tourism Highlights, 2003). Portugal is the third most frequently analysed markets, which appeared on five occasions. Portugal is also the tenth most popular tourist destination in Western Europe. Barbados, Denmark and Greece were examined four times, while Turkey, Singapore, South Korea, Hong Kong, France and Italy were analysed on three occasions. Destinations which appeared fewer than three times are given in Table 3.8.

Table 3.8   Tourism Destinations

Destinations	Frequency	Destinations	Frequency
Australia	12	Jamaica	1
Spain	8	Montserrat	1
Portugal	5	St Lucia	1
Barbados	4	St Vincent	1
Denmark	4	Trinidad and Tobago	1
Greece	4	Hong Kong	1
Turkey	3	Japan	1
Singapore	3	Taiwan	1
South Korea	3	Philippines	1
Hong Kong	3	Indonesia	1
France	3	England (Rural)	1
Italy	3	British Columbia (Canada)	1
Aruba	2	Netherlands	1
The Bahamas	2	USA	1
Thailand	2	Austria	1
New Zealand	2	Belgium	1
Germany	2	UK	1
Fiji	2	Switzerland	1
South Africa	1	Tenerife (Spain)	1
Cayman Islands	1	Yugoslavia	1
Dominica	1	Croatia	1
Dominican Rep.	1		

Destination-market classification of tourism demand. The 53 papers reviewed have been categorised into a destination-market classification. This classification is warranted because only six papers examine tourism demand between a single destination and a single market, and such analyses have a declining trend. Recently, data maintenance on tourist arrivals has been comprehensive. Surprisingly, data are available at high frequency from few least developed countries, disaggregated into tourist source countries and can be obtained without much difficulty. As a result, researchers have chosen the path of analysis of more than one market or destination. A summary of these categories and the frequency of occurrence of papers under each category is given in Table 3.9.

Table 3.9   Destination-Market Classification of Tourism Studies

Type	Classification	Frequency
I	Single Destination-Total Arrivals, Expenditure, or Revenue	11
II	Multiple Destination-Total Arrivals, Expenditure, or Revenue	4
III	Single Destination-Single Source Country	7
IV	Single Destination-Multiple Source Countries	24
V	Multiple Destinations-Single Source Country	5
VI	Multiple Destination-Multiple Source Countries	2
Total		*53*

Type I. Tourism demand to a single destination is measured in terms of total arrivals, total tourist expenditure or total tourist revenues. Of the 11 papers in this category, Downward (2003) is a regional tourism demand study, while González and Moral (1995, 1996) measure tourism demand to Spain in terms of total tourist receipts and expenditures. The basis for identifying tourism demand to Croatia in Payne and Merva (2002) is total tourism revenues. The rest of the eight papers in this category measures tourism demand on aggregated total international tourist arrivals.

Type II. The papers which are in this classification are explained as having analysed tourism demand to multiple destinations based on aggregated figures, such as international tourist arrivals, tourist expenditures and tourism revenues. These include Carey (1991), which analyses total international tourist arrivals for a group of countries in the Caribbean. Chu (1998) assesses the demand for international tourism in 10 destinations in Asian-Pacific destinations, Lanza et al. (2003) investigate the share of tourism expenditure in consumption in 13 OECD countries, and Romilly et al. (1998) identify economic and social determinants of tourism spending in 138 countries.

Type III. There are seven studies which specifically examine the demand for tourism from a specific source country to a specific destination, namely Burger et al. (2001), Hui and Yuen (1998, 2002), Lim and McAleer (1999), Qu and Lam (1997), Venegas and Croes (2000) and Yoon and Shafer (1996).

Such research may not be regarded as particularly useful because it does not provide a comparative assessment between source markets and its implications for the tourism industry of the destination country as a whole. A comparative assessment is always desirable to the destination country, so that policy as well as marketing strategies, both at micro and macro level, can be prescribed based on the comparative results.

Type IV. The largest number of papers, or 24 of 53, analyse tourism demand to a single destination from multiple source countries. This type of research on tourism demand is beneficial to the destination country since it would give them a perspective analysis of tourism demand from respective source countries, for that specific period of time and also due to the shortcomings of analyses in papers categorised under Type III.

Type V. Tourists from a single market to multiple destinations are examined in five papers, which assess the outbound tourism demand from UK in four instances, and from Australia on one occasion, namely De Mello et al. (2002), Kulendran and Witt (2001), Song et al. (2000), Turner et al. (1998) and Webber (2001). All five papers used tourism departures as a measure of outbound tourism demand. This type of tourism demand analysis would be particularly useful for tour operators because it would enable them to identify the markets that they would need to concentrate on to expand their commercial activities.

Type VI. Analyses of tourism demand from multiple sources to multiple destinations occur only twice, and we conclude that such an analysis is not very popular among researchers. Although computational problems are not of great concern these days, one reason of the unpopularity of such research could be that the analysis is too cumbersome. Moreover, the scope is too broad, particularly Wong (1997), who covers the entire world.

Functional form of tourism demand models. The demand for tourism in destination x by tourists in source country y is written as follows:

$$D_{xy} = f(Price_x, CP_y, Y_y, T_y, PR_{xy}, \varepsilon_{xy}) \tag{3.1}$$

where, D_{xy} is the quantity of tourism product demanded by tourists from source country y in destination x; $Price_x$ is the price a tourist from country y pays to visit destination x; CP_y is the price paid by source country y tourists to competitor destinations; Y_y is the level of income in source country y; T_y is the consumers' tastes in source country y; PR_{xy} is the promotional expenditure by destination x in country y; ε_{xy} is a random disturbance term, which is independently and identically distributed, with mean zero and constant variance. In essence, this term will account for all the other factors that influence tourism demand in destination x from source country y.

Determinants of tourism demand. In this sub-section, we analyse the possible choice of variables that can be considered for an empirical model in determining tourism demand. There are various reasons for which tourists travel outside their country of residence. The general definition of a tourist is someone who travels for pleasure, a temporary visitor staying at least 24 hours in the country visited for purposes classified as holiday (recreation, leisure, sports and visits to family, friends and relatives), business, official mission, convention or medical treatment. As mentioned above, a large proportion of empirical studies on tourism demand is based on total tourism visits, which include the above-mentioned purposes.

In general, the determinants of tourism demand are somewhat similar among the many types of tourism demand analysed because the hypotheses tested are based on microeconomic theory. The quantity of tourism product demanded by tourists from a particular destination, at a given point in time, is bounded by a series of constraints, and is defined as tourism demand. The tourist is the consumer, whose utility is maximised by the consumption of the tourism product, which is a conglomerate of tourism goods and services consisting of travel costs to and boarding and lodging at the destination. The constraints on the consumer (tourist) include the costs of travel and living in the destination, the costs of reaching and living in competitor destinations, tourists' tastes and preferences, social, cultural and political factors, international terrorism, and promotional expenditures.

The dependent variable. There are several measures of international tourism demand, and the most common measure is a physical head count of arriving tourists at a particular destination at a given point in time. Other measures of international travel demand include income received through tourism or expenditures by tourists, at a destination and at a particular point in time. On rare occasions, the number of bednights spend by arriving tourists, at a particular destination at a given point in time, is also used. Data on international tourist arrivals are usually obtained at the airport immigration counters, tourist registration information at hotels and resorts, sample surveys, and so forth.

Song and Witt (2000) assert that, on arrival at airports, there are circumstances where arriving tourists are counted as inbound tourists. They also argue that when entries are done for checking in tourists in hotels, day trippers, visiting family and friends, business tourists are excluded. In order to minimise the degree of measurement error, Song and Witt (2000) propose that entry and exit sample surveys may be applied and, for outbound tourist demand, a household survey should be undertaken. Under these two scenarios, the only drawback would be the small size, but the advantage would be the accuracy in finding a precise dependent variable. Such an exercise would certainly be worthwhile because it would enable more realistic inferences regarding the estimates.

Table 3.10 gives an illustration of the various choices of dependent variables that have been used in the 53 papers analysed. Except for 10 of the 53 papers, all have transformed the variables used into logarithms prior to undertaking the empirical analysis. There are many reasons why researchers transform the data into logarithms as a precursor to regression analysis. The first objective is to achieve linearity in the variables. The next is to achieve constant variance or homogeneity in the variance around the regression line. Normality in the random error term, or at least spherical symmetry about the regression line, should be accomplished.

Table 3.10   Dependent Variables

Dependent Variable	Frequency
1. Logarithm of Number of Tourist Arrivals	27
2. Logarithm of Tourist Expenditure	4
3. Logarithm of Travel Receipts	4
4. Logarithm of Number of Nights Spent	3
5. Logarithm of Per Capita Real Tourist Expenditure	3
6. Logarithm of Tourist Departures	3
7. Logarithm of per capita Tourist Arrivals	2
8. Logarithm of Real Tourist Expenditure	1
9. Logarithm of Visitors Lodged in Hotel and Apartments	1
10. Logarithm of Per Capita Tourism Visits	1
11. Number of Tourist Arrivals	7
12. Daily Room Occupancy Rate	2
13. Share of Tourist Expenditure in Consumption	1
Total	*59*

Note: Garcia-Ferrer and Queralt (1997) used 2 dependent variables; González and Moral (1995) used 3; González and Moral (1996) used 2; Jensen (1998) used 2; and Lim and McAleer(2001b) used 2.

A transformation into logarithms that achieves one of these objectives may also achieve all three. This is possible because, when the random sample has a multivariate normal distribution, homogeneity and linearity will follow. Hence, either of the three which makes a random sample appear normal in one respect, may also make it appear to be multivariate normal in the other two respects.

Independent variables. The choice of independent variables used in the empirical model is divided into five board categories, namely economic, social, commercial, geographical and qualitative. They are drawn according to the frequency of their usage in the 53 papers reviewed. Economic variables are the most frequently used independent variables since the demand for tourism is primarily based on the economic viability of the decision to purchase a tourism product. Altogether there are 48 explanatory variables used in the 53 papers, of which 28 are economic variables, seven are social variables, six are commercial variables, six are qualitative variables, and one is a geographical variable. Qualitative variables are incorporated in order to capture unique events that are perceived to affect tourism demand. The different choices of explanatory variables that appeared in the 53 papers surveyed, and their frequencies of occurrence, are given in Table 3.11. In order to emphasize concepts, only the important variables are discussed.

Income (expressed as GDP and GNP, as well as in their associated transformations) has the highest frequency of inclusion of 30 as an independent economic variable in the 53 papers. This variable is perceived to be the principal determinant of tourism demand. Generally, in tourism demand models the income of tourists or their aggregate consumption is reflected in the per capita GDP. This is applicable if the dependent variable is also expressed in per capita terms. Because tourism demand is categorized into various forms, the appropriate income variable needs to be chosen with care. As far as holiday tourism and visiting friends and relatives are concerned, the suitable income variable would be per capita consumption, for which data can be obtained from GDP estimates (see Kulendran and Witt, 2001; Qu and Lam, 1997 and Turner et al. 1998).

When world aggregate tourism demand is modelled for Thailand, Vogt and Wittayakorn (1998) use aggregated world income. If the model is examining business tourism, then the appropriate income variable would be per capita GDP (see Kulendran and Witt, 2003 and Kulendran and Wilson, 2000). GDP, GNP and their constituent parts are estimates based on the System of National Accounts (SNA) of the United Nations. Hence, the most appropriate variable to use as a proxy for income would be Broad Money (also known as M2), which consists of notes and coins and demand deposits in the banking system. Although it is a stock figure, this variable clearly provides the most accurate reflection of what residents of any country hold as income. High frequency data for this variable are published quarterly in the IMF/IFS. In the 53 papers surveyed, the national income (GDP or GNP) of the tourist source country was included on 36 occasions.

The price of tourism cannot be determined with any precision because the tourism product per se is a conglomerate of goods and services. Price of tourism is divided into two distinct parts, namely the cost of transport and the

Table 3.11   Choice of Explanatory Variables

Type of Explanatory Variables Used	Frequency
Economic Variables	
1. National Income of Tourist Source Country	30
2. Relative Cost of Living between Source and Destination	25
3. Lagged Tourist Arrivals	14
4. Air Travel Costs	13
5. Price of Competitor Destinations	11
6. Nominal Bilateral Exchange Rate	6
7. Exports and Imports	4
8. Price of Hotel Rooms	3
9. Personal Disposable Income	3
10. Real Effective Exchange Rate	3
11. Consumption Expenditure	2
12. Tourism Price	2
13. Income of Destination Country	2
14. Relative airfare to competitor destinations	2
15. Tourist Expenditure	1
16. Oil Price	1
17. Capital Stock in Destination	1
18. Surface Travel Costs	1
19. CPI in Tourism Source Country	1
20. Number of Inbound Holiday Tourists	1
21. Number of Outbound Holiday Tourists	1
22. Real Exchange Rate	1
23. Real Exchange Rate Volatility	1
24. World Tourism Price	1
25. World Income	1
26. Trip Cost	1
27. Exchange Rate Volatility	1
Social Variables	
1. Population	2
2. Tastes and Preferences	2
3. Age	1
4. Gender	1
5. Household Size	1

Table 3.11   Choice of Explanatory Variables (continued)

Type of Explanatory Variables Used	Frequency
6. Adult Literacy	1
7. Net Migration	1
Geographical Variables	
1. Distance to Destination	1
Commercial Variables	
1. Hotel Capacity	4
2. Promotional Expenditure	4
3. Openness to Trade	2
4. Lagged Hotel Nights	1
5. Nights spend	1
6. Number of Bed Nights Spent	1
7. Retail Sales	1
8. Business Confidence (Survey)	1
Qualitative Variables	
1. Dummy Variables	14
2. Seasonal Component	6
3. Deterministic Trend	4
4. Stochastic Time Trend	3
5. Stochastic Seasonal Component	2
6. Cyclical Component	1

cost of living in the destination. Transport costs are often omitted, primarily because they are directly correlated with other explanatory variables. Moreover, some authors have mentioned the difficulty in obtaining data for transport costs. Air travel costs were included as travel costs in 13 cases, reflecting the third most important explanatory variable appearing in the 53 papers, while surface travel costs and oil price appeared only once.

For the second component of the price of the tourism product, the consumer price index in the destination country is used as a proxy for the cost of living. Normally, CPI calculation is based on a representative basket of goods and services consumed locally. Such a basket usually does not incorporate tourist prices, such as hotel costs. Tourism is not regarded as a leisure activity but as a way of life in SITEs. Hence, it is not likely for it to appear in a representative consumption basket of a developing country.

Spain is the only country that seems to compile a Tourism Price Index (TPI). González and Moral (1995) assert that the Spanish TPI is not available for all of Spain's tourist client countries. The majority of the papers in this review used relative CPI between the tourism source country and destination to reflect the tourism price in 25 cases, which is the second most widely used explanatory variable. A rational tourist will make a decision to travel based on the relative purchasing power between the currencies against the currency of the destination. This can be done by making adjustments to the destination prices through the bilateral exchange rate. On six occasions, the nominal bilateral exchange rate was applied.

However, international tourism to SITEs is through package holidays that are operated by large multinational tour operators. Therefore, prices of such packages incorporate transport costs and the cost of living combined. Pricing of such packages is based on the general level of prices where they are sold (see Yoon and Shafer, 1996). Therefore, it would be sensible to incorporate the bilateral exchange rate of the tourist source country against the US dollar, the world's most widely used currency, to give a clear indication of the purchasing power of the tourism source country currency. Bilateral exchange rates may provide a better representation of the cost of living in a destination because most international travellers are comprised of nationals from the most economically advanced countries. The majority of the people who travel from such countries to international destinations have a reasonable knowledge of their bilateral exchange rates.

Furthermore, real exchange rate, real effective exchange rate and nominal exchange rate volatility are also used. The real exchange rate is nominal exchange rate adjusted for inflation. It is called the real effective exchange rate when it is weighted against principal trading partners. A cautionary note on including exchange rates is suggested in Martin and Witt (1987) because, while a favourable exchange rate to a destination country exists, that may be counterbalanced by high inflation. In such circumstances, using exchange rate alone may not be sensible. Moreover, Carey (1989, 1991, 1992) employed the price of hotel rooms, while Greenidge (2001) and Vogt and Wittayakorn (1998) applied a composite price of tourism adjusted for inflation.

The next most important independent variable incorporated in tourism demand models is the price of substitutes. Substitute prices are incorporated in two distinct ways. They are substitutes between domestic tourism and foreign tourism. In such circumstances, substitute prices are specified as the relative cost of living of tourists between home and abroad. However, it has been argued in the international tourism literature that tourism at home and tourism abroad are two different products, and so cannot be regarded as direct substitutes. Therefore, it may not be sensible to use the method of substitute prices.

Substitution is made between two overseas destinations, where domestic tourism is directly comparable to a group of destinations such as SITEs, or even two destinations with similar characteristics or themes, such as heritage tourism in the Taj Mahal and the Great Wall of China. In this instance, substitute prices are formulated to reflect the relative cost of two competing destinations or destinations within a group of destinations which depict similar attributes. The price of competitor destinations appears on 11 occasions, recording the fifth most widely used economic variable of the 53 papers, while relative airfares to competitor destinations occurred on two occasions.

It has been widely acknowledged in the international tourism literature that habit persistence in tourism is highly prevalent. In order to identify and evaluate the magnitude of habit persistence, an autoregressive term in the form of a lagged dependent variable is incorporated as an explanatory variable. On 14 instances, one period lagged tourist arrivals appeared, recording the third most widely used explanatory variable incorporated in the 53 papers reviewed, while on three occasions one period lagged hotel nights were included.

The incorporation of the lagged dependent variable reflects repeat visits and the effect of dissemination of knowledge to others through experience from previous visits to a destination. Innovations in the non-stationary behaviour of the lagged aggregate international tourists' arrivals would very likely become an important source of explaining international arrivals fluctuations. A significant coefficient on the lagged dependent variable will certainly explain that visitors in the preceding period had made a significant impact on the current level of tourist arrivals. It could be that a higher proportion of the last period visitors are repeaters and the last period visitors' word-of-mouth has been spread, having an impact on the current level.

Like any other good or service, tastes and preferences about tourism product have a profound impact on tourism demand. Tastes are influenced by the travellers' socio-economic background, such as age, sex, education, marital status, and so forth. Such characteristics are time varying because tourist destinations and source countries increase due to the emergence of new nations. Relevant examples are the formation of new countries due to the collapse of the former Soviet Union and its Eastern Bloc partners, and the independence of East Timor. The growth of world affluence, competitive airfares and greater awareness about the world due to the advent of the internet are factors that affect tastes and preferences of tourists.

The opening of a new airport in a remote destination to accommodate wide-bodied aircrafts, and population growth in tourism source countries, also affect tourism demand. Incorporation of a variable to indicate tastes and preferences is rather difficult due to data constraints. González and Moral (1995) argue that it is not only difficult to measure, but also that tastes are conceptually difficult to separate. Of the 53 papers, only in two instances were tastes and preferences explicitly incorporated in the tourism demand model.

Song et al. (2000) incorporated a derived variable called the destination preference index, defined as number of visits to a particular destination by total number of visits abroad. Downward (2003) incorporated tastes and preferences by obtaining data on visitor preferences in a tourism demand survey in rural Herefordshire, UK. In the international tourism literature, a convenient way to capture how popular a destination has been over time is by incorporating a time trend. In the 53 papers, inclusion of a time trend is not clearly stated, but on four occasions a deterministic time trend, and on three occasions a stochastic time trend, are used. Due to multicollinearity between time and income, time is typically deleted from the analysis.

Although population is perceived to be one of the most important variables in any economic analysis, it has unequivocally been incorporated as an explanatory variable in determining tourism demand only on two occasions in the 53 papers examined. However, it has been used indirectly on several occasions to determine per capita explanatory variables. Tourism demand from a particular source is determined by the size of its population since tourists are a subset of that population. Furthermore, the changes to the population are quite frequently ignored owing to the fact that tourism demand is not commonly modelled as the growth rate of tourist arrivals.

As mentioned previously, one of the primary reasons for not including population in the model is due to the direct correlation between income and population. Realistic tourism demand models are based on monthly and quarterly tourist arrivals, and occasionally on weekly or daily frequencies. In such short periods of time, significant changes in population in tourist source countries are unlikely to occur, so that it may not be sensible to incorporate it. In studies which measure tourism demand in terms of annual data, population may be incorporated.

Academics and practitioners in tourism advocate that effective promotional expenditures are the key to success in selling tourism products, so they play an important role in determining the level of tourist arrivals at destinations. There are countless ways in which tourism marketing is conducted, and is carried out through the media, travel fairs and expositions, among others. Nowadays, tourism advertising is not only undertaken by tour operators, but also by state-funded national tourism promotion organisations.

Generally, tour operator advertising is carried out on a collective basis, for a group of destinations with similar attributes that complement each other. Its desired impact is insignificant. Promoting tourism from the national promotional perspective has a direct and positive impact on international tourist arrivals. On four occasions, promotional expenditure was used as an explanatory variable in the 53 papers surveyed.

There are other qualitative explanatory variables in the form of dummy variables that are incorporated to analyse tourism demand. These include seasonal dummy variables and dummy variables to quantify the effects of one-off events, domestically or worldwide, that may have affected tourism demand. One of the important features of international tourism demand is seasonality, and frequently seasonal dummy variables are incorporated to determine the magnitude of how it affects tourism demand. Such dummy variables are normally incorporated in empirical models which use monthly and quarterly data to capture the high degree of seasonality that is persistent in tourism demand.

Tourism demand is usually influenced by a specific time of the year relating to a particular season or school holidays. Garín-Muñoz and Amaral (2000, p. 525) state that 'annual data are used to avoid seasonality problems...', and it is quite clear that in the international tourism literature some authors have avoided analysing seasonality. A monthly international tourism demand model should include 12 seasonal dummy variables, while in quarterly tourism demand analysis four seasonal dummy variables are typically included. Of the 53 papers analysed in this survey, seasonal dummy variables are included in eight instances.

There are also other independent variables in the form of dummy variables incorporated to capture one-off events that may have influenced worldwide travel. In turn, this affects travel to a particular destination or events that pertain to the destination itself, which subsequently affect the number of international tourist arrivals. In the 53 papers investigated, 24 events of special significance appeared on 37 occasions. Details of the events and their frequency of occurrence are given in Table 3.12.

Analysis of models
This section examines the empirical characteristics, such as recognition of omitted variables, as well as inclusion of proxy variables, specifications used in models of tourism demand, the various methods of estimation that have been used, reported descriptive statistics, and diagnostic testing in the 53 papers reviewed.

Recognition of omitted variables and use of proxy variables. As in the case of many economic relationships, the theoretical models postulated to assess tourism demand are quite frequently specified in terms of variables that are not directly observable. In order to derive the empirical specification of these models, proxy variables are used in place of the unobserved variables. The theoretically postulated variables in determining tourism demand, as well as their proxy variable counterparts that appeared in the 53 papers and their frequency of appearance in descending order, are represented in Table 3.13.

Table 3.12   Events of Special Significance for Tourism Demand

Qualitative Variable or Event	Frequency
1. Hotels of Different Quality	1
2. Spain's Membership in EFTA	1
3. Inception of Portugal's negotiations on EU membership	1
4. Japanese government policy on encouraging foreign travel	3
5. America's Cup 1986	2
6. 1991 Gulf War	5
7. Relaxation of outbound South Korean travel visa in 1988	1
8. Bird Flu Epidemic in Hong Kong 1997–98	1
9. Reversion of Hong Kong's Sovereignty to China in 1997	1
10. 1974 Oil Crisis	2
11. 1979 Oil Crisis	2
12. 1986 Bombing of Libya	2
13. Australia's Bicentennial Exposition in Brisbane in 1988	2
14. Australian Pilots' Strike 1989	2
15. Popularity of Australian Films Abroad 1985–86	1
16. Seoul Olympics 1988	1
17. Coups d'état of 1987 and 2000 in Fiji	2
18. Military action in Croatia in 1995	1
19. Tiananmen Square Incident 1989	1
20. Chinese visa relaxation to travel to Hong Kong in 1993	1
21. German Reunification 1991	1
22. Chernobyl Disaster 1986	1
23. Effects of US Recession 1979–81	1
24. Problems of airlift in Aruba 1986	1
Total	*37*

The inclusion of proxy variables in empirical analysis clearly indicates the presence of measurement errors since the correct variable is not used. The presence of measurement error has adverse implications for Ordinary Least Squares (OLS) estimation. The assumption that the variables are exogenous is violated by including inappropriately measured variables. Therefore, it is likely that the explanatory variables and error term in the regression are correlated, so that OLS produces biased and inconsistent estimators. Garber and Klepper (1980) provide a detailed and instructive explanation to deal with problems of errors-in-variables due to incorrectly measured variables.

Table 3.13   Omitted Variables and Proxy Variables

Theoretically Postulated Variable	Proxy Variable Used and Variables that are Omitted	Frequency
Income	1. GDP	8
	2. Real GDP	8
	3. Per Capita Real GDP	4
	4. Real Personal Disposable Income	4
	5. GNP	3
	6. Income expressed as an Index	3
	7. Per Capita Real GNP	2
	8. Share of Expenditure in Tourism	2
	9. Real GNP	1
	10. Per Capita Real Expenditure	1
	11. Real Private Consumption	1
	12. National Disposable Income	1
	13. Level of Per Capita Personal Disposable Income	1
	14. Per Capita Private Consumption Expenditure	1
	Total 1/	*40*
	Number of Papers omitted Income	*16*
Price	COST OF LIVING (CL)	
	1. Relative CPI between Destination and Source	14
	2. Exchange Rate Adjusted CPI in Destination	7
	3. Exchange Rate adjusted Relative CPI between Destination and Source	6
	4. Exchange Rate Adjusted Hotel Price in Destination	2
	5. Bilateral Nominal Exchange Rate	2
	6. Real Exchange Rate	2
	7. Real Effective Exchange Rate	2
	8. CPI of Destination	2
	9. Average Per Diem Expenditure	1
	10. CPI of Destination Adjusted by Implicit Price Deflator in Source	1
	Total 2/	*39*
	COST OF TRANSPORTATION (CT)	
	1. CPI Adjusted Economy Class Return Airfare	7
	2. CPI Adjusted Economy Class One-Way Airfare	2

Table 3.13   Omitted Variables and Proxy Variables (continued)

Theoretically Postulated Variable	Proxy Variable Used and Variables that are Omitted	Frequency
	3. Average Economy Class Return Airfare	1
	4. Cost of Travel by Surface	1
	5. Economy Class Airfare	1
	6. Geometric Mean of Different Classes of Airfare between destination and Source	1
	7. Oil Price	1
	8. Distance between Tourist Source and Destination	1
	Total	*15*
	Number of Papers omitted Cost of Transportation	*21*
	Number of Papers nested CL and CT in Spending and Trip Cost	*2*
	Number of Papers omitted both CL and CT	*15*
Substitute Prices	1. Relative CPI between Destination and Competitor Destinations	14
	2. Price of Substitute Hotels	2
	3. Relative Airfare between Destination and Competitor Destinations	2
	4. Relative Price Index between Destination and Competitor Destinations	1
	Total 3/	*19*
	Number of Papers omitted both CL and CT	*36*

Notes:
1. Jensen (1998), Kim and Song (1998), Kulendran and King (1997) and Kulendran (1996) used two variables for income. Downward (2003) used a survey based income measure.
2. Lee et al. (1996), Venegas and Croes (2000) and Webber (2001) used two variables for price.
3. Kulendran and Witt (2003) and Turner et al. (1998) used two variables for substitute prices.

If one proxy variable is used in a linear regression model, the absolute value of the estimate of the coefficient lies between zero and the absolute value of the parameter. The degree of absolute bias in the estimated coefficients of proxy variables and the correctly measured variables are negligible if the degree of measurement error is negligible in the proxy variable. Additionally, it is always favourable to use a proxy variable in the model than to delete it, otherwise the model will suffer from omitted variables bias.

In situations where more than one proxy variable is used, together with correctly measured variables, the estimates of the parameters of the proxy variables will not satisfy the conditions described above. Hence, reducing the measurement error in proxy variables may not necessarily improve the associated estimates of the correctly measured variables. In this scenario, excluding the proxy variables may be desirable rather than including them. As a result, the preferred option would be to use instrumental variables, which have to be chosen with care. Although it is frequently difficult to obtain a suitable instrumental variable, a prerequisite in choosing such a variable would be such that it is correlated with the incorrect proxy variable and uncorrelated with the error term.

As can be seen from Table 3.13, in the 53 papers examined, several proxy variables have been used. Few authors have acknowledged the use of proxy variables for the unobserved variables. However, it is evident that none of the papers has shown particular concern for the econometric implications of the use of proxy variables for estimation and inference. Income is proxied with 14 different types of variables on 40 different occasions. Of these, GDP and real GDP were used on eight occasions, respectively, while per capita real GDP and real personal disposable income appeared in four papers each. GNP and aggregate income expressed as an index were used in three instances, while per capita real GNP and the share of tourism in expenditure were used on two occasions. Per capita real expenditure, real private consumption, national disposable income, level of per capita personal disposable income and per capita private consumption expenditure appeared only once.

As an explanatory variable, income was not included in 16 papers which analysed tourism demand based on univariate time series modelling. In Jensen (1998), Kim and Song (1998), Kulendran (1996) and Kulendran and King (1997), two separate variables were proxied for income. Downward (2003) used correctly measured income of tourists due to a survey, and this was the only instance where income was not proxied among the 53 papers reviewed.

One of the components of tourism price is the cost of living, and it was represented by 10 different proxy variables on 39 occasions. Of the papers which included cost of living in their analysis, 35 per cent, or 14 of 53 papers, used the relative CPI between the destination and tourism source countries. Seven papers used the exchange rate adjusted CPI in the destination, while six papers used the exchange rate adjusted relative CPI between the destination and source countries. The exchange rate adjusted hotel price in destination, bilateral nominal exchange rate, real exchange rate, and the CPI of the destination were each used as a proxy on at least two occasions, while average per diem expenditure and CPI of destination adjusted by the implicit price deflator was included only on one occasion. Of the 53 papers, all of the papers which considered the multivariate analysis of tourism demand included a proxy variable for price.

The next component of tourism price is the cost of transportation, which was approximated by eight different proxy variables on 15 occasions. The CPI adjusted economy class airfare recorded the highest frequency with seven, compared with the CPI adjusted economy class one-way airfare, which only appeared in Kulendran (1996) and Kulendran and King (1997). Average return airfare, economy class airfare, and the geometric mean of different class of airfare between destination and tourist source, appeared on only one occasion. Ledesma-Rodriguez and Navarro-Ibanez (2001) used oil price as a proxy for the cost of transportation, while Daniel and Ramos (2002) used surface costs. There were 21 of the 53 papers which did not use transportation costs. In Downward (2003) and Yoon and Shafer (1996), the cost of living and transport costs are both nested in spending and trip cost, respectively. Of the 53 papers, 15 papers excluded both the cost of living and transportation costs. Finally, Lee et al. (1996), Venegas and Croes (2000) and Webber (2001) used two proxy variables for price in their papers.

The price of substitutes is generally regarded as the third most important determinant, and is proxied with four different variables in 19 of the 53 papers. The relative CPI between the destination and competitor destinations proved to be the most widely used proxy variable, with the highest occurrence of 14, while the price of substitute hotels and relative airfares between the destination and tourist source country each appeared in two papers. The relative price index between the destination and competitor destinations was used only once. Kulendran and Witt (2003) and Turner et al. (1998) used two proxy variables for substitute prices.

Model specification and types of models used. Consumer demand theory states that there exists a relationship between tourist arrivals and the price of tourism product, income of tourists, and the price of substitute destinations, among many others, and suggests how these factors are perceived to influence tourism demand. However, it cannot state that a relationship should have a particular specification. Hence, the choice of specification is based partly on convenience of estimation and ease of interpretation. The types of empirical specifications to test the economic hypotheses of interest and their associated models are listed in Table 3.14.

In the 53 papers there are 57 specifications, of which Garcia-Ferrer and Queralt (1997), Kulendran (1996), Kulendran and King (1997) and Song et al. (2003) each specified two models. The most popular specification is the multivariate log-linear single equation model, which appeared in 30 papers, or 55 per cent of the total. In almost all of the papers, it has been acknowledged that this type of specification was chosen due to the

Table 3.14   Model Specifications for International Tourism Demand

Estimated Models	Frequency
1. Multivariate Log-Linear Single Equation	30
2. Univariate Time Series Single Equation	16
3. Multivariate (Structural Time Series) Log-Linear Single Equation	7
4. Multivariate Log-Linear Systems of Equations	3
5. Log-Linear Time Series Single Equation	1
Total	*57*

Type of Model Estimated	Frequency
1. Autoregressive Integrated Moving Average (ARIMA)	16
2. Simple Linear Regression Model	15
3. Error Correction Model (ECM)	15
4. Vector Autoregressive (VAR)	14
5. Naive I	7
6. Structural Time Series Model	7
7. Exponential Smoothing	6
8. Seemingly Unrelated Regression Estimation (SURE)	5
9. Moving Average	4
10. Almost Ideal Demand System (AIDS)	4
11. Naïve II	3
12. Pooled Estimation	3
13. Autoregressive Model	3
14. Seasonal ARIMA	3
15. ARMA(p,q)	3
16. AR(1)	3
17. Artificial Neural Networks	2
18. Genetic Regression	1
19. Trend Curve	1
20. Sine Wave	1
21. Holt-Winters Forecasting	1
22. Dynamic Harmonic Regression	1
23. Holt-Winters Exponential Smoothing	1
24. Moving Average ARIMA	1
25. Transfer Function Model	1
26. Don't Know	1
27. AR (12)	1

Table 3.14   Model Specifications for International Tourism Demand
(continued)

Type of Model Estimated	Frequency
28. Cochrane-Orcutt	1
29. Ridge Regression	1
30. Autoregressive Distributed Lag Model (ADLM)	1
31. Johansen Maximum Likelihood	1
32. Reduced ADLM	1
33. Time Varying Parameter	1
34. Economic Structural (LISREL)	1
Total	*130*

Note: Garcia-Ferrer and Queralt (1997), Kulendran and King (1997), Kulendran (1996) and Song et al. (2003) specified two models.

convenience of interpreting the estimated coefficients as elasticities. Moreover, inference can be undertaken relatively easily.

Univariate time series single-equation specifications were used on 16 of 53 occasions, being the second most widely used specification. The attractiveness of this particular specification is associated with the difficulty in obtaining long horizon time series data in a multivariate framework. Until recently, Structural Time Series Models (STSMs) have not been used in estimating tourism demand. Previous surveys of empirical tourism demand have not even mentioned the use of STSMs, but in this survey there are seven papers which have applied STSMs. The special characteristics of modelling STSMs is that the specification incorporates the explanatory variables of tourism demand, as well as a seasonal component, a cyclical component and a time trend. According to Harvey (1989), this is the General Structural Model (GSM). Then the seasonal, cyclical and the trend components are specified separately and estimated, which is called the Basic Structural Model (BSM) (Harvey, 1989).

In the modelling procedure, the BSM is estimated, then it is incorporated into the GSM, and followed by the final estimation. Turner and Witt (2001, p. 137) state: 'the large number of parameters already contained in the STM may be exacerbated by adding additional parameters'. However, according to Greenidge (2001), including the explanatory variables improved the estimates in the general model. De Mello et al. (2002), Divisekera (2003) and Papatheodorou (1999) were the only papers which specified their models in the form of multivariate log-linear systems of equations.

The Box-Jenkins (1976) family of models is the most widely used specification for estimating tourism demand, with the ARIMA representation appearing 16 times among the different models estimated in the 53 papers. Moreover, there are 30 models in the Box-Jenkins (1976) family of models that have been estimated. In 15 instances, the simple linear regression model was used, recording the second highest type of model estimated.

Estimation methods. Table 3.15 shows the methods of estimation used in the 53 papers. It is worth noting that only Lanza et al. (2003) used more than one method of estimation. OLS is the most frequently used method of estimation. This is consistent with the findings in Lim (1997c), who also found that OLS was the most widely used estimation method. While it was apparent that OLS was used, the method of estimation was not stated on one occasion. Thus, OLS remains the most widely used method of estimation in tourism demand. Generalised least squares (GLS) was used on seven occasions, while non-linear least squares were used only once.

Table 3.15   Estimation Methods Used

Estimation Method	Frequency
1. Ordinary Least Squares	45
2. Generalised Least Squares	7
3. Non-Linear Least Squares	1
4. Presumably OLS?	1
Total	*54*

Note: Lanza et al. (2003) used 2 methods of estimation.

Descriptive statistics. Table 3.16 provides the frequency with which the various types of descriptive statistics have been reported. The descriptive statistics provide a benchmark against how well the model fits the data, with some adjustment for parsimony. The t-statistic was the most frequently reported descriptive statistic. In some cases the t-statistic was the only reported statistic of any kind for a regression model. P-values, as an alternative to reporting t-statistics, have been reported on six occasions. The coefficient of multiple determination (R^2) and $\bar{R}^2$ were the second and third most widely reported descriptive statistics, respectively, and were frequently used to indicate the statistical adequacy of a model. There were also cases where $\bar{R}^2$ was the only reported descriptive statistic of any kind for a regression model.

The F-statistic of the overall regression, which tests the significance of the

Table 3.16   Descriptive Statistics Reported

Reported Descriptive Statistics	Reporting Incidence
1. t-statistics	30
2. R^2	23
3. $\bar{R}^2$	22
4. F-Statistic of the Regression	13
5. Asymptotic Standard Errors	11
6. Mean Absolute Percentage Error (MAPE)	8
7. Root Mean Square Error (RMSE)	8
8. Mean Absolute Percentage Error (MAPE)	8
9. p-values	6
10. Standard Error of the Regression	6
11. Seasonally Adjusted R^2 ($R_D{}^2$)	4
12. Akaike Information Criterion (AIC)	4
13. Schwarz Bayesian Criterion (SBC)	4
14. Root Mean Square Percentage Error (RMSPE)	3
15. One Step Ahead Prediction Error Variance	3
16. Thiel's Inequality Coefficient	2
17. Standard Deviation of Variables Used	2
18. Mean Absolute Sum of Squared Errors (MABSE)	1
19. Mean Square Error (MSE)	1
20. Mean Absolute Deviation (MAD)	1
21. Pearson Product Moment Correlation Coefficient (PPMCC)	1
22. Mean of Variables Used	1
23. Variances Associated with Seasonal, Trend and Cyclical Component	1
24. Residual Sum of Squares	1
25. Goodness of Fit Index	1
26. Aggregated Goodness of Fit Index	1
27. No Descriptive Statistics Reported	4
Total	*172*

joint effect of the explanatory variables, is reported 13 times, making it the fourth highest descriptive statistic reported.

In order to evaluate and compare the number of competing regression models, a number of measures of the regression error are used. On 11 occasions, the asymptotic standard error of the regression, and on six instances asymptotic standard errors of the estimates, are reported as a measure of the variability of an estimated regression model.

The in-sample estimation and the out-of-sample forecasting ability of (competing) models are compared on the basis of error measures. These include the mean absolute percentage error, root mean square error, mean absolute percentage error, root mean square percentage error, one-step ahead prediction error variance, mean absolute sum of squared errors, mean square error, and mean absolute deviation, all of which appeared on 39 occasions.

Information criteria are used on eight occasions, including Schwarz's Bayesian Criterion (SBC) and Akaike's Information Criterion (AIC). SBC and AIC are used by Dharmaratne (1995) and Lim and McAleer (1999, 2001a, 2002) to evaluate, compare and contrast the competing regression models.

Diagnostic testing. In applied econometrics, diagnostic testing is concerned with establishing whether the estimated empirical model is an adequate explanation of the data. This process involves making several auxiliary assumptions regarding functional form, relevant variables, and adequate approximations of the 'true' variables of interest, and the stability of the model.

It is noted in Pesaran and Smith (1985, p. 138) that: 'A consequence of this procedure is that one cannot know whether the results of the statistical analyses reflect inferentially on the economic theory or on the auxiliary assumptions'. The statistical adequacy of the model is through diagnostic testing of the auxiliary assumptions and tests of a number of specific null hypotheses. These are listed below.

In the context of OLS, McAleer (1994) considers a linear regression model and lists the following auxiliary assumptions that require diagnostic testing: (a) correct functional form, (b) no heteroscedasticity, (c) no serial correlation, (d) exogeneity of the explanatory variables, (e) normality of the errors, (f) parameter consistency, (g) non-nested models (the model is adequate in the presence of non-nested alternative models), and (h) robustness to departures from the auxiliary assumptions.

McAleer (1994) also argues that there are foreseeable complications for estimation and inference when some or all of the auxiliary assumptions are not upheld. For instance, tests that reject the null hypothesis of incorrect functional form may be due to various possibilities, such as incorrect functional form, omitted variables, serial correlation, structural change, heteroscedasticity, or sample selection bias.

The auxiliary assumptions for which diagnostic tests were reported in the 53 empirical papers are given in Table 3.17. The most frequently tested

Table 3.17   Reported Diagnostic Tests in International Tourism Demand

Diagnostic Test	Frequency
SERIAL CORRELATION	
1. Breuch-Godfrey Test	26
2. Durban Watson Statistic	22
3. Box-Ljung Statistic	5
4. Box-Pierce Q-Statistic	1
5. Wallis Test	1
6. CRDW	1
NORMALITY	
7. Jarque-Bera Test	13
8. Other Tests	3
HETEROSCEDASTICITY	
9. White's Test	11
10. Breuch-Pagan Test	2
11. Other Tests	1
FUNCTIONAL FORM	
12. Ramsey's RESET Test	10
13. Chow Test	1
STRUCTURAL INSTABILITY	
14. Chow's Predictive Failure Test	9
OTHER TESTS FOR AUXILIARY ASSUMPTIONS	
15. Engle's ARCH Test	2
16. Hausman Test for Fixed Effects versus Random Effects	2
17. Likelihood Ratio Test for Homogeneity Restriction	1
18. Wald test for Joint Significance of Fixed Effects and First Differences	1
19. Wald Test for Homogeneity and Symmetry	1
20. Cointegration Durbin Watson Statistic	1
21. Wald Test for Restricted versus Unrestricted Models	1
22. Wald Test for Parameter Consistency	1
23. CUSUM Test Statistics	1
No Diagnostic Tests Reported	17
Total	*127*

auxiliary assumption was serial correlation. The Lagrange Multiplier (LM) test, or the Breusch (1978) and Godfrey (1978) test, appeared in 26 papers. The LM statistic is a more generally applicable test because it tests for higher-order serial correlation in the errors and accommodates the inclusion of a lagged dependent variable in the regression. The Durbin-Watson (DW) test (including the Cointegrating Regression DW test) was reported in 23 papers. However, the DW statistic is generally limited to detecting only first-order serial correlation.

Five papers used the Box-Ljung statistic, which generally has poor power, particularly in small samples. The following two tests implemented to detect serial correlation, namely the Box-Pierce Q-statistic, which appeared once in Dharmaratne (1995), has low power in small to medium-sized samples, while the Wallis test in Kulendran (1996) may have reasonable power.

The second most frequently tested auxiliary assumption is that of normality in the errors. The Jarque-Bera (1980) test is used in 13 papers. In small samples, if the assumption of normality in the errors is violated, then the t-statistics and the F-statistics in the estimated regression model are invalid. Three papers report other tests for serial correlation, such as the Kolmogorov-D statistic in Carey (1989, 1992), but it is not clearly stated which test was used in Downward (2003).

The auxiliary assumption of no heteroscedasticity is the third most frequently tested auxiliary assumption, appearing in 15 papers. The test developed by White (1980) was used in 11 papers. In this test, an auxiliary regression is estimated for the residuals from the regression equation against all the explanatory variables, together with their squares and cross-products. The Breusch-Pagan test for heteroscedasticity appeared in two papers, while Koenker's test appeared only in Payne and Merva (2002).

3.5   CONCLUSION

This chapter evaluated published empirical research with reference to the frequency of data used, choice of both dependent and explanatory variables, use of proxy variables, type of model chosen, economic hypotheses tested, methods of estimation, calculation of standard errors for inference, reported descriptive statistics, use of diagnostic tests of the auxiliary assumptions, use of information criteria, and empirical implications for tourism demand.

Compared with recent surveys of empirical examination in tourism analysis, particularly Lim (1997a), there is evidence to show that substantial change has occurred in reporting empirical results. Of the 53 papers examined in this chapter, nine failed to report diagnostic tests and three failed to report descriptive statistics. Lim (1997a) highlighted serious concern regarding the

100 papers surveyed of failing to report diagnostic tests and descriptive statistics, such that inferences regarding those results had to be made with caution. From the findings in this survey, the assertion made in Lim (1997a) would seem to have been well received in the tourism research community.

In this chapter, a relatively high frequency of applications of modern and innovative techniques, such as cointegration, ECM and Artificial Neural Networks, have been observed. The traditional empirical tourism analysis of a single destination and single tourism source country has appeared in only two papers. The most widely used analytical setting is a single destination and multiple tourism source countries. Such analyses are enabled through the availability of comprehensive data sets that are maintained by destination countries. This indicates the importance of empirical tourism analysis for individual economies as greater emphasis is now given to the tourism industry than ever before.

There has been substantial empirical research in tourism analysis over the period 1995–2003. It is evident that significant progress has been achieved in the application and presentation of empirical results compared with previous surveys of the international tourism literature.

REFERENCES

Akis, S. (1998), 'A compact econometric model of tourism demand for Turkey', *Tourism Management*, **19**(1), 99–102.

Box, G.E.P. and G.M. Jenkins (1976), *Time Series Analysis: Forecasting and Control*, Second Edition, San Francisco: Holden Day.

Breusch, T. (1978), 'Testing for autocorrelation in dynamic linear models', *Australian Economic Papers*, **17**, 334–55.

Burger, C.J.S.C., M. Dohnal, M. Kathrada and R. Law (2001), 'A practitioners' guide to time series methods for tourism demand forecasting: A case study of Durban, South Africa', *Tourism Management*, **22**, 403–9.

Carey, K. (1989), 'Tourism development in LDCs: Hotel capacity expansion with reference to Barbados', *World Development*, **17**(1), 59–67.

Carey, K. (1991), 'Estimation of Caribbean tourism demand: Issues in measurement and methodology', *Atlantic Economic Journal*, **19**(3), 32–40.

Carey, K. (1992), 'Optimal hotel capacity: The case of Barbados', *Social and Economic Studies*, **42**(2), 103–26.

Chan, Y.M., T.K. Hui and E. Yuen (1999), 'Modelling the impact of sudden environmental change on visitor arrival forecast: The case of the Gulf War', *Journal of Travel Research*, **37**(4), 391–4.

Cho, V. (2003), 'A comparison of three different approaches to tourist arrival forecasting', *Tourism Management*, **24**, 323–30.

Chu, F.L. (1998), 'Forecasting tourism demand in Asian-Pacific countries', *Annals of Tourism Research*, **25**(3), 597–615.

Crouch, G.I. (1994a), 'The study of international tourism demand: A survey of practice', *Journal of Travel Research*, **32**(4), 41–54.

Crouch, G.I. (1994b), 'The study of international tourism demand: A review of findings', *Journal of Travel Research*, **33**(1), 12–23.

Crouch, G.I. (1996), 'Demand elasticities in international marketing, a meta-analytical application to tourism', *Journal of Business Research*, **36**, 117–36.

Daniel, A.C.M. and F.F.R. Ramos (2002), 'Modelling inbound international tourism demand to Portugal', *International Journal of Tourism Research*, **4**, 193–209.

De Mello, M., A. Pack and T. Sinclair (2002), 'A system of equations model of UK tourism demand in neighbouring countries', *Applied Economics*, **34**, 509–21.

Dharmaratne, G.S. (1995), 'Forecasting tourist arrivals in Barbados', *Annals of Tourism Research*, **22**, 804–18.

Divisekera, S. (2003), 'A model of demand for international tourism', *Annals of Tourism Research*, **30**(1), 31–49.

Downward, P. (2003), 'Beyond the demand for day-visits: An analysis of visitor spending', *Tourism Economics*, **9**(1), 67–76.

Engle, R.F. and C.W.J. Granger (1987), 'Cointegration and error-correction: Representation, estimation and testing', *Econometrica*, **55**, 251–76.

Garber and Klepper (1980), 'Extending the classical normal errors-in-variable model', *Econometrica*, **48**, 1541–6,

Garcia-Ferrer, A. and R.A. Queralt (1997), 'A note on forecasting tourism demand in Spain', *International Journal of Forecasting*, **13**, 539–49.

Garín-Muñoz, T. and T.P. Amaral (2000), 'An econometric model for international tourism flows to Spain', *Applied Economics*, **7**, 525–9.

Godfrey, L.G. (1978), 'Testing for higher order serial correlation in regressors containing lagged dependent variables', *Econometrica*, **46**, 1303–10.

Goh, C. and R. Law (2002), 'Modelling and forecasting tourism demand for arrivals with stochastic non-stationary seasonality and intervention', *Tourism Management*, **23**, 499–510.

González, P. and P. Moral (1995), 'An analysis of tourism demand in Spain', *International Journal of Forecasting*, **11**, 233–51.

González, P. and P. Moral (1996), 'Analysis of tourism trends in Spain', *Annals of Tourism Research*, **11** (4), 233–51.

Greenidge, K. (2001), 'Forecasting tourism demand: An STM approach', *Annals of Tourism Research*, **28**(1), 98–112.

Harvey, A.C. (1989), *Forecasting, Structural Time Series Models and the Kalman Filter*, Cambridge: Cambridge University Press.

Hui, T.-K. and C.C. Yuen (1998), 'An econometric study on Japanese tourist arrivals in British Columbia and its implications', *The Service Industries Journal*, **18**(4), 38–50.

Hui, T.-K. and C.C. Yuen (2002), 'A study in the seasonal variations of Japanese tourist arrivals in Singapore', *Tourism Management*, **23**, 127–31.

Jarque, C.M. and A.K. Bera (1980), 'Efficient tests for normality, homoscedasticity and serial independence of regression residuals', *Economic Letters*, **6**, 255–9.

Jensen, T.C. (1998), 'Income and price elasticities by nationality for tourists in Denmark', *Tourism Economics*, **4**(2), 101–30.

Kim, S. and H. Song (1998), 'Analysis of inbound tourism demand in South Korea: A cointegration and error correction approach', *Tourism Analysis*, **3**, 25–41.

Kulendran, N. (1996), 'Modelling quarterly tourist flows to Australia using cointegration analysis', *Tourism Economics*, **2**(3), 203–22.

Kulendran, N. and M.L. King (1997), 'Forecasting international quarterly tourist flows using error correction and time series models', *International Journal of Forecasting*, **13**, 319–27.

Kulendran, N. and K. Wilson (2000), 'Modelling business travel', *Tourism Economics*, **6**(1), 47–59.

Kulendran, N. and S.F. Witt (2001), 'Cointegration versus least squares regression', *Annals of Tourism Research*, **28**(2), 291–311.

Kulendran N. and S.F. Witt (2003), 'Forecasting the demand for international business tourism', *Journal of Travel Research*, **41**(3), 265–71.

Lanza, A., P. Temple and G. Urga (2003), 'The implications of tourism specialisation in the long run: An econometric analysis for 13 OECD economies', *Tourism Management*, **24**, 315–21.

Lathiras, P. and C. Siriopoulos (1998), 'The demand for tourism to Greece: A cointegration approach', *Tourism Economics*, **4**(2), 171–85.

Ledesma-Rodriguez, F.J. and M. Navarro-Ibanez (2001), 'Panel data and tourism: A case study of Tenerife', *Tourism Economics*, **7**(1), 75–88.

Lee, C.K., T. Var and T.W. Blaine (1996), 'Determinants of inbound tourist expenditures', *Annals of Tourism Research*, **23** (3), 527–42.

Lim, C. (1997a), 'The functional specification of international tourism demand models', *Mathematics and Computers in Simulation*, **43**, 535–43.

Lim, C. (1997b), 'Review of international tourism demand models', *Annals of Tourism Research*, **24**(4), 835–49.

Lim, C. (1997c), 'An econometric classification and review of international tourism demand models', *Tourism Economics*, **3**(1), 69–81.

Lim, C. and M. McAleer (1999), 'A seasonal analysis of Malaysian tourist arrivals to Australia', *Mathematics and Computers in Simulation*, **48**, 573–83.

Lim, C. and M. McAleer (2001a), 'Monthly seasonal variations: Asian tourism to Australia', *Annals of Tourism Research*, **28**(1), 68–82.

Lim, C. and M. McAleer (2001b), 'Forecasting tourist arrivals', *Annals of Tourism Research*, **28**(4), 965–77.

Lim, C. and M. McAleer (2002), 'Time series forecasts of international travel demand for Australia', *Tourism Management*, **23**(4), 389–96.

Martin, C.A. and S.F. Witt (1987), 'Tourism demand forecasting models: Choice of appropriate variables to represent tourists' cost of living', *Tourism Management*, **8**, 233–46.

Morley, C. (1998), 'A dynamic international demand model', *Annals of Tourism Research*, **25**(1), 70–84.

McAleer, M. (1994), 'Sherlock Holmes and the search for the truth: A diagnostic tale', *Journal of Economic Surveys*, **8**, 317–370, reprinted in L. Oxley (ed.) (1994), *Surveys in Econometrics*, Oxford: Blackwell, pp. 91–138.

Narayan, P.K. (2003a), 'Determinants of tourism expenditure in Fiji: A cointegration approach', *Pacific Tourism Review*, **6**, 159–67.

Narayan, P.K. (2003b), 'Tourism demand modelling: Some issues regarding unit roots, cointegration and diagnostic tests', *International Journal of Tourism Research*, **5**, 369–80.

Nozawa, H. (1992), 'A marketing analysis of Japanese outbound travel', *Tourism Management*, **13**, 226–33.

Ong, C. (1995), 'Tourism demand models: A critique', *Mathematics and Computers in Simulation*, **39**, 367–72.

Papatheodorou, A. (1999), 'The demand for international tourism in the Mediterranean', *Applied Economics*, **31**, 619–30.

Payne, J. and A. Merva (2002), 'A note on modelling tourism revenues in Croatia', *Tourism Economics*, **8** (1), 103–9.

Pesaran, M.H. and R.P. Smith (1985), 'Keynes on economics', in T. Lawson and H.

Pesaran (eds), *Keynes' Economics: Methodological Issues*, London: Croom Helm, pp. 134–50.

Qu, H. and S. Lam (1997), 'A travel demand model for mainland Chinese tourists to Hong Kong', *Tourism Management*, **18**(8), 593–7.

Romilly, P., X. Liu and H. Song (1998), 'Economics and social determinants of international tourism spending: A panel data analysis', *Tourism Analysis*, **3**, 3–16.

Song, H. and S.F. Witt (2000), *Tourism Demand Modelling and Forecasting: Modern Econometric Approaches*, First Edition, Oxford: Pergamon Press.

Song, H., P. Romilly and X. Liu. (2000), 'An empirical study of outbound tourism demand in the UK', *Applied Economics*, **32**(5), 611–24.

Song, H., S.F. Witt and T.C. Jensen (2003), 'Tourism forecasting: Accuracy of alternative econometric models', *International Journal of Forecasting*, **19**, 123–41.

Sorensen, N.K. (1999), 'Modelling seasonality of hotel nights in Denmark by country and nationality', *Tourism Economics*, **5**(1), 9–23.

Turner, L.W., Y. Reisinger and S.F. Witt (1998), 'Tourism demand analysis using structural equation modelling', *Tourism Economics*, **4**(4), 301–23.

Turner, L.W. and S.F. Witt (2001), 'Forecasting tourism using univariate and multivariate structural time series models', *Tourism Economics*, **7**(2), 135–47.

Venegas, M. and R.R. Croes (2000), 'Evolution of demand, US tourists to Aruba', *Annals of Tourism Research*, **27**(4), 946–63.

Vogt, M.G. and C. Wittayakorn (1998), 'Determinants of the demand for Thailand's export of tourism', *Applied Economics*, **30**, 711–5.

Webber, A.G. (2001), 'Exchange rate volatility and cointegration in tourism demand', *Journal of Travel Research*, **39**, 398–405.

White, H. (1980), 'A heteroscedastic-consistent covariance matrix estimator and a direct test of heteroscedasticity', *Econometrica*, **48**, 817–38.

Witt, S.F. and C.A. Witt (1995), 'Forecasting tourism demand: A review of empirical research', *International Journal of Forecasting*, **11**, 447–75.

Wong, K.K.F. (1997), 'An investigation of the time series behaviour of international tourist arrivals', *Tourism Economics*, **3**(2), 185–99.

WTO (2003), 'Tourism highlights', http://www.world-tourism.org [last accessed: May 2007].

Yoon, J. and E.L. Shafer (1996), 'Models of US travel demand patterns for the Bahamas', *Journal of Travel Research*, **35**(1), 50–56.

APPENDIX 3.1 DESCRIPTIONS OF MODELS

	Author(s)	Title of Article	Publication (Journal)	Data Description	Dependent Variables	Independent Variables
1	Akis, S. (1998)	A Compact Econometric Model of Tourism Demand for Turkey	*Tourism Management*, **19**(1), 99–102	Annual data: 1980–1990	Logarithm of annual international tourist arrivals	Logarithm of national income of tourist generating country at constant prices Logarithm of the relative prices between destination and origin country
2	Burger, C.J.S.C., Dohnal, M., Kathrada, M. and Law, R. (2001)	A Practitioners' Guide to Time Series Methods for Tourism Demand Forecasting – A Case Study of Durban, South Africa	*Tourism Management*, **22**, 403–409	Monthly data: January 1992–December 1998	Monthly international tourist arrivals	Lagged values of monthly international tourist arrivals
3	Carey, K. (1992)	Optimal Hotel Capacity: The Case of Barbados	*Social and Economic Studies*, **42**(2), 103–126	Daily micro data pooled at individual firm level collected from 11 of the 27 luxury hotels in Barbados from December 1978 to December 1994. (The period of study covers one business cycle)	Daily room occupancy rates in hotel i on night t	Logarithm of income in countries generating tourists to hotel i in seasons s of year y Logarithm of (real) price of hotel i in month m deflated by the exchange rate Logarithm of capacity of hotel i in month m Logarithm of combined capacity of all luxury hotel rooms other than those in hotel i in month m Logarithm of promotional expenditure by hotel i in year y Dummy variable: $M = 1$ if month $= i$ (where $i =$ last half: Dec., Jan. or Feb.) and zero, otherwise. Dummy variables assigned to hotels of different quality

Appendix 3.1 Descriptions of Models (continued)

	Author(s)	Title of Article	Publication (Journal)	Data Description	Dependent Variables	Independent Variables
4	Carey, K. (1991)	Estimation of Caribbean Tourism Demand: Issues in Measurement and Methodology	*Atlantic Economic Journal*, **19**(3), 32–40	Annual data: 1977–1985 (Pooled)	Logarithm of the number of tourist arrivals at destination i from origin j in year y staying in hotels	Logarithm of real GDP per capita in tourist generating countries in US Dollars Logarithm of population of the country of origin Logarithm of price of hotel rooms in 1979 (adjusted by real exchange rate) Logarithm of distance in major city of embarkation in country of origin to destination Logarithm of promotional expenditure by host country
5	Carey, K. (1989)	Tourism Development in LDCs: Hotel Capacity Expansion with Reference to Barbados	*World Development*, **17**(1), 59–67	Daily micro data pooled at individual firm level collected from 11 of the 27 luxury hotels in Barbados from December 1978 to December 1994. (The period of study covers one business cycle)	Daily room occupancy rates in hotel i on night t	Logarithm of capacity of hotel i in month m Logarithm of combined capacity of all luxury hotel rooms other than those in hotel i in month m Logarithm of price of hotel i in month m deflated by the exchange rate Logarithm of income in countries generating tourists to hotel i in seasons s of year y Logarithm of promotional expenditure by hotel i in year y Dummy variable: $M = 1$ if month $= i$ (where $i =$ last half: Dec., Jan. or Feb.) and zero, otherwise

Appendix 3.1 Descriptions of Models (continued)

	Author(s)	Title of Article	Publication (Journal)	Data Description	Dependent Variables	Independent Variables
6	Chan, Y.M., Hui, T.K. and Yuen, E. (1999)	Modelling the Impact of Sudden Environmental Change on Visitor Arrival Forecast: The Case of the Gulf War	*Journal of Travel Research*, **37**(4), 391–394	Monthly data: August 1984–July 1990; August 1985–July 1991	Monthly international tourist arrivals	Lagged values of monthly tourist arrivals
7	Cho, V. (2003)	A Comparison of Three different Approaches to Tourist Arrival Forecasting	*Tourism Management*, **24**, 323–330	Monthly data: January 1974–December 2000	Monthly international tourist arrivals	Lagged values of monthly international tourist arrivals
8	Chu, F.L. (1998)	Forecasting Tourism Demand in Asian-Pacific Countries	*Annals of Tourism Research*, **25**(3), 597–615	Monthly data: January 1975–December 1994	Monthly international tourist arrivals	Lagged values of monthly international tourist arrivals
9	Daniel, A.C.M. and Ramos, F.F.R. (2002)	Modelling Inbound International Tourism Demand to Portugal	*International Journal of Tourism Research*, **4**, 193–209	Annual data: 1975–1997	Logarithm of the number of tourist arrivals	Logarithm of per capita real GDP

Logarithm of exchange rate adjusted relative CPI between destination and tourist source country

Logarithm of surface travel costs, using petrol price, distance, mean fuel consumption

Logarithm of air travel cost according to Passenger Air Tariff (PAT) |

Appendix 3.1 Descriptions of Models (continued)

Author(s)	Title of Article	Publication (Journal)	Data Description	Dependent Variables	Independent Variables
10 De Mello, M., Pack, A. and Sinclair, T. (2002)	A System of Equations Model of UK Tourism Demand in Neighbouring Countries	*Applied Economics*, **34**, 509–521	Annual data: 1969–1997	Logarithm of UK residents' expenditure in France, Spain and Portugal	Logarithm of the UK real per capita expenditure allocated to all destinations Logarithm of effective prices of tourism in each destination Dummy variables: 1980: Spain's membership in EFTA 1978: Inception of Portugal's negotiations with membership of EU Time trend
11 Dharmaratne, G.S. (1995)	Forecasting Tourist Arrivals in Barbados	*Annals of Tourism Research*, **22**, 804–818	Annual data: 1956–1991	Logarithm of international tourist arrivals	Lagged values of logarithm of annual international tourist arrivals
12 Divisekera, S. (2003)	A Model of Demand for International Tourism	*Annals of Tourism Research*, **30**(1), 31–49	Annual data: 1972–1995	Logarithm of travel receipts	Logarithm of price to destination (cost of living and travel costs) Logarithm of relative price of tourism between destination and competitor destinations Dummy variables: 1987: Japanese government policy on encouraging foreign travel during late 1987 1986: America's Cup

Appendix 3.1 Descriptions of Models (continued)

	Author(s)	Title of Article	Publication (Journal)	Data Description	Dependent Variables	Independent Variables
13	Downward, P. (2003)	Beyond the Demand for Day-visits: An Analysis of Visitor Spending	*Tourism Economics*, **9**(1), 67–76	Twelve weeks data: July–September 1999.	Logarithm of total spending by groups of tourists in Herefordshire	Logarithm of income Logarithm of nights spend in Herefordshire Logarithm of variables identifying group composition and motives for visiting
14	Garcia-Ferrer, A. and Queralt, R.A. (1997)	A Note on Forecasting Tourism Demand in Spain	*International Journal of Forecasting*, **13**, 539–549	Monthly data: January 1979– December 1993	Logarithm of monthly travel receipts Logarithm of monthly international tourist arrivals	Logarithm of monthly international income index Logarithm of monthly relative price index Logarithm of monthly competitor price index
15	Garin-Munoz, T. and Amaral, T.P. (2000)	An Econometric Model for International Tourism Flows to Spain	*Applied Economics*, **7**, 525–529	Annual data: 1985–1995 (Pooled)	Logarithm of per capita overnight stays in hotels in Spain	Logarithm of per capita GNP at PPP Logarithm of nominal bilateral exchange rate Logarithm of the relative price indexes Dummy variable: 1991: Gulf War

Appendix 3.1 Descriptions of Models (continued)

	Author(s)	Title of Article	Publication (Journal)	Data Description	Dependent Variables	Independent Variables
16	Goh, C. and Law, R. (2002)	Modelling and Forecasting Tourism Demand for Arrivals with Stochastic Non-stationary Seasonality and Intervention	*Tourism Management*, **23**, 499–510	Monthly data: January 1980–August 2000 and April 1991–August 2000	Monthly international tourist arrivals	Lagged values of monthly tourist arrivals Dummy Variables: November 1988: Relaxation of outbound travel visa in Korea December 1997 to January 1998: Bird Flu epidemic in Hong Kong Middle of 1997: Asian Economic Crisis July 1997: Reversion of Hong Kong to Chinese Sovereignty
17	Gonzalez, P. and Moral, P. (1996)	Analysis of Tourism Trends in Spain	*Annals of Tourism Research*, **11**(4), 233–251	Monthly data: January 1979–December 1993	Logarithm of real monthly travel receipts (expenditures) Logarithm of monthly tourist arrivals	Deterministic stochastic trend component Seasonal component constructed in terms of deterministic dummy variables

Appendix 3.1 Descriptions of Models (continued)

	Author(s)	Title of Article	Publication (Journal)	Data Description	Dependent Variables	Independent Variables
18	Gonzalez, P. and Moral, P. (1995)	An Analysis of Tourism Demand in Spain	*International Journal of Forecasting*, **11**, 233–251	Monthly data: January 1979–December 1993	Logarithm of real monthly travel receipts	Logarithm of monthly international income index
						Logarithm of monthly relative price index
						Logarithm of monthly competitor price index
						Seasonal component constructed in terms of deterministic dummy variables
19	Greenidge, K. (2001)	Forecasting Tourism Demand, An STM Approach	*Annals of Tourism Research*, **28**(1), 98–112	Quarterly data: 1968(Q1)–1997(Q4)	Logarithm of monthly tourist arrivals	Logarithm of real GDP
					Logarithm of tourist arrivals	Logarithm of price of tourism (measured as a ratio of tourism receipts and bed nights, of which bed nights are defined as arrivals multiplied by the duration of stay)
						Logarithm of the price index of the competitive tourist product
						Trend component
						Seasonal component
						Cyclical component
						Error component
20	Hui, T.-K. and Yuen, C.C. (2002)	A Study in the Seasonal Variations of Japanese Tourist Arrivals in Singapore	*Tourism Management*, **23**, 127–131	Monthly data: January 1985–December 1998	Logarithm of tourist arrivals	Lagged values of the logarithm of tourist arrivals

Appendix 3.1 Descriptions of Models (continued)

	Author(s)	Title of Article	Publication (Journal)	Data Description	Dependent Variables	Independent Variables
21	Hui, T.-K. and Yuen, C.C. (1998)	An Econometric Study on Japanese Tourist Arrivals in British Columbia and Its Implications	*The Service Industries Journal*, **18**(4), 38–50	Quarterly data: 1980(Q1)–1992(Q4)	Logarithm of the number of Japanese tourists	Logarithm of Japanese GDP Logarithm of lagged number of Japanese tourists Logarithm of nominal exchange rate Logarithm of RPI in Canada
22	Jensen, T.C. (1998)	Income and price elasticities by nationality for tourists in Denmark	*Tourism Economics*, 4(2), 101–130	Annual data: 1969–1995	Logarithm of number of nights spent Logarithm of daily spending	Logarithm of real income Logarithm of relative prices between destination and source Logarithm of relative prices between destination and competitors Time trend
23	Kim, S. and Song, Haiyan (1998)	Analysis of Inbound Tourism Demand in South Korea: A Cointegration and Error Correction Approach	*Tourism Analysis*, **3**, 25–41.	Annual data: 1962–1994	Logarithm of annual tourist arrivals	Logarithm of GDP in origin country Logarithm of South Korea CPI relative to tourist origin country Logarithm of Korean CPI relative to substitute destinations Logarithm of average return airfare to Seoul from source countries Logarithm of sum of exports and imports from destination to tourist source country

Appendix 3.1 Descriptions of Models (continued)

	Author(s)	Title of Article	Publication (Journal)	Data Description	Dependent Variables	Independent Variables
24	Kulendran, N. and Witt, S.F. (2003)	Forecasting the Demand for International Business Tourism	*Journal of Travel Research*, **41**(3), 265–271	Quarterly data: 1982 (Q1)–1996(Q4)	Logarithm of quarterly business tourist arrivals	Logarithm of GDP in origin country Logarithm of GDP in destination country Logarithm of sum of exports and imports from destination to tourist generating country Logarithm of nominal exchange rate Logarithm of air fare Logarithm of number of (volume) of holiday tourists Stochastic trend component Stochastic seasonal component

25	Kulendran, N. and Witt, S.F. (2001)	Cointegration Versus Least Squares Regression	*Annals of Tourism Research*, **28**(2), 291–311	Quarterly data: 1978(Q1)–1995(Q4)	Logarithm of outbound holiday tourism measured in terms of UK tourist visits to 8 destinations	Logarithm of per capita real personal disposable income
						Logarithm of relative cost of living tourists in destination country
						Logarithm of cost of living relative to competitive destination
						Logarithm of relative air fare to competitor destinations
						Lagged logarithm of outbound holiday tourist visits
						Dummy variables:
						  1979: Oil Crisis
						  1986: Bombing of Libya
						  1991: Gulf War

85

Appendix 3.1 Descriptions of Models (continued)

Author(s)	Title of Article	Publication (Journal)	Data Description	Dependent Variables	Independent Variables
26 Kulendran, N. and Wilson, K. (2000)	Modelling Business Travel	*Tourism Economics*, **6**(1), 47–59	Quarterly data:1982(Q1)–1996(Q4)	Logarithm of number of USA, UK, NZ and Japanese business tourists to Australia	Logarithm of origin country real income Logarithm of destination country real income Logarithm of openness to trade Logarithm of imports in origin country Logarithm of relative prices Logarithm of the number of holiday travellers.
27 Kulendran, N. and King, M.L. (1997)	Forecasting International Quarterly Tourist Flows using Error Correction and Time Series Models	*International Journal of Forecasting*, **13**, 319–327	Quarterly data:1975(Q1)–1990(Q4)	Logarithm of tourist arrivals	Logarithm of income Logarithm of one-way air fare Logarithm of relative prices Dummy variables: 1987: Japanese government policy encouraging overseas travel 1988: Australian Bicentennial Expo, Brisbane 1989: Australian Pilots' Strike

Appendix 3.1 Descriptions of Models (continued)

	Author(s)	Title of Article	Publication (Journal)	Data Description	Dependent Variables	Independent Variables
28	Kulendran, N. (1996)	Modelling Quarterly Tourist Flows to Australia using Cointegration Analysis	*Tourism Economics*, **2**(3), 203–222	Quarterly data:1975(Q1)–1990(Q4)	Logarithm of tourist arrivals at time t from origin i	Logarithm of income of origin i at time t Logarithm of the relative cost of living for a tourist from origin i Logarithm of cost of transport between origin i and Australia Seasonal Dummy Variables Dummy Variables: 1985–1986: Popularity of Australian films abroad 1986: America's Cup 1987: Japanese government policy encouraging overseas travel 1988: Australian Bicentennial Expo, Brisbane 1989: Australian Pilots' Strike
29	Lanza, A., Temple, P. and Urga, G. (2003)	The Implications of Tourism Specialisation in the Long Run: An Econometric Analysis for 13 OECD Economies'	*Tourism Management*, **24**, 315–321.	Annual data: 1975–1992	Share of the expenditure on tourist goods and services in total consumption expenditure	Logarithm of the relative price of the tourist bundle of goods and services to the consumer price deflator Logarithm of the total consumption expenditure deflated by Stone Price index
30	Lathiras, P. and Siriopoulos, C. (1998)	The Demand for Tourism to Greece: A Cointegration Approach	*Tourism Economics*, **4**(2), 171–185	Annual data: 1960–1995	Logarithm of per capita tourist arrivals	Logarithm of GDP per capita Logarithm of relative prices Logarithm of exchange rate Logarithm of substitute prices

Appendix 3.1 Descriptions of Models (continued)

	Author(s)	Title of Article	Publication (Journal)	Data Description	Dependent Variables	Independent Variables
31	Ledesma-Rodriguez, F.J. and Navarro-Ibanez, M. (2001)	Panel Data and Tourism: A Case Study of Tenerife	*Tourism Economics*, **7**(1), 75–88	Annual data: 1979–1997 (Pooled)	Logarithm of the number of visitors lodged in hotels and apartments	Logarithm of income Logarithm of lagged number of visitors lodged in hotels and apartments Logarithm of oil price per barrel Logarithm of exchange rate Logarithm of the capital stock of Tenerife Logarithm of promotional expenditure
32	Lee, C.K., Var, T. and Blaine, T.W. (1996)	Determinants of Inbound Tourist Expenditures	*Annals of Tourism Research*, **23**(3), 527–542	Annual data: 1970–1989	Logarithm of Total Real Tourist Expenditures divided by population in the origin country *i*	Logarithm of real per capita income in the origin country *i* Logarithm of relative prices between tourist source country and South Korea Logarithm of real exchange rate Dummy variables: 1974: Oil Crisis 1988: The Seoul Olympic Games
33	Lim, C. and McAleer, M. (2002)	Time Series Forecasts of International Travel Demand for Australia	*Tourism Management*, **23**(4), 389–396	Quarterly data: 1975(Q1)–1989(Q4)	Logarithm of tourist arrivals	Lagged values of logarithm of tourist arrivals
34	Lim, C. and McAleer, M. (2001a)	Monthly Seasonal Variations: Asian Tourism to Australia	*Annals of Tourism Research*, **28**(1), 68–82	Monthly data: January 1975–December 1996	Logarithm of tourist arrivals	Lagged values of logarithm of tourist arrivals

Appendix 3.1 Descriptions of Models (continued)

	Author(s)	Title of Article	Publication (Journal)	Data Description	Dependent Variables	Independent Variables
35	Lim, C. and McAleer, M. (2001b)	Forecasting Tourist Arrivals	*Annals of Tourism Research*, **28**(4), 965–977	Quarterly data: 1975(Q1)–1999(Q4)	Tourist arrivals; Logarithm of tourist arrivals	Lagged values of tourist arrivals; Lagged values of logarithm of tourist arrivals
36	Lim, C. and McAleer, M. (1999)	A Seasonal Analysis of Malaysian Tourist Arrivals to Australia	Mathematics and Computers in Simulation, **48**, 573–583	Quarterly data: 1975(Q1)–1996(Q4)	Logarithm of Malaysian tourist arrivals to Australia	Lagged values of logarithm of Malaysian tourist arrivals to Australia
37	Morley, C. (1998)	A Dynamic International Demand Model	*Annals of Tourism Research*, **25**(1), 70–84	Annual data: 1972–1992	Logarithm of the number of tourist arrivals	Logarithm of real GDP; Logarithm of relative prices between destination and tourist source; Logarithm of airfare between destination and tourist source; Dummy Variables: 1988: Australian Bicentennial Expo, Brisbane; 1989: National Pilots' Strike
38	Narayan, P.K. (2003a)	Determinants of Tourism Expenditure in Fiji: A Cointegration Approach	Pacific Tourism Review', **6**, 159–167	Annual data: 1970–2000	Logarithm of real tourist expenditure in Fiji in year t from tourists from country i (where i = Australia, US and New Zealand)	Logarithm of real GDP of the origin country in i in year t; Logarithm of relative prices between Fiji and tourist source country i in year t; Logarithm of real economy class air fare from tourist source country to Nadi; Dummy variables: 1987 and 1999: the *coups d'état*

Appendix 3.1 Descriptions of Models (continued)

	Author(s)	Title of Article	Publication (Journal)	Data Description	Dependent Variables	Independent Variables
39	Narayan, P.K. (2002)	A Tourism Demand Model for Fiji	Pacific Economic Bulletin, **17**(2), 103–116	Annual data: 1970–2000	Logarithm of visitor arrivals	Logarithm of per capita real GDP or origin country
						Logarithm of relative prices between Fiji and tourist source country *i* in year *t*
						Logarithm of substitute price index as the logarithm of CPI in Fiji relative to Bali for a tourist from country *i* in year *t*
						Logarithm of real economy class air fare
						Dummy variables: 1987 and 1999: the *corps d'état*
40	Papatheodorou, A (1999)	The Demand for International Tourism in The Mediterranean	*Applied Economics*, **31**, 619–630	Annual data: 1957–1990	Logarithm of percentage share of tourist expenditure in destination country	Logarithm of total per capita tourist expenditure in destination country
						Logarithm of exchange rate adjusted relative prices between origin and destination
						Logarithm of time trend
41	Payne, J. and Merva, A. (2002)	A Note on Modelling Tourism Revenues in Croatia	*Tourism Economics*, **8**(1), 103–109	Quarterly data: 1993(Q1)–1999(Q4)	Logarithm of real tourism revenue	Logarithm of European Union real GDP
						Logarithm of real effective exchange rate
						Dummy variable catering for military action during the first quarter of 1995
						Seasonal Dummy Variables

Appendix 3.1 Descriptions of Models (continued)

	Author(s)	Title of Article	Publication (Journal)	Data Description	Dependent Variables	Independent Variables
42	Qu, H. and Lam, S. (1997)	A Travel Demand Model for Mainland Chinese Tourists to Hong Kong	*Tourism Management*, **18**(8), 593–597	Annual data: 1957–1990	Number of mainland Chinese tourist arrivals in Hong Kong	Level of disposable income per capita in current Yuan Relative level of consumer prices, defined as the ratio between Hong Kong CPI and CPI in China, Bilateral nominal exchange rate. Dummy variables: Package site seeing to Hong Kong was introduced in 1987 Tiananmen Square Incident 1989 Gulf War 1990 Relaxation of Visa requirements 1993
43	Romilly, P., Liu, X. and Song, H. (1998)	Economics and Social Determinants of International Tourism Spending: A Panel Data Analysis	Tourism Analysis, **3**, 3–16	Annual data: 1989–1995 (Pooled) 138 countries	Logarithm of real per capita international tourism spending (US$) by country *i*	Logarithm of GDP per capita (US$) in country *i* Logarithm of real exchange rate Logarithm of real exchange rate volatility Logarithm of Age (the proportion of population of 16–64 year olds to total population in country *i*) Logarithm of the proportion of males in the total population in country *i* Logarithm of the average house hold size of country *i* (number of people) Logarithm of percentage of adult literacy rate Logarithm of the proportion of urban population to total population in country *i*

Appendix 3.1 Descriptions of Models (continued)

Author(s)	Title of Article	Publication (Journal)	Data Description	Dependent Variables	Independent Variables
44 Song, H., Witt, S.F. and Jensen, T.C. (2003)	Tourism Forecasting: Accuracy of Alternative Econometric Models	*International Journal of Forecasting*, **19**, 123–141	Annual data: 1969–1997	Logarithm of the number of nights spent by tourists	Logarithm of real private consumption expenditure per capita Logarithm of real cost of living for tourists measured by relative CPI Logarithm of tourism prices in substitute destination Logarithm of travel cost measured by airfare Log of time trend Dummy variables: 1974–1975 and 1975: Oil Crises 1990–91: Gulf War 1991: German Reunification 1986: Chernobyl Disaster 1986: US bombing of Libya
45 Song, H., Romilly, P. and Liu, X. (2000)	An Empirical Study of Outbound Tourism Demand in the UK	*Applied Economics*, **32**(5), 611–624	Annual data: 1965–1994	Logarithm of total per capita tourism visits	Logarithm of per capita UK personal disposable income Logarithm of cost of living index Logarithm of price of tourism in substitute destination measured as CPI of destination Logarithm of destination preference index (derived)
46 Sorensen, N.K. (1999)	Modelling seasonality of hotel nights in Denmark by country and nationality	*Tourism Economics*, **5**(1), 9–23	Monthly data: January 1970–December 1996	Logarithm of hotel nights	Lagged values of logarithm of hotel nights Stochastic Seasonal Dummy Variables

Appendix 3.1 Descriptions of Models (continued)

	Author(s)	Title of Article	Publication (Journal)	Data Description	Dependent Variables	Independent Variables
47	Turner, L.W. and Witt, S.F. (2001)	Forecasting Tourism Using Univariate and Multivariate Structural Time Series Models	*Tourism Economics*, 7(2), 135–147	Quarterly data: 1978(Q2)–1998(Q3)	Logarithm of total tourist visits	Logarithm of real GDP in origin country Logarithm of real air fare Logarithm of trade openness Deterministic stochastic trend component Seasonal components constructed in terms of deterministic dummy variables
48	Turner, L.W., Reisinger, Y. and Witt, S.F. (1998)	Tourism Demand Analysis Using Structural Equation Modelling	*Tourism Economics*, 4(4), 301–323	Quarterly data: 1978(Q1)–1995(Q4)	Logarithm of total tourists arrivals	Logarithm of UK population Logarithm of UK real personal disposable income per capita Logarithm of living costs in destination relative to UK Logarithm of living costs in destination relative to competing foreign destinations Logarithm of real air fare to destination Logarithm of real air fare to destination relative to competing foreign destinations Logarithm of UK real GDP Logarithm of UK real imports from destinations Logarithm of UK real exports to destinations Logarithm of migration into UK from destinations Logarithm of migration out of UK into destinations Logarithm of UK real retail sales The survey of UK business confidence

Appendix 3.1 Descriptions of Models (continued)

	Author(s)	Title of Article	Publication (Journal)	Data Description	Dependent Variables	Independent Variables

49	Venegas, M. and Croes, R.R. (2000)	Evolution of Demand, US Tourists to Aruba	*Annals of Tourism Research*, **27**(4), 946–963	Annual data: 1975–1996	Logarithm of tourist arrivals	Logarithm of US real GDP
						Logarithm of relative prices
						Logarithm of real effective exchange rates
						Lagged Logarithm of tourist arrivals
						Dummy Variables:
						  Effect of US recession in 1979–1981
						  Problems of airlift in Aruba 1986
						  Gulf War 1992

50	Vogt, M.G. and Wittayakorn, C. (1998)	Determinants of the demand for Thailand's export of tourism	*Applied Economics*, **30**, 711–715	Annual data: 1960–1993	Logarithm of real tourism expenditures	Logarithm of the price of tourism Logarithm of world price of tourism Logarithm of real effective exchange rate Logarithm of world income
51	Webber, A.G. (2001)	Exchange Rate Volatility and Cointegration in Tourism Demand	*Journal of Travel Research*, **39**, 398–405	Quarterly data: 1983 (Q1)–1997(Q4)	Logarithm of tourist departures	Logarithm of cost of living measured by CPI in destination adjusted by exchange rate of origin Logarithm of transportation cost Logarithm of substitute prices Logarithm of the variance of exchange rates Seasonal dummies
52	Wong, K.K.F. (1997)	An Investigation of the Time Series Behaviour of International Tourist Arrivals	*Tourism Economics*, **3**(2), 185–199	Annual data: 1964–1992	Logarithm of international tourist arrivals	Lagged values of logarithm of International tourist Arrivals
53	Yoon, J. and Shafer, E.L. (1996)	Models of US Travel Demand Patterns for the Bahamas	*Journal of Travel Research*, **35**(1), 50–56	Survey response of 6170 visitors to the Bahamas in each month in 1991	Logarithm of the number of visitors	Logarithm of the trip cost per visitor

APPENDIX 3.2 ANALYSIS OF MODELS

Author(s)	Recognition of Omitted Explanatory Variables and Use of Proxy Variables	Model Specification	Method of Estimation and Models Estimated	Reported Descriptive Statistics	Diagnostic Tests	Empirical Implications
1 Akis, S. (1998)	Tourist income is proxied with GDP Tourism price of tourism measured as relative CPI between destination and source country Transport costs are omitted Substitute prices are omitted Tastes and preferences are omitted Marketing expenditures are omitted	Multivariate Log Linear Single Equation	OLS (Simple Linear Regression Model)	R^2 t-statistics	Durban-Watson Statistic for first order serial correlation	This is a small compact model of tourism demand for Turkey. The model postulates that tourism demand to Turkey depends on the income of the tourist source country and relative price (foreign prices divided by domestic prices). The results indicate that there is a positive relationship between income and tourist arrivals, and a negative relationship between relative price and tourist arrivals. The elasticity of income is greater than 1, indicating that tourism to Turkey is a luxury good. The authors argue that this model is based on sound microeconomic theory, whereby only income and price is hypothesised to determine tourist demand to Turkey. Furthermore, they argue that such an hypothesis will alleviate the problems of multicollinearity and the loss of degrees of freedom.

Appendix 3.2   Analysis of Models (continued)

Author(s)	Recognition of Omitted Explanatory Variables and Use of Proxy Variables	Model Specification	Method of Estimation and Models Estimated	Reported Descriptive Statistics	Diagnostic Tests	Empirical Implications
2 Burger, C.J.S.C., Dohnal, M., Kathrada, M. and Law, R. (2001)	Tourist income is omitted Tourism prices are omitted Transport costs are omitted Substitute prices are omitted Tastes and preferences are omitted Marketing expenditures are omitted	Univariate Time Series Single Equation	OLS (Naïve, MA, Exponential Smoothing, ARIMA, Genetic Regression, Artificial Neural Networks)	Pearson Product Moment Correlation Coefficient (PPMCC)	Mean Absolute Percentage Error (MAPE)	According to the authors, a forecaster or policy maker makes best use of the available time series in the absence of structural data. Hence, they use numerous univariate time series methodologies, namely Naïve, Moving Average, ARIMA, Group Method of Data Handling (GMDH), Multiple Regression, and Artificial Neural Networks (ANNs). They test their accuracy against each another. The ANNs perform best by achieving the highest PPMCC and lowest MAPE. This is because of the high degree of freedom that ANNs have due to the large interconnection between the nodes. Therefore, there is a large parameter space that can be searched in order to obtain a higher r. In comparison, regression models are constrained by having fewer coefficients.

Appendix 3.2   Analysis of Models (continued)

	Author(s)	Recognition of Omitted Explanatory Variables and Use of Proxy Variables	Model Specification	Method of Estimation and Models Estimated	Reported Descriptive Statistics	Diagnostic Tests	Empirical Implications
3	Carey, K. (1992)	Tourist income proxied with real per capita GNP, converted to an index number Tourism price is proxied with exchange rate adjusted price of hotel rooms Substitute prices are proxied with price of substitute hotels Tastes and preferences are omitted Marketing expenditures are proxied with hotel promotional expenditures	Multivariate Log Linear Single Equation	OLS (Simple Linear Regression Model)	R^2 Kolmogorov D statistical test for normality in the errors	None	The primary objective of the paper is to model and estimate optimal hotel capacity in Barbados. The probability distribution of demand for Barbadian inbound tourism rather than historical occupancy rates is used to determine the probability of hotels being fully occupied. The income elasticity of 0.8 is the dominant determinant of demand for tourism. The small sample property has made it impossible to measure the effect of capacity with confidence. The sign of other hotel capacity changes to positive as a result of the mixed regression. Promotional expenditure is not significant.
4	Carey, K. (1991)	Tourist income is proxied with real per capita GDP Tourism price is proxied with relative CPI between destination and source country Transport costs are proxied with distance from source to destination Substitute prices are omitted Tastes and preferences are omitted Marketing expenditures are proxied with national promotional expenditures	Multivariate Log Linear Single Equation	GLS (Pooled-Estimation)	R^2 t-statistics	None	The income elasticity of demand is 1.209 and highly significant, whereas the price elasticity of demand is positive and insignificant. This indicates that there are factors other than price which influence the demand for tourism in Barbados. The coefficient of the distance between Barbados and the tourist-generating countries is highly significant and negative. The cost of airfare and travel time required appears to be more important than hotel prices. The promotional expenditure elasticity is 0.0577 and is highly significant.

Appendix 3.2   Analysis of Models (continued)

Author(s)	Recognition of Omitted Explanatory Variables and Use of Proxy Variables	Model Specification	Method of Estimation and Models Estimated	Reported Descriptive Statistics	Diagnostic Tests	Empirical Implications
5 Carey. K. (1989)	Tourist income is proxied with real per capita GNP, converted to an index number Tourism price is proxied with the exchange rate adjusted price of hotel rooms Substitute prices are proxied with price of substitute hotels Transport costs are omitted Tastes and preferences are omitted Marketing expenditures are proxied with hotel promotional expenditures	Multivariate Log Linear Single Equation	OLS (Simple Linear Regression Model)	R^2 t-statistics	Kolmogorov D statistical test for normality in the errors	The final judgement regarding the empirical findings was that there was excess capacity in tourism in Barbados. Therefore, the gains to other tourism sectors, such as food and local transport, are likely to compensate for the hotel sector losses.
6 Chan, Y.M., Hui, T.K. and Yuen, E. (1999)	Tourist income is omitted Tourism prices are omitted Transport costs are omitted Substitute prices are omitted Tastes and preferences are omitted Marketing expenditures are omitted	Univariate Time Series Single Equation	OLS (Naïve I and II, Exponential Smoothing, ARIMA, Trend Curve)	None	Mean Absolute Percentage Error (MAPE)	The accuracy of five competing methods of forecasting is compared using MAPE. For total tourist arrivals, Naïve II is the best performing technique of the five. Therefore, Naïve II best accommodates sudden environmental change because it adjusts the forecasts monthly and uses only the most recent data. However, the findings point to the need to examine the issue of environmental stability or instability more thoroughly rather than using cummy variables.

98

Appendix 3.2   Analysis of Models (continued)

Author(s)	Recognition of Omitted Explanatory Variables and Use of Proxy Variables	Model Specification	Method of Estimation and Models Estimated	Reported Descriptive Statistics	Diagnostic Tests	Empirical Implications
7 Cho, V. (2003)	Tourist income is omitted Tourism prices are omitted Transport costs are omitted Substitute prices are omitted Tastes and preferences are omitted Marketing expenditures are omitted	Univariate Time Series Single Equation	OLS (Naïve I and II, Exponential Smoothing, ARIMA, Artificial Neural Networks)	p-values	Root Mean Square Error (RMSE) Mean Absolute Percentage Error (MAPE)	The forecasting methods, namely exponential smoothing, ARIMA and Artificial Neural Networks (ANNs), were applied. The ANNs performed best for all countries, apart from the UK.
8 Chu, F.L. (1998)	Tourist income is omitted Tourism prices are omitted Transport costs are omitted Substitute prices are omitted Tastes and preferences are omitted Marketing expenditures are omitted	Univariate Time Series Single Equation	OLS (ARIMA, Sine Wave, Hotl-Winters Forecasting)	None	Thiel's Inequality Coefficient MAPE	In this paper, six different techniques for forecasting tourist arrivals in ten countries were examined. Seasonal and Non-Seasonal ARIMA was found to be the most accurate methods.

Appendix 3.2   Analysis of Models (continued)

Author(s)	Recognition of Omitted Explanatory Variables and Use of Proxy Variables	Model Specification	Method of Estimation and Models Estimated	Reported Descriptive Statistics	Diagnostic Tests	Empirical Implications
9 Daniel, A.C.M. and Ramos, F.F.R. (2002)	Tourist income is represented as real per capita GDP Tourism price is proxied with the relative exchange rate adjusted CPI between destination and tourism source country Transport costs are proxied with air costs (air fare) and surface costs (a composite price index of fuel prices, distance to travel and mean fuel consumption) Substitute prices are omitted Tastes and preferences are omitted Marketing expenditures are omitted	Multivariate Log Linear Single Equation Model	OLS (VAR, ECM)	$\bar{R}^2$ t-statistics F-statistic of the regression	Durban-Watson Statistic for first order serial correlation	The long-run specification of the model shows that there is substantial influence from income and cost of living indicators on tourism demand. With regard to the higher influence of income on tourism demand, it reaffirms that Portugal is a destination of mass tourism.

Appendix 3.2 Analysis of Models (continued)

Author(s)	Recognition of Omitted Explanatory Variables and Use of Proxy Variables	Model Specification	Method of Estimation and Models Estimated	Reported Descriptive Statistics	Diagnostic Tests	Empirical Implications
10 De Mello, M., Pack, A. and Sinclair, T. (2002)	Tourist income is proxied with the UK real per capita expenditure allocated to all destinations Price of tourism is proxied with the relative CPI between destination and source country Transport costs are omitted Substitute prices are omitted Tastes and preferences are omitted	Multivariate Log Linear Systems of Equations	GLS (SURE, AIDS)	$\bar{R}^2$ t-statistics F-statistic of the regression	Mean Absolute Sum of Squared Errors (MABSE) Root Mean Square Error (RMSE) Durban-Watson Statistic for first order serial correlation LM test for serial correlation of the errors Wald test for homogeneity and symmetry	The absolute percentage change in expenditure share due to a percentage change in own price indicates that tourism in Spain is a luxury (elastic), whereas for France it is a necessity (inelastic) for tourists from the UK. For Portugal it was insignificant. The dummy variables for political influences, such as membership of EFTA and negotiations of Portugal's membership to the EU, were positive and significant. The effect of the oil price shocks during the period 1975 to 1981 had negative effects on Spain and Portugal, whereby UK tourist's preference moved in favour of France relative to Portugal and Spain. The cross price elasticities were positive and indicated substitutability between the three destinations.
11 Dharmaratne, G.S. (1995)	Income is omitted Tourism prices are omitted Transport costs are omitted Substitute prices are omitted Tastes and preferences are omitted Marketing expenditures are omitted	Univariate Time Series Single Equation	OLS (AR, MA, ARIMA)	Asymptotic Standard Errors AIC SBC	Box-Pierce Q-Statistic for heteroscedasticity Mean Absolute Percentage Error (MAPE)	There were two alternative models used, namely ARIMA (2,1,1) and (1,1,1). The ARIMA (2,1,1) model shows that there are reasonable accurate *ex-post* forecasts. The model with assumed cycles is inferior in forecasting. It would be appealing to observe whether the five-year cycles continue.

Appendix 3.2   Analysis of Models (continued)

Author(s)	Recognition of Omitted Explanatory Variables and Use of Proxy Variables	Model Specification	Method of Estimation and Models Estimated	Reported Descriptive Statistics	Diagnostic Tests	Empirical Implications
12 Divisekera, S. (2003)	Tourist income is proxied with the share of expenditure allocated to tourism Price of tourism is proxied with (1) average per diem expenditure and (2) the geometric mean of economy, excursion and seasonal airfares between origin and destination. Substitute prices are omitted Tastes and preferences are omitted Marketing expenditures are omitted	Multivariate Log Linear Systems of Equations	GLS/SURE (AIDS)	t-statistics F-statistic of the regression	F-test for constrained and unconstrained model LR test for homogeneity restriction	The estimates of the models show that tourism in Australia, UK, New Zealand and USA are normal goods, and are gross substitutes with varying degrees of substitutability. However, Japanese tourist demand to Australia and New Zealand is complementary. The UK and USA have smaller expenditure and price elasticities, indicating they are traditional destinations, whereas, Australia, New Zealand and Japan have larger own price and expenditure elasticities, indicating they are emerging destinations. The estimated model proved to be consistent with theory but the presence of autocorrelation cannot be ruled out due to the lack of testing procedures for serial correlation in the system of demand equations. There may be further bias in the parameter estimates due to the use of a limited number of alternative destinations (small sample bias). Ideally, one should include all likely substitute and complementary destinations in each system, but data limitations prevented incorporation of these issues.

Appendix 3.2   Analysis of Models (continued)

Author(s)	Recognition of Omitted Explanatory Variables and Use of Proxy Variables	Model Specification	Method of Estimation and Models Estimated	Reported Descriptive Statistics	Diagnostic Tests	Empirical Implications
13 Downward, P. (2003)	Price of tourism is nested in spending Transport costs are nested in spending Substitute prices are omitted Tastes and preferences are identified as factors of attraction Marketing expenditures are omitted	Multivariate Log Linear Single Equation	OLS (Simple Linear Regression Model)	R^2 $\bar{R}^2$ t-statistics Mean of variables used Standard deviation of variables used	F-test of overall significance of the regression Ramsey's RESET test Test for functional form White's test for heteroscedasticity Normality	The number of tourists in a group, the number of nights spent and income were the main determinants of visitor spending. The coefficient estimates imply that the determinants of visitor spending are inelastic. A persistent problem was that the residuals of the regression failed the test for normality. This is not a surprising result as data on spending and income are typically skewed.

Appendix 3.2   Analysis of Models (continued)

Author(s)	Recognition of Omitted Explanatory Variables and Use of Proxy Variables	Model Specification	Method of Estimation and Models Estimated	Reported Descriptive Statistics	Diagnostic Tests	Empirical Implications
14 Garcia-Ferrer, A. and Queralt, R.A. (1997)	Tourist income is proxied with a seasonally adjusted international income index as a weighted average of industrial production index from the main tourist generating countries to Spain Price of tourism is proxied with the relative CPI between destination and origin converted to an index. Substitute prices are proxied with the relative CPI between destination and potential competitor destinations Transport costs are omitted Tastes and preferences are omitted Marketing expenditure are omitted	Log Linear Time Series Single Equation Multivariate Log Linear Single Equation	OLS (Dynamic Harmonic Regression (DHM), ARIMA, STSM)	R^2 Standard errors Prediction Error Variance	Root Mean Square Error (RMSE)	This paper is about re-estimation of the models advanced by González and Moral (1995) for the same data set. Here the authors find the contributions of inputs of existing models to alternative univariate models are negligible. One-step-ahead forecast accuracy measures or RMSEs are particularly useful measures of prediction accuracy when dealing with tourist flows to Spain. The use of traditional accuracy measures help very little in explaining competing measures.

Appendix 3.2   Analysis of Models (continued)

Author(s)	Recognition of Omitted Explanatory Variables and Use of Proxy Variables	Model Specification	Method of Estimation and Models Estimated	Reported Descriptive Statistics	Diagnostic Tests	Empirical Implications
15 Garin-Munoz, T. and Amaral, T.P. (2000)	Tourist income is proxied with the GDP of tourist source country in PPP US Dollars Price of tourism is proxied with Spanish CPI divided by the CPI of tourist source country Transport costs are omitted Tastes and preferences are omitted	Multivariate Log Linear Single Equation	OLS (Pooled) GLS (Pooled)	$\bar{R}^2$ t-statistics	Wald test for joint significance of fixed effects and first differences. Tests first and second order autocorrelation of the errors	The estimated income elasticity of demand is +1.41 and is within the range found in most empirical studies, confirming the hypothesis that tourism to Spain is a luxury. The estimated price elasticity is –0.30, which is inelastic. A direct comparison of this figure to that found in the literature is not warranted because different studies use different measures of prices, and there is substantial variation in the estimated price elasticities across studies. To test for the possibility that prices not only have an instantaneous effect on current tourist arrivals, but also past prices have an effect on current tourist arrivals, a lagged price term was incorporated and was insignificant. This confirms that lagged effects are likely to occur when tourism source countries are geographically distant from the tourism destination. The estimated exchange rate elasticity is +0.5 and significant, indicating that a devaluation of the Peseta will increase international tourists to Spain.

Appendix 3.2 Analysis of Models (continued)

Author(s)	Recognition of Omitted Explanatory Variables and Use of Proxy Variables	Model Specification	Method of Estimation and Models Estimated	Reported Descriptive Statistics	Diagnostic Tests	Empirical Implications
16 Goh, C. and Law, R. (2002)	Tourist income is omitted Tourism prices are omitted Transport costs are omitted Substitute prices are omitted Tastes and preferences are omitted Marketing expenditures are omitted	Univariate Time Series Single Equation	OLS (Exponential Smoothing, Holt and Winter's Exponential Smoothing, Naïve I, Naïve II, ARIMA, SARIMA, MARIMA)	*t*-statistics	Thiel's Inequality Coefficient MAPE MSE RMSPE RMSE Mean Absolute Deviation (MAD)	All the time series from the ten different sources of tourist arrivals to Hong Kong are stochastic, seasonal, and non-stationary, with seasonal unit roots. Five of the series tested have significant external intervention in and around July 1997 when the Bird Flu was most prevalent. The forecasting accuracy of the ten models for each series was assessed against six criteria. It was found that the Multivariate ARIMA model outperformed all the other models, although there was significant intervention in the series. SARIMA maintained the second best mean ranking, but the individual performance of the model depended on the country of origin. SARIMA preformed best for the USA, UK, China and Singapore, whereas it performed worst for Korea and Japan.

Appendix 3.2   Analysis of Models (continued)

Author(s)	Recognition of Omitted Explanatory Variables and Use of Proxy Variables	Model Specification	Method of Estimation and Models Estimated	Reported Descriptive Statistics	Diagnostic Tests	Empirical Implications
17 Gonzalez, P. and Moral, P. (1996)	Tourist income is omitted Tourism prices are omitted Transport costs are omitted Substitute prices are omitted Tastes and preferences are omitted Marketing expenditures are omitted	Multivariate (Structural Time Series) Log Linear Single Equation	OLS (STSM, ARIMA)	R_D^2 (convent'l) R_S^2 (seasonal) One step ahead prediction error variance t-statistics Asymptotic standard errors	Jarque-Bera test for normality in the errors Box-Ljung Statistic for first order autocorrelations White's test for heteroscedasticity	Two indicators of international tourism demand, namely tourist expenditures and international tourist arrivals, have been used. Estimation of trends, seasonality and the underlying growth yield results that are somewhat different for the indicators, so that the two analyses become complementary. For the tourist expenditure series, the diagnostic results are satisfactory since there is no statistical evidence of autocorrelation, heteroscedasticity or non-normality of the errors. A newly proposed coefficient of determination by Harvey (1990), which takes into account the seasonal patterns in the series, was applied. The estimated model is able to explain 25 per cent more of the variation in real tourist expenditures than a very simple model that includes a lagged endogenous variable and a deterministic seasonal component. As far as the tourist arrivals series are concerned, the effect of Easter is significant, with a coefficient of 0.16, which means that in Easter tourist arrivals increase by 16 per cent. The diagnostics are satisfactory, but there is a large departure from normality of the model, suggesting the existence of outliers.

Appendix 3.2 Analysis of Models (continued)

Author(s)	Recognition of Omitted Explanatory Variables and Use of Proxy Variables	Model Specification	Method of Estimation and Models Estimated	Reported Descriptive Statistics	Diagnostic Tests	Empirical Implications
18 Gonzalez, P. and Moral, P. (1995)	Tourist income is proxied with a seasonally adjusted international income index as a weighted average of industrial production index from the main tourist generating countries to Spain Price of tourism is proxied with the relative CPI between destination and origin converted to an index. Substitute prices are proxied with the relative CPI between destination and potential competitor destinations Transport costs are omitted Tastes and preferences are omitted Marketing expenditures are omitted	Multivariate (Structural Time Series) Log Linear Single Equation	OLS (STSM, ARIMA, Transfer Function Model, ECM)	R_D^2 (convent'l) R_S^2 (seasonal) Prediction error variance t-statistics Asymptotic standard errors	Jarque-Bera test for normality in the errors Box-Ljung Statistic for first order autocorrelations White's test for heteroscedasticity	The diagnostics are quite satisfactory for the structural time series model (STSM) with tourist expenditures. This shows that the price indexes are relevant variables to explain foreign tourism expenditure, with very similar coefficients but with very different dynamics, so that their aggregation is not recommended. The income index is insignificant, showing that tourist expenditure in Spain do not seem to be affected by the level of income. The two price indexes are significant and the elasticities are similar. For many travellers there is a higher degree of elasticity of substitution, so that higher than expected prices in Spain may result in a change of destination rather than in a decision to forego travelling abroad. The authors allowed for a stochastic trend by using a causal STM to forecast tourism demand. Since they transformed the variables to logarithms and estimated fixed parameters on the causal variables, their demand elasticities were constant. The STSM with number of tourists show an estimated trend component with a level that varies very smoothly over time with a constant slope. The estimated coefficients have the expected signs and are all statistically significant.

Appendix 3.2 Analysis of Models (continued)

Author(s)	Recognition of Omitted Explanatory Variables and Use of Proxy Variables	Model Specification	Method of Estimation and Models Estimated	Reported Descriptive Statistics	Diagnostic Tests	Empirical Implications
19 Greenidge, K. (2001)	Tourist income is proxied with real GDP of tourist-generating country Tourism prices are proxied with an index of relative CPI between destination and origin Substitute prices are expressed as relative CPI source and other potential destinations Transport costs are omitted Tastes and preferences Marketing expenditures are omitted	Multivariate (Structural Time Series) Log Linear Single Equation	OLS (STSM)	R_D^2 (convent'l) R_S^2 (seasonal) Prediction error variance t-statistics Asymptotic Standard errors	Durban-Watson Statistic for first order serial correlation Jarque-Bera test for normality in the errors Box-Ljung Statistic for first order autocorrelations White's test for heteroscedasticity Asymptotic standard errors Chow test for model consistency	The STM is able to capture most of the information that is normally left in the residuals of standard tourism demand regression models. Unlike Dharmaratne (1995), this paper takes into account the components which have direct interpretations and can give the planner further insights into tourism behaviour. This study incorporates seasonality into the analysis because it is a dominant feature in the time series and has been unsatisfactorily treated in previous models of tourism demand. It has also provided improved results for the coefficient estimates compared with previous studies, particularly the coefficient on the relative price variable, which has turned out to be correct.

Appendix 3.2 Analysis of Models (continued)

Author(s)	Recognition of Omitted Explanatory Variables and Use of Proxy Variables	Model Specification	Method of Estimation and Models Estimated	Reported Descriptive Statistics	Diagnostic Tests	Empirical Implications
20 Hui, T.-K. and Yuen, C.C. (2002)	Tourist income is omitted Tourism prices are omitted Transport costs are omitted Substitute prices are omitted Tastes and preferences are omitted Marketing expenditures are omitted	Univariate Time Series Single Equation	Presumably OLS?	R^2 p-values t-statistics	None	The seasonal indices estimated were quite stable, peaking in August because this is the school summer holidays season in Japan. However, except for August and December, all the indexes estimated were found to be insignificant. In general, the seasonal indexes are around 1, showing that Japanese tourists visit Singapore throughout the year due to geographical proximity and frequent flights. A simple linear trend model fitted to annual data from 1985 to 1998 led to the slope of the trend line being significant, with $R^2 = 0.6918$. However, when the model was fitted to data from 1985 to 1997 (to exclude the effect of the Asian financial crisis), the fit of the model improved to $R^2 = 0.9265$. This finding shows the need to include the effect of unexpected events which affect the validity of the analysis.

Appendix 3.2   Analysis of Models (continued)

Author(s)	Recognition of Omitted Explanatory Variables and Use of Proxy Variables	Model Specification	Method of Estimation and Models Estimated	Reported Descriptive Statistics	Diagnostic Tests	Empirical Implications
21 Hui, T.-K. and Yuen, C.C. (1998)	Tourist income is proxied with the GDP of tourist generating country Tourism price is proxied with the logarithm of the retail price index in destination country Transport costs are omitted Substitute prices are omitted Tastes and preferences are omitted Marketing expenditures are omitted	Multivariate Log Linear Single Equation	OLS (Simple Linear Regression Model)	$\bar{R}^2$ t-statistics	Durban-Watson Statistic for first order serial correlation RMSPE	There are nine estimation periods in the entire period of analysis. During the nine periods, the income elasticity has been varying significantly. The exchange rate was significant only when the Japanese yen was appreciating against the US$, which clearly affects visitor arrivals. Habit persistence has also been significant throughout, but with a declining trend. This indicates there is growing popularity among competitor destinations. Seasonality has been significant mainly in the summer due to good weather, but winter tourists have been increasing due to the popularity of Canadian winter sports. However, the estimation for the fourth quarter dummy variable contradicts the above results.

Appendix 3.2   Analysis of Models (continued)

Author(s)	Recognition of Omitted Explanatory Variables and Use of Proxy Variables	Model Specification	Method of Estimation and Models Estimated	Reported Descriptive Statistics	Diagnostic Tests	Empirical Implications
22 Jensen, T.C. (1998)	Tourist income is represented as real GDP and real private consumption in tourist generating country Tourism price is proxied with the relative CPI between tourism source country and destination Substitute prices are the relative price between the destination and competitor destinations Transport costs are omitted Tastes and preferences are expressed with a time trend Marketing expenditures are omitted	Multivariate Log Linear Single Equation	OLS (Simple Linear Regression Model)	R^2 Standard Deviation of the variables used	Durban-Watson Statistic for first order serial correlation t-statistics Lagrange Multiplier test for first order serial correlation in the errors	The choice of income variables matters, but not in a systematic way. Therefore, results with real private consumption are given. For almost all countries, there is evidence of multicollinearity with the time trend. The long-run price and income elasticities are, in general, significantly different from zero, with the exception of Norway. The income elasticity for Germany is close to 2, but Germans do not seem to act on Danish tourism in prices and income. The income elasticity for most countries is higher than 1 and the price elasticity is less than −1, with the exception of the UK and the Netherlands. UK visitors have very low income and price elasticities, indicating a high share of business tourists. Dutch visitors are very price sensitive, especially in terms of the choice of destination, but the elasticities are equally sensitive to the specification. The price elasticity for the USA is highly significant and has consistently been very close to −1 in all formulations. Well defined long-run relationships between the variables are found for Germany, USA and Sweden.

Appendix 3.2 Analysis of Models (continued)

Author(s)	Recognition of Omitted Explanatory Variables and Use of Proxy Variables	Model Specification	Method of Estimation and Models Estimated	Reported Descriptive Statistics	Diagnostic Tests	Empirical Implications
23 Kim, S. and Song, Haiyan (1998)	Tourist income is proxied with GDP or National Disposable Income (NDI) Tourism price is proxied with CPI in destination countries Transport costs are proxied with average airfare between destination and tourist source country Substitute prices are proxied with the relative CPI between destination and competitors Tastes and preferences are omitted Marketing expenditures are omitted	Multivariate Log Linear Single Equation	OLS (Naïve, AR(1) ARMA (p,q) Simple Exponential Smoothing, Simple Moving Average, ECM, VAR)	R^2 $\bar{R}^2$ Standard error of the regression	Cointegration Durbin-Watson Statistic Jarque-Bera test for normality in the errors Breusch-Godfrey test for serial correlation Engle's ARCH test White's test for heteroscedasticity Ramsey's RESET test Chow's predictive failure test	The cointegration and ECM tests are used to analyse the inbound tourism demand in South Korea, by four major tourist source countries. The Engle-Granger procedure showed that there is a long-run cointegrating vector among the variables. However, it is acknowledged that the procedure is likely to suffer from small sample bias. Therefore, the Johansen procedure is suggested but not used. The estimated income elasticities range from 1.5 to 3.0 in the long-run models, implying that tourism to South Korea is a luxury for Japanese, German, UK and US tourists. The trade volume variable is highly significant, implying that there is significant business travel to South Korea from the four sources. The relative price of Korean tourism is highly significant for UK and US, but not German and Japanese tourists, implying that German and Japanese tourists are less concerned about the cost of travel than their UK and US counterparts. Finally, in terms of the significance of substitute prices, Malaysia and China tend to be perfect substitute destinations, whereas Singapore and Thailand tend to be complementary destinations.

Appendix 3.2 Analysis of Models (continued)

Author(s)	Recognition of Omitted Explanatory Variables and Use of Proxy Variables	Model Specification	Method of Estimation and Models Estimated	Reported Descriptive Statistics	Diagnostic Tests	Empirical Implications
24 Kulendran, N. and Witt, S.F. (2003)	Tourist income is proxied with GDP Tourism price is proxied with the bilateral exchange rate adjusted CPI Airfares are explicitly excluded in tourism price since they are not perceived to have any effect on business tourism Substitute prices are omitted Tastes and preferences are omitted Marketing expenditures are omitted	Multivariate (Structural Time Series) Log Linear Single Equation	OLS (STSM, ARIMA, VAR, ECM)	R_D^2 (convent'l) R_S^2 (seasonal) t-statistic Variances associated with seasonal, trend and cyclical component Asymptotic Standard errors	Durbin-Watson Statistic for first order serial correlation Jarque-Bera test for normality in the errors Box-Ljung Statistic for first order autocorrelations White's test for heteroscedasticity	Contrary to Greenidge (2001), the empirical results suggest that the addition of explanatory variables to the univariate STSM does not improve the forecasting accuracy. Seven models were tested for forecasting accuracy, providing the most comprehensive comparison to date of the performance of modern forecasting techniques in the context of the demand for international business tourism. For Japan and UK, there is only deterministic seasonality. The volume of holiday tourists is also influential for business tourism. Trade openness and origin income appear in each relationship in the cointegration models. The volume of holiday tourism appears in each causal STM relationship, but features only twice in the long-run models. For short-term forecasting, ARIMA and BSM models generate the best forecasts. For medium-term forecasts, the seasonal no-change model generates the most accurate forecasts. The empirical results demonstrate that adding explanatory variables to the univariate model does not improve forecasting performance.

Appendix 3.2 Analysis of Models (continued)

Author(s)	Recognition of Omitted Explanatory Variables and Use of Proxy Variables	Model Specification	Method of Estimation and Models Estimated	Reported Descriptive Statistics	Diagnostic Tests	Empirical Implications
25 Kulendran, N. and Witt, S.F. (2001)	Tourist income is proxied with the UK per capita real personal disposable income Tourism price is proxied with (1) the relative CPI between destination and origin; and (2) unrestricted economy class air fares Substitute prices are omitted Tastes and preferences are omitted Marketing expenditures are omitted	Multivariate Log Linear Single Equation	OLS (Naïve, Simple Linear Regression Model, ARIMA, VAR, ECM)	$\bar{R}^2$ F-Statistic of the regression	Durban-Watson Statistic for first order serial correlation Lagrange multiplier test for fourth order serial correlation of the errors Ramsey's RESET test for functional form Breush-Pagan test for heteroscedasticity Chow's predictive failure test	The paper compares and contrasts the forecasting ability of the linear regression, cointegration/ECM, ARIMA, and structural time series models. The empirical results show that the combined effects of diagnostic checking and the adoption of cointegration/ECM methods lead to more accurate tourism demand forecasts than those generated by linear regression models. However, when the forecasting performance of these models is compared, the ECM generates more accurate forecasts than the traditional model by only 25 per cent. Moreover, the ECM fails to outperform the univariate time series models.

Appendix 3.2   Analysis of Models (continued)

Author(s)	Recognition of Omitted Explanatory Variables and Use of Proxy Variables	Model Specification	Method of Estimation and Models Estimated	Reported Descriptive Statistics	Diagnostic Tests	Empirical Implications
26 Kulendran, N. and Wilson, K. (2000)	Tourist income is proxied with real GDP of origin country and destination country Tourism price is proxied with the relative exchange rate adjusted CPI between destination and origin. Transport costs are explicitly excluded since such costs are not perceived to have any effect on business tourism Substitute prices Marketing expenditure Tastes and preferences	Multivariate Log Linear Single Equation	OLS (Naïve, ARIMA, VAR, ECM)	$\bar{R}^2$ F-statistic of the regression	Durban-Watson Statistic for first order serial correlation LR test for the null hypothesis that the parameters are zero MAPE RMSPE Lagrange multiplier test for fourth order serial correlation of the errors	Business tourism to four pairs of destination-to-origin is modelled, and the results are found to be quite diverse. Origin country income and openness to trade appear in the business travel long run relationships, and are significant at the 5 per cent level in three cases. Since the NZ economy has been integrated with the Australian economy, modelling business travel from NZ to Australia seems to be more problematic compared with the traditional trading partners such as Japan, UK and USA.

Appendix 3.2   Analysis of Models (continued)

Author(s)	Recognition of Omitted Explanatory Variables and Use of Proxy Variables	Model Specification	Method of Estimation and Models Estimated	Reported Descriptive Statistics	Diagnostic Tests	Empirical Implications
27 Kulendran, N. and King, M.L. (1997)	Tourist income is proxied with real GDP for UK, real GNP for USA and Japan and production based real GDP for New Zealand Price of tourism is proxied with the relative measure of exchange rate adjusted CPI between destination and origin. Transport costs as real one-way airfare Substitute prices are omitted Tastes and preferences are omitted Marketing expenditures are omitted	Univariate Time Series Single Equation Multivariate Log Linear (Structural Time Series) Single Equation	OLS (Simple Linear Regression Model, STSM, AR, AR(12), ARIMA, SARIMA, VAR, ECM)	$\bar{R}^2$ Asymptotic Standard errors F-statistic of the regression	Durban–Watson Statistic for first order serial correlation Lagrange multiplier test for fourth order serial correlation of the errors Thiel's inequality coefficient MAPE PMSPE RMSE	The performance of the ECM relative to time series models is weak. However, ECMs should perform better because they are multivariate, whereas time series models are univariate. Six models were tested for forecasting accuracy, and were gauged against MAPE, RMSPE and RMSE, as well as Thiel's U statistic. The AR(1) model outperforms AR(12). The regression model is the best overall for the USA, but arguably the worst for UK and New Zealand. The ARIMA models show a clear tendency to be relatively less accurate than other procedures as time increases. On the other hand, the AR model improves with increasing lead times, and provides the best period forecasts for four countries. The BSMs perform relatively well, while the ECMs perform relatively poorly. While AR model performs best for the UK, the ARIMA model provides the best short-term forecast for New Zealand. For Japanese tourists, it much harder to be clear-cut about the best model. The main feature of the results is the poor performance of the ECMs. Unlike time series models, ECMS use exogenous variables and their known values were used to forecast. But why do ECMs perform so poorly? A possible answer is the use of hypothesis testing to choose the level of differencing and seasonal differencing. There is also concern in the literature on the lack of power of unit roots null hypothesis.

Appendix 3.2 Analysis of Models (continued)

Author(s)	Recognition of Omitted Explanatory Variables and Use of Proxy Variables	Model Specification	Method of Estimation and Models Estimated	Reported Descriptive Statistics	Diagnostic Tests	Empirical Implications
28 Kulendran, N. (1996)	Tourist income is proxied with real GDP for UK, real GNP for USA and Japan and production based real GDP for New Zealand Price of tourism is proxied by the relative measure of exchange rate adjusted CPI between destination and origin. Substitute prices are omitted Tastes and preferences are omitted Exclusion of marketing expenditures are acknowledged	Multivariate Log Linear Single Equation Univariate Time Series Single Equation	OLS (VAR, ECM)	R^2 t-statistics Asymptotic Standard errors F-statistic of the regression	Durbin-Watson Statistic for first order serial correlation Lagrange multiplier test for fourth order serial correlation of the errors Wallis test to test for fourth order serial correlation in the errors Ramsey's RESET test for functional form Engle's ARHC test Chow's predictive failure test Jarque-Bera test for normality in the errors Breush-Pagan test for heteroscedasticity	For countries of origin, namely USA, UK and New Zealand, the estimated long-run income elasticity of demand is greater than one, and is considerably higher for Japan. The results imply that income is the most significant variable in the determination of tourist arrivals to Australia. The higher income elasticities may be due to the geographical isolation of Australia. UK tourists are more susceptible to changes in airfare than changes in income since a larger proportion travels to Australia to visit friends and relatives. The long-run estimated relative price elasticity for Japan is close to unity. This means that a percentage rise in the relative price level (that is, the price of tourism in Australian relative to Hawaii) will cause a drop in the percentage of tourist arrivals from Japan to Australia.

Appendix 3.2   Analysis of Models (continued)

Author(s)	Recognition of Omitted Explanatory Variables and Use of Proxy Variables	Model Specification	Method of Estimation and Models Estimated	Reported Descriptive Statistics	Diagnostic Tests	Empirical Implications
29 Lanza, A., Temple, P. and Urga, G. (2003)	Tourist income is proxied with GDP and GNP of tourist source country Tourism prices are omitted Transport costs are omitted Substitute prices are omitted Tastes and preferences are omitted Marketing expenditures are omitted	Multivariate Log Linear Single Equation	OLS/GLS (AIDS, SURE, VAR, ECM)	None	None	The price elasticity of demand, as well as the income elasticity of demand of tourism in 13 different OECD countries, are highly elastic (all of them exceed 1) and significant. International tourism is a luxury good for consumers in industrial countries. The demand for international tourism grows more than proportionally with respect to an increase in total expenditure over the observed ranges. The elasticities of substitution between tourism and manufacturing are all less than one and significantly less than 1 for 9 of the 13 countries. Moreover, the econometric evidence suggests that the terms of trade effect may be strong, and needs to be considered in evaluating the long-run growth prospects of regions specialising in tourism.

Appendix 3.2   Analysis of Models (continued)

Author(s)	Recognition of Omitted Explanatory Variables and Use of Proxy Variables	Model Specification	Method of Estimation and Models Estimated	Reported Descriptive Statistics	Diagnostic Tests	Empirical Implications
30 Lathiras, P. and Siriopoulos, C. (1998)	Tourist income is proxied with GDP of tourist source country Tourism price is proxied with the exchange rate adjusted relative CP between destination and tourist source country Substitute prices are expressed as the exchange rate adjusted relative CPI between destination and substitute destinations Transport costs are omitted Tastes and preferences are omitted Marketing expenditures are omitted	Multivariate Log Linear Single Equation	OLS (VAR, ECM)	R^2 t-statistics Standard Error of the Regression	Durban-Watson Statistic for first order serial correlation Lagrange multiplier test for serial correlation of the errors Ramsey's RESET test for functional form Chow's predictive failure test Jarque-Bera test for normality in the errors	All the long-run equilibrium parameters have the expected signs. There are two cointegrating vectors for Italy and three for the UK, indicating that the demand system is stationary in more than one direction, and hence is more stable. The negative income coefficient for the long run equation for the Netherlands indicates that tourism in Greece is an inferior good for Dutch tourists. However, for the rest of the tourist-generating countries, tourism is more of a luxury. Although past empirical work does not indicate clearly that ECMs outperform regression models in forecasting, results based on Theil's U, stability and predictive failure tests show that estimated short-run demand models have good forecasting power.
31 Ledesma-Rodriguez, F.J. and Navarro-Ibanez, M. (2001)	Tourist income is proxied with GDP of tourist source country Tourism price is proxied with the bilateral exchange rate Transport costs are proxied with price of oil Marketing expenditures are included in the regression Tastes and preferences are omitted	Multivariate Log Linear Single Equation	GLS (Pooled) SURE	t-statistics	Durban-Watson Statistic for first order serial correlation Hausman test for fixed versus random effects Wald test for restricted versus unrestricted model	The results indicate that the number of visitors lodged in Tenerife exhibits high elasticity with respect to real income per capita, considering the luxury good nature of the tourism product. In first differences, the estimate of the income elasticity is smaller, and the exchange rate and cost of travel have a significant influence on the number of visitors. Expenditures on infrastructure and promotion show their importance in tourism activity.

Appendix 3.2   Analysis of Models (continued)

Author(s)	Recognition of Omitted Explanatory Variables and Use of Proxy Variables	Model Specification	Method of Estimation and Models Estimated	Reported Descriptive Statistics	Diagnostic Tests	Empirical Implications
32 Lee, C.K., Var, T. and Blaine, T.W. (1996)	Tourist income is proxied with the real GDP of tourist source country Tourism price is proxied with (1) the relative CPI between tourist source country and the destination and (2) the real exchange rate between destination and tourism source country Transport costs are omitted Marketing expenditures are omitted Tastes and preferences are omitted	Multivariate Log Linear Single Equation	OLS (Simple Linear Regression Model, Cochrane-Orcutt, R.dge Regression)	R^2	Durban-Watson Statistic for first order serial correlation	The results show that four of eight models accounted for greater than 90 per cent of the variation in the dependent variable (per capita tourist expenditure), two models explain just over 80 per cent, and the other two models explain just below 70 per cent of the variation in per capita tourist expenditure. The poor fit of the latter two models, which is due to the omission of variables, is acknowledged. The income elasticities are found to be in the range 1.18 for Taiwan to 14.32 for the Philippines, indicating tourism to South Korea is a luxury. This also implies that their expenditures in South Korea are very responsive to income and continued economic growth in the source countries, so that tourism to South Korea should expand substantially. The coefficient of relative prices had the expected sign, except for Taiwan and Canada, but was insignificant. Moreover, for the Philippines, Japan and UK, the coefficients were quite elastic, indicating that Korea needs to remain competitive in order to attract tourists from these countries. The coefficient of the exchange rate variable had the expected sign for all countries, except for UK, but was insignificant. In general, it is regarded as a fundamental determinant of tourism to Korea.

Appendix 3.2   Analysis of Models (continued)

Author(s)	Recognition of Omitted Explanatory Variables and Use of Proxy Variables	Model Specification	Method of Estimation and Models Estimated	Reported Descriptive Statistics	Diagnostic Tests	Empirical Implications
33 Lim, C. and McAleer, M. (2002)	Tourist income is omitted Tourism prices are omitted Transport costs are omitted Substitute prices are omitted Tastes and preferences are omitted Marketing expenditures are omitted	Univariate Time Series Single Equation	OLS (ARIMA, SARIMA)	t-statistics AIC SBC	RMSE	This paper compares the respective RMSE, lowest post sample forecast errors, when the Holt-Winters additive and multiplicative models were used. Expenential smoothing models are one of the simplest and most widely used techniques for forecasting tourism demand. The paper raises the issue that seasonality is of corcern when forecasting tourism demand to Australia. The existence of unit roots does not seem to be an important issue, in general, in forecasting, as the model seem to perform better (with lower RMSE) when tourist arrivals are not adjusted for the presence of unit roots.

Appendix 3.2 Analysis of Models (continued)

Author(s)	Recognition of Omitted Explanatory Variables and Use of Proxy Variables	Model Specification	Method of Estimation and Models Estimated	Reported Descriptive Statistics	Diagnostic Tests	Empirical Implications
34 Lim, C. and McAleer, M. (2001a)	Tourist income is omitted Tourism prices are omitted Transport costs are omitted Substitute prices are omitted Tastes and preferences are omitted Marketing expenditures are omitted	Univariate Time Series Single Equation	OLS (AR, MA, ARMA)	*t*-statistics AIC SBC	Lagrange Multiplier test for serial correlation of the errors	The 12-month moving averages for the estimation of seasonal patterns of tourist arrivals from Hong Kong, Malaysia and Singapore, in Australia show considerable differences. In terms of the levels of the variables, the strongest concentrations are from Hong Kong, Malaysia, and Singapore, and seem to work in Australia's favour in that they do not coincide in the same months. The peak months of inbound tourists from Hong Kong, Malaysia and Singapore are February, November and December, respectively. Although a redistribution of the arrivals to bring about a change in seasonal concentration is not crucial, it would be beneficial for Australia to reduce the seasonal range and ratio between the peak and trough months through marketing and promotional efforts. The assumption of constant seasonal patterns over time may not be adequate to describe the behaviour of arrivals to Australia.

Appendix 3.2   Analysis of Models (continued)

Author(s)	Recognition of Omitted Explanatory Variables and Use of Proxy Variables	Model Specification	Method of Estimation and Models Estimated	Reported Descriptive Statistics	Diagnostic Tests	Empirical Implications
35 Lim, C. and McAleer, M. (2001b)	Tourist income is omitted Tourism prices are omitted Transport costs are omitted Substitute prices are omitted Tastes and preferences are omitted Marketing expenditures are omitted	Univariate Time Series Single Equation	OLS (Exponential Smoothing)	*t*-statistics	RMSE	The inherent volatility in tourism demand, which is attributed to the discretionary nature of its spending, raises some serious difficulties in forecasting international tourism demand. Therefore, accurate forecasting becomes an essential requirement for decision makers. Forecasting accuracy measures have been computed for both the levels and logarithm of tourist arrivals. The use of procedures such as tests for unit roots improves the validity of using ARIMA models for forecasting, and allows the forecaster to make an informed judgment at each step of the modelling cycle. This paper shows that by comparing the RMSE, lowest post-sample forecast errors were obtained when time series methods such as Box-Jenkins ARIMA and seasonal ARIMA models were used.
36 Lim, C. and McAleer, M. (1999)	Tourist income is omitted Tourism prices are omitted Transport costs are omitted Substitute prices are omitted Tastes and preferences are omitted Marketing expenditures are omitted	Univariate Time Series Single Equation	OLS (ARIMA)	*p*-values AIC SBC	Lagrange Multiplier test for serial correlation of the errors Jarque-Bera test for normality in the errors	The Box-Jenkins seasonal ARIMA process, which includes seasonal and non-seasonal differencing, is likely to be a more appropriate model of the data. There is evidence of a varying seasonal pattern. The findings suggest that previous studies of international tourism demand, which included seasonal dummies to explain seasonal patterns, are likely to be fragile if seasonal unit roots are present.

124

Appendix 3.2   Analysis of Models (continued)

Author(s)	Recognition of Omitted Explanatory Variables and Use of Proxy Variables	Model Specification	Method of Estimation and Models Estimated	Reported Descriptive Statistics	Diagnostic Tests	Empirical Implications
37 Morley, C. (1998)	Tourist income is proxied with the real per capita GDP of tourist source country Tourism price is the exchange rate adjusted relative CPI between destination and tourist source country Transport costs are origin country CPI adjusted air fares Substitute prices are omitted but acknowledges that they should be included to achieve more accuracy Tastes and preferences are omitted Marketing expenditures are omitted	Multivariate Log Linear Single Equation	NLLS	Asymptotic Standard Errors	MAPE	The diffusion type model for seven major sources of tourists to Australia fits the data well and yields meaningful results. The diffusion model does not give constant elasticities (indeed, the elasticities are complex functions of the parameters, explanatory variables and past demand), so the impact of changes in the explanatory variables has to be calculated by substitution into the fitted models. Income elasticities vary across origins and within origins over time. Income elasticities are generally greater than 1 due to the destination life cycle hypothesis, which considers how customer income, changes in tastes and previous experience may lead to changes in travel choices. The fare and price elasticities need to be cautioned because of the possibility of data and measurement biases in airfares. The differences in price and airfares elasticities for each origin tend to validate the decision to include them as separate variables rather than all-inclusive single price variables, as in most studies. The Bicentennial Expo and Pilots' Strike had positive and negative estimates, respectively.

Appendix 3.2   Analysis of Models (continued)

Author(s)	Recognition of Omitted Explanatory Variables and Use of Proxy Variables	Model Specification	Method of Estimation and Models Estimated	Reported Descriptive Statistics	Diagnostic Tests	Empirical Implications
38 Narayan, P.K. (2003a)	Tourism income is proxied with real GDP of tourist source country Tourism price is proxied with the exchange rate adjusted relative CPI between tourist source country and destination Transport costs are proxied with the logarithm of real economy class airfare between tourist source country and the destination Tastes and preferences are omitted Exclusion of marketing expenditures and that they should be included to achieve more accuracy is acknowledged	Multivariate Log Linear Single Equation	OLS (VAR, ECM)	$\bar{R}^2$ t-statistics Asymptotic Standard errors Standard Error of the Regression	Breusch-Godfrey LM test for autocorrelation of the errors Jarque-Bera test for normality in the errors Ramsey's RESET test for functional form and omitted variables White's test for heteroscedasticity Chow's predictive failure test	The empirical analysis shows that in the long run, a 1 per cent increase in real income in Australia, USA and New Zealand leads to an increase in tourist expenditures from these countries to Fiji by 2.1 per cent, 2.2 per cent and 2.6 per cent, respectively. An elasticity of income greater than or e implies that tourism in Fiji is a luxury for these three countries. This also implies that, with continued economic growth in Fiji's main tourist sources, their tourist expenditure in Fiji will continue to grow The relative price coefficient estimate implies that a percentage increase in prices in Fiji relative to Queensland (a substitute to Fiji) leads to a fall in tourist expenditures in Fiji by 0.3 per cent (Australians), 1.3 per cent (Americans) and 0.7 per cent (New Zealanders). Long-run transport cost elasticities range from –0.99 to –2.10, indicating the need to lower airfares to Fiji. Importantly, the coups of 1987 and 2000 are statistically significant.

Appendix 3.2   Analysis of Models (continued)

Author(s)	Recognition of Omitted Explanatory Variables and Use of Proxy Variables	Model Specification	Method of Estimation and Models Estimated	Reported Descriptive Statistics	Diagnostic Tests	Empirical Implications
39 Narayan, P.K. (2002)	Tourist income is proxied with real GDP of tourist source country Tourism price is proxied with the exchange rate adjusted relative CPI between tourist source country and destination Transport costs are proxied with the logarithm of real economy class airfare between tourist source country and the destination Tastes and preferences are omitted Exclusion of marketing expenditures and they should be included to achieve more accuracy is acknowledged	Multivariate Log Linear Single Equation	OLS (VAR, ECM)	$\bar{R}^2$ Asymptotic Standard errors of the estimates Standard Error of the Regression t-statistics	Breusch-Godfrey LM test for autocorrelation of the errors Jarque-Bera test for normality in the errors Ramsey's RESET test for functional form and omitted variables White's test for heteroscedasticity Chow's predictive failure test	In the short run, income is the only significant determinant in the case of tourists arriving from Australia. It follows that short-run changes in prices are unlikely to influence travel decisions significantly, as most trips are planned in advance. In the short run, increases in prices in Fiji relative to Bali increases tourism, which is an anomaly as the CPI is unable to capture the full effects of price changes related to tourist consumption of goods and services. In the long run, income is the main factor in influencing visitor flows to Fiji, with long-run elasticities ranging from 2.16 to 3.34. The long run relative price elasticities ranged from −0.37 to −3.11, while the substitute price elasticities ranged from −0.18 to −2.89. This indicates that Bali is a substitute for Fiji for Australian, New Zealand and US tourists. Long run results of transport cost elasticities range from −0.4 to −2.87, showing the importance of travel costs to Fiji.

127

Appendix 3.2   Analysis of Models (continued)

Author(s)	Recognition of Omitted Explanatory Variables and Use of Proxy Variables	Model Specification	Method of Estimation and Models Estimated	Reported Descriptive Statistics	Diagnostic Tests	Empirical Implications
40 Papatheodorou, A (1999)	Tourist income is proxied with tourists' share of expenditure in buying tourism products Price of tourism is a weighted average of the bilateral exchange rate adjusted relative CPI Transport costs are omitted Tastes and preferences is determined through time trend Marketing Expenditure	Multivariate Log Linear Systems of Equations	GLS/SURE (AIDS)	$\bar{R}^2$ t-statistics	Wald test for parameter constancy Durban-Watson Statistic for first order serial correlation	The results do not seem to be particularly novel. The aim of the analysis was to give a consistent quantification of the tourist economic relations in the Mediterranean region, rather than to support econometrically a new theory of location. All of the estimates were found to be statistically significant. The reported results seem to support the view that a major reason for changes in the share of tourist receipts lie in changing tastes for different destinations. Expenditure elasticities seem to be similar among all countries. Italy and Spain exhibit the highest expenditure elasticities since they have a bigger tourist infrastructure to cater for a larger market. The cross-price elasticities suggest that Portugal and Spain are substitutes and share common characteristics. Greece and Turkey are considered complements due to the effect of the distance travelled, which is not entirely plausible.

Appendix 3.2 Analysis of Models (continued)

Author(s)	Recognition of Omitted Explanatory Variables and Use of Proxy Variables	Model Specification	Method of Estimation and Models Estimated	Reported Descriptive Statistics	Diagnostic Tests	Empirical Implications
41 Payne, J. and Merva, A. (2002)	Tourist income is proxied with aggregate GDP for European Union Price of tourism product is proxied with real effective exchange rate Substitute prices are omitted Transport costs are omitted Tastes and preferences are omitted Marketing expenditures are omitted	Multivariate Log Linear Single Equation	OLS (Simple Linear Regression Model)	$\bar{R}^2$ p-values t-statistics F-statistic of the regression	Durban-Watson Statistic for first order serial correlation Lagrange Multiplier test for higher order autocorrelation Koenker's test for heteroscedasticity Jarque-Bera test for normality in the errors Ramsey's RESET test for functional form and omitted variables CUSUM test statistics	The results indicate that EU income, REER and the 1995 military actions were significant in explaining real revenues from international tourism to Croatia. The estimated coefficients suggest that Croatian tourism revenues are highly sensitive to EU GDP. The dummy variable indicating military action in 1995 was negative and highly significant, indicating how vulnerable the Croatian tourism sector is to the lack of peace, both domestically and in the border region of a potential tourist destination. The quarterly seasonal dummy variables are all significant, suggesting the third quarter as the most influential in attracting tourism. The empirical model passed a battery of diagnostic tests.

Appendix 3.2   Analysis of Models (continued)

Author(s)	Recognition of Omitted Explanatory Variables and Use of Proxy Variables	Model Specification	Method of Estimation and Models Estimated	Reported Descriptive Statistics	Diagnostic Tests	Empirical Implications
42 Qu, H. and Lam, S. (1997)	Tourist income is proxied with the level of personal disposable income in tourist source country. Tourism price is proxied with the relative CPI between origin and destination. Substitute prices are omitted. Transport costs are omitted. Tastes and preferences are omitted. Marketing expenditures are omitted.	Multivariate Log Linear Single Equation	OLS (Simple Linear Regression Model)	R^2 $\bar{R}^2$ F-statistic of the regression	Durban-Watson Statistic for first order serial correlation	The only two significant variables were disposable income and the dummy variable indicating a relaxation of visa regulations by the Chinese government during 1993–1995. Exchange rate and relative prices were insignificant. Relative price and exchange rate are more appropriate in measuring the tourism expenditure elasticity since they are more likely to change the purchasing power of tourists. The exchange rate and disposable income had very high collinearity, so that the exchange rate deleted from the model. As a result, one can conclude that the exchange rate and relative price variables may not be appropriate in this model.

Appendix 3.2   Analysis of Models (continued)

Author(s)	Recognition of Omitted Explanatory Variables and Use of Proxy Variables	Model Specification	Method of Estimation and Models Estimated	Reported Descriptive Statistics	Diagnostic Tests	Empirical Implications
43 Romilly, P., Liu, X. and Song, H. (1998)	Tourist income is proxied with the real per capita GDP of tourist source country Tourism price is proxied with real exchange rate Transport costs are omitted Substitute prices are omitted Tastes and preferences are omitted Marketing expenditures are omitted	Multivariate Log Linear Single Equation	GLS (Pooled)	$\bar{R}^2$ R^2 t-statistics F-statistic of the regression Residual Sum Squares	Hausman test for fixed versus random effects Durban-Watson Statistic for first order serial correlation	The analysis showed that the data can be pooled in the form of a heterogeneous intercept and homogenous slope coefficient. The choice between fixed and random effects was inconclusive. The significant variables are real per capita GDP, the real exchange rate, age structure and urbanisation. The most significant variable is real GDP, with a pooled income elasticity of 0.86. The estimated income elasticities are lower than reported in the literature, and is considerably lower than time series estimates. However, income elasticities under the two different estimation methods are conceptually different. The results imply that the price level in the origin and destination countries are more important than nominal exchange rates in determining international tourism spending. The significance of the social variables to determine tourism may change over time, given the nature of the tourism source country, though one should not neglect their temporal effects.

Appendix 3.2   Analysis of Models (continued)

Author(s)	Recognition of Omitted Explanatory Variables and Use of Proxy Variables	Model Specification	Method of Estimation and Models Estimated	Reported Descriptive Statistics	Diagnostic Tests	Empirical Implications
44 Song, H., Witt, S.F. and Jensen, T.C. (2003)	Tourist income is proxied with private consumption expenditure per capita in tourism source country Tourism price is proxied with the relative CPI between destination and tourist source countries Substitute prices are proxied with the relative CPI of destination against a weighted average of CPIs of alternative destinations Transport costs proxied with real economy class airfare Tastes and preferences are omitted Marketing expenditures are omitted	Univariate Time Series Single Equation Multivariate Log Linear Single Equation	OLS (ADLM, ECM, JML, Reduced ADLM, VAR, TVP, ARIMA)	R^2 Standard Error of Regression F-statistic of the regression	LM test for autocorrelation of the errors Durban-Watson Statistic for first order serial correlation Jarque-Bera test for normality in the errors Ramsey's RESET test for functional form and omitted variables White's test for first order heteroscedasticity Chow's predictive failure test	The paper uses annual data to test for accuracy in univariate models. Seasonality, which is one of the most prominent features in tourist demand, is neglected. Six different models are applied to tourism demand for Denmark. The static model reveals that per capita private consumption expenditure is the most significant variable. The significance of own price is weaker than for income. The Chernobyl disaster had a significant effect in the static model. Three choices of ADLM models, namely ECM, reduced ADLM, time-varying parameter model, VAR and univariate time series, are used for forecasting. According to the two accuracy measures used, namely RMSPE and MAPE, the TVP model and the static models are ranked equal best. Moreover, the TVP model generates the most accurate one-year-ahead forecasts, the static model generates the second most accurate forecasts, while the no-change model is also reasonably accurate.

Appendix 3.2   Analysis of Models (continued)

Author(s)	Recognition of Omitted Explanatory Variables and Use of Proxy Variables	Model Specification	Method of Estimation and Models Estimated	Reported Descriptive Statistics	Diagnostic Tests	Empirical Implications
45 Song, H., Romilly, P. and Liu, X. (2000)	Tourist income is proxied with the UK personal disposable income at 1990 prices Tourism price is proxied with CPI in destination deflated by UK implicit deflator of total consumer expenditure abroad Substitute prices are proxied with CPI of destination deflated by UK implicit deflator of total consumer expenditure abroad Transport costs are omitted Tastes and preferences are omitted Marketing expenditures are omitted	Multivariate Log Linear Single Equation	OLS (ARMA(p,q), VAR, ECM)	R^2 Standard Error of Regression	Durban-Watson Statistic for first order serial correlation Breusch-Godfrey LM test for autocorrelation of the errors Jarque-Bera test for normality in the errors Ramsey's RESET test for functional form and omitted variables White's test for Heteroscedasticity Chow's predictive failure test	In this paper, annual data are used because they are the most consistent data set available. Of the 12 destinations tested for cointegration, France is the only destination which had no cointegration. This could be due to omission of non-air travel modes, which could be an important tourism demand determinant to France. All standard diagnostic tests are reported, and 6 of the 12 destination-equations pass. The estimated long-run income elasticities range from 1.7 to 3.9, with a mean value of 2.4. These results suggest that international tourism is a luxury good for British tourists. The own price elasticities are negative for all but two, and are inelastic. In this paper, the 12 countries chosen are viewed as both substitutes and complements. The relative price of tourism to Ireland is significant in 10 of the 12 cointegrating regressions, which suggests Ireland is the perfect substitute for domestic tourism in UK. Through the RMSE, MAPE and Theil's inequality coefficient, the paper also compares the forecasting performance of the Naïve I, II, AR(1), ARMA(p,q), UVAR and ECM models. The ECM has the best forecasting performance for UK outbound tourism.

Appendix 3.2 Analysis of Models (continued)

Author(s)	Recognition of Omitted Explanatory Variables and Use of Proxy Variables	Model Specification	Method of Estimation and Models Estimated	Reported Descriptive Statistics	Diagnostic Tests	Empirical Implications
46 Sorensen, N.K. (1999)	Income is omitted Tourism prices are omitted Transport costs are omitted Substitute prices are omitted Tastes and preferences are omitted Marketing expenditures are omitted	Univariate Time Series Single Equation	OLS (AR(1))	None	None	The paper showed that more than one-quarter of the hotel nights are concentrated in the Copenhagen city area because of the extensive tourist infrastructure. The most important foreign consumers of hotel nights in Denmark are Germans, Swedes and Norwegians, who account for more than one-half of hotel nights spent by foreigners. There is a close correlation between hotel nights spent by foreign tourists and their bilateral exchange rates. The seasonal patterns have varied considerably in the six Danish counties and the six nationalities investigated. Of these, the most varying seasonal patterns have been for the Scandinavians, English and Italians, while the most stable were the Germans, Japanese and Americans. The paper concludes than this feature should be taken into account in modelling tourist demand for Denmark.

Appendix 3.2   Analysis of Models (continued)

Author(s)	Recognition of Omitted Explanatory Variables and Use of Proxy Variables	Model Specification	Method of Estimation and Models Estimated	Reported Descriptive Statistics	Diagnostic Tests	Empirical Implications
47 Turner, L.W. and Witt, S.F. (2001)	Tourist income is proxied with UK real personal disposable income per capita Tourism price is proxied with relative CPI multiplied by the exchange rate Acknowledges that substitute prices are omitted because, '...they are not considered to be particularly relevant on the account of medium-to-long-haul nature of travel involved between the source countries and New Zealand, and also the unique character of the destination' Tastes and preferences are omitted Marketing expenditures are omitted	Multivariate (Structural Time Series) Log Linear Single Equation	OLS (STSM)	R^2 *t*-statistics	Durban-Watson Statistic for first order serial correlation Bowman-Shenton Statistic for normality in the errors White's test for heteroscedasticity Box-Ljung Statistic for first order autocorrelations	The primary purpose of the paper is to test the hypothesis that multivariate STSM are capable of generating more accurate forecasts than univariate STMS. Although explanatory variables can be included in the STSM, and while this may provide a theoretical explanation as to why demand is rising or falling, it does not necessarily follow that forecasting accuracy will improve. STSM are capable of providing reasonably accurate univariate and multivariate forecasts. However, there is little or no evidence that inclusion of explanatory variables improves forecasting accuracy. Univariate estimates have proved to be more accurate in forecasting tourism. The overall forecast error for the multivariate STSM is higher than for the basic structural model. Moreover, the empirical findings are consistent with previous studies, indicating that univariate models provide the most accurate forecasts. The finding that causal structural time series models can reduce the overall forecast error by 2–3 per cent against the naive no-change model is important because this has not been found to be the case for other causal models. It appears that tourism forecasting accuracy may be improved by using structural time series models that incorporate explanatory variables rather than other causal models.

Appendix 3.2   Analysis of Models (continued)

Author(s)	Recognition of Omitted Explanatory Variables and Use of Proxy Variables	Model Specification	Method of Estimation and Models Estimated	Reported Descriptive Statistics	Diagnostic Tests	Empirical Implications
48 Turner, L.W., Reisinger, Y. and Witt, S.F. (1998)	Tourist income is proxied with UK real personal disposable income per capita Tourism price is proxied with relative CPI multiplied by the exchange rate Substitute prices are proxied with, (1) relative CPI between the destination and competing destinations multiplied by the exchanger rate and (2) the real airfare to destination relative to competing destinations Tastes and preferences are omitted Marketing expenditures are omitted	Multivariate (Structural Time Series) Log Linear Single Equation	OLS (Economic Structural Modelling LISREL Model)	$\bar{R}^2$ t-statistics Goodness of fit index Aggregated goodness of fit Index	RMSEA	Three types of tourism, namely holiday, business and visiting friends and relatives (VFR), are modelled for UK outbound tourists for seven European destinations simultaneously. The results show significant distinctions among the independent variables which influence tourism demand to different destinations, for a given purpose of visit. Economic variables play a dominant role in explaining business travel to seven destinations, whereas social factors feature in just two variables. However, social variables feature more in terms of explaining holiday tourism. Contrary to expectations, social variables play a less influential role in explaining tourism of VFRs, while economic variables are seen to be more important in explaining VFRs.

Appendix 3.2 Analysis of Models (continued)

Author(s)	Recognition of Omitted Explanatory Variables and Use of Proxy Variables	Model Specification	Method of Estimation and Models Estimated	Reported Descriptive Statistics	Diagnostic Tests	Empirical Implications
49 Venegas, M. and Croes, R.R. (2000)	Tourist income is proxied with real GDP of USA Price of tourism is proxied with (1) relative CPI between destination and origin CPI (2) real effective exchange rate Transportation costs are omitted Tastes and preferences are omitted Marketing expenditures are omitted	Multivariate Log Linear Single Equation	OLS (Simple Linear Regression Model)	$\bar{R}^2$ F-statistic of the regression	Durban–Watson Statistic for first order serial correlation	A total of 12 tourism demand models of linear and log-linear equations were estimated. All the estimates have extremely high $\bar{R}^2$ values that are close to 1, indicating that the variables are likely to be non-stationary and the regressions are spurious. In this case, cointegration analysis should be used. However, the estimates from log-linear equations are discussed here. The effect of income dominates those of exchange rates and relative price. The short-run income elasticity is 1.38 and the long-run income elasticity is 3.12. Relative prices are not significant, but the authors claim that the demand for US tourism to Aruba is inelastic.
50 Vogt, M.G. and Wittayakorn, C. (1998)	Income of tourists are proxied with world income expressed as an index Price of tourism is proxied with CPI of Thailand Substitute prices are omitted Transport costs are omitted Tastes and preferences are omitted Marketing expenditures are omitted	Multivariate Log Linear Single Equation	OLS (Simple Linear Regression Model)	$\bar{R}^2$ t-statistics F-statistic of the regression	None	This is only one of the 53 papers surveyed which has not found any significant variables in determining demand for tourism. Of the four estimated price elasticities, two have the incorrect signs while the other two are significant. The two income elasticities have the correct sign but are insignificant. There are fundamental flaws in this analysis.

137

Appendix 3.2 Analysis of Models (continued)

Author(s)	Recognition of Omitted Explanatory Variables and Use of Proxy Variables	Model Specification	Method of Estimation and Models Estimated	Reported Descriptive Statistics	Diagnostic Tests	Empirical Implications
51 Webber, A.G. (2001)	Tourist income is proxied with Australian real income Price of tourism is proxied with, (1) the relative CPI of tourist destinations against origin and (2) the bilateral exchange rate between origin and tourist destinations Substitute prices are omitted Transport costs are omitted Tastes and preferences are omitted Marketing expenditures are omitted	Multivariate Log Linear Single Equation	OLS (VAR, ECM)	*p*-values	None	Personal disposable income is the strongest determinant of tourist departures, followed by substitute prices, real exchange rates and the variance of exchange rates. Exchange rate volatility appears to be a deterrent for Australian tourists travelling to the Philippines, Singapore and Thailand, but a stimulus for those travelling to Japan. The countries that appear to be explained by the greatest variety of long-run variables are Japan, Singapore and Thailand, for which all the explanatory variables are significant. The UK has low explanatory power from the core variables, so that income and seasonal factors appear to be the most significant. There is broad similarity between income and substitute price elasticities. The significant estimates are predominantly in the inelastic range for both variables, with income tending to be close to unity and substitute prices towards between zero and unity.

Appendix 3.2   Analysis of Models (continued)

Author(s)	Recognition of Omitted Explanatory Variables and Use of Proxy Variables	Model Specification	Method of Estimation and Models Estimated	Reported Descriptive Statistics	Diagnostic Tests	Empirical Implications
52 Wong, K.K.F. (1997)	Income is omitted Tourism prices are omitted Transport costs are omitted Substitute prices are omitted Tastes and preferences are omitted Marketing expenditures are omitted	Univariate Time Series Single Equation	OLS (AR(11))	$\bar{R}^2$	None	The paper examines the time series properties of tourist arrivals in regions and countries over a period of 17 to 35 years. A majority of the time series investigated was consistent with non-stationarity. This implies that any shocks to the time series will have a permanent effect as the shock will exert its influence indefinitely on tourist arrivals. Therefore, shocks such as the oil price shocks of 1973 and 1979 will exert their influence on tourist arrivals around the world. The paper addresses the results of prior tourism demand studies that used OLS to estimate demand functions under the incorrect assumption of stationary tourist arrivals series. In such circumstances, the OLS estimates are not asymptotically normal and inferences were invalid, thereby leading to misleading conclusions.
53 Yoon, J. and Shafer, E.L. (1996)	Tourist income is omitted Price of tourism is nested in trip cost Transport costs are nested in trip cost Substitute prices are omitted Tastes and preferences are omitted Marketing expenditures are omitted	Multivariate Log Linear Single Equation	OLS (Simple Linear Regression Model)	R^2 p-values	None	A log-linear regression model of US tourist arrivals in the Bahamas on trip cost was estimated based on a survey of 6170 respondents. The study analysed how the trip cost (which can be controlled by tourism destination planners) can affect the number of visitors in a given time period (one year) for eight different sub-markets. The absolute value of the price elasticities was greater than 1 for seven of eight submarkets, indicating that travellers are quite sensitive to trip cost changes.

4. Economic Profiles, Tourism Composition and Trends in Country Risk in Small Island Tourism Economies[1]

4.1 INTRODUCTION

This chapter provides a detailed assessment of the economic profiles of the twenty SITEs mentioned in Chapter 2. It has already been established that these countries are relatively small in population, GDP and land area, among other measures. Considering these features, some SITEs are diversified in a unique way, while others are struggling with one or two dominant economic activities. This chapter assesses the main economic activities in these SITEs, and examines the importance of their primary economic activities to economic welfare. In general, tourism is the dominant economic activity for each of these SITEs.

Considering the importance of inbound tourism demand, we analyse the composition of international tourists who visit six of these SITEs using the available data. It is well known that the trends in tourism earnings coincide with the economic trends of the tourism source countries. The principal tourism source countries are the G7 countries, and any adverse economic impacts in these tourism sources can affect the trends in international tourist arrivals, and hence tourism earnings. Moreover, new and emerging source countries appear as globalisation and democratisation continue at current rates of progress. The break-up of the former Soviet Union created new and relatively wealthy economies which have become new tourism sources to some SITEs. In time, these source markets will begin to influence tourism earnings across SITEs and, as a result, the composition of the tourism source base will be affected. The threat of terrorism, global conflicts, and rising oil prices, among others, affect the trends in tourism in SITEs. Since SITEs are remotely located, the effect on airfares due to changing oil prices and terrorism-related activities will affect air travel. Such consequences are also likely to influence travel and tourism globally.

It is imperative that we examine the structure of international tourist arrivals in SITEs because it is an important prerequisite in the assessment of tourist demand. This will primarily entail establishing whether these SITEs represent features of competitive or complementary tourism markets through comparing the cross-correlation coefficients. The cross-correlations for international tourist arrivals are calculated using the annual numbers of international tourist arrivals from the eighteen principal markets to the six destination SITEs during the period 1980–2000 for which data are available.

The structure of this chapter is as follows. In Section 4.2, country economic profiles are presented for 20 individual SITEs. For the Bahamas, Dominican Republic, Haiti, Jamaica, Cyprus and Malta, special emphasis will be given to how the economic, political and financial performance of these economies have affected the respective country risk ratings, which will be analysed in Chapter 7. Thereafter, the compositions of tourist arrivals in SITEs are examined in Section 4.3. This is followed by a presentation of some concluding remarks in Section 4.4.

4.2   COUNTRY ECONOMIC PROFILES

In order to compile these country economic profiles, information regarding the economic, financial and political sectors for the 20 SITEs has been pooled from four widely respected international sources. These sources include the US Department of State (2003), BBC News (2003), *The Economist* (2003) and the Central Intelligence Agency of the United States of America (2003).

Antigua and Barbuda

The economy of Antigua and Barbuda is based mainly on service industries such as tourism, financial and government services, which also provide the main source of employment. Antigua is considered one of the success stories of economic prosperity in the West Indies. Tourism is the principal economic activity, accounting for nearly one-half of GDP. Although Antigua has achieved higher living standards than most Caribbean countries, it also faces the challenge of defending against vulnerability to violent environmental consequences. A series of violent hurricanes since 1995 have damaged a large part of the tourism infrastructure and ever since there has been a decline in tourist arrivals. To circumvent such disasters which affect tourism unfavourably, Antigua has sought to diversify its economy, and transport, communications and financial services have become important economic sectors. Despite experiencing environmental calamities in the recent past, the Antiguan tourism sector has continued on a path of recovery. In 2002, more than half a million tourists visited this island nation, of which the majority are European and US cruise ship tourists. Tourism receipts reached USD 240 million and the real economy grew at 2.7 per cent per annum in 2002. The financial services sector has also been adversely affected by sanctions imposed by the UK and USA due to the loosening of its money-laundering controls. The Antiguan government has made efforts to comply with the demands of the international community in order to lift the sanctions, and was listed as a tax haven by the OECD in 2000. The limited agricultural sector produces only for domestic consumption, and growth is constrained by the limited water supply and labour shortages. There is a growing manufacturing sector, which comprises furniture and assembly of electronic components. The medium growth prospects depend on the timely recovery of the US economy as more than one-third of its tourist arrivals are from the USA.

The Bahamas

The Bahamas, which is an archipelago of approximately 700 islands, is one of the most popular tourist destinations in the western hemisphere. With few domestic resources and little industry, the Bahamas imports nearly all of its foodstuffs and manufactured goods from the USA. It is also a major provider of offshore financial services, and has one of the world's largest open-registry shipping fleets. The economy is entirely dependent on tourism and offshore financial services. Tourism alone provides more than two-thirds of GDP and employs two-fifths of the Bahamian workforce. In 2002, four million tourists visited the Bahamas, of which 80 per cent were from the USA. Offshore financial services are the second most important sector in the Bahamian economy, accounting for 15 per cent of GDP, which is due to the country's status as a tax haven and offshore financial centre. Despite the government's incentives aimed at manufacturing and agriculture, together they contribute only 10 per cent of GDP and show little growth. The principal sources of government revenue are import tariffs and royalties. The challenge faced by the Bahamian government is to liberalise trade, which will be a difficult option since its volume of merchandise exports is insignificant. The Bahamas is a stable, developing nation, and the overall real growth prospects in the short run will depend mainly on the fortunes of the tourism sector, which eagerly awaits a speedy recovery in the US economy.

Barbados

Since independence in 1966, the Barbadian economy has been transformed from a low income to a middle income country. Today, Barbados is regarded as the intellectual capital of the West Indies, which is also home to the headquarters of many regional multilateral agencies and think-tanks. In the past, the Barbadian economy was dependent on sugarcane cultivation and associated activities. However, in recent years it has diversified into manufacturing and tourism, which is now categorised as a high middle income country. The inception of the Port Charles Marina Project in Speightown helped to expand the tourism industry over the period 1996–2000. Moreover, offshore financial and information services are important foreign exchange earners. There has been a sharp economic downturn in the early 1990s due to macroeconomic mismanagement. After some difficult times, the economy began to grow in 1993, averaging growth of 3 to 5 per cent per annum until the events of 11 September, 2001. The general global economic downturn over the last four years, the decline in US tourist arrivals, and the impact of the depreciated Euro on sugar exports, have been the main factors responsible for the slump in economic activity. The continued recession has led to a rise in unemployment in all sectors of the economy, compared with a net decrease in employment in the tourism sector. The largest employer in Barbados is the public sector. The government continues its efforts to curb unemployment, encourage direct foreign investment and privatise state-owned enterprises. The real economic growth prospects depend on the recovery of the US economy, the growth in international tourist arrivals, particularly from the USA, and forecasts that it would be steady in the short to medium term.

Comoros

Comoros is one of the poorest and least developed countries in the world, with an estimated per capita GDP of USD700. Comoros comprises three islands that have inadequate transportation links, a young and rapidly increasing population, and few natural resources. Although the quality of land differs from island to island, most of the widespread lava-encrusted soil formations are unsuitable for agriculture. As a result, inhabitants make their living from subsistence agriculture and fishing. The low educational level of the labour force contributes to a subsistence level of economic activity, high unemployment, and a heavy dependence on foreign grants and technical assistance. Agriculture, including fishing, hunting and forestry, contributes 40 per cent to GDP, employs 80 per cent of the labour force, and provides most of the exports. Services including tourism, which provided more than 20 per cent of total export earnings, construction and commercial activities constitute the remainder of GDP. Plantations engage a large proportion of the population in producing the major cash crops for exports, namely vanilla, cloves, perfume essences and copra. Comoros is the world's largest producer of ylang-ylang essence that is used in manufacturing perfume, and is also the world's second largest producer of vanilla. Principal food crops are coconuts, bananas and cassava. The country is not self-sufficient in food production, so that the bulk of the rice consumed is imported. In Comoros, the infrastructure necessary for development is virtually non-existent, and the seaport systems are rudimentary. Some settlements are not even linked to the main road system and are isolated. Long-distance and ocean-going ships must lie offshore and be unloaded by small boats. During the cyclone season, this procedure is dangerous and most ships are reluctant to visit. In such circumstances, freight is sent to Mombassa in Kenya or La Reunion, an archipelagic French territory in the Indian Ocean, and then transhipped. France is Comoros' major trading partner and finances some development projects. The USA receives a large proportion of Comoros' exports, but US imports are negligible. The government, which is hampered by internal political disputes, is struggling to upgrade education and technical training, privatise commercial and industrial enterprises, improve health services, diversify exports, promote tourism and reduce the high population growth rate. Increased foreign support is essential if the goal of 4 per cent annual GDP growth is to be achieved.

Cyprus

The economy of Cyprus had been transformed from a totally agricultural economy to an open, free market and service-based economy. Cyprus is considered among the most prosperous nations in the Mediterranean, but is highly sensitive to external shocks. The real economic growth rates have been erratic during the 1990s, reflecting the economy's vulnerability to the volatility in international tourist arrivals, caused by political instability on the island, coupled with the adverse fluctuations in economic conditions in Western Europe. Cypriot economic policy has been focused on meeting the criteria for admission to the European Union (EU). There is a growing water shortage problem in the Turkish sector, and installations of several desalination plants are planned. The Turkish Cypriot economy has about 20 per cent of the population and one-third of the per capita GDP of the Greek Cypriot south. Moreover, it is recognized only by Turkey and has greater difficulty in obtaining foreign capital. Investors are reluctant to invest due to the high risk. The main sectors are agriculture and government services, which together employ about one-half of the labour force. Moreover, the small, vulnerable economy has suffered because the Turkish lira is the legal tender. In order to compensate for the economy's weakness, Turkey provides direct and indirect aid to tourism, education and industry, among others.

Dominica

The Dominican economy depends on agriculture and is highly vulnerable to climatic conditions, notably tropical storms. Agriculture, primarily bananas, accounts for 21 per cent of GDP and employs 40 per cent of the labour force. Dominica is mostly volcanic and has few beaches. Compared with neighbouring islands, the development of tourism in Dominica has been relatively slow, due mainly to the lack of an international airport. Nevertheless, Dominica's high, rugged mountains, rainforests, freshwater lakes, hot springs, waterfalls and diving spots make it an attractive tourist destination. Cruise ship stopovers have increased following the development of modern docking and waterfront facilities in the capital. Eco-tourism is also a growing industry. The banana sector is highly vulnerable to weather conditions and to external events affecting commodity prices. Hurricane Luis devastated the country's banana crop in September 1995, and tropical storms wiped out one-quarter of the crop in 1994. In view of the European Union's (EU) phasing out of preferred access of bananas to its markets, agricultural diversification is a priority. Dominica has made some progress, with the export of small quantities of citrus fruits and vegetables, particularly coffee, patchouli, aloe vera, mangoes, guavas and papayas. The subsequent recovery from the devastations caused by the severe climatic conditions has been fuelled by increases in construction, soap production, and tourist arrivals. Dominica also recently entered the offshore financial services industry in order to diversify the island's production base. Dominica is a member of the Eastern Caribbean Currency Union (ECCU). The Eastern Caribbean Central Bank (ECCB) issues a common currency to all eight members of the ECCU, manages monetary policy, and regulates and supervises commercial banking activities in its member countries. Dominica is a beneficiary of the US Caribbean Basin Initiative (CBI). In 2001, exports totalled USD47 million, with the USA receiving nearly 9 per cent of these exports. Dominica's imports amounted to USD100 million, 41 per cent from the USA. Dominica is also a member of the fourteen-member Caribbean Community and Common Market (CARICOM) and of the Organization of Eastern Caribbean States (OECS).

Dominican Republic

Sharing the Island of Hispaniola with Haiti, the country has become one of the most popular tourist destinations in the Caribbean, with tourism and free-trade zones as key sources of foreign exchange. While still one of the poorest countries in the Caribbean, with a large wealth gap between rich and poor, the Dominican economy has experienced a fast growth rate over the past decade. Although the country has long been viewed primarily as an exporter of sugar, coffee and tobacco, in recent years the service sector has overtaken agriculture as the economy's largest employer, due to growth in tourism and free trade zones. The country suffers from marked income inequality. The poorest half of the population receives less than one-fifth of GNP, while the richest 10 per cent enjoy 40 per cent of national income. In December 2000, the new administration passed broad new tax legislation which it hopes will provide sufficient revenue to offset rising oil prices and to enable servicing of foreign debt.

Fiji

Fiji is the most developed island economy in the Pacific Ocean, although it remains a developing country with a subsistence agricultural sector, endowed with forest, mineral and fish resources. Sugar exports and the tourism industry are the main economic activities, while sugar processing accounts for one-third of the industrial sector. The effects of the Asian economic and financial crises, as well as political turmoil, resulted in a substantial drop in the GDP in 1997 and 1998. Positive growth returned in 1999 with the aid of a devaluation in the Fijian Dollar. According to the Asian Development Bank, the economy contracted by 4.7 per cent in 2000, but recovered quickly and grew by an estimated 5.1 per cent in 2001. This recovery was supported by growth in international tourist arrivals, improved performance in the mining sector, and the harvesting and processing of mahogany and fresh fish exports. Tourism has expanded rapidly since the 1980s and is the main economic activity, with over half a million tourists visiting Fiji in recent years. The major tourist markets are Australia, New Zealand and the USA. In the wake of the events of 11 September, 2001, US tourist arrivals declined, but have recovered over the last two years. Gross earnings from the Fijian tourism sector continue to be Fiji's principal source of foreign currency. Fiji runs persistently large trade deficits, although its tourism revenue yields a positive services account, which keeps the current account roughly in balance. Australia is the biggest trading partner, with 35 per cent of its trade, while USA, UK and Japan account for between 15 to 30 per cent. Fiji's two main exports are sugar and garments, which are responsible for one-quarter of export revenues. The potential collapse of the Fijian sugar industry is due to poor quality, lack of administration and the phasing out of the preferential price agreement with the EU, which will come into effect in 2007. The textile industry expanded rapidly due to the introduction of tax exemptions, and subsequently the industry output has expanded more than ten-fold. However, the lower labour costs of Chinese competitors, and the softening of a trade preference agreement with Australia, have resulted in many closures of garment factories. Long-term economic problems include low investment rates and uncertain property rights. Investment laws have been reviewed to make them more business friendly, and work permit requirements have been relaxed. In April 2002, Moody's Investor Services upgraded its sovereign ratings for Fiji from negative to stable, noting that, despite continuing domestic political uncertainty, the country's external financial position has improved dramatically improved over the past two years. Prospects for the Fijian economy are optimistic.

Grenada

The economy of Grenada is based primarily upon agricultural production of nutmeg, mace and cocoa, and was brought to a near standstill by Hurricane Ivan on 7 September, 2004. There were 37 fatalities caused by the hurricane, and approximately eight to ten thousand people were left homeless. Hurricane Ivan damaged or destroyed 90 per cent of the buildings on the island, including some tourist facilities. Reconstruction is expected to require time and substantial resources. In this island economy, progress in fiscal reforms and prudent macroeconomic management has kept annual growth steady since 1998. Strong performances in construction and manufacturing, together with the development of an offshore financial industry, have also contributed to growth in national output. Grenada relies on tourism as its main source of foreign exchange, especially since the construction of an international airport in 1985. Major short-term concerns are the rising fiscal deficit and the deterioration in the external account balance. Grenada shares a common central bank and a common currency with seven other members of the Organization of Eastern Caribbean States (OECS). Grenada is a member of ECCU and ECCB, and is also a member of CARICOM. Most goods can be imported into Grenada under open general license, but some goods require specific licenses. Goods that are produced in the Eastern Caribbean receive additional protection. In May 1991, the CARICOM common external tariff (CET) was implemented. The CET aims to facilitate economic growth through intra-regional trade by offering duty-free trade among CARICOM members and duties on goods imported from outside CARICOM.

Haiti

Haiti is probably the poorest country in the western hemisphere. Haiti has been plagued by political instability, violence, poverty, unemployment, migration and environmental degradation for much of its history since independence in 1804 from France. Since the 1980s these factors have led to economic stagnation and damaged Haiti's image as a major tourist destination. The country's infrastructure has deteriorated, and drug trafficking has corrupted both the judicial system and police force. Approximately 80 per cent of the Haitian population lives in abject poverty. Nearly 70 per cent of all Haitians depend on the agriculture sector, which consists mainly of small-scale subsistence farming and employs about two-thirds of the economically active work force. Haiti's real GDP growth turned negative in 2001 after six years of continuous growth, and has since become highly volatile. Macroeconomic instability is adversely affected by political instability, the collapse of the informal banking cooperatives, high budget deficits, low investment and reduced international capital flows. Haiti's economy stabilised in 2003 and the government agreed to a staff monitoring programme with the IMF. The IMF predicts real growth of 1 per cent in 2004, with real per capita GDP of USD425, which will continue to decline as population grows at an estimated 1.6 per cent per annum.

Jamaica

The key natural resources in this island economy, famous for its dark rum, are bauxite and a climate that is conducive to agriculture and tourism. The discovery of bauxite in the 1940s, and subsequent establishment of the bauxite-alumina industry, transformed this island economy from sugar and bananas. By the 1970s, Jamaica had emerged as a world leader in exports of these minerals, and foreign investment increased. The country is confronted with serious obstacles, but has the potential for growth and modernisation. These problems include high interest rates, increased foreign competition, and the weak financial condition of business, in general, resulting in receiverships or closures, downsizing of companies, shifts in investment portfolios to non-productive, short-term high yield instruments, a depreciating exchange rate, widening merchandise trade deficit, and the growing internal debt of the government to bail out various ailing sectors of the economy, particularly the financial sector. After four years of subsequent negative growth, the Jamaican economy improved, with a GDP growth rate of 0.8 per cent in 2000. Since assuming office in 1992, Prime Minister Patterson has eliminated most price control measures, streamlined tax schedules and privatised government enterprises. Although inflationary pressures are mounting, continued tight monetary and fiscal policies have helped slow inflation and stabilise the exchange rate. Inflation fell from 25 per cent in 1996 to 7 per cent in 2001. Depressed economic conditions in 1999–2000 led to increased civil unrest, including a mounting crime rate. Jamaica's medium-term prospects will depend on encouraging investment in the productive sectors, maintaining a competitive exchange rate, stabilising the labour environment, selling off reacquired firms, and implementing proper fiscal and monetary policies.

Maldives

Development has been centred upon the tourism industry and its complementary service sectors, transport, distribution, real estate, construction and government. Taxes on the tourist industry have been directed towards infrastructure development, and have been used to improve technology in the fisheries and agricultural sectors. The Maldivian tourism industry is the largest sector, accounting for 31 per cent of GDP and more than 60 per cent of Maldivian foreign exchange receipts. Over 90 per cent of government tax revenue comes from import duties and tourism-related taxes. Over half a million tourists visit the islands annually. Distribution is the second largest sector, accounting for 14 per cent, with the government a further 12 per cent. The fishery industry, which accounts for just 8 per cent of GDP, was the mainstay of the economy until tourism took over in the early 1980s. The GDP in 2002 totalled USD640 million, or about USD2200 per capita. The Maldives has experienced relatively low inflation in recent years. Real GDP growth averaged about 10 per cent in the 1980s. It expanded by an exceptional 16.2 per cent in 1990, declined to 4 per cent in 1993, grew to 10 per cent in 1998, and has since levelled to the 5–7 per cent range. The Maldives has been running a merchandise trade deficit in the range of USD200 to USD260 million since 1997. The trade deficit declined to USD208 million in 2002 from USD233 million in 2001. The Maldivian Government began an economic reform programme in 1989, initially by lifting import quotas and opening some exports to the private sector. Subsequently, it has liberalised regulations to allow more foreign investment. Agriculture and manufacturing continue to play a minor role in the economy, constrained by the limited availability of cultivable land and the shortage of domestic labour. Most staple foods must be imported. Industry, which consists mainly of garment production, boat building and handicrafts, accounts for about 18 per cent of GDP. Maldivian authorities worry about the impact of erosion and possible global warming on their low-lying country as 80 per cent of the total land area is one metre or less above sea level. International shipping to and from the Maldives is operated mainly by the private sector, with only a small fraction of the tonnage carried on vessels operated by the national carrier. Over the years, the Maldives has received substantial economic assistance from multilateral development organisations, including the United Nations Development Program (UNDP), Asian Development Bank and the World Bank. Individual donors, including Australia, Japan, India, and European and Arab countries, including Islamic Development Bank and the Kuwaiti Fund, also have contributed. A 1956 bilateral agreement gave the UK the use of Gan in Addu Atoll in the far south of the country for 20 years as an air facility in return for British aid. The agreement ended in 1976, shortly after the British closed the Gan air station.

Malta

Malta achieved independence from the British in 1964. Although this island economy was politically divided on whether to join the EU, it was the smallest of the ten countries to join the EU in May 2004. Malta has limited native raw materials and has a very small domestic market. The main natural resources are limestone, a favourable geographic location, which fosters tourism and boasts a productive labour force. It produces one-fifth of its food consumption and has limited fresh water supplies. The Maltese economy is entirely dependent on foreign trade, manufacturing of textiles and electronics, with a substantial tourism sector accounting for nearly one-third of GDP. Tourist arrivals and the associated foreign exchange earnings have steadily increased since the second oil shock of the late 1970s. Following the events of 11 September, 2001, Malta also paid a hefty price for the decline in tourist arrivals by 7 per cent in 2001 and 2002. At the same time, the bursting of the high-tech bubble took its toll on the electronics manufacturing industry, which resulted in reduction in exports and private investment. In spite of these setbacks, the relatively flexible workforce kept unemployment steady. After the recession of 2001, a slow recovery began with the help of increased tourist arrivals. The continued sluggishness in the global economy is holding back Maltese exports, tourism is increasing moderately, and the real growth rate for 2003 is estimated to be around 3 per cent.

Mauritius

Mauritius has developed from a low-income, agriculture-based economy to a middle-income diversified economy with growing industrial, financial and tourist sectors. Since independence from the UK in 1968, Mauritius has become one of the strongest economies in Africa. The economy has sustained 6 per cent annual growth rate for the last two decades, driven by sugar, textiles and apparel, tourism, and most recently by financial services. With a per capita income of USD 3800, Mauritius is now classified as a middle-income country. The Human Development Index of the 173 UN member nations ranks Mauritius 67th globally, 40th among the developing countries, and second in Africa. Resulting from lower growth in sugar and tourism sectors, economic growth slowed to 5.8 per cent in 2001 from 9.3 per cent in 1999. In 2002, the economy expanded by more than 4 per cent, boosted considerably by increased trade through the Africa Growth and Opportunity Act (AGOA) legislation. Over the past several years, Mauritius registered balance-of-payments surpluses, leading to a comfortable external reserves position, currently equivalent to more than nine months of imports, an external debt service ratio of only 7 per cent, and modest single-digit inflation, on average. The inflation rate increased from 4.2 per cent in 2000 to 5.4 per cent in 2001. It reached 6.3 per cent in 2002, owing to the recent increase in the rate of VAT from 12 per cent to 15 per cent, as well as large increases in government spending. However, the rising trend in unemployment and the deterioration in public finances are matters of concern. The unemployment rate increased steadily from 2.7 per cent in 1991 to 9.2 per cent in 2001, representing 48 000 unemployed. It reached slightly more than 10 per cent in 2002. While Mauritius relies heavily on exports of sugar, textiles, garments and tourism, services like free port, offshore business and financial services comprise other pillars of the economy. The offshore sector is playing an increasingly important role in the financial services sector, and is emerging as a growth vehicle for the economy. At the end of October 2002, the number of companies registered in the offshore sector reached 20 111. Mauritius is a major regional distribution, transhipment and marketing centre. There has been growing realisation on the part of the government that the traditional industries of sugar, textile and tourism are no longer capable of sustaining further wealth and job creation. Accordingly, the government is giving high priority to the development of Information and Communications. Although the near-term outlook for growth is encouraging, the challenges facing Mauritius in the long term are daunting. On the domestic front, the decline in fertility and the aging of the population will decrease the available pool of labour for the economy, thereby reducing the long-term growth potential.

Samoa

The economy of Samoa has traditionally been dependent on development aid, family remittances from overseas, agriculture, fishing and tourism. The country is vulnerable to devastating storms. Global climatic change concerns Samoa's position as a low-lying island state. The effects of three natural disasters in the early 1990s were overcome by the middle of the decade, but economic growth declined again with the regional economic downturn. Two major cyclones hit Samoa at the beginning of the 1990s. Cyclone Ofa left an estimated 10 000 islanders homeless in February 1990. Cyclone Val caused 13 deaths and hundreds of millions of dollars in damage in December 1991. As a result, GDP declined by nearly 50 per cent from 1989 to 1991. Long-run development depends upon upgrading the tourist infrastructure, attracting foreign investment and further diversification of the economy. The service sector accounts for more than one-half of GDP and employs approximately 30 per cent of the labour force. Tourism is the single largest activity, more than doubling in visitor numbers and revenue over the last decade. More than 85 000 visitors came to Samoa in 1999, contributing over USD12 million to the local economy. One-third came from American Samoa, 28 per cent from New Zealand and 11 per cent from the USA. Arrivals increased in 2000, as visitors to the South Pacific avoided the political strife in Fiji by travelling to Samoa instead. The primary sectors are agriculture, forestry, and fishing, employing nearly two-thirds of the labour force and producing 17 per cent of GDP. Important products include coconuts and fish. The manufacturing sector mainly processes agricultural products. The decline of fish stocks in the area is a continuing problem. Industry accounts for over one-quarter of GDP, while employing less than 6 per cent of the work force. Samoa's principal exports are coconut products and fish. Its main imports are food and beverages, industrial supplies and fuels. The collapse of taro exports in 1994 has had the unintended effect of modestly diversifying Samoa's export products and markets. The largest industrial venture is Yazaki Samoa, a Japanese-owned company processing automotive components for export to Australia under a concessional market-access arrangement. The Samoan Government has called for deregulation of the financial sector, encouragement of investment, and continued fiscal discipline, while protecting the environment. Observers point to the flexibility of the labour market as a basic strength for future economic advances. Foreign reserves are in a relatively healthy state, the external debt is stable and inflation is low. As a result of these economic reforms, GDP growth rebounded to over 6 per cent in both 1995 and 1996, before slowing again towards the end of the decade. Polynesian Airlines reached a financial crisis in 1994, which disrupted the tourist industry and eventually required a government bailout. New Zealand is Samoa's principal trading partner, typically providing between 35 per cent and 40 per cent of imports, and purchasing 45 to 50 per cent of exports. Australia, American Samoa, USA and Fiji also are important trading partners. The more than 100 000 Samoans who live overseas provide direct remittances, recently amounting to   USD 12 million per year. Samoa also receives USD7.6 million annually in official development assistance from sources led by Australia, Japan and New Zealand. The three main sources of revenue, namely tourism, private transfers and official transfers, allow Samoa to cover its persistently large trade deficits.

Seychelles

Since independence from the UK in 1976, per capita output in this Indian Ocean archipelago has expanded more than seven-fold, from USD1000 per capita in 1976 to USD7600 today. GDP growth in 2001 was 3.3 per cent. Growth has been led by the tourist sector, which accounts for about 13 per cent of GDP, employs about 30 per cent of the labour force, and provides more than 70 per cent of foreign currency earnings. The vulnerability of the tourist sector was illustrated by the sharp drop in 1991–92, due mainly to the Gulf War. Although the industry has rebounded, the government recognizes the continuing need for upgrading the sector in the face of stiff international competition. Tourism arrivals, which are one of the two main indicators of vitality in the sector, grew by 4.1 per cent in 2000. A strong marketing effort by the Seychelles Tourism Marketing Authority (STMA) and the introduction of several new five-star hotels seems to have spurred growth. Officials hoped that the planned new hotels and expanded airline service to the island would help offset the possibility of reduced global travel following the events of 11 September, 2001. In 2003, tourism earnings accounted for USD680 million and 122 000 visitors, comprising 82 per cent from the UK, Italy, France, Germany and Switzerland. Any decline in tourism quickly translates into a fall in GDP, a decline in foreign exchange receipts and budgetary difficulties. However, the country's economy is extremely vulnerable to external shocks. Not only does it depend on tourism, but it imports more than 90 per cent of its total primary and secondary production inputs. The manufacturing and construction sectors, including industrial fishing, accounted for about 28.8 per cent of GDP. The public sector, comprising government and state-owned enterprises, dominates the economy in terms of employment (two-thirds of the labour force) and gross revenue. Public consumption absorbs over one-third of the gross GDP. Industrial fishing in Seychelles, notably tuna fishing, is an increasingly significant factor in the economy. Recent changes in the climate have greatly affected the tuna industry. In 1995, Seychelles saw the privatisation of the Seychelles Tuna Canning Factory, 60 per cent of which was purchased by the American food company, Heinz Inc. Other industrial activities are limited to small-scale manufacturing, particularly agro-processing and import substitution. Despite attempts to improve its agricultural base and emphasise locally manufactured products and indigenous materials, Seychelles continues to import 90 per cent of consumption goods. The exceptions are some fruits and vegetables, fish, poultry, pork, beer, cigarettes, paint, and a few locally-made plastic items.

St Kitts and Nevis

The economy of St Kitts and Nevis has traditionally depended on the growing and processing of sugarcane, and the country was the last sugar monoculture in the Eastern Caribbean. The government of St Kitts and Nevis embarked on a programme of economic diversification when the sugar industry collapsed. Tourism, export-oriented manufacturing and offshore banking activity have assumed larger roles. The government instituted a programme of investment incentives for businesses considering the possibility of locating to St Kitts and Nevis, thereby encouraging both domestic and foreign private investment. Government policies provide liberal tax holidays, duty-free imports of equipment and materials, and subsidies for training provided to local personnel. Tourism has shown the greatest growth. By 1987, tourism had surpassed sugar as the major foreign exchange earner for St Kitts and Nevis. The economy of St Kitts and Nevis experienced strong growth for most of the 1990s, but hurricanes in 1998 and 1999 contributed to a sharp slowdown. In 2002, real growth was 0.75 compared with 4.3 per cent in 2001. The economy experienced a mixed performance during 2002, with some sectors experiencing positive growth while others experienced varying levels of decline. The construction sector recorded a 4.5 per cent decline, manufacturing and hotels and restaurants also recorded significant declines of 4 and 10 per cent, respectively, and sugar production fell by 5 per cent. Significant new investment in tourism, including a 648-room Marriott hotel and convention centre that opened in December 2002, as well as continued government efforts to diversify the economy, are expected to improve the economic performance. Over the past few years, consumer prices have risen moderately. The inflation rate was 3 to 4 per cent for most of the 1990s. Most food is imported. St Kitts and Nevis is also working to improve revenue collection in order to better fund social programmes. In late September 1998, Hurricane Georges caused approximately USD445 million in damages and limited GDP growth for the year. St Kitts and Nevis is also a member of ECCU and ECCB. St Kitts and Nevis is a member of the Eastern Caribbean Telecommunications (ECTEL) authority, which is developing the regulations to liberalise the telecommunications sector in the region by 2004.

St Lucia

St Lucia's economy depends primarily on revenue from banana production and tourism, with some input from small-scale manufacturing. There are numerous small and medium-sized agricultural enterprises. Revenue from agriculture has supported the noticeable socioeconomic changes that have occurred in St Lucia since the 1960s. Eighty per cent of merchandise trade earnings came from banana exports to the UK in the 1960s. In view of the EU's announced phase-out of preferred access to its markets by Windward Island bananas by 2006, agricultural diversification is a priority. An attempt is being made to diversify production by encouraging the establishment of tree crops such as mangos and avocados. A variety of vegetables is produced for local consumption. Recently, St Lucia added small computer-driven information technology and financial services as development objectives. Agriculture, tourism and small-scale manufacturing have become the leading revenue earners in St Lucia. This has largely benefited from infrastructure improvements in roads, communications, water supply, sewerage and port facilities. Until the events of 11 September, 2001, the tourism sector had made significant gains, experiencing a boom despite some untimely and destructive hurricanes. Stay-over visitors and cruise arrivals declined in 2001, and several hotels declared bankruptcy, including the Hyatt. The development of the tourism sector remains a priority, and the government is committed to providing a favourable investment environment. Incentives are available for building and upgrading tourism facilities. There has been liberal use of public funds to improve the physical infrastructure of the island, and the government has made efforts to attract cultural and sporting events and to develop historical sites. Foreign investors have also been attracted by the infrastructure improvements, as well as by the educated and skilled work force and relatively stable political conditions. The largest investment is in a petroleum storage and transhipment terminal built by Hess Oil. St Lucia is a member of ECCU and the ECCB, a beneficiary of the US CBI, a member of the CARICOM and the OECS, and is also the headquarters of the Eastern Caribbean Telecommunications (ECTEL) authority, which is developing the regulations to liberalise the telecommunications sector in the region by 2004.

St Vincent and the Grenadines

The St Vincent economy is highly dependent on agriculture. Bananas alone account for more than 60 per cent of the workforce and 50 per cent of merchandise exports. Such reliance on a single crop makes the economy vulnerable to external factors. The continuing dependence on a single crop represents the biggest obstacle to development, and tropical storms wiped out substantial portions of crops in both 1994 and 1995. St Vincent's banana growers benefited from preferential access to the European market. As in the case of St Lucia, the EU announcement of the phase-out of this preferred access means that economic diversification is a priority. The government has been relatively unsuccessful in introducing new industries, and a high unemployment rate persists. Tourism has grown to become a very important part of the economy. In 1993, tourism supplanted banana exports as the chief source of foreign exchange. The Grenadines have become a favourite of up-market yachting customers. The trend toward increasing tourism revenues will likely continue. In 1996, new cruise ship and ferry berths came on-line, sharply increasing the number of passenger arrivals. In 2002, total visitor arrivals stood at 250 971, with US visitors constituting 8.5 per cent. A relatively small number of Americans reside on the islands. St Vincent and the Grenadines is a beneficiary of the US Caribbean Basin Initiative. The country belongs to CARICOM, which has signed a framework agreement with the USA to promote trade and investment in the region. The services sector, based mainly on a growing tourist industry, is also important. The tourism sector has considerable potential for development over the next decade. Recent growth has been stimulated by strong activity in the construction sector and improvements in tourism. There is a small manufacturing sector and a small offshore financial sector, for which the particularly restrictive secrecy laws have caused some international concern.

Vanuatu

The economy of Vanuatu is primarily agricultural, with 80 per cent of the population engaged in agricultural activities that range from subsistence farming to smallholder farming of coconuts and other cash crops. Copra, cocoa, kava and beef account for more than 60 per cent of Vanuatu's total exports by value, and agriculture accounts for approximately 20 per cent of GDP. Kava root extract exports also have become important. Economic development is hindered by a dependence on relatively few commodity exports, vulnerability to natural disasters, and long distances from main markets and between constituent islands. A severe earthquake in November 1999, followed by a tsunami (huge tidal wave), caused extensive damage to the northern Island of Pentecote and left thousands homeless. Another powerful earthquake in January 2002 caused extensive damage in the capital, Port-Vila, and surrounding areas, and was also followed by a tsunami. GDP growth rose less than 3 per cent, on average, in the 1990s. In response to foreign concerns, the government has promised to tighten regulation of its offshore financial centre. The government has maintained Vanuatu's pre-independence status as a tax haven and international financial centre. About 2000 registered institutions offer a wide range of offshore banking, investment, legal, accounting, and insurance and trust-company services. Vanuatu also maintains an international shipping register in New York City. Tourism is Vanuatu's fastest-growing sector, having comprised 40 per cent of GDP in 2000. Average tourist arrivals over the period 1999–2002 have been 50 000 per annum. Australia and New Zealand are the main suppliers of tourists and foreign aid. Industrial production declined from 15 per cent to 10 per cent of GDP between 1990 and 2000, and government consumption accounted for about 27 per cent of GDP. Vanuatu is a small country, with only a few commodities, and imports exceeded exports by a ratio of nearly 4 to 1. However, this was offset by high services income from tourism, which kept the current account balance fairly even. Vanuatu claims an exclusive economic zone of 680 000 square kilometres and possesses substantial marine resources. Currently, only a limited number of *ni*-Vanuatu are involved in fishing, while foreign fleets exploit this potential. In 1997 the government, with the aid of the Asian Development Bank, committed itself to a 3-year comprehensive reform programme. During the first year of the programme, the government has adopted a value-added tax, consolidated and reformed government-owned banks, and started a 10 per cent downsizing of the public service. The programme was derailed when Barak Sope became Prime Minister. Under Prime Minister Edward Natapei, reform programmes have slowly been reintroduced. Economic growth expanded moderately in 2003.

4.3   COMPOSITION OF TOURIST ARRIVALS IN SITES

Table 4.1 shows the mean percentages of the composition of the principal eighteen nationalities of tourist arrivals to the 20 SITEs examined in Chapter 2. This information was obtained from the WTO. Tourism arrivals from these 18 major markets represent a significant proportion of the total international tourist arrivals to SITEs. On average, 64 per cent of tourists who visited during the period 1980–2000 are from these 18 tourist source countries. Among these 18 markets are the world's richest 7 countries, the G7, and the rest of the source countries belong to the OECD, which are also among the richest countries in the world.

These 18 countries are geographically located with varying measures of distance relative to the 20 SITEs. These countries are also diverse in their social and economic cultures, but explain more than two-thirds of the composition of international tourist arrivals in all SITEs, except for Antigua and Barbuda, Dominican Republic, Dominica, Grenada, Samoa and St Vincent and the Grenadines. The capacities of the tourism industries in these six SITEs are relatively small and the tourism industry characteristics are moderately different as compared with the rest of SITEs. Moreover, the relatively small magnitudes of mean percentages of tourists from a wide variety of nationalities to these six SITEs is the dominant feature, besides US tourists dominating the visitor profile, except for Samoa, accounting for just above 20 per cent of total tourist arrivals. During the same period, in Cyprus, Maldives, Malta and Seychelles, international tourist arrivals account for more than 11 of the 18 tourist source countries, with Maldives welcoming the highest number of source countries, accounting for 14 of the 18. Grenada received tourists from 9 of the 18 most tourist-generating countries, while Barbados, Dominican Republic and St Lucia each welcomed tourists from 8 of the 18 sources countries. During 1980–2000, there were tourist visits from 7 of the 18 main tourist source countries to Antigua and Barbuda, Fiji, Samoa and St Vincent and the Grenadines. Comoros, Dominica, Jamaica and Vanuatu welcomed tourists from 6 of the 18 main tourist-generating countries, while Haiti and St Kitts and Nevis received tourists from 3 and 4 tourist-generating countries, respectively.

Table 4.1 Mean Proportion of Annual International Tourist Arrivals to SITEs, 1980–2000

Source Market	Antigua	Bahamas	Barbados	Comoros	Cyprus	Dominica	Dom. Rep.	Fiji	Grenada	Haiti	Jamaica	Maldives	Malta	Mauritius	Samoa	Seychelles	St Kitts	St Lucia	St Vincent	Vanuatu
Australia								27				2	1	2	10					55
Austria		6			2							4	1	1		1		1		
Belgium				3			1					1	1	1		1				
Canada	3		15			4	5	5	5	10	12				1		10	9	7	
Denmark					1								2							
France	1			45	2	4	1		1	3		6	5	22		14		2		
Germany	2	1	3	3	8	2	5	2	4		2	24	12	8	2	10	5	5	3	2
Italy	1	1	1	3	1		2		1		1	18	7	5		11		1	1	
Japan								7			1	8			1	2			1	4
New Zealand								12							22					11
Norway					2															
South Africa				19								1		14		3				
Spain					6		2		1			1				1				
Sweden			2		4							2	2							
Switzerland	1		1		2	1			1			6		3		4		1	1	
The Netherlands			1		2				1			1	3							
UK	10	2	24		43	9	2	5	12		7	8	52	7	2	12	8	20	11	1
United States	16	82	30	4	3	17	13	14	23	57	69	1	1	1	11	2	38	27	22	3
Total	34	92	76	75	73	37	30	72	49	70	93	82	87	63	48	61	61	65	46	76

Source: World Tourism Organisation (WTO) and the respective Government Statistics Offices and Bureaux.

As can be seen from Table 4.1, the USA, UK, France, Germany, Canada, Italy and Switzerland are the dominant markets for tourists to these SITEs. Moreover, these seven markets also correspond to quite substantial mean percentages across most of the SITEs. Although the USA is the world's largest and richest economy, their prominence in international tourist arrivals is significant only in the Caribbean SITEs, most notably in The Bahamas, followed by Jamaica, Haiti, St Kitts and Nevis, Barbados, St Vincent and the Grenadines, and St Lucia. In the Indian Ocean SITEs, US tourists feature with very low mean percentages. However, UK tourists are spread more evenly among the 20 SITEs compared with US tourists. UK tourists are the most widely travelled in all of the SITEs compared with the 18 tourism markets, arguably because of the British colonial heritage attached to these SITEs. Generally, European tourists seem to travel to island destinations compared with US and Canadian tourists. German tourists have smaller magnitudes than their UK counterparts, but they feature in all 18 SITEs. The Germans are followed by French and Italian tourists, with 14 SITE visits, and travel particularly more to the Indian Ocean SITEs as compared with their Mediterranean and Caribbean counterparts. Canadians appear somewhat evenly across the 11 Caribbean SITEs, Fiji and Samoa. According to this analysis, the Swiss are the fifth most widely travelled tourists covering 11 SITEs in all regions except the Pacific. Australian, Austrian, Belgian, Dutch, Japanese and Swedish tourist arrivals appear among six SITEs, with varying visitor profiles. Australian tourists are dominant in the Pacific, and moderate in the Indian Ocean and the Mediterranean SITEs. Japanese tourists make tourist visits to all SITE regions, while Austrian, Belgian, Dutch and Swedish tourists are present among all the regions, except the Pacific. New Zealand tourists travel only in the Pacific SITEs, while Danish and Norwegian tourists only appear in the Mediterranean. Spain is also an upcoming tourism source country, featuring in the Indian Ocean as well as in the Caribbean.

A preliminary analysis of the cross-correlations of international tourism provides useful information on policies on long-term tourism planning and marketing. In the literature on tourism demand, destinations are considered as substitutes when they are in the same geographic region or share similar characteristics. If the cross-correlation coefficients are calculated to be negative, they are considered to be substitutes. Conversely, complementarity among destinations is recognised when the estimated cross-correlation coefficients are calculated to be positive.

In the tourism literature, the findings on substitutability or complementarity of a destination are mixed. Anastasopoulos (1991) states that destinations that are close to each other have positive and relatively large correlation coefficients. Additionally, such correlations are very low or negative among destinations which are far apart. Syriopoulos and Sinclair

(1993) indicate that destinations show a wide range of substitutability and complementarity, depending on the tourist originating countries. Yannopoulos (1987) concluded that, while econometric evidence suggests a complementary relationship between two destinations, the relationship may not necessarily be symmetric. Thus, an increase in international tourist arrivals to Sri Lanka may increase international tourist arrivals to the Maldives. Nevertheless, an increase in international tourist arrivals to the Maldives may not increase international tourist arrivals to Sri Lanka, even though the duration of air travel between the two countries is one hour. White (1985) found both substitutability and complementarity among destinations for travellers originating from several different countries. Rosensweig (1988) found a degree of both competitive and complementary elasticities for tourism in the Caribbean. In a study based on limited data, Leiper (1989) determined the main destination ratios for several destinations for tourists from Japan, New Zealand and Australia.

The cross-correlations of annual international tourist arrivals from 11 different source countries, namely the USA, Canada, UK, Germany, France, Italy, Switzerland, Sweden, Japan, Australia and New Zealand, to six SITEs, namely Barbados, Cyprus, Dominica, Fiji, Maldives and Seychelles, for which data are available, are given in Tables 4.2(a) to 4.2(l). This analysis show that the growth in international tourism arrivals grew simultaneously in all the six SITEs (see Table 4.2(a)). The cross-correlation coefficients for total international tourist arrivals to all six SITEs have a range of 0.75 to 0.96, and are relatively large. For total monthly international tourist arrivals to these SITEs, the estimated cross-correlation coefficients suggest that the six SITEs featured are complements. The main reason for the high estimated cross-correlation coefficients is that these six SITEs have very similar economic, social and geophysical characteristics. These results are consistent with previous findings in the literature. The correlations were calculated such that the relationship between two series x and y are given by:

$$r_{xy}(l) = \frac{c_{xy}(l)}{\sqrt{c_{xx}(0)}\sqrt{c_{yy}(0)}} \qquad (4.1)$$

and

$$c_{xy}(l) = \begin{cases} \sum_{t=1}^{T-1}[(x_t - \overline{x})(y_{t+1} - \overline{y})]/T \\ \sum_{t=1}^{T+1}[(y_t - \overline{y})(x_{t-1} - \overline{x})]/T \end{cases} \qquad (4.2)$$

Table 4.2   *Cross Correlations of Annual Total International Tourist Arrivals and by Source Country*

(a) All Tourists

	BAR	CYP	DOM	FIJ	MAL	SEY
BAR	1	·	·	·	·	·
CYP	0.84	1	·	·	·	·
DOM	0.83	0.95	1	·	·	·
FIJ	0.75	0.86	0.77	1	·	·
MAL	0.87	0.94	0.96	0.78	1	·
SEY	0.82	0.92	0.94	0.86	0.93	1

(b) American Tourists

	BAR	CYP	DOM	FIJ	MAL	SEY
BAR	1	·	·	·	·	·
CYP	0.13	1	·	·	·	·
DOM	−0.16	0.34	1	·	·	·
FIJ	0.45	0.44	0.50	1	·	·
MAL	−0.19	0.38	0.91	0.54	1	·
SEY	−0.42	−0.11	0.74	0.11	0.67	1

(c) Canadian Tourists

	BAR	CYP	DOM	FIJ	MAL	SEY
BAR	1	·	·	·	·	·
CYP	−0.40	1	·	·	·	·
DOM	−0.35	0.86	1	·	·	·
FIJ	0.34	−0.70	−0.62	1	·	·
MAL	−0.37	0.97	0.88	−0.71	1	·
SEY	0.11	0.92	0.79	−0.72	0.93	1

(d) British Tourists

	BAR	CYP	DOM	FIJ	MAL	SEY
BAR	1	·	·	·	·	·
CYP	0.85	1	·	·	·	·
DOM	0.81	0.87	1	·	·	·
FIJ	0.89	0.85	0.81	1	·	·
MAL	0.96	0.84	0.78	0.94	1	·
SEY	0.53	0.64	0.82	0.51	0.46	1

(e) German Tourists

	BAR	CYP	DOM	FIJ	MAL	SEY
BAR	1	·	·	·	·	·
CYP	0.42	1	·	·	·	·
DOM	−0.06	0.32	1	·	·	·
FIJ	0.30	−0.18	−0.41	1	·	·
MAL	−0.46	−0.17	0.68	−0.35	1	·
SEY	−0.49	0.75	0.79	0.63	0.73	1

(f) French Tourists

	BAR	CYP	DOM	FIJ	MAL	SEY
BAR	1	·	·	·	·	·
CYP	0.80	1	·	·	·	·
DOM	0.76	0.88	1	·	·	·
FIJ	0.49	0.60	0.71	1	·	·
MAL	0.71	0.71	0.76	0.63	1	·
SEY	0.85	0.86	0.90	0.61	0.88	1

(g) Italian Tourists

	BAR	CYP	DOM	FIJ	MAL	SEY
BAR	1	·	·	·	·	·
CYP	0.76	1	·	·	·	·
DOM	0.82	0.67	1	·	·	·
FIJ	0.46	0.69	0.58	1	·	·
MAL	0.53	0.90	0.35	0.57	1	·
SEY	0.55	0.73	0.31	0.37	0.78	1

(h) Swiss Tourists

	BAR	CYP	DOM	FIJ	MAL	SEY
BAR	1	·	·	·	·	·
CYP	0.62	1	·	·	·	·
DOM	0.38	0.21	1	·	·	·
FIJ	0.38	0.78	0.08	1	·	·
MAL	0.47	0.91	0.00	0.71	1	·
SEY	−0.22	0.38	−0.05	0.47	0.46	1

Table 4.2   Cross Correlations of Annual Total International Tourist Arrivals and by Source Country (continued)

(i) Swedish Tourists

	BAR	CYP	DOM	FIJ	MAL	SEY
BAR	1	·	·	·	·	·
CYP	0.53	1	·	·	·	·
DOM	0.21	–0.16	1	·	·	·
FIJ	0.00	–0.11	0.66	1	·	·
MAL	0.80	0.58	–0.10	–0.31	1	·
SEY	0.51	0.59	0.28	0.31	0.44	1

(j) Japanese Tourists

	BAR	CYP	DOM	FIJ	MAL	SEY
BAR	1	·	·	·	·	·
CYP	0.30	1	·	·	·	·
DOM	0.43	–0.01	1	·	·	·
FIJ	0.45	0.20	0.75	1	·	·
MAL	0.63	0.70	0.59	0.70	1	·
SEY	–0.67	–0.30	–0.23	–0.31	–0.53	1

(k) Australian Tourists

	BAR	CYP	DOM	FIJ	MAL	SEY
BAR	1	·	·	·	·	·
CYP	na	1	·	·	·	·
DOM	na	na	1	·	·	·
FIJ	0.30	na	na	1	·	·
MAL	0.52	na	na	0.15	1	·
SEY	0.07	na	na	–0.49	–0.30	1

(l) New Zealand Tourists

	BAR	CYP	DOM	FIJ	MAL	SEY
BAR	1	·	·	·	·	·
CYP	na	1	·	·	·	·
DOM	na	na	1	·	·	·
FIJ	0.70	na	na	1	·	·
MAL	0.62	na	na	0.56	1	·
SEY	–0.35	na	na	0.00	–0.49	1

Note: BAR, CYP, DOM, FIJ, MAL and SEY refer to Barbados, Cyprus, Dominica, Fiji, Maldives and Seychelles, respectively.

Source: World Tourism Organisation (WTO) and the respective Government Statistics Offices and Bureau.

where $l = 0, \pm 1, \pm 2, \ldots$ Specifications given in equations (4.1) and (4.2) are given in EViews 4.1, Users Guide (2003, p. 214). For the 11 markets, the cross-correlation coefficients of international tourist arrivals show considerable variability. Thus, tourists from some markets consider some destinations as substitutes, while tourists from other markets consider them as complements. According to the estimated cross-correlation coefficients, British, French and Italian tourists consider all six SITEs examined as complements, while the other nine markets consider some SITEs as substitutes and some as complements.

The magnitudes of the cross-correlation coefficients reveal that British, French and Italian tourists judge these six SITEs with substantially different perceptions. From the estimated coefficients, British and French tourists judge these six destinations in a similar manner, while Italians seem to show some discretion in their judgment. The US, Canadian, German and Swedish tourists show a great deal of cautious perception about the six SITEs, with a higher degree of variability in the magnitudes of the estimated coefficients. Swiss tourists consider most of the six SITEs as complements, while revealing that there is a great deal of substitutability between Seychelles, Barbados and Dominica. Japanese tourists consider Seychelles to be substitutable with the other five SITEs.

An important aspect of policy formulation on tourism planning and promoting is to assess and identify the complementary and substitute destinations. To assess the competitive and complementary relationships of international tourism demand among SITEs, the broadest possible market structure (tourism originating countries) is considered. In this chapter, the total international tourist arrivals to 20 SITEs for the period 1980–2000 approximate the total inbound international tourism demand. Pairwise correlation coefficients are calculated based on the most reliable and available measure of tourism demand to obtain some background information. Despite the limited availability of data, pairwise correlations of International Tourism Receipts for the 20 SITEs are presented in Table 4.3. The magnitudes of these correlation coefficients are relatively large and are close to 1, indicating that the tourism product of these 20 SITEs are complementary. The only SITE which displays substitutability is Haiti.

4.4   CONCLUSION

In this chapter, the country economic profiles of 20 SITEs were presented in detail. It is evident from these descriptions that a large proportion of these SITEs was dependent on agriculture, and have now diversified their economies to become more service oriented, based on tourism. Tourism development requires substantial financial capital, but only requires unskilled or semi-skilled labour. Therefore, in these SITEs it is relatively easy to expand if it is well managed. Hence, in most of these SITEs, tourism is the predominant activity. The composition of tourist arrivals in these SITEs is mainly from the world's richest nations geographically located in the temperate zone. The most widely travelled tourists are from the UK, visiting all of the 20 SITEs included in the assessment. The relative cross-correlation coefficients of monthly international tourist arrivals showed that the six SITEs, namely Barbados, Cyprus, Dominica, Fiji, Maldives and Seychelles, are complementary destinations as far as total monthly international tourist arrivals are concerned. However, when the monthly arrivals from 11 different tourist source markets to these six economies are examined separately, some markets consider these SITEs as substitutes as well as complements. Furthermore, when international tourism receipts for the 20 SITEs are considered together, all SITEs except Haiti are deemed to be complements.

Table 4.3   *Cross-correlations of International Tourism Receipts (ITRs) for 20 SITEs*

SITE	Antigua	Bahamas	Barbados	Comoros	Cyprus	Dominica	Dom. Rep.	Fiji	Grenada	Haiti	Jamaica	Maldives	Malta	Mauritius	Samoa	Seychelles	St Kitts	St Lucia	St Vincent	Vanuatu
Antigua	1																			
Bahamas	0.9	1																		
Barbados	0.8	0.8	1																	
Comoros	0.9	0.7	0.7	1																
Cyprus	0.9	0.8	0.8	0.9	1															
Dominica	0.9	0.8	0.8	0.9	1.0	1														
Dom. Rep.	0.9	0.8	0.9	0.9	1.0	1.0	1													
Fiji	0.8	0.7	0.7	0.9	0.9	0.9	0.9	1												
Grenada	0.9	0.9	0.8	0.9	1.0	1.0	1.0	0.9	1											
Haiti	-0.5	-0.2	0.0	-0.3	-0.3	-0.2	-0.1	-0.1	-0.3	1										
Jamaica	0.9	0.9	0.8	0.9	1.0	1.0	0.9	0.9	1.0	-0.3	1									
Maldives	0.9	0.8	0.8	0.9	1.0	1.0	0.9	0.9	1.0	-0.2	1.0	1								
Malta	0.9	0.7	0.5	0.8	0.8	0.8	0.7	0.7	0.8	-0.4	0.9	0.9	1							
Mauritius	0.9	0.8	0.9	0.9	1.0	1.0	1.0	0.9	1.0	-0.1	0.9	1.0	0.7	1						
Samoa	0.6	0.6	0.7	0.5	0.7	0.7	0.7	0.6	0.7	0.1	0.7	0.7	0.6	0.7	1					
Seychelles	0.9	0.8	0.9	0.9	1.0	1.0	1.0	0.9	1.0	-0.1	0.9	1.0	0.7	1.0	0.7	1				
St Kitts	0.6	0.6	0.9	0.7	0.8	0.8	0.9	0.8	0.8	0.1	0.7	0.8	0.4	0.9	0.6	0.9	1			
St Lucia	0.9	0.8	0.8	0.9	0.9	1.0	0.9	0.9	1.0	-0.2	0.9	1.0	0.8	0.9	0.7	1.0	0.8	1		
St Vincent	0.9	0.8	0.9	0.9	1.0	1.0	1.0	0.9	1.0	-0.1	1.0	1.0	0.8	1.0	0.8	1.0	0.8	1.0	1	
Vanuatu	0.7	0.5	0.6	0.9	0.8	0.9	0.8	0.8	0.8	0.0	0.9	0.9	0.8	0.9	0.7	0.9	0.7	0.8	0.8	1

Source: World Development Indicators (2002), The World Bank.

164

NOTE

1. Parts of Sections 4.2 and 4.3 of this chapter have been presented at the International Conference on Tourism and Sustainable Development Macro and Micro Issues, jointly organized by the Centre for North South Economic Research, University of Cagliari, Fondazione Eni Enrico Mattei (FEEM) and the World Bank, Sardinia, Italy, September, 2003, and the PhD Conference on Economics and Business, University of Western Australia, Perth, Australia, November 2003.

REFERENCES

Anastasopoulos, P. (1991), 'Demand for travel', *Annals of Tourism Research*, **18**, 663–66.

BBC News (2003), 'Country profiles and timeline', http://news.bbc.co.uk/1/shared/bsp/hi/country_profiles/html/default.stm [last accessed: May 2007].

Central Intelligence Agency (2003), 'The world factbook 2002', http://www.odci.gov/cia/publications/factbook/index.html [last accessed: May 2007].

EViews 4.1 User's Guide (2003), Quantitative Micro Software.

Leiper, N. (1989), 'Main destination ratios: Analyses of tourist flows', *Annals of Tourism Research*, **16**, 530–41.

Rosensweig, J.A. (1988), 'Elasticities of substitution in Caribbean tourism', *Journal of Development Economics*, **29**, 89–100.

Syriopoulos, T.C. and M.T. Sinclair (1993), 'An econometric study of tourism demand: The AIDs model of US and European tourism in Mediterranean countries', *Applied Economics*, **25**, 1541–52.

The Economist (2003), 'Country Briefings', http://www.economist.com/countries/.

US Department of State (2003), *Countries and Regions*, http://www.state.gov/countries/ [last accessed: May 2007].

White, K.J. (1985), 'An international travel demand model: US travel to Western Europe', *Annals of Tourism Research*, **12**, 529–45.

Yannopoulos, G.N. (1987), 'Intra-regional shifts in tourism growth in Mediterranean area', *Travel and Tourism Analyst*, November, 15–24.

5. Models of Symmetric and Asymmetric Conditional Volatility: Structure, Asymptotic Theory and Applications to Tourism Demand

5.1 INTRODUCTION

Over the last 20 years, there has been concern among many economists, practitioners and academics regarding the volatility in asset returns. The future is uncertain and investors do not know with certainty whether the economy will be growing rapidly or experiencing a recession. As such, they do not know what rate of return their investments will yield. Therefore, decisions are based on expectations about the future. The expected rate of return on a stock represents the mean of the probability distribution of possible future returns. The volatility of the expected return on an asset is defined as the square of the deviation from the mean of the expected return of the asset during any given period.

There are several reasons why we need to model and forecast the volatility in international tourist arrivals or country risk returns. First, governments as well as tour operators need to examine the underlying uncertainty that is intrinsic in the total number, as well as in the growth rate, of international tourist arrivals. Similarly, investors need to analyse the riskiness in investing in SITEs, through an analysis of the volatility in country risk returns. Second, in the time series econometrics literature it is widely believed that the forecast confidence interval is time varying. Therefore, more accurate confidence intervals can be obtained by modelling the conditional variance of the errors. Finally, if the heteroscedasticity in the errors is carefully examined and modelled accurately, more efficient estimators of the parameters in the conditional mean can be obtained.

Theoretical developments in finance have made numerous attempts to formulate optimal portfolios, or a set of various assets, which is determined by the variances and covariances of the returns of the assets incorporated in the portfolio. The Capital Asset Pricing Model (CAPM) is one such theoretical advance, as are the option pricing model and the Value-at-Risk (VaR) threshold model.

The volatility in returns of an asset has been known to cluster, besides having thicker or fatter tails than the density of the normal distribution. Although these two prominent features of volatility have been known for some time, returns were still modelled ignoring such deviations from empirical regularities. There are numerous examples of such empirical work in the time series econometrics literature. However, Engle (1982) made a significant breakthrough in describing time-varying volatility by way of the Autoregressive Conditional Heteroscedasticity (ARCH) model. Over the last 20 years, there have been major extensions to the basic model, including Bollerslev (1986), Bollerslev et al. (1992), Bollerslev et al. (1994) and Li et al. (2002), among others, to extend the ARCH model to the Generalized ARCH (or GARCH) model by adding various lags of the conditional variance.

One of the most intriguing features of asset returns is 'news', and the nature of the effect on asset returns due to good or bad news. The ARCH model of Engle (1982) and the GARCH model of Bollerslev (1986) assume there is symmetry in the variances of the asset returns. In order to accommodate asymmetric behaviour between positive and negative shocks, Glosten, Jagannathan and Runkle (1992) (GJR) introduced the Threshold ARCH (or TARCH) model to allow for the effects of good and bad news to have different effects on volatility. Furthermore, Nelson (1991) proposed the Exponential GARCH (EGARCH) model to accommodate asymmetry in the conditional variance. The GJR and EGARCH models are the two most widely applied models of asymmetry in modelling conditional volatility. With the introduction of the ARCH model, the theoretical developments and applications in economic and financial data have expanded significantly.

In this monograph, applications of the ARCH family of models, particularly the symmetric GARCH(r,s) and the asymmetric GJR(r,s) models in univariate and multivariate settings, are undertaken to examine the features of conditional volatility in monthly international tourism arrivals and monthly country risk returns in SITEs. The primary purpose of this chapter is to review the theoretical developments and structural properties in GARCH research. In what follows, monthly international tourist arrivals and monthly country risk returns will be referred to as tourism demand and country risk, respectively.

The plan of this chapter is as follows. The developments and statistical properties of univariate and multivariate models of conditional volatility are examined in Sections 5.2 and 5.3, respectively. In Section 5.4, an interpretation of the conditional correlation coefficients of the standardised shocks obtained from the estimated conditional variance is presented. The data used for the applications of the conditional volatility models are discussed in Section 5.5. Empirical results for the univariate and multivariate models are presented in Sections 5.6 and 5.7, respectively. Conclusions from the findings are given in Section 5.8.

5.2   UNIVARIATE MODELS OF CONDITIONAL VOLATILITY

In this section, some of the recent theoretical results on univariate GARCH models are discussed. Detailed surveys of theoretical and empirical developments associated with univariate GARCH models are given in Bollerslev et al. (1992), Bollerslev et al. (1994), Bera and Higgins (1993) and Li et al. (2002). It was only recently that the structural and asymptotic properties underlying these models were determined. A survey of recent theoretical results regarding the structure and asymptotic theory for GARCH models is given in Li et al. (2002). Theoretical results underlying the structure and estimation of GARCH models include convenient sufficient conditions for strict stationarity and ergodicity, the existence of moments, and for the (quasi-) maximum likelihood estimators (QMLE) to be consistent and asymptotically normal. The theoretical results regarding the structure have been recognised for some asymmetric models. McAleer et al. (2008) established the consistency and asymptotic normality of the multivariate GJR(p,q), or asymmetric vector ARMA-AGARCH model, under empirically verifiable conditions. An extensive review and analysis of univariate and multivariate conditional and stochastic financial volatility models is given in McAleer (2005).

The ARCH Model

In model building, econometricians usually attempt to parameterise the conditional mean of a set of variables. Furthermore, at a given point in time there is a realisation of an array of variables Y_t and X_t, where Y_t is typically a scalar and X_t is a set of variables which may also include lagged values of Y_t. Consequently, we write an econometric model for Y_t such that:

$$Y_t = E(Y_t | X_t) + \varepsilon_t \qquad (5.1)$$

where the conditional mean, $E(Y_t | X_t)$, is the expected value of Y_t given X_t, and the expected value of the error term is $E\{\varepsilon_t | X_t\} = 0$, so that ε_t is a series of uncorrelated random variables with mean zero. The unconditional variance of ε_t is σ^2 and is typically assumed to be constant over time. However, Engle (1982) reconsidered this assumption, stating that if the unconditional variance σ^2 existed, the conditional variance of the error term, ε_t, may be time varying. This suggestion enables an explanation of the time-varying conditional variance, and simultaneously estimates the conditional mean and the conditional variance. The error term, ε_t, was defined as follows:

$$\varepsilon_t = \eta_t \sqrt{h_t} \tag{5.2}$$

where the standardized residuals, η_t, is assumed to be a standard white noise process with mean zero and variance one. Hence, the conditional variance, h_t, is written as follows.

$$h_t = E(\varepsilon_t^2 | I_t) = \alpha_0 + \sum_{i=1}^{r} \alpha_i \varepsilon_{t-i}^2 \tag{5.3}$$

where, $\alpha_0 > 0$ and $\alpha_i \geq 0$ for $i = 1,...,r$ are sufficient (but not necessary) conditions to ensure that the conditional variance $h_t > 0$. In (5.2), $\varepsilon_t = Y_t - E[Y_t | X_t]$ and the information set is $I_t = \{\varepsilon_{t-i}; i \geq 1\}$. Equation (5.3) is the ARCH(r) model of Engle (1982), which implies that the conditional variance is a function of past values of squared unconditional shocks and varies over time. This is in contrast with the traditional assumption that ε_t has a constant unconditional variance over time.

Such a model is particularly useful in examining the volatility in tourism demand and country risk since it captures the tendency for tourism demand growth and country risk returns to move in largely unpredictable directions, while the magnitudes of these changes are allowed to be correlated.

Engle (1982) parameterised the conditional variance on the assumption that large unconditional errors ε_t are followed by large ε_t, and vice-versa, such that the conditional variances tend to cluster. This is evident from equation (5.3), where the current period's conditional variance depends on the square of the previous unconditional shocks, ε_{t-i}^2, for $i = 1,...,r$.

The GARCH Model

In general, among high frequency data the unconditional errors tend to show a relatively slow decaying autocorrelation function of the unconditional variances, ε_t^2. To represent this stylised fact in high frequency data, we require an ARCH model with a longer lag. Therefore, the right-hand side of equation (5.3) is augmented to include past values of the conditional variance, h_t, so that a more parsimonious representation is achieved. Bollerslev (1986) developed the GARCH(r,s) model, which takes the following form:

$$\varepsilon_t = \eta_t \sqrt{h_t}$$
$$h_t = \alpha_0 + \sum_{i=1}^{r} \alpha_i \varepsilon_{t-i}^2 + \sum_{i=1}^{s} \beta_i h_{t-i} \tag{5.4}$$

where $\alpha_0 > 0$, $\alpha_i \geq 0$ and $\beta_i \geq 0$ are sufficient (but not necessary) conditions for $h_t > 0$. The GARCH(1,1) model is the most widely used conditional volatility model.

The ARCH (or α_i) effect captures the short-run persistence of shocks, while the GARCH (or β_i) effect measures the contribution of shocks to long-run persistence,

$$\sum_{i=1}^{r}\alpha_i + \sum_{i=1}^{s}\beta_i \; .$$

The first number in the brackets denotes the number of autoregressive lags of the unconditional shock, or ARCH terms, that appears in the model, while the second number signifies the number of moving average, or GARCH, terms included in the model. It is sometimes necessary to estimate models with more than one lag to find an adequate conditional variance forecast.

It is important to consider the statistical properties of the GARCH model. It was only recently that all the statistical properties of the GARCH model were fully established under verifiable conditions. Bollerslev (1986) proved that

$$\sum_{i=1}^{r}\alpha_i + \sum_{i=1}^{s}\beta_i < 1, \qquad\qquad (5.5)$$

which is the necessary and sufficient condition for the second-order stationarity of equation (5.4). It has been shown by Ling and McAleer (2003) that the QMLE of GARCH(r,s) is consistent if the second moment is finite. The well known necessary and sufficient condition for the existence of the second moment of ε_t for GARCH(1,1), which is given in equation (5.5), is also sufficient for consistency of the QMLE. Jeantheau (1998) showed that the weaker log-moment condition is sufficient for consistency of the QMLE for the univariate GARCH(r,s) model. Hence, a sufficient condition for the QMLE of GARCH(1,1) to be consistent and asymptotically normal is given by:

$$E[\ln(\alpha_1\eta_t^2 + \beta_1)] < 0 . \qquad\qquad (5.6)$$

The above condition (5.6) allows $\alpha_1 + \beta_1$ to be greater than one, which implies that $E(\varepsilon_t^2)$ is not finite. This result is achieved by applying Jensen's inequality,

$$E[\ln(\beta_1 + \alpha_1\eta_t^2)] < \ln[E(\beta_1 + \alpha_1\eta_t^2)] , \qquad\qquad (5.7)$$

so that $0 < \alpha_1 + \beta_1 < 1$. McAleer et al. (2008) argue that the result in equation (5.6) is not straightforward to check in practice as it involves the expectation of a function of an unknown random variable and unknown parameters. Moreover, the second moment condition is far more straightforward to check in practice, although it is a stronger condition.

In equation (5.4), the parameters are typically estimated by maximum likelihood to obtain QMLE in the absence of normality of η_t. The conditional log-likelihood function is given as follows:

$$\sum_{i=1}^{r} \ell_i = -\frac{1}{2} \sum_{i=1}^{r} \left(\log h_i + \frac{\varepsilon_i^2}{h_i} \right).$$ (5.8)

Asymmetric GARCH Models

So far we have discussed symmetric GARCH models. One of the most intriguing features of asset returns or high frequency time series data is 'news' and the effect of good or bad news on asset returns. Black (1976) observed that the volatility in asset returns tends to increase more with negative returns than with positive returns. Furthermore, Black (1976) hypothesised that the reduction in the price of shares led to an increase in the ratio of debt to equity, making stock returns more volatile. Nevertheless, Black (1976) showed that the leverage effect, or the tendency for volatility to decline when asset returns rise, and to rise when asset returns fall, could not explain this empirical stylised fact.

Both the ARCH and GARCH models assume that there is symmetry in the conditional variances. GARCH models are able to explain volatility clustering but are unable to accommodate the leverage effect. Hence, the asymmetric model of Glosten, Jagannathan and Runkle (1993) was developed.

Asymmetric behaviour is captured in the GJR model, for which GJR(r,s) is defined as follows:

$$h_t = \omega_0 + \sum_{i=1}^{r} \alpha_i \varepsilon_i^2 + \sum_{i=1}^{r} \gamma_i I_i(\eta_{i-1}) \varepsilon_{i-1}^2 + \sum_{i=1}^{s} \beta_i h_{i-1}$$ (5.9)

where $\omega_0 > 0$, $\Sigma_{i=1}^{r} \alpha_i + \Sigma_{i=1}^{r} \gamma_i \geq 0$ and $\Sigma_{i=1}^{s} \beta_i \geq 0$ are sufficient conditions for $h_t > 0$, and $I(\eta_t)$ is an indicator variable defined by:

$$I(\eta_t) = \begin{cases} 1, & \eta_t < 0 \\ 0, & \eta_t \geq 0 . \end{cases}$$ (5.10)

The indicator variable distinguishes between positive and negative shocks such that asymmetric effects are captured by γ_i, with $\gamma_i > 0$. In the GJR model, the asymmetric effect, γ_i, measures the contribution of shocks to both short-run persistence,

$$\sum_{i=1}^{r} \alpha_i + \sum_{i=1}^{r} (y_i / 2),$$

and long-run persistence,

$$\sum_{i=1}^{r} \alpha_i + \sum_{i=1}^{r} (y_i / 2) + \sum_{i=1}^{s} \beta_i.$$

The necessary and sufficient condition for the existence of the second moment of GJR(1,1) under symmetry of η_t is given in Ling and McAleer (2002) as:

$$\sum_{i=1}^{r} \alpha_i + \sum_{i=1}^{r} \left(\frac{\gamma_i}{2} \right) + \sum_{i=1}^{s} \beta_i < 0 \qquad (5.11)$$

The weaker sufficient log-moment condition for GJR(1,1) is given by McAleer et al. (2008) as follows:

$$E \left\langle \log \left\{ [\alpha_1 + \gamma_1 I(\eta_t)] \eta_t^2 + \beta_1 \right\} \right\rangle < 0. \qquad (5.12)$$

It is also demonstrated that the QMLE of the parameters are consistent and asymptotically normal if the log-normal condition is satisfied.

5.3   MULTIVARIATE MODELS OF CONDITIONAL VOLATILITY

The following presentation closely follows that of McAleer et al. (2008). There are three different multivariate GARCH models of volatility discussed in this section, namely the Constant Conditional Correlation Univariate GARCH(r,s) model of Bollerslev (1990), hereafter CCC-MGARCH(r,s), the Vector ARMA-GARCH(r,s) model of Ling and McAleer (2003), hereafter VARMA-GARCH(r,s), and the Vector ARMA-AGARCH(r,s) model of McAleer et al. (2008), hereafter VARMA-AGARCH(r,s). These three models are estimated using monthly international tourist arrivals data for seven SITEs in Section 5.6 of this chapter. In Chapter 5 and Chapter 6, the CCC-MGARCH(r,s) model is estimated for monthly international tourist arrivals for seven SITEs, and from eight principal source countries, to the

Maldives, respectively. The models and their structural and statistical properties are presented below.

Consider the Constant Conditional Correlation (CCC) multivariate GARCH model of Bollerslev (1990), which is given as follows:

$$Y_t = E(Y_t \mid F_{t-1}) + \varepsilon_t, \qquad t = 1, \ldots, n$$
$$\varepsilon_t = D_t \eta_t \qquad\qquad\qquad\qquad\qquad\qquad (5.13)$$
$$Var(\varepsilon_t \mid F_{t-1}) = D_t \Gamma D_t$$

where F_t is the information set available to time t, $D_t = diag\,(h_{it}^{1/2})$, $i = 1, \ldots, m$, is a diagonal matrix of the conditional variances, for which m is the total number of assets, markets or sources, and

$$\Gamma = \begin{pmatrix} 1 & \rho_{12} & \cdots & \rho_{1m} \\ \rho_{21} & 1 & \rho_{23} & \cdots \\ & & \cdots & \\ \rho_{m1} & \cdots & \rho_{m,m-1} & 1 \end{pmatrix}$$

is the matrix of static (or constant) conditional correlations, in which $\rho_{ij} = \rho_{ji}$ for $i, j = 1, \ldots, m$. The main feature of this model is that the conditional correlations, given by

$$E(\varepsilon_{it} \varepsilon_{jt} \mid F_{t-1}) \Big/ \sqrt{E(\varepsilon_{it}^2 \mid F_{t-1}) E(\varepsilon_{jt}^2 \mid F_{t-1})} = \rho_{ij}$$

are constant over time, where $i \neq j$, $i, j = 1, \ldots, m$, and ε_{it} is the ith element of ε_t. Bollerslev (1990) assumed that

$$h_{it} = \omega_i + \sum_{l=1}^{r} \alpha_{il} \varepsilon_{it-l}^2 + \sum_{l=1}^{s} \beta_{il} h_{it-l}, \qquad i = 1, \ldots, m \qquad (5.14)$$

in which there is no interdependence between h_{it} and $(\varepsilon_{jt-k}, h_{jt-l})$ for $i \neq j$; $i, j = 1, \ldots, m$; $k = 1, \ldots, r$; and $l = 1, \ldots, s$, and hence no relationship of volatilities across different tourist source countries, country risk returns, assets or markets. Thus, the multivariate effects are determined solely through the static (or constant) conditional correlation matrix, Γ. The multivariate constant conditional correlation model based on equations (5.13) and (5.14) is denoted CCC-MGARCH(1,1).

Equation (5.14) is the standard GARCH(r,s) model of Bollerslev (1986) for asset i, in which $\Sigma_{i=1}^{r} \alpha_i$ denotes short-run persistence (or the ARCH effects of shocks) and $\Sigma_{i=1}^{r} \alpha_i + \Sigma_{i=1}^{s} \beta_i$ denotes long-run persistence (in which $\Sigma_{i=1}^{s} \beta_i$ are the GARCH effects).

In order to allow for interdependencies of volatilities across different assets or markets, Ling and McAleer (2003) proposed the following VARMA-GARCH model:

$$\Phi(L)(Y_t - \mu) = \Psi(L)\varepsilon_t$$
$$\varepsilon_t = D_t \eta_t$$

(5.15)

$$H_t = W + \sum_{l=1}^{r} A_l \vec{\varepsilon}_{t-l} + \sum_{l=1}^{s} B_l H_{t-l}$$

(5.16)

where $D_t = diag(h_{it}^{1/2})$, A_l and B_l are each $m \times m$ matrices with typical elements given by α_{ij} and β_{ij}, respectively, for $i, j = 1,...,m$, $\Phi(L) = I_m - \Phi_1 L - ... - \Phi_p L^p$ and $\Psi(L) = I_m - \Psi_1 L - ... - \Psi_q L^q$ are polynomials in L, is the $k \times k$ identity matrix, and $\vec{\varepsilon}_t = (\varepsilon_{1t}^2,...,\varepsilon_{mt}^2)'$.

It is clear that when A_l and B_l are diagonal matrices, equation (5.16) reduces to equation (5.17), so that the VARMA-GARCH model in equation (5.16) has CCC-MGARCH as a special case. Ling and McAleer (2003) established the structural and statistical properties of the model, including the necessary and sufficient conditions for stationarity and ergodicity by deriving the causal expansion. This is a useful approach as it yields proofs of stationarity and ergodicity without assuming the existence of moments. Ling and McAleer (2003) also provided the necessary and sufficient condition for the existence of the $2m$th moment, namely

$$\rho[E(A_t^{\otimes m})] < 1,$$

where

$$A_t = \begin{bmatrix} \tilde{\eta}_t A_1 & \cdots & \tilde{\eta}_t A_r & \tilde{\eta}_t B_1 & \cdots & \tilde{\eta}_t B_s \\ I_{m(r-1)} & O_{m(r-1)\times m} & & O_{m(r-1)\times ms} & \\ A_1 & \cdots & A_r & B_1 & \cdots & B_s \\ O_{m(s-1)\times mr} & & & I_{m(s-1)} & O_{m(s-1)\times m} \end{bmatrix}$$

and $\tilde{\eta}_t = diag(\eta_{1t},...,\eta_{1mt})$.

McAleer et al. (2008) extended the VARMA-GARCH model of Ling and McAleer (2003) to accommodate asymmetric impacts of the unconditional shocks on the conditional variances, and proposed the VARMA-AGARCH model as follows:

$$\Phi(L)(Y_t - \mu) = \Psi(L)\varepsilon_t$$
$$\varepsilon_t = D_t \eta_t \tag{5.17}$$

$$h_{it} = \omega_i + \sum_{l=1}^{r} \alpha_{il}\varepsilon_{it-l}^2 + \sum_{l=1}^{r} \gamma_{il}I(\eta_{it-l})\varepsilon_{it-l}^2 + \sum_{l=1}^{s} \beta_{il}h_{it-l}, \quad i = 1,...,m \tag{5.18}$$

in which $\varepsilon_{it} = \eta_{it}\sqrt{h_{it}}$ for all i and t, and $I(\eta_{it})$ is an indicator function such that

$$I(\eta_{it}) = \begin{cases} 1, & \eta_{it} < 0 \\ 0, & \eta_{it} \geq 0. \end{cases}$$

It is clear that if $m = 1$, equation (5.18) collapses to the asymmetric GARCH, or GJR, model of Glosten et al. (1992). If $\gamma_{il} = 0$ for $\forall l = 1,...,r$ equations (5.17) and (5.18) reduce to the VARMA-GARCH model of Ling and McAleer (2003). McAleer et al. (2008) established the structural properties of the VARMA-AGARCH model. As in Ling and McAleer (2003), these included the necessary and sufficient conditions for stationarity and ergodicity, sufficient conditions for the existence of moments, and sufficient conditions of consistency and asymptotic normality of the QMLE.

The necessary and sufficient conditions for stationarity and ergodicity of (5.17) and (5.18) were established by McAleer et al. (2008) using the same techniques as Ling and McAleer (2003), namely by deriving the causal expansion. Hence, their proofs of stationarity and ergodicity did not require the existence of any moments.

Moreover, McAleer et al. (2008) showed that the necessary and sufficient condition for the existence of the $2m$th moment is:

$$\rho[E(\tilde{A}_t^{\otimes m})] < 1,$$

where

$$\tilde{A}_t = \begin{bmatrix} \tilde{\eta}_t A_1^* & \cdots & \tilde{\eta}_t A_r^* & \tilde{\eta}_t B_1 & \cdots & \tilde{\eta}_t B_s \\ I_{m(r-1)} & O_{m(r-1)\times m} & O_{m(r-1)\times ms} \\ A_1^* & \cdots & A_r^* & B_1 & \cdots & B_s \\ O_{m(s-1)\times mr} & I_{m(s-1)} & O_{m(s-1)\times m} \end{bmatrix}$$

and $A_l^* = A_l + \gamma_l I(\vec{\eta}_{t-l})$, $l = 1,...,r$

The parameters of equations (5.15) and (5.16) are typically estimated by MLE under a joint normal density, namely

$$\hat{\theta} = \max_{\theta} -\frac{1}{2}\sum_{t=1}^{T}\left(\log|H_t| + |\varepsilon_t' H_t^{-1}\varepsilon_t|\right), \qquad (5.19)$$

where $|A|$ denotes the determinant of a matrix A. When η_t does not follow a joint normal distribution, equation (5.19) is defined as the QMLE. Ling and McAleer (2003) showed that the existence of the second moment is sufficient for consistency, while the existence of the fourth moment is sufficient for asymptotic normality of the QMLE.

As in the case of the VARMA-GARCH(r,s) model, VARMA-AGARCH(r,s) is also typically estimated by QMLE, as defined in equation (5.19). McAleer et al. (2007) showed that the existence of the second moment is sufficient for consistency, while the existence of the fourth moment is sufficient for asymptotic normality.

A comparative summary of the various multivariate GARCH models is provided in McAleer et al. (2007), including Engle and Kroner's (1995) Vech (or VAR) model, Bollerslev et al. (1988) Diagonal model, Engle and Kroner's (1995) BEKK model, and the Dynamic Conditional Correlation (DCC) model of Engle (2002), which is closely related to the Varying Conditional Correlation Multivariate GARCH (VCC-MGARCH) model of Tse and Tsui (2002). The objective of the BEKK model is to model the conditional covariances, which may be used to obtain multivariate confidence intervals, whereas the primary purpose of the other multivariate models described above is to analyse the conditional correlations, which can be used to determine an optimal financial or tourism portfolio.

5.4   CONSTANT CONDITIONAL CORRELATIONS OF STANDARDISED SHOCKS AND THEIR MEANINGS

In this monograph, we place special significance on the interpretation of CCCs of the standardised shocks in the GARCH(1,1), GJR(1,1) VARMA-GARCH(1,1), and VARMA-AGARCH(1,1) models. Furthermore, we assess the implications of the CCC coefficients, particularly in the context of analysing the conditional volatility in tourism demand. There are two aspects to the interpretation, namely (i) we need to identify the effects of constant conditional correlations of the standardised shocks regarding the measure of tourism demand or the choice of dependent variable used, and (ii) the sign and magnitude of the CCC coefficients have relevance to policy formulation for national governments and in the development of marketing strategies by tour operators.

In the case where tourism demand is measured as the number of monthly tourist arrivals (that is, in levels), the correlation coefficients of the standardised shocks show how a conditional shock in one source country

affects the number of international tourist arrivals from another tourist source country. However, if the dependent variable is defined in logarithms, the conditional correlations explain how a conditional shock in one source country affects the logarithm of the number of monthly international tourist arrivals from another tourist source county. Furthermore, if tourism demand is measured in first differences, the conditional correlations illustrate how a shock to the absolute one-period change in tourist arrivals will affect the absolute one-period change in the monthly international tourist arrivals from another tourist market. If the monthly growth rate of international tourist arrivals is the measure of tourism demand, the conditional correlations of the standardised residuals describe how a conditional shock to the growth rate in monthly international tourist arrivals will affect the monthly growth rate of international tourist arrivals from another tourist source market.

When the estimated conditional correlations are close to +1, it means that there is a positive linear relationship between the conditional shocks in tourist source countries. A conditional shock in one tourist source market will have similar effects on international tourist arrivals from other tourist source countries. In this case, the objective for governments and tour operators would be to specialise in promotional efforts in the tourist source countries which produce the highest numbers in international tourist arrivals.

When the estimated conditional correlations are close to −1, there is a negative linear relationship between the conditional shocks in tourist source countries. That is to say, a conditional shock on one tourist source country will have an opposite effect in international tourist arrivals from other sources. In such circumstances, efforts should be to diversify promotional activities in the preferred tourism source countries, depending on the choice made by tour operators or national governments.

When the estimated conditional correlations are equal to zero, a relationship of conditional shocks of the standardised shocks between tourist source countries does not exist. Therefore, the tourist source countries are segmented. As a result, the tour operators and governments will have to pay particular attention to the volatilities in international tourist arrivals as well as the number of international tourist arrivals independently. All efforts in tourism promotion will have to be considered, independently of each tourist source country.

5.5 DATA

The empirical section in this chapter models the conditional volatility of the logarithm of monthly international tourist arrivals and the growth rate of monthly international tourist arrivals in seven SITEs. The growth rate and log

　　　　　The Economics of Small Island Tourism

differences of monthly international tourist arrivals are used synonymously. For these SITEs, the frequency of the data is monthly and the samples are as follows: Barbados, January 1973 to December 2002; Cyprus, January 1976 to September 2004; Dominica, January 1990 to December 2001; Fiji, January 1968 to August 2004; Maldives, January 1986 to December 2003; Malta, January 1968 to February 2004 and Seychelles, January 1971 to September 2004.

The descriptive statistics for the logarithms of monthly tourist arrivals and the log-differences of the monthly international tourist arrivals are presented in . These statistics show that there is very little variability in the means across the seven SITEs, with a relatively short range of 2.783. The highest mean is recorded for Cyprus with 11.244, while the lowest is for

Table 5.1　　*Descriptive Statistics for Logarithms and Log-differences of Monthly International Tourist Arrivals to SITEs*

Logarithms	Barbados	Cyprus	Dominica	Fiji	Maldives	Malta	Seychelles
Mean	10.333	11.244	8.461	9.829	9.978	10.687	8.629
Median	10.401	11.333	8.480	9.857	10.010	10.812	8.825
Max.	10.910	12.830	9.128	10.845	10.973	11.978	9.624
Min	9.329	8.262	7.771	8.288	8.501	7.398	4.727
S.D.	0.328	1.008	0.301	0.461	0.565	0.825	0.802
Skewness	−0.868	−0.431	−0.159	−0.616	−0.350	−0.607	−2.238
Kurtosis	3.391	2.380	2.380	3.543	2.330	2.905	9.382
J-B	47.490	16.189	2.917	33.237	8.437	26.841	1025.474
Prob.	0.000	0.000	0.233	0.000	0.015	0.000	0.000
n	360	345	144	440	216	434	405

Log-differences	Barbados	Cyprus	Dominica	Fiji	Maldives	Malta	Seychelles
Mean	0.003	0.013	0.005	0.005	0.007	0.006	0.010
Median	0.015	0.012	0.003	−0.009	0.009	0.031	0.011
Max.	0.526	0.984	0.835	1.136	0.580	2.437	0.683
Min	−0.653	−0.920	−0.885	−0.955	−0.550	−1.427	−0.547
S.D.	0.231	0.359	0.385	0.186	0.215	0.316	0.196
Skewness	−0.335	−0.243	−0.159	−0.296	−0.146	0.646	0.121
Kurtosis	3.148	2.921	2.308	8.905	3.133	10.750	3.157
J-B	7.064	3.479	3.456	644.160	0.924	1113.872	1.398
Prob.	0.029	0.176	0.178	0.000	0.630	0.000	0.497
n	359	344	143	439	215	433	404

Dominica with 8.461, which also has the smallest sample among the seven SITEs. The standard deviation does not vary substantially across the seven SITEs and has a range of 0.707, with the highest standard deviation of 1.008 recorded for Cyprus and the lowest of 0.301 for Dominica. All of the seven series are skewed to the left, where the magnitude of skewness is a maximum for Seychelles while the least skewed is Dominica. Except for Dominica, the Jarque-Bera test decisively rejects the null hypothesis of normality, while the other six series are leptokurtic.

In the same table, the descriptive statistics for the growth rate or log-differences of monthly international tourist arrivals for the seven SITEs are given. The most interesting series among them are for Fiji and Malta, where the distribution of the series is similar to financial time series.

All seven SITEs exhibit distinct seasonal patterns and positive trends. The most frequently used method, the ratio-to-moving average method, is computed using EViews 4.1, and is illustrated in Table 5.2. The seven SITEs are located either in the tropical or subtropical regions of the world, so that the peak tourist seasons in these countries coincide with the northern hemisphere winter months. Examining the seasonal indexes in Table 5.2, for the two SITEs in the Caribbean, namely Barbados and Dominica, nearly one-half of the tourist arrivals are in December to April. In Barbados almost one-fifth of the tourists arrive during July and August, coinciding with the northern hemisphere summer, where family holidays are particularly popular. For the Mediterranean SITEs, namely Cyprus and Malta, the tourist season is almost

Table 5.2   Seasonal Indices for Monthly International Tourist Arrivals to SITEs

Month	Barbados	Cyprus	Dominica	Fiji	Maldives	Malta	Seychelles
January	1.11	0.40	0.90	0.97	1.28	0.46	1.00
February	1.16	0.47	1.30	0.86	1.29	0.57	1.10
March	1.19	0.79	1.01	0.96	1.28	0.85	1.17
April	1.08	1.17	0.99	0.91	1.05	1.06	1.05
May	0.85	1.35	0.95	0.93	0.70	1.24	0.85
June	0.76	1.38	0.89	0.92	0.62	1.30	0.79
July	1.12	1.86	1.46	1.11	0.90	1.69	1.02
August	1.11	1.84	1.27	1.25	1.08	1.81	1.12
September	0.71	1.60	0.62	1.06	0.94	1.45	0.90
October	0.86	1.35	0.91	1.05	0.95	1.20	1.03
November	1.03	0.70	0.80	1.00	1.00	0.74	0.96
December	1.18	0.61	1.21	1.04	1.19	0.65	1.10

identical, where almost 80 per cent of the tourist arrivals take place from April to October. Similarly, for the Indian Ocean SITEs of Maldives and Seychelles, their peak tourist season coincides well with the European winter months. As for Fiji in the Pacific, its major tourist source countries being Australia, New Zealand and USA, their tourist season is the latter half of the calendar year, peaking in August which is the coldest month in Australia.

The primary reason for modelling the logarithms and log-differences of monthly international tourist arrivals rather than in levels is the presence of unit roots in some of the series. The Phillips and Perron (1990) (PP) test for stationarity with truncated lags of order 5 was conducted using EViews 4.1 for the seven SITEs. In Table 5.3, the PP test results are presented for the respective sample periods for the seven SITEs. Except for Maldives, the test reveals that the logarithms of monthly tourist arrivals are stationary, while the hemisphere summer, where family holidays are particularly popular. For the tests, different lags were used but the results are robust to the various changes.

Table 5.3   *Unit Root Tests for Logarithms and Log-differences of Monthly International Tourist Arrivals to SITEs*

	Barbados			Cyprus		
	Obs.	Stat.	CVs	Obs.	Stat.	CVs
Logarithms	359	−6.83	5% 10%	344	−4.54	5% 10%
Log Difference		−23.94	−2.87 −2.57		−12.03	−2.87 −2.57

	Dominica			Fiji		
	Obs.	Stat.	CVs	Obs.	Stat.	CVs
Logarithms	143	−10.35	5% 10%	439	−3.54	5% 10%
Log Difference		−37.10	−2.88 −2.58		−29.18	−2.87 −2.57

	Maldives			Malta		
	Obs.	Stat.	CVs	Obs.	Stat.	CVs
Logarithms	215	−2.24	5% 10%	433	−5.09	5% 10%
Log Difference		−11.09	−2.88 −2.57		−17.32	−2.87 −2.57

	Seychelles		
	Obs.	Stat.	CVs
Logarithms	404	−5.05	5% 10%
Log Difference		−29.58	−2.87 −2.57

Note: The null hypothesis is that monthly international tourist arrivals have a unit root.

The PP test is considered superior to the more popular Augmented-Dickey Fuller (ADF) test because the ADF takes into account only serial correlation, while the PP test accommodates both serial correlation and heteroscedasticity.

The logarithm of international tourist arrivals to each of these SITEs exhibits distinct seasonal patterns and positive trends, and are illustrated in Figure 5.1. For Barbados, there are some cyclical effects, which coincide with the business cycles in the US economy. These business cycles are the boom period in the latter half of the 1970s, the slump due to the second oil price shock of 1979, and the recession in the early 1990s. In Cyprus, the only visible change in monthly international tourist arrivals is the outlier of the 1991 Gulf War. In Dominica and the Maldives, there are no apparent changes during the respective sample periods. In Malta the first oil price shock of 1973 adversely affected monthly international tourist arrivals, and thereafter continued to grow gradually. However, in Fiji, the coups of 1987 and 2000 are quite noticeable. Until the second oil shock of 1979, tourism was rapidly increasing in Seychelles, after which the growth rate of monthly international tourist arrivals has stabilised.

The volatilities of the logarithm of the deseasonalised and detrended monthly tourist arrivals are illustrated in Figure 5.2. These volatilities were calculated from the square of the estimated residuals, ε_t^2, using non-linear least squares from the following regression model, which is the empirical equivalent of the conditional mean equation (5.1):

$$\log TA_t = ARMA(1,1) + \sum_{i=1}^{12} \phi_i D_{it} + \theta_1 t + \theta_2 t^2 + \theta_3 t^* + \varepsilon_t \qquad (5.21)$$

$$Vol(\varepsilon_t) = \varepsilon_t^2 \qquad (5.22)$$

where TA_t is the total monthly international tourist arrivals at time t; D_{ti} (= 1 in month $i = 1, 2, \ldots, 12$, and = 0 elsewhere) denotes 12 seasonal dummies; $t = 1, \ldots, T$, where $T = 360$, 345, 144, and 216 for Barbados, Cyprus, Dominica and Maldives, respectively; $T = 88$ and $t^* = 89, \ldots, 440$ for Fiji; and $T = 150$ and $t^* = 151, \ldots, 405$ for Seychelles. The most visible cases of volatility clusterings in monthly international tourism demand are Barbados, Cyprus and Seychelles. In Barbados, in the first third of the sample, monthly international tourism arrivals have been highly volatile owing to the economic cycles in the US economy. For Cyprus and Seychelles, there is volatility clustering in the late-1970s to mid-1980s due to the second oil price shock. For Fiji, volatility clusterings are virtually non-existent, whereas for Dominica and Maldives, volatility seems to be accompanied by seasonality in monthly international tourist arrivals.

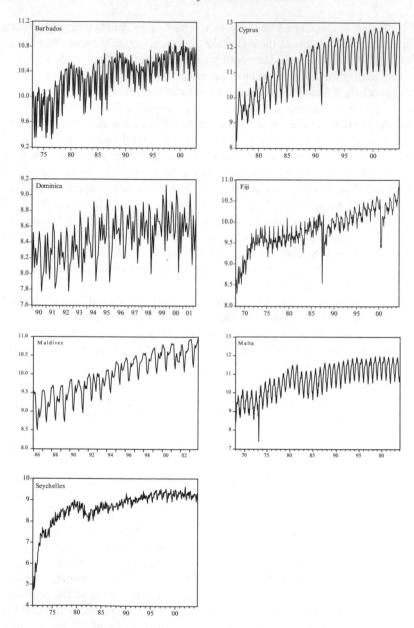

Figure 5.1   Logarithms of Monthly International Tourist Arrivals

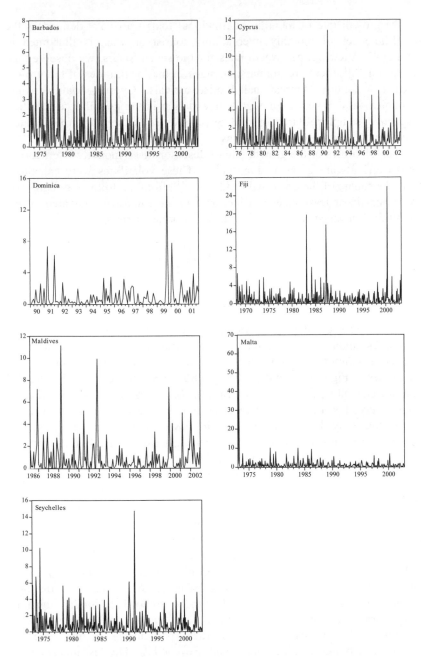

Figure 5.2   Volatility of the Logarithms of Monthly Deseasonalised and Detrended International Tourism Arrivals

The growth rate of monthly international tourist arrivals, defined as the log-differences of monthly international tourist arrivals, is illustrated in Figure 5.3. Viewing the growth rates for the seven SITEs, we observe that, except for Fiji, there are dramatic changes in the magnitudes of the growth rates of monthly international tourist arrivals. Cyprus, Maldives and Dominica show a very high degree of variation in the growth rates, in their respective samples. Barbados and Seychelles share similar growth rates, while Fiji shows the lowest variations.

The volatilities of the growth rate of deseasonalised monthly international tourist arrivals are given in Figure 5.4. These volatilities were calculated from the square of the estimated residuals, v_t^2, from the following regression using non-linear least squares, which is also the empirical equivalent of the conditional mean equation (5.1) for the transformed series:

$$\Delta \log TA_t = ARMA(1,1) + \sum_{i=1}^{12} \phi_i D_{it} + v_t \qquad (5.23)$$

$$Vol(v_t) = v_t^2 . \qquad (5.24)$$

In this case, the dependent variable is the log-differences of TA_t. The volatilities among the seven SITEs show slightly different patterns over the respective sample periods, with the simple correlation coefficients for the volatilities in Figures 5.2 and 5.4 being 0.86, 0.93, 0.91, 0.98, 0.82, 0.92 and 0.60 for Barbados, Cyprus, Dominica, Fiji, Maldives, Malta and Seychelles, respectively. For Barbados, there is clear evidence of volatility clustering during the early 1970s and in the mid-1980s, after which there is little evidence of volatility clustering. Volatility clustering is visible for Cyprus in the mid-1970s. In Dominica, in late 1999 and early 2000, there is volatility clustering. The volatility structure of Fiji resembles that of a financial time series, with volatility clustering not so profound, except for outliers, which signify the coups of 1987 and 2000. In the case of Malta, around the first oil shock of 1973, there is clear evidence of volatility clustering. In Seychelles, volatility clustering is noticeable in the early 1970s, whereas in the Maldives, there are few extreme observations and little volatility clustering.

It is important to note that the volatilities of the logarithm of monthly international tourist arrivals and the growth rate of monthly international tourist arrivals to the seven SITEs show somewhat similar dynamic behavioural patterns. However, there are visible differences in the magnitudes of the calculated volatilities, particularly in the cases of Barbados, Dominica, Fiji, Malta and Seychelles. This is plausible for monthly international tourist arrivals, so there would seem to be a strong case for estimating both symmetric and asymmetric conditional volatility models

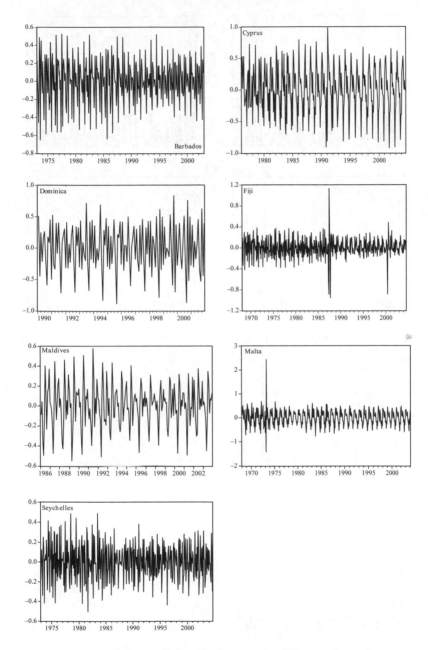

Figure 5.3   Growth Rate of Monthly International Tourist Arrivals

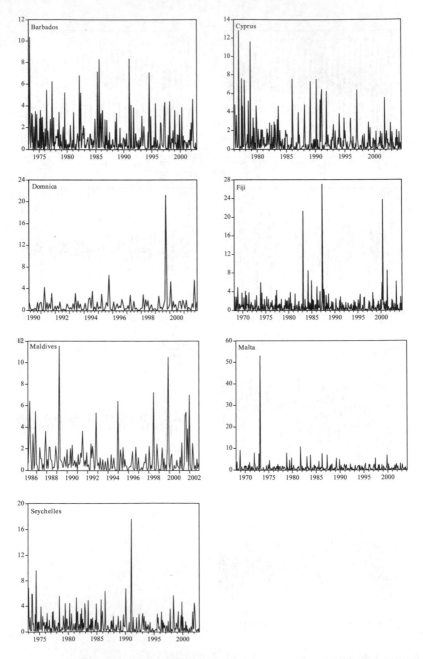

*Figure 5.4   Volatility of the Growth Rate of Deseasonalised Monthly
             International Tourist Arrivals*

for both the logarithm of monthly international tourism arrivals and their log-differences to these seven SITEs.

5.6   EMPIRICAL EVALUATION

This section models the volatility of the logarithm of monthly international tourist arrivals and the growth rate of monthly international tourist arrivals using the GARCH(1,1) and GJR(1,1) models, as defined in equations (5.4) and (5.9) for the respective sample periods for the seven SITEs. Similar assessments were undertaken by Shareef and McAleer (2005) and Chan et al. (2005). In order to accommodate the presence of seasonal effects and various deterministic time trends, the logarithm of tourist arrivals is given by the conditional mean equation (5.21), while for the growth rate of monthly international tourist arrivals, the conditional mean is given by equation (5.23).

Modelling the mean equation is important to estimate accurately the unconditional shocks, ε_t, from which to estimate the conditional variance, h_t. Time series data on monthly international tourist arrivals shows a considerable degree of persistence. The literature on univariate time series analysis of tourism demand has shown that ARMA models fit the data reasonably well. Moreover, for the seven SITEs examined, there is evidence of non-linearity in the series. In the monthly tourist arrivals series for Fiji and Seychelles, there appear to be structural breaks in early 1975 and mid-1983, respectively. These structural breaks have been taken into consideration when estimating the conditional means. Hence, an ARMA(p,q) specification is estimated with monthly seasonal dummies and various deterministic time trends, possibly with breakpoints. In this chapter, various ARMA order specifications have been examined and the ARMA(1,1) seems to be the optimal specification using AIC and SBC.

Estimates of the parameters of the conditional mean and the conditional variance for the three models using the seven samples are given in Tables 5.4–5.11. The Berndt-Hall-Hall-Hausman (1974) algorithm incorporated in EViews 4.1 is used to obtain the estimates of the parameters. Where iterations fail to converge, the Marquandt algorithm is used. The three entries correspond to the estimate (in bold), asymptotic t-ratio and the Bollerslev-Wooldridge (1992) robust t-ratio. A linear trend is used for Fiji before the breakpoint (denoted by BP-t) at April 1975, and a separate linear trend is used thereafter. Both a linear and quadratic trend is used for Seychelles before the breakpoint (denoted by BP-t) at June 1983, and a separate linear trend is used thereafter.

The log-moment and second moment conditions for the GARCH(1,1) model are the empirical versions of equations (5.5) and (5.6), respectively,

Table 5.4 Conditional Mean Estimates for the Logarithms of Deseasonalised and Detrended Monthly International Tourist Arrivals

Barbados

	AR(2)					D1	D2	D3	D4	D5	D7	D8	D11	D12
	0.968					0.412	0.312	0.393	0.300	0.023	0.614	0.710	0.697	0.642
	10.605					16.951	9.963	15.417	12.073	1.300	15.960	32.907	23.557	23.254
	6.492					16.941	14.776	17.084	12.602	0.742	31.699	27.409	30.832	28.782

Cyprus

	AR(1)	MA(1)	t	t^2	D1	D2	D3	D4	D5	D6	D7	D8	D11	D12
	0.983	−0.386	4.5E-04	−7.3E-07	−0.197	0.292	0.713	0.522	0.336	0.143	0.384	0.158	−0.564	−0.111
	15.705	−6.199	0.934	−0.923	−7.051	8.688	22.665	16.183	11.577	3.782	9.721	2.317	−16.028	−4.107
	15.084	−6.243	0.881	−0.888	−6.438	11.009	26.702	21.190	10.773	5.814	17.266	9.749	−21.026	−3.881

Dominica

	AR(1)	MA(1)	t	D1	D2	D3	D4	D5	D6	D7	D8	D9	D10	D11	D12
	−0.671	0.772	0.006	12.136	12.273	12.238	12.063	12.004	11.928	12.391	12.543	11.698	11.633	11.789	12.127
	−18.026	9.123	9.960	54.663	61.533	57.327	62.138	63.310	63.666	63.318	56.303	58.427	63.095	54.582	52.847
	−3.451	4.415	7.022	8.487	8.956	8.476	8.640	8.592	8.588	8.988	8.562	8.074	8.950	8.607	8.979

Fiji

	AR(1)	MA(1)	BP-t	t	D1	D2	D3	D4	D5	D6	D7	D8	D9	D10	D11	D12
	0.941	−0.589	1.9E-04	3.4E-04	0.478	0.409	0.631	0.426	0.653	0.509	0.721	0.687	0.346	0.552	0.505	0.579
	74.305	−10.123	3.975	2.018	4.035	3.450	5.460	3.706	5.683	4.497	5.955	5.847	2.960	4.537	4.291	4.912
	72.165	−9.756	4.234	2.511	3.949	3.439	5.333	3.582	5.307	4.106	6.133	5.607	2.762	4.625	4.157	4.826

Maldives

	AR(1)	MA(1)	AR(2)	t^2	t	D1	D3	D4	D5	D6	D8	D9	D10	D12
	0.037	0.717	0.737	−1.8E-05	0.013	0.109	−0.052	−0.266	−0.655	−0.621	0.289	−0.081	−0.176	0.113
	2.163	10.059	13.931	−17.149	8.282	3.939	−1.228	−6.128	−15.147	−17.859	5.836	−1.740	−5.866	4.586
	1.311	4.546	6.092	−5.680	5.781	3.101	−2.608	−7.690	−16.827	−12.981	5.944	−2.310	−6.291	3.302

Table 5.4   Conditional Mean Estimates for the Logarithms of Deseasonalised and Detrended Monthly International Tourist Arrivals (continued)

	AR(1)	AR(2)	MA(2)	t		D1	D2	D3	D4	D5	D6	D7	D8	D9	D10	D11	D12
Malta	0.562	0.383	−0.222	1.7E−04		0.178	0.655	1.014	0.888	0.809	0.669	0.819	0.743	0.432	0.329	−0.002	0.189
	47.892	56.190	−3.938	3.805		3.122	12.425	17.654	15.044	13.283	11.085	13.464	11.814	7.021	5.517	−0.036	3.303
	4.473	3.425	−3.544	1.795		0.690	2.550	3.733	3.039	2.812	2.303	2.879	2.463	1.479	1.202	−0.008	0.765
	AR(1)	AR(2)	MA(2)	t		D1	D2	D3	D4	D5	D6	D7	D8	D9	D10	D11	D12
Seychelles	0.537	0.404	−0.378	1.9E−04		0.456	0.536	0.580	0.398	0.224	0.298	0.662	0.674	0.338	0.542	0.470	0.564
	15.677	14.641	−5.914	2.444		3.475	4.184	4.357	3.022	1.721	2.401	5.276	5.254	2.640	4.341	3.680	4.403
	9.088	6.459	−6.221	1.965		2.344	2.729	2.956	2.001	1.128	1.489	3.487	3.566	1.717	2.732	2.421	2.850

Note: The three entries associated with each parameter are their respective estimate, the asymptotic *t*-ratio and the Bollerslev-Wooldridge (1992) robust *t*-ratios.

*Table 5.5   Conditional Variance Estimates of GARCH(1,1) for the
Logarithms of Deseasonalised and Detrended Monthly
International Tourist Arrivals*

SITE	ω	α	β	Log Moment	Second Moment
Barbados	0.006	0.223	0.390	−0.580	0.613
	1.988	2.733	1.740		
	2.480	2.876	2.026		
Cyprus	0.001	0.213	0.752	−0.077	0.965
	2.145	4.580	14.154		
	1.461	2.094	7.792		
Dominica	0.009	0.281	0.250	−0.891	0.531
	2.675	3.471	1.807		
	1.672	1.227	0.656		
Fiji	0.006	0.506	0.208	−0.747	0.714
	5.479	6.868	2.420		
	3.515	2.279	1.840		
Maldives	2.0E–04	0.026	0.954	−0.024	0.980
	0.917	2.960	44.627		
	0.492	1.340	17.848		
Malta	0.002	0.416	0.375	−0.413	0.791
	7.169	13.695	16.010		
	3.102	0.782	1.478		
Seychelles	1.7E–04	0.047	0.941	−0.017	0.988
	0.554	1.900	29.795		
	0.652	1.747	23.933		

Note: The three entries associated with each parameter are their respective estimate, the asymptotic *t*-ratio and the Bollerslev-Wooldridge (1992) robust *t*-ratios.

and the log-moment and second moment conditions for the GJR(1,1) model are the empirical versions of equations (5.11) and (5.12), respectively. The empirical version of the second moment conditions (5.5) and (5.11) are evaluated from the respective QMLE of the conditional volatility models. To calculate the empirical version of the log-moment condition, the QMLE of the parameters of the conditional variance are substituted into equations (5.6) and (5.12), along with the estimated standardised residuals from the respective conditional volatility models. These empirical moment conditions offer practical diagnostic checks of the regularity conditions on the validity of the models estimated.

Table 5.6 Conditional Mean Estimates for the Logarithms of Deseasonalised and Detrended Monthly International Tourist Arrivals

	AR(1)	AR(2)	MA(1)				D1	D2	D3	D4	D5	D6	D7	D8	D9	D10	D11	D12
Barbados	.	0.967	.	.	.		0.427	0.330	0.422	0.299	0.013	.	0.627	0.672	.	.	0.699	0.636
		10.938					18.991	11.353	17.503	13.951	0.731	.	19.388	28.863	.	.	29.131	28.890
		7.136					18.909	16.961	19.939	12.176	0.442	.	34.985	30.554	.	.	34.075	28.187
Cyprus	0.993	.	-3.4E-04	5.3E-07	-0.206		0.301	0.709	0.512	0.307	0.144	0.372	0.153	-0.567	.	.	-0.107	-0.409
	2.529		-1.041	0.958	-7.278		9.545	24.471	16.543	11.432	3.846	8.227	2.427	-17.972	.	.	-4.072	-7.400
	3.956		-3.047	4.181	-7.011		11.928	25.104	21.241	9.246	5.980	19.818	9.443	-19.404	.	.	-3.685	-7.675
Dominica	-0.782	.	0.007	12.939	.		13.085	13.096	12.853	12.811	12.744	13.186	13.376	12.495	12.377	12.607	12.904	0.824
	-2.501		13.077	76.189			77.875	73.454	83.347	86.010	78.652	79.048	75.008	80.592	82.433	69.488	76.061	11.975
	-4.431		7.593	10.090			10.614	9.984	10.143	10.152	10.157	10.620	10.122	9.579	10.564	10.150	10.558	4.808
Fiji	0.937	.	4.1E-04	2.2E-04	0.510	0.107 (BP-t)	0.437	0.665	0.461	0.694	0.541	0.756	0.725	0.392	0.591	0.541	0.615	-0.527
	6.535		2.104	3.975	3.821	4.274	3.284	5.208	3.539	5.395	4.189	5.671	5.494	2.965	4.373	4.107	4.648	-8.274
	6.415		2.604	4.257	3.769	3.147	3.291	5.040	3.429	5.198	3.886	5.770	5.270	2.801	4.410	3.978	4.579	-8.242
Maldives	0.034	0.013	0.750	-1.7E-05	.		-0.050	.	-0.266	-0.657	-0.631	0.293	.	-0.082	-0.177	0.113	.	0.718
	0.367	5.764	8.146	-5.681			-1.474	.	-7.341	-16.728	-16.315	5.960	.	-2.104	-6.387	5.217	.	6.248
	0.310	5.868	6.835	-5.686			-2.624	.	-7.705	-17.708	-14.526	6.320	.	-2.424	-6.269	3.338	.	4.905

191

Table 5.6   Conditional Mean Estimates for the Logarithms of Deseasonalised and Detrended Monthly International Tourist Arrivals (continued)

	AR(1)	AR(2)	MA(2)	t		D1	D2	D3	D4	D5	D6	D7	D8	D9	D10	D11	D12
Malta	0.570	0.382	1.4E–04	0.114	.	0.589	0.970	0.808	0.730	0.601	0.761	0.671	0.367	0.257	–0.079	0.126	–0.292
	30.882	14.029	2.169	0.943	.	4.790	8.563	7.106	6.025	4.899	5.949	5.407	2.837	1.912	–0.582	0.960	–4.781
	5.535	3.819	1.724	0.645	.	3.301	5.560	4.346	3.882	3.168	3.973	3.362	1.868	1.350	–0.420	0.680	–5.112
	AR(1)	AR(2)	MA(2)	t		D1	D2	D3	D4	D5	D6	D7	D8	D9	D10	D11	D12
Seychelles	0.567	0.373	–0.336	1.7E–04	.	0.459	0.547	0.582	0.400	0.238	0.306	0.681	0.678	0.333	0.55:	0.478	0.586
	23.015	15.652	–5.288	2.075	.	3.043	3.708	3.832	2.661	1.567	2.061	4.677	4.605	2.272	3.734	3.234	3.976
	9.800	6.161	–5.457	1.716	.	2.397	2.820	3.034	2.049	1.222	1.564	3.684	3.651	1.716	2.845	2.510	3.012

Note: The three entries associated with each parameter are their respective estimate, the asymptotic *t*-ratio and the Bollerslev-Wooldridge (1992) robust *t*-ratios.

Table 5.7   *Conditional Variance Estimates of GJR(1,1) for the Logarithms of Deseasonalised and Detrended Monthly International Tourist Arrivals*

SITE	ω	α	γ	$\alpha+\gamma/2$	β	Log-Moment	Second Moment
Barbados	0.002	−0.102	0.415	0.106	0.747	−0.245	0.853
	2.593	−2.659	3.793		8.008		
	3.272	−3.615	4.372		10.424		
Cyprus	0.001	0.052	0.413	0.258	0.725	−0.099	0.984
	2.559	1.262	3.188		13.293		
	1.978	0.872	2.837		10.950		
Dominica	0.005	0.383	−0.374	0.196	0.507	−0.467	0.702
	1.538	2.031	−1.160		3.620		
	1.038	0.844	−0.840		1.205		
Fiji	0.007	0.604	0.019	0.614	0.121	−0.930	0.734
	5.333	4.047	0.091		1.250		
	4.253	2.665	0.056		1.391		
Maldives	0.000	0.051	−0.033	0.034	0.938	−0.026	0.972
	0.674	1.387	−0.675		19.179		
	0.452	1.155	−0.794		12.004		
Malta	0.003	0.049	0.447	0.273	0.390	−0.590	0.663
	11.111	3.495	10.600		12.236		
	3.372	0.599	0.471		1.262		
Seychelles	0.001	0.039	0.087	0.082	0.848	−0.081	0.930
	1.293	1.266	1.300		10.692		
	1.243	0.759	1.198		9.513		

Note: The three entries associated with each parameter are their respective estimate, the asymptotic t-ratios and the Bollerslev-Wooldridge (1992) robust t-ratios.

Empirical Estimates for Univariate GARCH(1,1) and GJR(1,1) for the Logarithms of Monthly International Tourist Arrivals

The conditional mean estimates of GARCH(1,1) and GJR(1,1) for the logarithm of monthly international tourist arrivals are given in Tables 5.4 and 5.6, respectively. The conditional mean estimates for GARCH(1,1) and

Table 5.8   Conditional Mean Estimates for the Log-differences of Deseasonalised and Detrended Monthly International Tourist Arrivals

Barbados

	AR(1)	MA(1)	D1	D2	D4	D5	D7	D8	D9	D10	D11	D12
	0.423	-0.824	-0.120	0.069	-0.087	-0.184	0.423	-0.206	-0.398	0.373	0.081	0.062
	7.693	-21.763	-5.664	4.099	-5.314	-10.775	19.135	-7.086	-20.654	11.747	3.289	2.548
	7.054	-18.804	-5.909	3.999	-5.157	-7.924	23.010	-6.955	-19.838	12.607	4.071	3.387

Cyprus

	AR(1)	MA(1)	D1	D2	D4	D5	D7	D8	D9	D10	D11	D12
	0.655	-0.899	-0.188	0.621	0.298	-0.165	0.188	-0.156	-0.134	-0.081	-0.585	0.236
	14.337	-53.426	-6.191	26.527	4.826	-3.201	4.510	-2.268	-1.929	-2.098	-25.012	5.778
	7.340	-22.608	-4.349	11.883	4.999	-2.677	7.281	-5.628	-9.500	-2.976	-13.778	3.241

Dominica

	AR(1)	MA(1)	D2	D4	D7	D9	D11	D12
	-0.516	-0.829	0.153	-0.243	0.430	-0.737	0.110	0.344
	-15.269	-15.287	3.971	-7.746	11.612	-19.612	1.337	4.654
	-7.844	-14.947	5.066	-8.316	15.145	-16.884	3.502	11.709

Fiji

	AR(1)	MA(2)	D1	D2	D3	D4	D5	D6	D7	D8	D9	D10	D11
	-0.446	-0.467	-0.052	-0.141	0.059	-0.061	0.063	0.064	0.184	0.209	-0.131	-0.071	-0.034
	-6.712	-7.536	-2.288	-6.103	2.988	-3.442	4.070	4.410	4.991	9.097	-4.621	-2.481	-1.418
	-6.381	-9.924	-3.455	-10.613	2.628	-1.887	1.945	2.290	10.756	9.840	-7.429	-3.545	-2.438

Maldives

	AR(1)	MA(1)	D1t	D4t	D5t	D6t	D7t	D8t	D9t	D11t	D12t
	0.517	-9.0E-01	1.1E-05	-5.1E-04	-8.9E-04	2.6E-04	1.1E-03	6.6E-05	-5.0E-04	2.1E-04	3.3E-04
	6.421	-18.909	0.124	-6.870	-9.373	1.891	11.672	0.649	-6.055	3.130	3.514
	6.156	-19.861	0.112	-7.026	-9.642	2.220	11.770	0.495	-5.817	2.648	3.807

Table 5.8 *Conditional Mean Estimates for the Log–differences of Deseasonalised and Detrended Monthly International Tourist Arrivals (continued)*

Malta	AR(1)	MA(1)				D1	D2	D3	D4	D5	D7	D9	D10	D11
	0.268	−0.683				−0.250	0.336	0.312	0.124	0.056	0.230	−0.206	−0.127	−0.461
	10.270	−14.572				−14.308	19.044	20.796	7.033	3.673	11.614	−10.611	−7.735	−33.727
	11.432	−12.238				−14.663	20.860	16.784	7.479	3.081	25.011	−17.490	−8.088	−24.825

Seychelles	AR(1)	MA(1)	t	t^2	BP-t	D2	D3	D5	D7	D8	D9	D10	D12
	0.034	−0.631	−4.6E−04	6.7E−07	−1.7E−04	0.167	0.112	−0.148	0.315	0.170	−0.116	0.229	0.194
	0.631	−12.285	−5.614	3.904	−4.150	7.743	4.446	−5.320	11.793	5.546	−4.327	9.655	7.680
	0.600	−11.947	−6.130	4.414	−3.956	5.590	4.261	−5.733	12.566	6.600	−4.853	8.886	7.704

Note: The three entries associated with each parameter are their respective estimate, the asymptotic t-ratio and the Bollerslev-Wooldridge (1992) robust t-ratios.

Table 5.9　　Conditional Variance Estimates of GARCH(1,1) for the Log-differences of Deseasonalised and Detrended Monthly International Tourist Arrivals

SITE	ω	α	β	Log-Moment	Second Moment
Barbados	1.402E–04	0.045	0.932	–0.024	0.977
	1.051	1.741	23.853		
	0.918	1.927	25.792		
Cyprus	0.006	0.619	0.313	–0.393	0.932
	3.248	4.910	3.580		
	3.339	5.165	2.984		
Dominica	0.006	0.312	0.423	–0.444	0.735
	1.584	1.952	1.588		
	1.089	1.020	1.027		
Fiji	0.005	0.372	0.340	–0.565	0.712
	4.980	5.910	3.742		
	2.814	1.639	1.942		
Maldives	1.883E–04	0.071	0.908	–0.025	0.978
	1.270	1.686	19.895		
	0.590	1.551	12.742		
Malta	3.288E–04	0.445	0.653	–0.054	1.099
	1.464	5.998	12.721		
	1.037	2.860	16.819		
Seychelles	4.436E–04	0.057	0.903	–0.044	0.959
	1.204	1.906	16.638		
	0.907	1.470	12.886		

Note:　The three entries associated with each parameter are their respective estimate, the asymptotic *t*-ratio and the Bollerslev-Wooldridge (1992) robust *t*-ratios.

GJR(1,1) are somewhat different in the seven SITEs. The AR(1) estimates for GARCH(1,1) and GJR(1,1) are highly significant for all SITEs, showing a high degree of persistence of tourist arrivals to these destinations. The estimated parameters for AR(1) in GARCH(1,1) and GJR(1,1) are very close to one for Barbados, Cyprus and Fiji. This may indicate the presence of a unit root, so that it may be appropriate to take first differences or log-

Table 5.10   Conditional Mean Estimates for the Log-differences of Deseasonalised and Detrended Monthly International Tourist Arrivals

Barbados

AR(1)	MA(1)	D1	D2	D4	D5	D7	D8	D9	D10	D11	D12
0.396	-0.803	-0.111	0.064	-0.092	-0.200	0.419	-0.186	-0.411	0.367	0.086	0.064
6.930	-22.902	-5.649	3.837	-5.978	-11.879	18.272	-6.844	-22.965	11.485	3.782	2.823
7.682	-18.519	-5.863	3.678	-5.221	-9.138	26.153	-6.568	-22.096	13.913	4.620	3.778

Cyprus

AR(1)	MA(1)	D1	D2	D4	D5	D7	D8	D9	D10	D11	D12
0.652	-0.898	-0.203	0.615	0.293	-0.167	0.191	-0.147	-0.136	-0.078	-0.585	0.241
13.107	-43.003	-6.415	24.941	5.053	-3.646	4.471	-2.260	-2.035	-2.071	-23.600	5.546
8.170	-25.912	-5.000	11.012	4.943	-2.882	7.777	-5.848	-9.219	-2.785	-13.695	3.530

Dominica

AR(1)	MA(1)	D2	D4	D7	D9	D11	D12
-0.530	-0.806	0.124	-0.216	0.444	-0.709	0.070	0.363
-11.286	-14.168	3.829	-7.456	14.687	-16.687	1.509	8.022
-13.155	-23.228	5.747	-8.283	19.883	-29.628	2.412	13.220

Fiji

AR(1)	MA(2)	D1	D2	D3	D4	D5	D6	D7	D8	D9	D10	D11
-0.422	-0.329	-0.043	-0.137	0.049	-0.066	0.079	0.057	0.190	0.192	-0.133	-0.065	-0.035
-45.816	-9.564	-1.985	-5.579	3.072	-4.468	3.996	4.181	5.644	14.179	-5.062	-2.704	-1.566
-10.452	-7.107	-3.119	-11.825	2.534	-2.437	3.261	2.172	12.711	9.539	-6.845	-4.829	-2.532

Maldives

AR(1)	MA(1)	D1t	D4t	D5t	D6t	D7t	D8t	D9t	D11t	D12t
-0.243	0.338	2.8E-04	-5.8E-04	-1.3E-03	-6.6E-04	1.0E-03	9.1E-04	-2.7E-04	2.2E-04	5.2E-04
-1.101	1.742	2.139	-9.041	-8.482	-2.501	9.802	3.498	-1.398	2.220	6.154
-2.126	3.362	3.824	-5.685	-13.134	-4.309	9.946	6.141	-2.450	2.787	6.601

Table 5.10   Conditional Mean Estimates for the Log-differences of Deseasonalised and Detrended Monthly International Tourist Arrivals (continued)

Malta

	AR(1)	MA(1)	t	t^2	BP-t	D1	D2	D3	D4	D5	D7	D9	D10	D11
	0.263	−0.695	.	.	.	−0.252	0.333	0.315	0.132	0.060	0.229	−0.207	−0.126	−0.463
	10.341	−15.113	.	.	.	−14.473	18.578	20.590	7.412	3.994	11.577	−10.057	−7.233	−33.362
	10.750	−14.949	.	.	.	−14.280	20.235	17.386	7.974	3.206	24.500	−18.118	−8.111	−24.805

Seychelles

	AR(1)	MA(1)	t	t^2	BP-t	D2	D3	D5	D7	D8	D9	D10	D12
	0.026	−0.632	−4.6−04	6.7E−07	−1.7E−04	0.164	0.110	−0.153	0.317	0.170	−0.117	0.228	0.198
	0.468	−12.203	−5.865	3.981	−4.137	7.656	4.464	−5.476	11.566	5.475	−4.293	9.535	7.996
	0.470	−12.368	−9.764	8.181	−4.060	5.573	4.459	−6.715	13.658	6.655	−5.172	9.691	8.678

Note: The three entries associated with each parameter are their respective estimate, the asymptotic *t*-ratio and the Bollerslev-Wooldridge (1992) robust *t*-ratios.

Table 5.11   *Conditional Variance Estimates of GJR(1,1) for the Log-differences of Deseasonalised and Detrended Monthly International Tourist Arrivals*

SITE	ω	α	γ	$\alpha+\gamma/2$	β	Log-Moment	Second Moment
Barbados	3.4E–05	–0.050	0.102	2.9E–04	0.996	–0.008	0.996
	1.251	–2.853	2.795		12.647		
	0.893	–3.273	3.119		6.810		
Cyprus	0.006	0.406	0.465	0.638	0.338	–0.368	0.976
	3.115	3.165	1.672		3.608		
	3.064	3.265	1.414		3.079		
Dominica	0.001	0.224	–0.434	0.007	0.967	–0.084	0.974
	2.113	3.712	–4.767		18.940		
	1.634	2.683	–2.730		37.160		
Fiji	0.010	0.552	0.024	0.564	–0.083	–1.810	0.482
	9.905	4.438	0.154		–2.270		
	6.053	2.631	0.061		–1.442		
Maldives	0.008	–0.142	0.275	–0.005	0.328	–1.230	0.323
	1.497	–3.105	2.091		0.684		
	3.399	–6.689	2.385		1.591		
Malta	2.8E–04	0.496	–0.173	0.410	0.677	–0.048	1.087
	1.266	4.282	–1.143		12.435		
	1.062	2.208	–0.904		18.391		
Seychelles	0.001	0.009	0.096	0.057	0.869	–0.080	0.926
	1.781	0.206	1.929		15.163		
	1.000	0.224	1.272		8.364		

Note: The three entries associated with each parameter are their respective estimate, the asymptotic t-ratio and the Bollerslev-Wooldridge (1992) robust t-ratios.

differences to obtain stationarity, which we have already taken into account. Moreover, it is important to note the negative coefficient of the AR(1) term for Dominica in the case of GARCH(1,1) and GJR(1,1), while the moving average estimates are highly significant for all but Barbados. The significance of the moving average term indicates that the unconditional shock in the previous periods accounts for the determination of tourist arrivals in the current period.

The large majority of the coefficients of the 12 seasonal dummies incorporated in the conditional mean are significant, indicating that there is strong seasonality in monthly international tourist arrivals in these SITEs. The estimates for the seasonal dummies significantly indicate consistency with the seasonal indexes that are presented in Table 5.2. For the logarithm of monthly international tourist arrivals, the estimates of the conditional volatility using GARCH(1,1) and GJR(1,1) are highly satisfactory. The sufficient conditions $\omega > 0$, $\alpha_i \geq 0$, $\beta_i \geq 0$ to ensure positivity of the conditional variance are met for all seven SITEs, where both the ARCH and GARCH effects are significant for GARCH(1,1). However, for GJR(1,1) the only satisfactory estimates are available for Cyprus and Malta, where the ARCH, GARCH and the asymmetric effects are all significant. Although the asymmetric estimate for Barbados in GJR(1,1) is significant, the ARCH component has a negative sign, which suggests that the model may be misspecified.

It is worth noting that the log-moment and second moment conditions are satisfied for both GARCH(1,1) and GJR(1,1) for all seven SITEs, which is a strong empirical result. Therefore, the moments exist, and the QMLE of the coefficients of the conditional variance for both these models are consistent and asymptotically normal. Hence, inferences regarding these estimates can be implemented for policy analysis and formulation. The estimates of α, or short-run persistence, and β, which is the contribution of the shocks to long-run persistence, are all significant. It is worth noting that, in the case of Maldives, the GARCH effect is very strong. The significance of the asymmetric effect, γ, for both Cyprus and Malta is worth noting. If there is a negative shock to the growth rate of monthly international tourist arrivals to either of these two countries, then there would be greater uncertainty about tourist arrivals in subsequent periods. Cyprus has had a volatile political climate for an extended period, which has created greater uncertainty for tourists. Similarly, as mentioned in Chapter 4, it has been well documented that the events of 11 September, 2001 created greater uncertainty in tourist arrivals in the months thereafter.

Empirical Estimates for Univariate GARCH(1,1) and GJR(1,1) for the Growth Rate of Monthly International Tourist Arrivals

The conditional mean estimates for GARCH(1,1) and GJR(1,1) for the growth rate of monthly international tourist arrivals are given in Tables 5.8 and 5.10, respectively. The conditional means for both GARCH(1,1) and GJR(1,1) vary among the seven destination countries, but not substantially. Generally, the conditional mean estimates are highly satisfactory for the growth rate of monthly international tourist arrivals. The AR(1) estimates for

GARCH(1,1) and GJR(1,1) are significant for all seven SITEs, except for Seychelles. The MA(1) estimates for GARCH(1,1) are significant for all SITEs, and MA(2) estimates are significant for Fiji. Virtually all of the estimates of the seasonal dummy variables in both GARCH(1,1) and GJR(1,1) are significant at the 5 per cent level.

The estimates of the conditional volatility using GARCH(1,1) and GJR(1,1) for the growth rate of monthly international tourist arrivals in Tables 5.9 and 5.11 are highly satisfactory for all SITEs. The second moment condition is satisfied for all SITEs except Malta. However, the weaker log-moment condition holds for Malta, so the QMLE are consistent and asymptotically normal. It can be observed from the conditional variance estimates that the α and β estimates are significant. The highest GARCH effects are estimated for Barbados, Maldives and Seychelles, respectively. This is perfectly plausible because, in the case of Barbados, the adverse effects of US business cycles on tourist arrivals are prolonged, while in the Maldives the macroeconomic conditions in Europe hamper tourist arrivals more than anticipated. It is also evident for Seychelles that the effects of the second oil shock of 1979 and the 1991 Gulf War reduced tourist arrivals for the periods subsequent to those events.

An interesting feature of the results in Table 5.11 is that the estimate of the asymmetric effect in GJR(1,1) is negative for Dominica. This outcome implies that the short- and long-run effects of a negative shock in the growth rate of monthly international arrivals will result in less uncertainty in subsequent periods for Dominica. However, for Barbados, Maldives and Seychelles, if there is a negative shock to the expected growth rate of monthly international tourist arrivals, there will be greater uncertainty in subsequent periods. This is perfectly plausible, particularly in the case of Barbados where the major tourist source market is the USA, and any negative shock such as the US recession of the early 1980s and the events of 11 September, 2001 undermines the perceptions of international travellers.

The estimates for the univariate analysis presented above shows satisfactory results, particularly the GARCH(1,1) estimates for the logarithms and the log-differences in monthly international tourist arrivals. The GJR(1,1) models are preferable to GARCH(1,1) models since the GJR(1,1) captures the asymmetric effects, where more information is available for policy formulation and marketing strategy design. Therefore, for logarithms, the estimated asymmetric models for Cyprus and Malta, and for the log-differences, the estimated asymmetric models for Dominica and Maldives, are preferable. The preferred model for the remaining series is the symmetric GARCH(1,1) model.

5.7 EMPIRICAL ESTIMATES FOR MULTIVARIATE MODELS OF VOLATILITY

This section presents the estimates for various multivariate models. First, the CCC-MGARCII (Bollerslev, 1990) estimates are presented. These results are the common sample conditional correlation coefficients of the standardised residuals from the GARCH(1,1) model in equation (5.4) and the GJR(1,1) model in equation (5.9). This will be followed by discussion of estimates for the VARMA-GARCH(1,1) model of Ling and McAleer (2003) and the VARMA-AGARCH(1,1) model of McAleer et al. (2008).

Empirical Estimates of CCC for Univariate GARCH(1,1) and GJR(1,1) for the Logarithms and Growth Rate of Monthly International Tourist Arrivals

The CCC-MGARCH(1,1) estimates are presented in Tables 5.12–5.14. In general, the magnitude of these conditional correlation coefficients of the standardised residuals is relatively small in all seven cases. Therefore, shocks to monthly international tourist arrivals to these seven SITEs do not affect inbound tourism in the other SITEs. These results show that inbound tourism in these SITEs is complementary. The estimated conditional correlation coefficients for the GARCH(1,1) models for the logarithms and growth rate of monthly international tourist arrivals are very similar. The only negative estimate occurs between Maldives and Dominica.

For the logarithms and the growth rate series, the highest correlation coefficients, 0.371 and 0.368, respectively, are estimated between Malta and Seychelles. For the same two series, the lowest estimated correlation coefficients, –0.066 and –0.045, respectively, are estimated between Maldives and Dominica, which are also the only negative correlation coefficients for the GARCH(1,1) estimates. For these two SITEs, marketing efforts by tour operators and national governments will have to be diversified because a shock to monthly international tourist arrivals in either of these two SITEs will have opposite effects. Since the magnitude of the coefficient is negligible at close to zero, the effects of shocks to monthly international tourism demand in either of these two SITEs are independent. The same inference can be made for these two SITEs, in relation to the estimated CCCs in the growth rate of monthly tourist arrivals.

An interesting result can be observed in the estimated conditional correlation coefficients of the standardised residuals, where the highest estimates of 0.371 and 0.368 for the logarithms and the growth rate of monthly international tourist arrivals, respectively, are for the same pair of SITEs, namely Seychelles and Malta. The impacts of monthly international

Table 5.12 *Constant Conditional Correlations of Standardised Residuals of GARCH(1,1) for the Logarithms of Deseasonalised and Detrended Monthly International Tourist Arrivals*

SITE	Barbados	Cyprus	Dominica	Fiji	Maldives	Malta	Seychelles
Barbados	1						
Cyprus	0.204	1					
Dominica	0.038	0.072	1				
Fiji	0.160	0.024	0.067	1			
Maldives	0.066	0.142	−0.066	0.218	1		
Malta	0.093	0.168	0.225	0.170	0.059	1	
Seychelles	0.250	0.357	0.092	0.201	0.153	0.371	1

Table 5.13 *Constant Conditional Correlations of Standardised Residuals of GJR(1,1) for the Logarithms of Deseasonalised and Detrended Monthly International Tourist Arrivals*

SITE	Barbados	Cyprus	Dominica	Fiji	Maldives	Malta	Seychelles
Barbados	1						
Cyprus	0.067	1					
Dominica	0.124	−0.074	1				
Fiji	−0.003	−0.045	0.068	1			
Maldives	0.044	0.106	−0.022	0.253	1		
Malta	0.064	0.166	0.110	0.106	0.050	1	
Seychelles	0.195	0.297	0.098	0.128	0.039	0.303	1

Table 5.14 *Constant Conditional Correlations of Standardised Residuals of GARCH(1,1) for the Log-differences of Deseasonalised and Detrended Monthly International Tourist Arrivals*

SITE	Barbados	Cyprus	Dominica	Fiji	Maldives	Malta	Seychelles
Barbados	1						
Cyprus	0.241	1					
Dominica	0.155	0.020	1				
Fiji	0.147	0.026	−0.045	1			
Maldives	0.108	0.150	0.086	0.115	1		
Malta	0.268	0.118	0.175	0.136	0.122	1	
Seychelles	0.331	0.285	0.115	0.179	0.113	0.368	1

tourist arrivals in these two pairs of SITEs will lead to similar effects. Hence, tour operators will have to emphasise their promotional activities in selling holiday packages to SITEs which produce the highest growth rates in monthly international tourist arrivals. The estimated conditional correlation coefficients of standardised shocks in the growth rate of monthly international tourist arrivals are relatively larger in magnitude compared with the estimates for the logarithms of monthly international tourist arrivals. The highest conditional correlation coefficient estimate is 0.368 between Malta and Seychelles, followed by 0.331 between Barbados and Seychelles, and 0.285 between Seychelles and Cyprus. In general, these estimates indicate that the shocks to inbound tourism to these SITEs have similar effects to each other, so that the markets are segmented.

Table 5.13 shows the estimated conditional correlation coefficients of the logarithm of monthly tourist arrivals when asymmetric effects are taken into account. In this case, the highest and the lowest conditional correlation coefficients are estimated for the same pair of SITEs, as discussed above. When asymmetry is incorporated, three new negative correlation coefficients emerge, namely between Fiji–Barbados, Fiji–Cyprus and Dominica–Cyprus. These imply that shocks to the logarithm of monthly tourist arrivals in one of these SITEs have an opposite effect on the other. Taking into account the overall estimates of the conditional correlations of the standardised shocks to monthly international tourist arrivals to these seven SITEs, we can conclude that there is a moderate level of complementarity between the tourism products of the respective SITEs. The conditional correlation coefficients of the standardised shocks of GJR(1,1) for the growth rate of monthly tourist arrivals have not been estimated because the univariate results presented in Table 5.11 were only statistically significant for Seychelles, but not otherwise.

Empirical Estimates for VARMA-GARCH(1,1) and VARMA-AGARCH(1,1) for the Logarithms and Growth Rate of Monthly International Tourist Arrivals

This section discusses empirical estimates for the multivariate models that were discussed in Section 5.6, namely the VARMA-GARCH(1,1) and the VARMA-AGARCH(1,1) models, to investigate the country dependent and interdependent effects of the conditional volatilities from one SITE to another, and to capture the asymmetric behaviour of the unconditional shock on the conditional volatility.

The models are estimated using the longest sample available between SITEs, and such a sample of 434 observations is only available for Fiji and Malta from January 1968 to February 2004. The second longest sample with 398 observations is available for three SITEs, namely Fiji, Malta and

Seychelles from January 1971 to February 2004. For four SITEs, namely Barbados, Fiji, Malta and Seychelles, the third longest sample with 360 data points is from January 1973 to December 2002, and a final sample of 324 observations from January 1976 to December 2002 are taken for five SITEs, which are Barbados, Cyprus, Fiji, Malta and Seychelles. As the sample size decreases, the number of SITEs included in the sample increases. Furthermore, there are samples available including six and seven SITEs with 204 and 144 observations, respectively, but the empirical estimates of the QMLE for the models based on these two samples did not converge using either the Marquandt or the BHHH algorithm, and so are not included here. Statistically valid inference on the estimates for purposes of policy formulation and designing marketing strategies from the different sample periods are made independently. For the respective SITEs, the same conditional means of equations (5.21) and (5.23) were used in this analysis. For reasons of brevity, the conditional mean estimates are not presented.

The results for VARMA-GARCH(1,1) and VARMA-AGARCH(1,1) for the four separate sample periods are given in Tables 5.15–5.22, and suggest strong country effects for the logarithm of monthly tourist arrivals. From the estimates for Fiji and Malta in Table 5.15, there is evidence to suggest that contributions of shocks to long-run persistence in monthly international tourist arrivals to Fiji affect the monthly tourist arrivals to Malta, but the converse does not hold. This result is plausible because the effect of the *coups d'état* in 1988 and 2000 in Fiji affect the monthly international tourist

Table 5.15   Conditional Variance Estimates of VARMA-GARCH(1,1) of the Logarithms of Deseasonalised and Detrended Monthly International Tourist Arrivals in Fiji and Malta

Fiji	ω	α_{FJI}	β_{FJI}	α_{MLT}	β_{MLT}
	0.007	0.439	0.139	−0.003	0.001
	9.507	6.661	3.724	−3.501	0.128
	4.162	2.983	2.055	−1.409	−0.787
Malta	ω	α_{MLT}	β_{MLT}	α_{FJI}	β_{FJI}
	0.013	0.357	0.279	−0.007	−0.039
	4.173	6.088	1.912	−0.536	−2.424
	4.173	6.088	1.912	−0.536	−2.424

Notes:
The three entries associated with each parameter are their respective estimate, the asymptotic *t*-ratios and the Bollerslev-Wooldridge (1992) robust *t*-ratios.
The parameters in Equation (5.16) associated with Fiji and Malta are denoted by subscripts FJI and MLT.

Table 5.16　　*Conditional Variance Estimates of VARMA-GARCH(1,1) of the International Tourist Arrivals in Fiji, Malta and Seychelles*

Fiji	ω	α_{FJI}	β_{FJI}	α_{MLT}	β_{MLT}	α_{SYC}	β_{SYC}
	0.001	0.658	0.189	0.565	−0.097	−0.118	0.284
	0.401	5.209	2.682	5.197	−1.676	−6.580	2.305
	0.449	3.048	2.530	3.653	v2.443	v4.428	2.538
Malta	ω	α_{MLT}	β_{MLT}	α_{FJI}	β_{FJI}	α_{SYC}	β_{SYC}
	0.002	0.095	0.632	−0.008	0.009	0.028	−0.005
	2.475	1.891	15.088	−7.530	2.745	0.608	−0.069
	1.684	1.478	3.186	−5.273	1.059	0.862	−0.048
Seychelles	ω	α_{SYC}	β_{SYC}	α_{FJI}	β_{FJI}	α_{MLT}	β_{MLT}
	0.008	0.082	0.324	0.006	−0.009	0.007	−0.010
	2.057	1.261	1.103	0.243	−0.340	0.683	−1.408
	2.461	1.124	1.217	0.885	−1.028	1.096	−2.695

Notes:
The three entries associated with each parameter are their respective estimate, the asymptotic *t*-ratios and the Bollerslev-Wooldridge (1992) robust *t*-ratios.
The parameters in Equation (5.16) associated with Fiji, Malta and Seychelles are denoted by subscripts FJI, MLT and SYC.

arrivals in Malta. According to these results, the logarithm of monthly tourist arrivals to Fiji is only affected by its previous own short and long run shocks.

The estimates in Table 5.16, between Fiji, Malta and Seychelles, are indicative of substantial country effects in the monthly international tourist arrivals. The monthly international tourist arrivals in Fiji are affected by its own previous short- and long-run shocks, as well as those of Malta and Seychelles, whereas for Malta, the monthly international tourist arrivals are affected by its own short- and long-run shocks, coupled with the short- and long-run shocks to the conditional variance of the monthly international tourist arrivals to Fiji. These univariate results suggest that the tourism products of Malta and Fiji are complements, because there is evidence of strong interdependency between monthly international tourist arrivals between these two SITEs.

Based on the results in Table 5.17, the monthly international tourist arrivals to Barbados are affected by its own previous long-run shocks to the conditional variance, due to the effect of US business cycles and the previous short- and long-run shocks to the monthly international tourist arrivals in both Malta and Seychelles. The monthly international tourist arrivals in Fiji are affected by its own previous period short- and long-run shocks to the conditional variance, and the short-run shock to tourist arrivals in Seychelles.

Table 5.17   *Conditional Variance Estimates of VARMA-GARCH(1,1) of the Logarithms of Deseasonalised and Detrended Monthly International Tourist Arrivals in Barbados, Fiji, Malta and Seychelles*

Barbados	ω	α_{BRB}	β_{BRB}	α_{FJI}	β_{FJI}	α_{MLT}	β_{MLT}	α_{SYC}	β_{SYC}
	0.002	−0.022	0.005	−0.001	−3.9E−04	0.058	−0.065	0.014	−0.112
	10.979	−2.403	10.363	−0.180	−0.082	14.360	−15.616	2.888	−18.342
	12.509	−1.262	5.920	−0.310	−0.129	1.648	−1.605	2.856	−7.507
Fiji	ω	α_{FJI}	β_{FJI}	α_{BRB}	β_{BRB}	α_{MLT}	β_{MLT}	α_{SYC}	β_{SYC}
	0.017	0.158	0.461	−0.116	−0.204	−0.002	−0.003	−0.112	−0.170
	1.587	3.080	4.003	−1.439	−0.643	−0.323	−0.554	−3.300	−0.192
	2.275	0.791	1.774	−1.102	−0.807	−0.707	−0.513	−6.129	−0.284
Malta	ω	α_{MLT}	β_{MLT}	α_{BRB}	β_{BRB}	α_{FJI}	β_{FJI}	α_{SYC}	β_{SYC}
	0.020	0.083	0.497	−0.153	−0.236	−0.012	−0.020	−0.104	−0.288
	2.135	0.402	2.239	−1.146	−0.463	−0.509	−0.659	−1.569	−0.262
	1.244	1.438	2.897	−4.961	−1.258	−1.934	−1.528	−11.709	−0.282
Seychelles	ω	α_{SYC}	β_{SYC}	α_{BRB}	β_{BRB}	α_{FJI}	β_{FJI}	α_{MLT}	β_{MLT}
	0.003	0.106	0.574	0.056	0.045	−0.001	−0.001	−0.003	0.011
	1.461	1.727	2.289	0.800	0.286	−0.090	−0.057	−0.367	0.677
	1.233	1.352	2.007	0.594	0.395	−0.153	−0.085	−4.437	1.528

Notes:
The three entries associated with each parameter are their respective estimate, the asymptotic *t*-ratios and the Bollerslev-Wooldridge (1992) robust *t*-ratios.
The parameters in Equation (5.16) associated with Barbados, Fiji, Malta and Seychelles are denoted by subscripts BRB, FJI, MLT and SYC.

For Seychelles, the monthly tourist arrivals are only affected by its own short- and long-run shocks to the conditional variance in the previous period. These results indicate that inbound tourism to Barbados and Malta are interdependent, so that substitutability of the tourism product of these two SITEs is reasonably close. The tourism product of Seychelles is moderately substitutable because there is evidence of dependencies.

In the empirical results presented for the VARMA-GARCH(1,1) model in Table 5.18 for five SITEs, the estimates for Cyprus are all insignificant. For Fiji, the conditional variance of monthly international tourist arrivals is affected by its own short and long impacts, as well as those of Barbados, the previous short-run effects in Cyprus, and the lagged short- and long-run effects of Malta. Seychelles' monthly inbound international tourism is affected by its own short-run effect, the long-run effects of Barbados and Cyprus, and the short-run effects of Cyprus and Fiji.

Table 5.18   *Conditional Variance Estimates of VARMA-GARCH(1,1) of the Logarithms of Deseasonalised and Detrended Monthly International Tourist Arrivals in Barbados, Cyprus, Fiji, Malta and Seychelles*

Barbados	ω	α_{BRB}	β_{BRB}	α_{CYP}	β_{CYP}	α_{FJI}	β_{FJI}	α_{MLT}	β_{MLT}	α_{SYC}	β_{SYC}
	4.6E–05	0.031	0.673	0.018	–0.005	0.000	–0.003	0.057	0.074	0.002	0.046
	0.035	0.822	3.861	1.642	–0.349	0.148	–1.085	1.118	0.289	0.081	0.788
	0.039	0.788	3.698	1.707	–0.386	0.174	–1.371	1.026	0.325	0.074	0.654
Cyprus	ω	α_{CYP}	β_{CYP}	α_{BRB}	β_{BRB}	α_{FJI}	β_{FJI}	α_{MLT}	β_{MLT}	α_{SYC}	β_{SYC}
	0.004	0.133	0.075	0.193	0.038	–0.009	–0.020	–0.036	–0.161	0.124	1.536
	3.536	1.847	0.168	0.595	0.033	–0.596	–1.471	–0.158	–0.184	0.852	1.628
	0.279	1.293	0.209	1.086	0.019	–1.863	–1.601	–0.257	–0.302	0.460	1.438
Fiji	ω	α_{FJI}	β_{FJI}	α_{BRB}	β_{BRB}	α_{CYP}	β_{CYP}	α_{MLT}	β_{MLT}	α_{SYC}	β_{SYC}
	0.013	0.234	0.469	0.214	–0.756	0.095	–0.011	0.825	–1.318	–0.027	–0.169
	6.174	4.082	6.890	1.955	–2.702	4.188	–0.425	7.378	–5.092	–0.742	–1.160
	6.174	4.082	6.890	1.955	–2.702	4.188	–0.425	7.378	–5.092	–0.742	–1.160
Malta	ω	α_{MLT}	β_{MLT}	α_{BRB}	β_{BRB}	α_{CYP}	β_{CYP}	α_{FJI}	β_{FJI}	α_{SYC}	β_{SYC}
	0.001	0.091	0.373	–0.017	0.085	0.036	0.024	0.002	–0.005	–0.003	–0.006
	1.011	2.318	1.749	–0.560	0.426	2.846	0.895	0.302	–1.246	–0.179	–0.066
	0.915	1.511	1.430	–0.318	0.445	1.825	0.772	0.348	–1.317	–0.136	–0.064
Seychelles	ω	α_{SYC}	β_{SYC}	α_{BRB}	β_{BRB}	α_{CYP}	β_{CYP}	α_{FJI}	β_{FJI}	α_{MLT}	β_{MLT}
	0.008	0.203	–0.021	0.241	–0.791	–0.034	0.182	–0.004	–0.002	0.097	–0.037
	1.929	2.448	–0.088	1.744	–1.363	–1.899	2.650	–0.396	–0.217	0.731	–0.071
	2.886	2.590	–0.128	1.716	–2.191	–3.480	3.922	–2.000	–0.239	1.293	–0.119

Notes:
The three entries associated with each parameter are their respective estimate, the asymptotic *t*-ratios and the Bollerslev-Wooldridge (1992) robust *t*-ratios.
The parameters in Equation (5.16) associated with Barbados, Cyprus, Fiji, Malta and Seychelles are denoted by subscripts BRB, CYP, FJI, MLT and SYC.

Examining the results in Table 5.19, there is no evidence to detect asymmetry between Malta and Fiji. However, the results presented in Table 5.20 show the presence of asymmetric behaviour in the case of Fiji and Seychelles, and are 0.890 and 0.187, respectively. Furthermore, there is a significant impact of asymmetry for Fiji in the results presented in Table 5.21. This implies that a negative shock to the monthly international tourist arrivals in the case of Fiji and Seychelles has a greater impact on the conditional variance than a positive shock. This is perfectly plausible because, for the case of Fiji, the negative impact of the *coups d'état* of 1988

Table 5.19   *Conditional Variance Estimates of VARMA-AGARCH(1,1) of the Logarithms of Deseasonalised and Detrended Monthly International Tourist Arrivals in Fiji and Malta*

Fiji	ω	α_{FJI}	γ_{FJI}	β_{FJI}	α_{MLT}	β_{MLT}
	0.007	0.378	−0.017	0.227	−0.003	0.000
	7.204	4.354	−0.116	3.428	−6.463	−0.351
	7.204	4.354	−0.116	3.428	−6.463	−0.351
Malta	ω	α_{MLT}	γ_{MLT}	β_{MLT}	α_{FJI}	β_{FJI}
	0.026	0.145	0.047	0.559	−0.025	−0.063
	1.607	0.393	0.100	2.114	−0.970	−1.355
	1.464	0.545	0.177	1.809	−0.493	−0.622

Notes:
The three entries associated with each parameter are their respective estimate, the asymptotic *t*-ratios and the Bollerslev-Wooldridge (1992) robust *t*-ratios.
The parameters in Equation (5.18) associated with Fiji and Malta are denoted by subscripts FJI and MLT.

Table 5.20   *Conditional Variance Estimates of VARMA-AGARCH(1,1) of the Logarithms of Deseasonalised and Detrended Monthly International Tourist Arrivals in Fiji, Malta and Seychelles*

Fiji	ω	α_{FJI}	γ_{FJI}	β_{FJI}	α_{MLT}	β_{MLT}	α_{SYC}	β_{SYC}
	0.002	−0.013	0.890	0.391	0.393	−0.142	−0.082	0.161
	2.191	−0.178	4.507	5.698	4.214	−2.822	−2.701	1.893
	1.399	−0.423	2.148	5.496	4.086	−6.643	−2.815	1.584
Malta	ω	α_{MLT}	γ_{MLT}	β_{MLT}	α_{FJI}	β_{FJI}	α_{SYC}	β_{SYC}
	0.002	0.041	0.081	0.663	0.008	−0.007	0.014	0.040
	2.177	0.646	1.004	13.753	1.576	−2.787	0.298	0.513
	2.235	0.660	0.984	4.623	0.583	−1.276	0.527	0.621
Seychelles	ω	α_{SYC}	γ_{SYC}	β_{SYC}	α_{FJI}	β_{FJI}	α_{MLT}	β_{MLT}
	0.004	0.029	0.187	0.576	0.006	−0.004	−0.003	0.001
	1.762	0.457	1.967	2.966	0.230	−0.362	−0.170	0.057
	1.587	0.598	1.235	2.409	1.041	−1.363	−5.629	0.830

Notes:
The three entries associated with each parameter are their respective estimate, the asymptotic *t*-ratios and the Bollerslev-Wooldridge (1992) robust *t*-ratios.
The parameters in Equation (5.18) associated with Fiji, Malta and Seychelles are denoted by subscripts FJI, MLT and SYC.

*Table 5.21   Conditional Variance Estimates of VARMA-AGARCH(1,1) of
the Logarithms of Deseasonalised and Detrended Monthly
International Tourist Arrivals in Barbados, Fiji, Malta and
Seychelles*

Barbados	ω	α_{BRB}	γ_{BRB}	β_{BRB}	α_{FJI}	β_{FJI}	α_{MLT}	β_{MLT}	α_{SYC}	β_{SYC}
	0.001	0.017	0.093	0.621	0.003	−0.010	0.044	0.054	0.016	0.022
	0.540	0.230	0.985	4.368	0.667	−1.987	1.176	0.406	0.587	0.645
	0.473	0.262	1.114	7.929	1.423	−3.520	1.436	0.408	0.841	0.876
Fiji	ω	α_{FJI}	γ_{FJI}	β_{FJI}	α_{BRB}	β_{BRB}	α_{MLT}	β_{MLT}	α_{SYC}	β_{SYC}
	−0.002	0.721	−0.374	0.352	0.069	0.095	−0.008	0.191	0.405	−0.102
	−0.638	4.395	−2.052	4.939	0.997	0.358	−0.334	0.839	4.115	−1.680
	−0.590	2.607	−1.322	4.117	0.737	0.554	−0.408	0.737	2.961	−2.566
Malta	ω	α_{MLT}	γ_{MLT}	β_{MLT}	α_{BRB}	β_{BRB}	α_{FJI}	β_{FJI}	α_{SYC}	β_{SYC}
	0.021	0.084	−0.071	0.536	−0.147	−0.273	−0.015	−0.023	−0.094	−0.214
	3.348	0.346	−0.246	3.573	−0.882	−0.557	−0.616	−0.874	−0.826	−0.380
	1.734	0.430	−0.315	2.218	−3.556	−0.929	−1.720	−1.570	−5.797	−0.701
Seychelles	ω	α_{SYC}	γ_{SYC}	β_{SYC}	α_{BRB}	β_{BRB}	α_{FJI}	β_{FJI}	α_{MLT}	β_{MLT}
	0.002	0.047	0.134	0.590	0.036	0.040	0.001	−0.001	−0.003	0.013
	1.801	0.968	1.206	3.188	0.521	0.333	0.019	−0.056	−4.908	0.873
	1.412	0.590	0.996	2.599	0.531	0.407	0.064	−0.107	−4.415	1.587

Notes:
The three entries associated with each parameter are their respective estimate, the asymptotic
t-ratios and the Bollerslev-Wooldridge (1992) robust t-ratios.
The parameters in Equation (5.18) associated with Barbados, Fiji, Malta and Seychelles are
denoted by subscripts BRB, FJI, MLT and SYC.

and 2000 on monthly international tourist arrivals further aggravate the
uncertainty inbound tourism in subsequent months. Likewise, for the case of
Seychelles, the impact of the first oil shock of 1973 and the second oil shock
of 1979 adversely affected inbound tourism and carried forward the
uncertainty in subsequent periods. In the results presented in Table 5.22,
there are no significant asymmetric effects.

In essence, the empirical results presented in Tables 5.15 to 5.22 have
shown strong country effects, as well as significant asymmetric behaviour
that are worth noting. The results are mixed for the different sample periods.
However, the empirical results that are presented in Tables 5.16 and 5.20
estimated for the second longest sample for the three SITEs, namely Fiji,
Malta and Seychelles, are preferred.

The empirical results of the VARMA-GARCH(1,1) and VARMA-
AGARCH(1,1) models for the growth rate of monthly international tourist

Table 5.22   *Conditional Variance Estimates of VARMA-AGARCH(1,1) of the Logarithms of Deseasonalised and Detrended Monthly International Tourist Arrivals in Barbados, Cyprus, Fiji, Malta and Seychelles*

Barbados

	ω	α_{BRB}	γ_{BRB}	β_{BRB}	α_{CYP}	β_{CYP}	α_{FIJ}	β_{FIJ}	α_{MLT}	β_{MLT}	α_{SYC}	β_{SYC}
	0.001	−0.016	0.111	0.579	0.023	0.001	0.000	−0.004	−0.011	−0.010	0.031	0.155
	1.172	−0.652	1.304	5.862	2.614	0.067	0.244	−4.575	−0.895	−0.443	1.110	1.665
	0.790	−0.198	1.178	3.924	1.798	0.048	0.132	−2.652	−0.489	−0.211	0.724	0.926

Cyprus

	ω	α_{CYP}	γ_{CYP}	β_{CYP}	α_{BRB}	β_{BRB}	α_{FIJ}	β_{FIJ}	α_{MLT}	β_{MLT}	α_{SYC}	β_{SYC}
	0.015	0.147	0.004	−0.097	0.047	1.050	−0.009	−0.029	−0.005	0.456	−0.047	0.168
	5.454	1.451	0.033	−0.339	0.226	1.382	−0.501	−2.765	−0.036	0.992	−0.209	0.230
	5.454	1.451	0.033	−0.339	0.226	1.382	−0.501	−2.765	−0.036	0.992	−0.209	0.230

Fiji

	ω	α_{FIJ}	γ_{FIJ}	β_{FIJ}	α_{BRB}	β_{BRB}	α_{CYP}	β_{CYP}	α_{MLT}	β_{MLT}	α_{SYC}	β_{SYC}
	0.004	0.539	−0.186	0.297	0.139	−0.001	0.053	0.055	0.016	−0.188	0.663	−0.662
	2.048	2.772	−0.930	4.340	1.263	−0.003	2.781	2.402	0.331	−2.339	5.530	−4.840
	1.916	2.679	−0.632	3.435	1.486	−0.003	3.445	1.607	0.637	−3.426	3.424	−4.718

Malta

	ω	α_{MLT}	γ_{MLT}	β_{MLT}	α_{BRB}	β_{BRB}	α_{CYP}	β_{CYP}	α_{FIJ}	β_{FIJ}	α_{SYC}	β_{SYC}
	0.001	0.080	0.020	0.526	−0.024	0.044	0.051	0.003	0.004	−0.007	0.027	−0.069
	1.249	0.866	0.184	5.460	−0.527	0.233	3.401	0.257	2.056	−4.936	0.649	−1.311
	1.701	1.150	0.234	3.915	−0.513	0.342	3.344	0.213	0.493	−1.559	0.927	−1.356

Seychelles

	ω	α_{SYC}	γ_{SYC}	β_{SYC}	α_{BRB}	β_{BRB}	α_{CYP}	β_{CYP}	α_{FIJ}	β_{FIJ}	α_{MLT}	β_{MLT}
	0.008	0.071	0.153	0.197	0.202	−0.320	−0.033	0.098	−0.008	−0.003	0.105	−0.175
	3.374	0.954	1.209	1.136	1.729	−1.530	−2.613	2.018	−1.468	−0.425	0.908	−0.577
	4.098	1.065	1.114	1.192	1.473	−1.845	−2.959	3.287	−4.632	−0.667	1.501	−0.976

Notes: The three entries associated with each parameter are their respective estimate, the asymptotic *t*-ratios and the Bollerslev-Wooldridge (1992) robust *t*-ratios. The parameters in Equation (5.18) associated with Barbados, Cyprus, Fiji, Malta and Seychelles are denoted by subscripts BRB, CYP, FIJ, MLT and SYC.

211

The Economics of Small Island Tourism

arrivals are illustrated in Tables 5.23–5.30. Compared with the empirical results presented in Table 5.15 for the logarithms of monthly international tourist arrivals, the empirical results presented in Table 5.23 for the growth rate of monthly tourist arrivals in for Fiji and Malta show stronger country effects. Furthermore, there is strong evidence of interdependency in the growth rate of monthly tourist arrivals between these two SITEs. Although these two SITEs are geographically far apart, there is evidence to suggest the respective tourism products of these two countries feature substitutability.

Empirical estimates presented in Table 5.24 show that the growth rate in inbound tourism in Fiji is substantially affected by the previous short- and long-run impacts to the conditional variance of its own, as well as the previous short-run effect to the conditional variance of inbound tourism growth rate in Malta. However, the converse does not hold. The growth rate of tourist arrivals in Malta is affected by the previous long-run impact and the previous short-run impact of the conditional variance of the growth rate in monthly international tourism arrivals to Seychelles. The conditional variance of the growth rate in monthly international tourism in Seychelles is only affected by its own long-run impact to the conditional variance. Seychelles has shown weaker country effects both in the case of the logarithm of arrivals and growth rate in the analysis of the second largest sample.

When Barbados is incorporated into the analysis, the results of the estimates for this particular case of examining the multivariate effects of the growth rate of tourist arrivals for four SITEs are revealed in Table 5.25. The

Table 5.23   *Conditional Variance Estimates of VARMA-GARCH(1,1) of the Log-differences of Deseasonalised and Detrended Monthly International Tourist Arrivals in Fiji and Malta*

Fiji	ω	α_{FJI}	β_{FJI}	α_{MLT}	β_{MLT}
	0.008	0.438	0.133	−0.003	−0.001
	6.995	6.529	1.986	−3.727	−0.114
	3.681	1.790	0.900	−8.240	−0.418
Malta	ω	α_{MLT}	β_{MLT}	α_{FJI}	β_{FJI}
	0.002	0.669	0.369	0.025	−0.037
	4.525	6.755	7.625	1.219	−2.004
	4.918	2.669	5.440	3.471	−4.475

Notes:
The three entries associated with each parameter are their respective estimate, the asymptotic *t*-ratios and the Bollerslev-Wooldridge (1992) robust *t*-ratios.
The parameters in Equation (5.16) associated with Fiji and Malta are denoted by subscripts FJI, and MLT.

Table 5.24   *Conditional Variance Estimates of VARMA-GARCH(1,1) of the Log-differences of Deseasonalised and Detrended Monthly International Tourist Arrivals in Fiji, Malta and Seychelles*

Fiji	ω	α_{FJI}	β_{FJI}	α_{MLT}	β_{MLT}	α_{SYC}	β_{SYC}
	−4.47E−04	0.570	0.170	0.776	−0.025	−0.021	0.129
	−2.686	6.098	2.837	6.371	−0.355	−0.955	1.877
	−3.664	3.040	2.307	3.931	−1.055	−1.572	1.621
Malta	ω	α_{MLT}	β_{MLT}	α_{FJI}	β_{FJI}	α_{SYC}	β_{SYC}
	0.018	0.209	0.317	−0.007	−0.017	−0.094	−0.206
	5.109	1.564	4.317	−0.402	−1.007	−4.386	−1.385
	1.470	1.721	0.717	−0.685	−1.902	−8.799	−0.912
Seychelles	ω	α_{SYC}	β_{SYC}	α_{FJI}	β_{FJI}	α_{MLT}	β_{MLT}
	0.012	0.056	0.508	−0.009	−0.012	−1.328E−04	−0.002
	1.502	0.586	1.621	−0.537	−0.652	−0.024	−0.155
	2.782	0.974	2.772	−3.395	−3.116	−0.018	−0.284

Notes:
The three entries associated with each parameter are their respective estimate, the asymptotic *t*-ratios and the Bollerslev-Wooldridge (1992) robust *t*-ratios.
The parameters in Equation (5.16) associated with Fiji, Malta and Seychelles are denoted by subscripts FJI, MLT and SYC.

conditional variance of the growth rate of monthly international tourism to Barbados is affected by the previous short-run effects to the conditional variance of the monthly international tourist arrivals to Fiji, Malta and Seychelles, and its own and Malta's long-run shock. For Fiji, the volatility of the growth rate of tourist arrivals is affected by its own previous period short- and long-run shocks to the conditional variance, as well as the short-run shocks from Malta and Seychelles. For Malta, the conditional variance is affected by its own long-run shock and the short-run impact in the conditional variance of the monthly tourist arrivals in Seychelles. For Seychelles, the conditional variance of the growth rate is affected by the previous period short-run effect from Fiji and Malta. From these results, the short-run impact of the conditional variance of the growth rate of monthly international tourist arrivals is interdependent between Fiji and Seychelles.

The multivariate estimates of VARMA-GARCH(1,1) for the growth rate in monthly international tourist arrivals to five SITEs for the smallest sample considered, and the most number of SITEs included, are presented in Table 5.26. For Barbados, the growth rate of monthly international tourist arrivals gives significant estimates of country effects from Cyprus, Fiji, Malta and

Table 5.25   Conditional Variance Estimates of VARMA-GARCH(1,1) of the Log-differences of Deseasonalised and Detrended Monthly International Tourist Arrivals in Barbados, Fiji, Malta and Seychelles

Barbados	ω	α_{BRB}	β_{BRB}	α_{FJI}	β_{FJI}	α_{MLT}	β_{MLT}	α_{SYC}	β_{SYC}
	0.007	0.023	0.932	−0.003	0.003	0.145	−0.498	0.056	−0.504
	5.219	0.873	23.340	−1.397	0.862	1.954	−1.765	2.864	−3.147
	1.829	0.945	24.615	−2.041	1.887	2.326	−2.371	4.066	−4.112
Fiji	ω	α_{FJI}	β_{FJI}	α_{BRB}	β_{BRB}	α_{MLT}	β_{MLT}	α_{SYC}	β_{SYC}
	−0.009	0.425	0.251	0.041	0.495	0.672	−0.222	−0.068	0.894
	−1.491	3.846	3.337	0.574	1.643	4.307	−0.498	−2.524	1.682
	−1.559	2.271	2.265	0.460	1.641	2.921	−0.521	−4.926	1.791
Malta	ω	α_{MLT}	β_{MLT}	α_{BRB}	β_{BRB}	α_{FJI}	β_{FJI}	α_{SYC}	β_{SYC}
	0.006	0.071	0.515	−0.026	−0.058	−0.004	−0.008	−0.045	−0.092
	0.749	0.762	1.529	−0.330	−0.304	−0.824	−1.295	−2.678	−0.144
	1.828	1.156	2.387	−0.592	−0.437	−0.561	−1.348	−4.126	−0.539
Seychelles	ω	α_{SYC}	β_{SYC}	α_{BRB}	β_{BRB}	α_{FJI}	β_{FJI}	α_{MLT}	β_{MLT}
	0.004	0.081	0.142	0.064	−0.060	−0.010	0.007	0.222	0.362
	1.386	1.135	0.325	0.592	−0.218	−1.135	0.367	1.517	0.618
	2.141	1.054	0.683	0.635	−0.248	−8.296	0.915	2.391	1.142

Notes:
The three entries associated with each parameter are their respective estimate, the asymptotic *t*-ratios and the Bollerslev-Wooldridge (1992) robust *t*-ratios.
The parameters in Equation (5.16) associated with Barbados, Fiji, Malta and Seychelles are denoted by subscripts BRB, FJI, MLT and SYC.

Seychelles. As for Cyprus, in addition to its own previous period short- and long-run impacts, the previous period short- and long-run shocks from Fiji are significant. In the case of Fiji, the country effects on the conditional variance of the growth rate of tourist arrivals are from the previous period short-run impact from Cyprus and Seychelles, besides the previous period long-run impact from Malta. For Seychelles, the only significant impact on the conditional variance is from its own and Barbados' previous period long-run shocks. The results for the conditional variance for the growth rate of tourist arrivals are preferable to the results for the logarithms of monthly international tourist arrivals because there are more statistically significant results.

The asymmetric results for the growth rate of monthly international tourist arrivals are given in Tables 5.27–5.30. The only significant asymmetric behaviour in the conditional mean for the growth rate of monthly tourist

Table 5.26 Conditional Variance Estimates of VARMA-GARCH(1,1) of the Log-differences of Deseasonalised and Detrended Monthly International Tourist Arrivals in Barbados, Cyprus, Fiji, Malta and Seychelles

	ω	α_{BRB}	β_{BRB}	α_{CYP}	β_{CYP}	α_{FJI}	β_{FJI}	α_{MLT}	β_{MLT}	α_{SYC}	β_{SYC}
Barbados	-0.002	0.102	-0.212	-0.025	0.091	-0.003	0.003	0.057	0.165	0.106	0.304
	-0.606	1.484	-1.018	-2.825	1.751	-1.041	0.167	1.620	1.870	2.273	0.722
	-0.891	1.609	-1.116	-2.820	2.341	-6.211	0.582	2.059	2.083	3.533	1.005
Cyprus	0.005	0.012	0.008	0.157	0.603	-0.012	-0.008	0.014	0.015	0.009	0.001
	1.118	0.070	0.016	2.855	3.931	-2.497	-0.831	0.284	0.129	0.096	0.002
	1.078	0.077	0.013	1.716	4.580	-3.962	-2.120	0.206	0.160	0.065	0.002
Fiji	0.003	-0.068	0.369	0.101	-0.036	0.589	0.009	0.006	0.323	-0.051	-0.142
	0.985	-0.796	0.796	2.339	-0.714	5.744	0.125	0.127	2.248	-2.095	-1.763
	2.441	-1.253	0.589	1.501	-0.553	1.973	0.085	0.113	1.219	-0.535	-1.632
Malta	-0.002	0.031	1.216	0.077	-0.066	0.009	-0.017	0.175	0.420	0.103	-0.032
	-0.603	0.327	2.215	1.679	-1.352	0.730	-1.393	2.291	3.060	1.361	-0.085
	-0.778	1.026	3.091	2.348	-1.866	0.824	-2.197	2.675	3.987	1.572	-0.100
Seychelles	0.005	0.136	-0.658	0.009	0.058	-0.001	0.002	0.104	-0.013	0.045	0.530
	2.856	1.127	-2.216	0.432	1.492	-0.249	0.245	2.115	-0.207	0.788	3.018
	2.702	1.520	-2.296	0.383	2.281	-0.418	0.386	3.169	-0.270	0.741	3.218

Notes: The three entries associated with each parameter are their respective estimate, the asymptotic *t*-ratios and the Bollerslev-Wooldridge (1992) robust *t*-ratios. The parameters in Equation (5.16) associated with Barbados, Cyprus, Fiji, Malta and Seychelles are denoted by subscripts BRB, CYP, FJI, MLT and SYC.

Table 5.27   Conditional Variance Estimates of VARMA-AGARCH(1,1) of
the Log-differences of Monthly and Detrended Monthly
International Tourist Arrivals in Fiji and Malta

Fiji	ω	α_{FJI}	γ_{FJI}	β_{FJI}	α_{MLT}	β_{MLT}
	0.007	0.342	0.160	0.189	0.019	−0.008
	6.491	4.187	1.126	2.410	1.224	−2.615
	4.602	1.409	0.456	1.633	1.744	−4.149
Malta	ω	α_{MLT}	γ_{MLT}	β_{MLT}	α_{FJI}	β_{FJI}
	0.022	0.147	0.038	0.578	−0.026	−0.041
	1.902	0.510	0.083	2.489	−1.047	−1.031
	2.600	0.331	0.208	3.240	−1.690	−2.294

Notes:
The three entries associated with each parameter are their respective estimate, the asymptotic
t-ratios and the Bollerslev-Wooldridge (1992) robust *t*-ratios.
The parameters in Equation (5.18) associated with Fiji and Malta are denoted by subscripts FJI
and MLT.

Table 5.28   Conditional Variance Estimates of VARMA-AGARCH(1,1) of
the Log-differences of Monthly and Detrended Monthly
International Tourist Arrivals in Fiji, Malta and Seychelles

Fiji	ω	α_{FJI}	γ_{FJI}	β_{FJI}	α_{MLT}	β_{MLT}	α_{SYC}	β_{SYC}
	−0.001	0.766	−0.197	0.063	0.790	0.118	−0.029	0.096
	−0.965	5.397	−1.085	0.929	6.082	1.127	−1.825	1.545
	−0.812	2.766	−0.528	0.952	4.331	1.545	−1.492	1.262
Malta	ω	α_{MLT}	γ_{MLT}	β_{MLT}	α_{FJI}	β_{FJI}	α_{SYC}	β_{SYC}
	0.021	0.120	−0.080	0.490	−0.015	−0.018	−0.126	−0.221
	3.415	0.642	−0.451	4.352	−0.893	−0.845	−2.981	−0.976
	1.499	0.782	−0.241	1.429	−1.729	−1.761	−5.478	−0.800
Seychelles	ω	α_{SYC}	γ_{SYC}	β_{SYC}	α_{FJI}	β_{FJI}	α_{MLT}	β_{MLT}
	0.012	0.057	−0.037	0.513	−0.010	−0.011	0.001	−0.001
	1.705	0.527	−0.237	1.867	−0.505	−0.608	−0.016	−0.084
	2.924	0.749	−0.318	2.952	−3.493	−3.172	−0.017	−0.189

Notes:
The three entries associated with each parameter are their respective estimate, the asymptotic
t-ratios and the Bollerslev-Wooldridge (1992) robust *t*-ratios.
The parameters in Equation (5.18) associated with Fiji, Malta and Seychelles are denoted by
subscripts FJI, MLT and SYC.

Table 5.29   *Conditional Variance Estimates of VARMA-AGARCH(1,1) of the Log-differences of Deseasonalised and Detrended Monthly International Tourist Arrivals in Barbados, Fiji, Malta and Seychelles*

Barbados	ω	α_{BRB}	γ_{BRB}	β_{BRB}	α_{FJI}	β_{FJI}	α_{MLT}	β_{MLT}	α_{SYC}	β_{SYC}
	0.004	0.020	0.012	0.312	−0.004	0.004	0.177	−0.601	0.032	−0.059
	2.032	0.439	0.207	18.004	−3.263	2.038	2.235	−2.039	1.155	−0.586
	1.385	0.507	0.246	16.871	−2.075	1.979	4.219	−4.843	1.978	−0.744
Fiji	ω	α_{FJI}	γ_{FJI}	β_{FJI}	α_{BRB}	β_{BRB}	α_{MLT}	β_{MLT}	α_{SYC}	β_{SYC}
	0.001	−0.026	0.374	0.458	−0.061	0.554	0.916	−0.948	−0.032	0.226
	0.372	−0.795	3.506	8.827	−1.240	2.342	5.134	−1.827	−1.248	1.669
	0.343	−1.649	1.982	5.511	−1.175	2.429	4.064	−2.667	−3.430	0.977
Malta	ω	α_{MLT}	γ_{MLT}	β_{MLT}	α_{BRB}	β_{BRB}	α_{FJI}	β_{FJI}	α_{SYC}	β_{SYC}
	0.000	0.036	0.165	0.543	−0.009	0.470	0.001	−0.008	0.025	−0.110
	0.328	0.480	1.433	3.231	−0.193	1.961	1.890	−4.881	0.749	−0.715
	0.328	0.480	1.433	3.231	−0.193	1.961	1.890	−4.881	0.749	−0.715
Seychelles	ω	α_{SYC}	γ_{SYC}	β_{SYC}	α_{BRB}	β_{BRB}	α_{FJI}	β_{FJI}	α_{MLT}	β_{MLT}
	0.004	0.045	0.033	0.263	0.083	−0.117	−0.010	0.007	0.236	0.262
	1.432	0.484	0.304	0.647	0.741	−0.473	−3.130	0.497	1.586	0.440
	2.025	0.540	0.263	0.943	0.784	−0.592	−7.554	0.862	2.559	0.659

Notes:
The three entries associated with each parameter are their respective estimate, the asymptotic *t*-ratios and the Bollerslev-Wooldridge (1992) robust *t*-ratios.
The parameters in Equation (5.18) associated with Barbados, Fiji, Malta and Seychelles are denoted by subscripts BRB, FJI, MLT and SYC.

arrivals are evident in Table 5.29 for Fiji, and is perfectly plausible for the reasons given above. Furthermore, there is evidence of asymmetry in the case of Malta, which is suggestive of the impact of the events of September 11, 2001, which means that a negative growth rate in the monthly international tourist arrivals creates greater uncertainty in subsequent periods than does a positive shock.

From this analysis, we can conclude that there are few asymmetric effects in the logarithms and in the growth rate of monthly tourist arrivals. The preferred results are presented in Table 5.24 for Fiji, Malta and Cyprus, giving the largest number of statistically significant estimates. There is evidence to suggest that the tourism product of Fiji and Seychelles is highly interdependent, showing a reasonable level of substitutability between these two countries.

Table 5.30 *Conditional Variance Estimates of VARMA-AGARCH(1,1) of the Log-differences of Deseasonalised and Detrended Monthly International Tourist Arrivals in Barbados, Cyprus, Fiji, Malta and Seychelles*

Barbados

ω	α_{BRB}	γ_{BRB}	β_{BRB}	α_{CYP}	β_{CYP}	α_{FJI}	β_{FJI}	α_{MLT}	β_{MLT}	α_{SYC}	β_{SYC}
0.000	0.234	-0.158	-0.142	-0.027	0.114	-0.003	0.003	0.030	0.168	0.076	0.052
-0.227	1.711	-1.063	-0.891	-6.413	3.084	-1.279	0.205	1.302	2.234	2.082	0.482
-0.245	2.197	-1.492	-0.784	-6.041	2.461	-2.658	0.543	1.095	2.046	2.631	0.538

Cyprus

ω	β_{CYP}	γ_{CYP}	β_{CYP}	α_{BRB}	β_{BRB}	α_{FJI}	β_{FJI}	α_{MLT}	β_{MLT}	α_{SYC}	β_{SYC}
0.004	0.083	0.179	0.706	0.126	0.403	-0.013	0.006	0.027	-0.097	0.096	-0.360
1.142	1.224	1.738	8.644	0.694	1.004	-3.134	1.038	0.411	-1.294	1.135	-1.128
1.027	1.081	1.555	7.674	1.335	1.594	-5.264	1.992	0.933	-1.813	1.195	-1.040

Fiji

ω	α_{FJI}	γ_{FJI}	β_{FJI}	α_{BRB}	β_{BRB}	α_{CYP}	β_{CYP}	α_{MLT}	β_{MLT}	α_{SYC}	β_{SYC}
0.003	0.589	0.009	-0.068	0.369	0.101	-0.036	0.006	0.323	-0.051	-0.247	0.003
0.985	5.744	0.125	-0.796	0.796	2.339	-0.714	0.127	2.248	-2.095	-0.690	0.985
1.441	1.973	0.085	-1.253	0.589	1.501	-0.553	0.113	1.219	-0.535	-0.958	1.441

Malta

ω	α_{MLT}	γ_{MLT}	β_{MLT}	α_{BRB}	β_{BRB}	α_{CYP}	β_{CYP}	α_{FJI}	β_{FJI}	α_{SYC}	β_{SYC}
0.003	-0.083	0.497	0.405	-0.006	0.015	0.053	0.004	0.010	-0.019	0.056	-0.396
0.984	-2.623	3.210	3.856	-0.073	2.664	1.269	0.103	0.773	-1.841	0.907	-1.717
1.039	-3.442	4.250	3.178	-0.067	2.702	1.435	0.129	0.919	-2.891	0.778	-1.590

Seychelles

ω	α_{SYC}	γ_{SYC}	β_{SYC}	α_{BRB}	β_{BRB}	α_{CYP}	β_{CYP}	α_{FJI}	β_{FJI}	α_{MLT}	β_{MLT}
0.004	0.025	0.089	0.536	0.140	-0.442	-0.028	0.085	4.3E-04	0.001	0.075	-0.062
3.080	0.321	1.037	3.593	1.421	-2.033	-1.542	1.819	0.068	0.061	2.454	-1.418
2.961	0.364	0.882	3.495	1.682	-2.580	-2.413	4.961	0.113	0.108	2.505	-1.987

Notes: The three entries associated with each parameter are their respective estimate, the asymptotic t-ratios and the Bollerslev-Wooldridge (1992) robust t-ratios. The parameters in Equation (5.18) associated with Barbados, Cyprus, Fiji, Malta and Seychelles are denoted by subscripts BRB, CYP, FJI, MLT and SYC.

Empirical Estimates of CCC for VARMA-GARCH(1,1) and VARMA-AGARCH(1,1) for the Logarithms and Growth Rate of Monthly Tourist Arrivals

Tables 5.31–5.40 display the CCC coefficients of the standardised residuals for the VARMA-GARCH(1,1) and VARMA-AGARCH(1,1) models estimated for the respective samples. The magnitudes of the CCC coefficients for these models are quite similar to those of their univariate counterparts.

For the logarithms of monthly international tourist arrivals, the CCC coefficients of the standardised shocks estimated for the VARMA-GARCH(1,1) model presented in Table 5.15 is 0.022, and between Malta and Fiji and for its asymmetric counterpart it is 0.018. Since these multivariate estimates are very close to zero, they imply that the shocks to the conditional variances in these two markets are independent, so that marketing efforts have to be implemented separately. Tables 5.31 and 5.33 present the CCC estimates for VARMA-GARCH(1,1) and VARMA-AGARCH(1,1) for Fiji,

Table 5.31   *Constant Conditional Correlations of VARMA-GARCH(1,1)*
                Conditional Variance Estimates of the Logarithms of
                Deseasonalised and Detrended Monthly International Tourist
                Arrivals in Fiji, Malta and Seychelles

SITE	Fiji	Malta	Seychelles
Fiji	1		
Malta	−0.033	1	
Seychelles	0.222	0.176	1

Table 5.32   *Constant Conditional Correlations of VARMA-GARCH(1,1)*
                Conditional Variance Estimates of the Logarithms of
                Deseasonalised and Detrended Monthly International Tourist
                Arrivals in Barbados, Fiji, Malta and Seychelles

SITE	Barbados	Fiji	Malta	Seychelles
Barbados	1			
Fiji	0.154	1		
Malta	0.174	0.030	1	
Seychelles	0.264	0.194	0.233	1

Malta and Seychelles, with the highest CCC estimates of 0.222 and 0.244, respectively, recorded between Seychelles and Fiji, and the lowest estimates of –0.033 and –0.015, respectively, between Fiji and Malta.

The CCC estimates presented in Tables 5.35–5.40 are for the VARMA-GARCII(1,1) and VARMA-AGARCH(1,1) models based on the growth rate

Table 5.33   *Constant Conditional Correlations of VARMA-AGARCH(1,1) Conditional Variance Estimates of the Logarithms of Deseasonalised and Detrended Monthly International Tourist Arrivals in Fiji, Malta and Seychelles*

SITE	Fiji	Malta	Seychelles
Fiji	1		
Malta	–0.015	1	
Seychelles	0.224	0.186	1

Table 5.34   *Constant Conditional Correlations of VARMA-AGARCH(1,1) Conditional Variance Estimates of the Logarithms of Deseasonalised and Detrended Monthly International Tourist Arrivals in Barbados, Fiji, Malta and Seychelles*

SITE	Barbados	Fiji	Malta	Seychelles
Barbados	1			
Fiji	0.048	1		
Malta	0.195	–0.074	1	
Seychelles	0.255	–0.067	0.236	1

Table 5.35   *Constant Conditional Correlations of VARMA-GARCH(1,1) Conditional Variance Estimates of the Log-differences of Deseasonalised and Detrended Monthly International Tourist Arrivals in Fiji, Malta and Seychelles*

SITE	Fiji	Malta	Seychelles
Fiji	1		
Malta	0.041	1	
Seychelles	0.323	0.131	1

Table 5.36   *Constant Conditional Correlations of VARMA-GARCH(1,1)*
Conditional Variance Estimates of the Log-differences of
Deseasonalised and Detrended Monthly International Tourist
Arrivals in Barbados, Fiji, Malta and Seychelles

SITE	Barbados	Fiji	Malta	Seychelles
Barbados	1			
Fiji	0.187	1		
Malta	0.149	−0.043	1	
Seychelles	0.244	0.244	0.213	1

Table 5.37   *Constant Conditional Correlations of VARMA-GARCH(1,1)*
Conditional Variance Estimates of the Log-differences of
Deseasonalised and Detrended Monthly International Tourist
Arrivals in Barbados, Cyprus, Fiji, Malta and Seychelles

SITE	Barbados	Cyprus	Fiji	Malta	Seychelles
Barbados	1				
Cyprus	0.174	1			
Fiji	0.148	0.022	1		
Malta	0.065	0.140	−0.043	1	
Seychelles	0.238	0.259	0.207	0.168	1

Table 5.38   *Constant Conditional Correlations of VARMA-AGARCH(1,1)*
Conditional Variance Estimates of the Log-differences of
Deseasonalised and Detrended Monthly International Tourist
Arrivals in Fiji, Malta and Seychelles

SITE	Fiji	Malta	Seychelles
Fiji	1		
Malta	0.058	1	
Seychelles	0.323	0.158	1

of monthly international tourist arrivals. From the estimates in Table 5.35, the highest CCC of 0.323 is recorded between Fiji and Seychelles, and when asymmetry is incorporated, the estimate as given in Table 5.38 shows that it

*Table 5.39   Constant Conditional Correlations of VARMA-AGARCH(1,1)
Conditional Variance Estimates of the Log-differences of
Deseasonalised and Detrended Monthly International Tourist
Arrivals in Barbados, Fiji, Malta and Seychelles*

SITE	Barbados	Fiji	Malta	Seychelles
Barbados	1			
Fiji	0.184	1		
Malta	0.185	−0.001	1	
Seychelles	0.244	0.243	0.233	1

*Table 5.40   Constant Conditional Correlations of VARMA-AGARCH(1,1)
Conditional Variance Estimates of the Log-differences of
Deseasonalised and Detrended Monthly International Tourist
Arrivals in Barbados, Cyprus, Fiji, Malta and Seychelles*

SITE	Barbados	Cyprus	Fiji	Malta	Seychelles
Barbados	1				
Cyprus	0.178	1			
Fiji	0.192	0.049	1		
Malta	0.089	0.148	−0.018	1	
Seychelles	0.233	0.247	0.222	0.174	1

is identical. The lowest estimate is recorded between Fiji and Malta. For the second largest sample for four SITEs, the CCC estimates given in Table 5.36 show that the highest estimate of 0.244 is between Barbados and Seychelles, and it is identical when asymmetric behaviour is accommodated.

The lowest estimated CCC is between Fiji and Malta, and is negative. Furthermore, Seychelles has CCC estimates with the highest magnitude, while Malta has the lowest CCC estimates. For five SITEs in the smallest sample, the estimates in Tables 5.37 and 5.40 show that the highest CCC estimates are between Cyprus and Seychelles, while the lowest   CCC estimates are between Fiji and Malta. The same could be said for the estimates of the CCCs in Table 5.40 when asymmetry is incorporated. The most interesting feature of these conditional correlations is that Seychelles has consistently maintained the highest CCC estimates throughout the analysis, while Malta has maintained the lowest magnitudes of the estimated CCCs.

5.8 CONCLUSION

This chapter reviewed the most recent theoretical results for the univariate GARCH models of conditional volatility developed by Engle (1982), with subsequent developments by Bollerslev (1986, 1990), and the recently developed VARMA-GARCH model of Ling and McAleer (2003) and VARMA-AGARCH model of McAleer et al. (2008).

The associated volatilities of the logarithms of monthly international tourist arrivals, and the growth rate of monthly tourist arrivals, for seven SITEs, namely Barbados, Cyprus, Dominica, Fiji, Maldives, Malta and Seychelles, were examined. The conditional means of the logarithms of monthly international tourist arrivals, and the growth rate of monthly international tourist arrivals, were specified for each SITE as ARMA(p,q) models, with 12 monthly seasonal dummy variables in each case, and a combination of linear and quadratic time trends for the monthly tourism arrivals. Two models, namely GARCH(1,1) and GJR(1,1), were used to estimate the conditional volatility of the shocks to monthly international tourist arrivals to each of these SITEs.

The constant conditional correlations were estimated for the univariate GARCH(1,1) and GJR(1,1) models. Furthermore, the VARMA-GARCH(1,1) and VARMA-AGARCH(1,1) models, which also assumed constant conditional correlations, were estimated for four separate samples, with two, three, four and five SITEs in each sample.

REFERENCES

Bera, A.K. and M.L. Higgins (1993), 'ARCH models: Properties, estimation and testing', *Journal of Economic Surveys*, **7**, 305–366; reprinted in L. Oxley et al. (eds), *Surveys in Econometrics*, Oxford: Blackwell, pp. 215–72.

Berndt, E.K., B.H. Hall, R.E. Hall and J.A. Hausman (1974), 'Estimation and inference in nonlinear structural models', *Annals of Economic and Social Measurement*, **3**, 653–65.

Black, F. (1976), 'Studies of stock price volatility changes', *Proceedings of the 1976 Meeting of the American Statistical Association, Business and Economics Statistics Section*, pp. 177–81.

Bollerslev, T. (1986), 'Generalised autoregressive conditional heteroscedasticity', *Journal of Econometrics*, **31**, 307–27.

Bollerslev, T. (1990), 'Modelling the coherence in short-run nominal exchange rate: A multivariate generalized ARCH approach', *Review of Economics and Statistics*, **72**, 498–505.

Bollerslev, T. and J.M. Wooldridge (1992), 'Quasi-maximum likelihood estimation and inference in dynamic models with time-varying covariances', *Econometric Reviews*, **11**, 143–73.

Bollerslev, T., R.Y. Chou and K.F. Kroner (1992), 'ARCH modelling in finance: A review of the theory and empirical evidence', *Journal of Econometrics*, **52**, 5–59.

Bollerslev, T., R.F. Engle and J.M. Wooldridge (1988), 'A capital asset pricing model with time varying covariance', *Journal of Political Economy*, **96**, 116–31.

Bollerslev, T., R.F. Engle and D.B. Nelson (1994), 'ARCH models', in R.F. Engle and D.L. McFadden (eds), *Handbook of Econometrics*, Vol. 4, Amsterdam: North-Holland, pp. 2961–3038.

Chan, F., S. Hoti, M. McAleer and R. Shareef (2005), 'Forecasting international tourism demand and uncertainty for Barbados, Cyprus and Fiji', in A. Lanza, A. Markandya and F. Pigliaru (eds), *The Economics of Tourism and Sustainable Development*, Cheltenham, UK and Northampton, MA, USA: Edward Elgar, pp. 30–55.

Engle, R.F. (1982), 'Autoregressive conditional heteroscedasticity with estimates of the variance of United Kingdom inflation', *Econometrica*, **50**, 987–1007.

Engle, R.F. (2002), 'Dynamic conditional correlation: A new simple class of multivariate GARCH models', *Journal of Business and Economic Statistics*, **20**, 339–50.

Engle, R.F. and K.F. Kroner (1995), 'Multivariate simultaneous generalized ARCH', *Econometric Theory*, **11**, 122–50.

Glosten, L., R. Jagannathan and D. Runkle (1992), 'On the relation between the expected value and volatility of nominal excess return on stocks', *Journal of Finance*, **46**, 1779–801.

Jeantheau, T. (1998), 'Strong consistency of estimators for multivariate ARCH models', *Econometric Theory*, **14**, 70–86.

Li, W.K., S. Ling and M. McAleer (2002), 'Recent theoretical results for time series models with GARCH Errors', *Journal of Economic Surveys*, **16**, 245–69. Reprinted in M. McAleer and L. Oxley (eds), *Contributions to Financial Econometrics: Theoretical and Practical Issues*, Oxford: Blackwell, pp. 9–33.

Ling, S. and M. McAleer (2002), 'Stationarity and the existence of moments of a family of GARCH processes', *Journal of Econometrics*, **106**, 109–17.

Ling, S. and M. McAleer (2003), 'Asymptotic theory for a vector ARMA-GARCH model', *Econometric Theory*, **19**, 278–308.

McAleer, M. (2005), 'Automated inference and learning in modeling financial volatility', *Econometric Theory*, **21**, 232–61.

McAleer, M., F. Chan and D. Marinova (2007), 'An econometric analysis of asymmetric volatility: Theory and application to patents', *Journal of Econometrics*, **139**, 259–84.

McAleer, M., S. Hoti and F. Chan (2008), 'Structure and asymptotic theory for multivariate asymmetric conditional volatility', *Econometric Reviews*, forthcoming.

Nelson, D.B. (1991), 'Conditional heteroscedasticity in asset returns: A new approach', *Econometrica*, **59**, 347–70.

Phillips, P.C.B. and P. Perron (1990), 'Testing for a unit root in time series regressions', *Biometrika*, **75**(2), 335–46.

Shareef, R. and M. McAleer (2005), 'Modelling international tourism demand and volatility in small island tourism economies', *International Journal of Tourism Research*, **7**, 313–33.

Tse, Y.K. and A.K.C. Tsui (2002), 'A multivariate generalized autoregressive conditional heteroscedasticity model with time-varying correlations', *Journal of Business and Economic Statistics*, **20**, 351–62.

6. Modelling Uncertainty in International Tourist Arrivals to Maldives

6.1 INTRODUCTION

The discussion in this chapter is an extension of the analysis in Shareef and McAleer (2007). A primary purpose is to model the uncertainty in monthly international tourist arrivals from the eight major tourist source countries to Maldives, which falls into the definition of SITEs. Maldives is probably the only SITE which relies entirely on tourism for the economic well-being of the nation. Tourism accounts for a substantial proportion of foreign exchange earnings, which enables importation of consumer as well as capital goods for economic development, leads to a significant share of government revenue, is a key determinant of development expenditure, and provides employment for a considerable proportion of the workforce.

This chapter gives estimates of the conditional mean, the conditional variance (or uncertainty) and static conditional correlations of monthly international tourist arrivals from tourist source countries to a particular SITE, namely Maldives. Such empirical analysis permits a distinction to be made between the short- and long-run persistence of shocks to international tourist arrivals, which provides useful information regarding the effects of shocks on the associated uncertainty. Moreover, the conditional correlation coefficients give an indication of the relationship between shocks to monthly international tourist arrivals, as well as the direction of causality in the monthly international tourist arrivals across the eight main international tourist sources to Maldives. For Maldives, it is crucial to obtain an accurate estimate of the uncertainty surrounding monthly international tourist arrivals based on historical data. In this chapter, we examine the associated volatilities of monthly tourist arrivals from the eight major tourist source countries, namely Italy, Germany, UK, Japan, France, Switzerland, Austria and The Netherlands, for the period 1994–2003.

The structure of this chapter is as follows. In Section 6.2, a brief overview of the Maldivian economy is given. Section 6.3 gives a detailed account of tourism development in Maldives since its inception in 1973. An outline of the tourist resort concept in Maldives is advanced in Section 6.4. The trends and composition of tourist arrivals are examined in Section 6.5, followed by a careful scrutiny of the characteristics of the data series in Section 6.6. The choice of conditional mean models is given in Section 6.7. Finally, some concluding remarks are given in Section 6.8.

6.2   THE MALDIVIAN ECONOMY: AN OVERVIEW

The Republic of Maldives was a former British protectorate, which became independent in 1965. It is an archipelago in the Indian Ocean, comprising 1192 islands, of which 199 are inhabited. The Exclusive Economic Zone of Maldives is 859 000 square kilometres, and the aggregated land area is roughly 290 square kilometres. The total population of Maldives is 270 101 in the 2000 census, and is estimated to have grown at 2.4 per cent per annum over the period 1990–2000.

In spite of the small size, limited natural resource base, small population and remoteness, Maldives has shown an impressive economic growth record over the last 20 years, with an average growth rate of 7 per cent per annum. This growth rate enabled Maldives to attain an estimated real per capita GDP of USD2261 in 2003, which is considerably above average for a small island developing country, which has an average per capita GDP of USD1500. The engine of growth in Maldives has been the tourism industry, which is regarded as the most important industry in the economy, accounting for one-fifth of GDP, a third of fiscal revenue, and two-thirds of gross foreign exchange earnings in recent years. The fisheries sector remains the largest sector in terms of employment, accounting for about one-quarter of the labour force. It is still an important source of foreign exchange earnings. Due to the high salinity content in the soil, agriculture continues to play a minor role. The government, which employs about 20 per cent of the labour force, plays a dominant role in the economy, both in the production process and through its regulation of the economy.

6.3   TOURISM DEVELOPMENT

As a tourist destination, Maldives was not known to the world until 1972, when the first tourist resort was established. Ever since, tourism has been the most important sector in the economy. A significant part of the Maldivian tourism industry is comprised of package tour operations, mainly from Western Europe. European tourists accounted for more than three-quarters of total international tourist arrivals in Maldives for the period 1981–2003. A significant impact in the rate of growth of international tourist flow to Maldives has been due to major infrastructure developments, such as the international airport and increasing bed capacity in tourist resorts. During the 1980s, tourism contributed an annual average of more than 16 per cent to real GDP, accounted for more than 21 per cent of total government revenue, and provided 41 per cent of gross foreign exchange earnings. The significance of tourism's contribution to the economy rose to 18 per cent of GDP in the 1990s, provided 18 per cent of government revenue, and more than 62 per cent of foreign exchange receipts. The tourism sector also employs about one-third of the expatriate labour force, and employment from the domestic labour force has grown from 1 per cent in the 1970s to 11 per cent in the 1990s. In addition to the direct benefit from tourism, there are also considerable multiplier effects on other sectors, such as commerce, transportation and telecommunications. Tourism has also given impetus to fisheries and agriculture. Many fishermen sell their daily catch directly to the resorts. The construction sector has also benefited directly from the development and upgrading of tourism-related infrastructure and accommodation. There are altogether 89 resorts built to date, on independent self-contained islands with a total bed capacity of 16 318. In 1981, the total bed capacity was 3228, and the bed capacity has increased at an annual growth rate of 7.7 per cent.

In Maldives, tourism has a direct impact on fiscal policy, which determines development expenditure. More than one-fifth of government revenue comes from tourism-related levies. The most important tourism-related revenues are the tourism tax, the resort lease rents, resort land rents, and royalties. Except for tourism tax, the other sources of tourism-related revenues are based on contractual agreements with the government of Maldives. Tourism tax is levied on every occupied bed night by tourists from all tourist establishments, such as hotels, tourist resorts, guest houses and safari yachts. This tax was introduced through legislation in 1978, with an initial levy of USD3, and was then doubled to USD6 in 1988. After 16 years without a change in the tax rate, from November 2004 it was increased to USD8. This tax is a regressive tax, as it does not take into account the profitability of the tourist establishments. Moreover, this tax does not incorporate inflation, such that the tax yield has eroded over time.

The tax is collected by the tourist establishments and is deposited at the Inland Revenue Department at the end of every month. Current revenue is used directly to finance the government budget on a monthly basis. Since the tax is levied directly on the tourist, any uncertainty that surrounds international tourist arrivals will affect the tax receipts, and hence fiscal policy. Any adverse affect on international tourist arrivals may result in the suspension of planned development expenditures.

6.4   TOURIST RESORT CONCEPT OF THE MALDIVES

The make-up of tourist resorts in Maldives is unique. Almost all the land belongs to the state, and most of the existing resorts are built on islands that have been set aside for tourism development. They are all leased from the government on fixed-term contracts, with annual rents determined through competitive bidding.

The development of the resorts that exist in Maldives today would not have been possible without conserving the delicate ecosystems surrounding Maldives, and protecting the Maldivian culture and traditions from any controversy arising through international tourism. Therefore, tourism development is the greatest challenge in the history of Maldives, and has led to the creation of distinctive resort islands. In Domroes (1985, 1989, 1993, 1999), it is asserted that these islands are deserted and uninhabited, but have been converted into 'one-island–one-hotel' schemes. The tourism industry is strictly regulated by the government of Maldives through extensive statutory authority provided to the Ministry of Tourism and the Ministry of Home Affairs, Housing and Environment. There are 87 carefully chosen islands to develop exclusively tourist resorts which incorporate all tourist requirements. The criteria for choosing the resorts for development are not disclosed by the government of Maldives to the private sector.

The building of physical and social infrastructure of the resort islands must abide by strict standards to protect the flora, fauna and the marine environment of the islands, while basic facilities for sustainability of the resort have to be maintained. The architectural design of the resort islands in Maldives vary profoundly in their character and individuality. Only 20 per cent of the land area of an island is allowed to be developed, which is imposed to restrict the capacity of tourists on every island. All tourist accommodation must face a beach front area of five metres. In most island resorts, bungalows are built as single or double units. Recently, there has been an extensive development of water bungalows on stilts along the reef adjacent to beaches. All the conveniences for tourists are available on each island, and are provided by the onshore staff.

6.5   PATTERNS OF INTERNATIONAL TOURIST ARRIVALS

This section explains the trends in international tourist arrivals to Maldives over the period 1981–2004, in which international tourist arrivals have recorded a growth rate of 9.7 per cent per annum. Table 6.1 gives an overview of the numbers of tourist arrivals and their respective shares in total international arrivals.

Over the same period, tourists from Europe, particularly Western Europe, showed an annual growth rate of 10.1 per cent, 8.5 per cent from Asian tourists, 10.1 per cent from African tourists, 7.6 per cent from the Americas and 11.9 per cent from tourists from Oceania. There are over 200 different tourist source countries, for which the Ministry of Tourism maintains international tourist arrivals data. Of these tourist source countries, 21 are from Western Europe, 35 are from Eastern Europe, 13 are from South and South-East Asia, 25 are from the Middle East, 52 from Africa, 36 from South America and 10 from Oceania.

The single biggest tourist source is Western Europe, which accounts for more than four-fifths of international tourist arrivals to Maldives. In 2003, Italy was the single largest source country, while there was one tourist from each of the Vatican City, Burundi, Cape Verde, Comoros, Gambia, Guinea Bissau, Mali, Ecuador, Guatemala, Guyana, Samoa, Marshall Islands, New Caledonia, Norfolk Island, Solomon Islands and Tonga. Although UK was ranked fourth among the highest tourist-generating countries during the period 1994–2004, it is also considered the most important tourist-source country because, as can be seen from Figure 6.1, British tourist arrivals have shown a continuously increasing linear trend. The single biggest emerging market is Russia, with an annual growth rate of 35.2 per cent per annum over the period 1991–2003.

The top eight tourist generating countries to Maldives over the period 1994–2004 were Italy, Germany, UK, Japan, France, Switzerland, Austria and The Netherlands. Tourists from Italy increased steadily at an annual rate of 14.5 per cent during the period 1981–1992, while accounting for just over 21 per cent of the total international tourist arrivals. From the beginning of the European recession in 1992, the growth rate of Italian tourist arrivals to Maldives fell dramatically to 2.4 per cent per annum until 1997. Thereafter, the annual growth rate recorded an all-time high of 15 per cent per annum from 1998 to 2003, accounting for just over 20 per cent of the total share of total tourist arrivals. Currently, Italy generates the highest number of tourist arrivals, and has also been the single biggest source country for six consecutive years since 1998.

Germany is the single most prominent tourist source country in the history of tourism in Maldives, maintaining its dominance in the composition of tourist arrivals for 17 consecutive years since 1981, with an average share of 27.7 per cent and an annual growth rate of 9.4 per cent. From 1998, Germany lost its dominance to Italy, coinciding with an average share of 16.7 per cent during the period 1998–2004, while recording an annual growth rate of –1.2 per cent per annum. The main purpose of German tourism to Maldives is the attraction of scuba diving.

British tourists have been keen visitors to Maldives, accounting for the third largest tourist source country over the period 1981–2004. An analysis of British tourist arrival figures illustrates an increasing linear trend, accounting for an annual average share of 10.3 per cent of the total international tourist arrivals, and leads to 16.1 per cent annual growth rate. However, as can be seen from Figure 6.1, during the period 1981–1990, British tourist arrivals grew at 14.2 per cent per annum, and then plummeted to 15 500 tourists in 1992 compared with 22 684 in 1990. From 1992 onwards, the annual growth rate in British tourist arrivals returned to the pre-slump growth rate of 14 per cent. This slump was due to the 1991 Gulf War. In 2003, British tourists accounted for the second-highest number of international tourists from a single source.

Japanese tourists are well known for overseas travel due to their economic prosperity, change in lifestyles caused by increased disposable income, and stronger Yen, all of which contributed to the higher demand for international travel. Japan is one of the principal source markets for inbound tourism to Maldives, and was the third highest tourist-generating country during the period 1981–1996. This is due to the significant role played by the Japanese government in promoting overseas travel in order to reduce their large trade surpluses. To this effect, the Japanese government unveiled the 'Ten Million People Program' and established the International Tourism Institute of Japan to promote travel abroad. There was also a relaxation of Japanese emigration policies by making international bilateral agreements with countries so that overseas travel would become easier. However, during the period 1994–2003, Japan dropped to fourth position in market share, which is attributable to the effect of emerging source countries. Nevertheless, Japanese tourists have recorded an annual growth rate of 15.6 per cent over the last 23 years, with the exception of the 1998–1999 Asian economic and financial crises.

French tourists have been visiting Maldives since the inception of tourism in Maldives in 1972. France has been the fifth largest tourist source market throughout the last 23 years, and recorded an annual growth rate of 8.3 per cent over the period. Although French tourists have been increasing in numbers, the share of French tourists has been declining, most notably during the period 1981–1988. Nevertheless, the share in tourist arrivals increased after 1988, but was hampered by the European recession of 1992 and continued to decline after 1997. After 1997, French tourist arrivals have been increasing steadily, and in 2003 their share reached a record 7.7 per cent.

There has been an increasing trend in visitor arrivals from Switzerland over the last 23 years, accounting for an annual growth rate of 9.2 per cent. As can be seen from Figure 6.1, the share of Swiss tourists to Maldives has been changing dramatically over time, averaging 5.7 and 5.9 per cent during the periods 1981–1993 and 1994–2004, respectively. The reasons for the

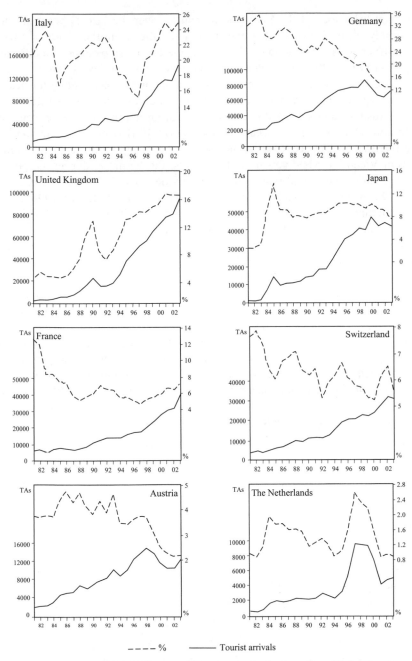

Figure 6.1   *Trends and Shares of Tourist Arrivals from Top Eight Tourist Sources, 1981–2003*

erratic behaviour of the Swiss tourist market over the last 23 years are not entirely clear. However, the explanation for the declining share of Swiss tourist arrivals in the period 1991–1993 is the European recession, and for the period 1996 to 2000 it was due to the depreciation of the Swiss Franc.

Austria is the seventh largest tourist source country, accounting for nearly 3 per cent of total international tourists to Maldives. Over the last 23 years, the Austrian tourist arrival rate has grown at an impressive 8.4 per cent per annum. During these 23 years, in the period 1981–1993 Austrian tourists arrived at 13.2 per cent per annum due to the inauguration of direct flights from Vienna to Maldives in the late 1980s. Furthermore, during the period 1994–2003, the arrival rate dropped to a modest 3.4. This drop is explained by the negative annual growth rate of 11.6 per cent during 1998–2001, accounting for the depreciation of the Austrian Shilling against major hard currencies. The trend for Austrian tourists has been declining in both the growth rate and the share of total tourist arrivals. This could be due to the faster growth rate of tourist arrivals from emerging markets such as Russia and other Eastern European states.

As given in Table 6.1, inbound tourism from The Netherlands has always remained in eighth position among the eight major tourist source countries to Maldives. The number of Dutch tourist arrivals has increased steadily over the last 23 years at an annual rate of 10.3 per cent. Their share in total tourist arrivals has been changing over the same period, peaking at 2.6 per cent in 1997. Dutch tourist travel has been highly susceptible to exchange rate movements in the Guilder against the other major currencies. This is evident

Table 6.1   Tourist Arrivals and Shares, 1981–2003

1981–1993			1994–2003		
Source Country	Head Count	% Share	Source Country	Head Count	% Share
Germany	451 803	24.62	Italy	852 389	20.78
Italy	347 019	18.91	Germany	730 453	17.81
Japan	134 207	7.31	UK	603 501	14.72
UK	126 716	6.91	Japan	381 374	9.30
France	112 063	6.11	France	238 638	5.82
Switzerland	104 392	5.69	Switzerland	237 245	5.79
Austria	69 296	3.78	Austria	118 324	2.89
The Netherlands	23 251	1.27	The Netherlands	60 011	1.46
Total International Tourist Arrivals	*1 835 037*	*100.00*	*Total International Tourist Arrivals*	*4 101 028*	*100.00*

during the period 1994–1997, when the arrival rate was 35 per cent per annum, and was largely attributable to the appreciation of the Guilder. However, the current trend for Dutch tourist arrivals to Maldives is declining.

6.6 DATA

For the analysis in this chapter, we use monthly international tourist arrivals from the eight major tourist sources countries to Maldives during the period 1994–2003, as obtained from the Ministry of Tourism, Republic of Maldives. The number of tourist arrivals, logarithms (logs), annual differences, log-differences and their associated uncertainties, are examined. The plots of these series, together with their associated volatilities, are given in Figures 6.2–6.5.

Of the eight major tourist source countries, Italy, UK, Japan, France and Switzerland exhibit upward trends in the numbers of tourist arrivals and in their logarithms. These five countries also show clear seasonal and cyclical patterns in the two series. There is strong evidence to suggest that the associated uncertainties or volatilities in monthly international tourist arrivals have strong correlations with the seasonality in tourism in Maldives. The issue of seasonality in monthly tourist arrivals in Maldives will be dealt with in Section 6.4. As can be seen from Figure 6.2, there is a sudden increase in uncertainty in the number of Italian tourist arrivals during the 2002–2003 peak tourist season, while in logarithms there is evidence to show that there is uncertainty at the beginning of the series. For the UK, in levels and in logarithms, there is little evidence of volatility, except that some uncertainty is visible at the beginning of the levels series, while they appear at the end of the logarithmic series. Uncertainty appears throughout the series and is largely influenced by seasonal variations for Japanese tourist arrivals in levels but, for the same series in logarithms, they are smaller in magnitude. The uncertainty associated with French tourist arrivals is very similar to that of Italy, with noticeable variations towards the latter half of the sample, while in the logarithmic series they are much smaller in magnitude. It is evident from these figures that the volatilities in tourist arrivals from Switzerland are increasing in magnitude, together with the growth in arrivals, but this pattern is reversed in the case of logarithms.

Surprisingly, during the same period, Germany, Austria and The Netherlands show no clear trend. Interestingly, they show very similar seasonal patterns, owing to the fact that they are from Western Europe, which is the principal source of tourism to Maldives. It is evident from Figures 6.2 and 6.3 that German tourist arrivals grew steadily for the three subsequent years after 1994, stagnated from 1997 to 1999, declined thereafter, and then increased the growth rate during the last three years of the sample period.

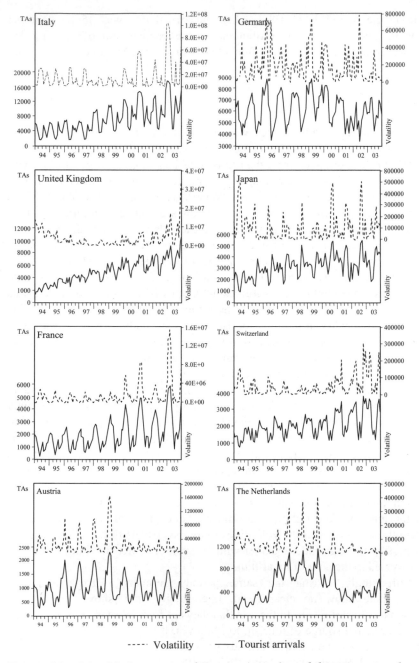

Figure 6.2   Monthly International Tourist Arrivals and their Associated Volatilities, 1994–2003

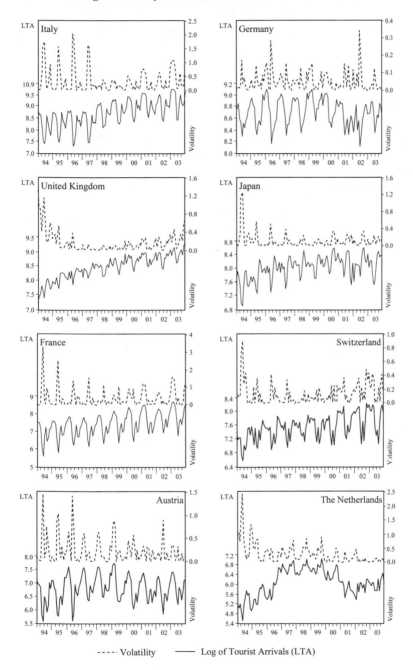

Figure 6.3   Logarithms of Monthly International Tourist Arrivals and their Associated Volatilities, 1994–2003

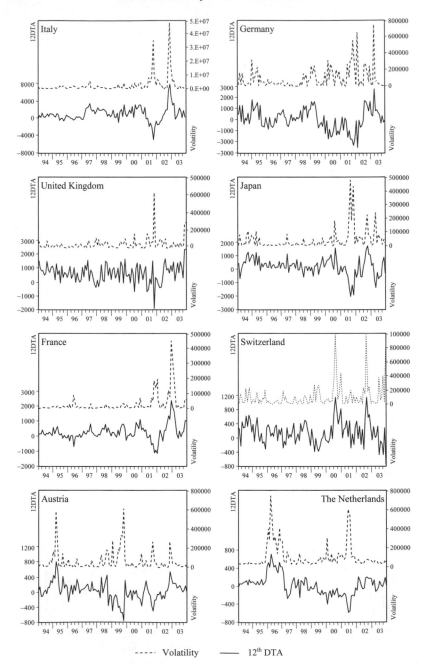

Figure 6.4   Annual Difference of Monthly International Tourist Arrivals and their Associated Volatilities, 1994–2003

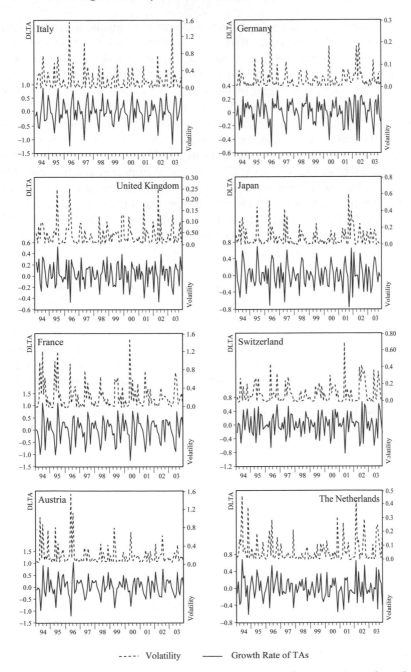

----- Volatility   ——— Growth Rate of TAs

Figure 6.5   *Log-Difference of Monthly International Tourist Arrivals and*
             their Associated Volatilities, 1994–2003

Their associated volatilities have been widespread in levels, with clustering around 1995, 1998 and 2002, while in logarithms the clusterings are only apparent in 1996 and 2002. For Austria, tourist arrivals as well as their logarithmic counterparts increased steadily from 1994 to 1999, and then showed a sudden decline thereafter until the end of the sample period. The associated uncertainty in levels for Austria is quite evident for the period 1996–1999, and in logarithms the volatilities are widespread during the first half of the series. As for The Netherlands, arrivals increased from 1994 to 1996. From 1997, there was a sudden surge in Dutch tourist arrivals, which was maintained at a high level until 2000, and then declined to the pre-1997 trend until the end of the sample period. In this series, there is clear evidence of a structural break in tourist arrivals through the influence of the value of the Dutch Guilder. Furthermore, during the period 1997–1999, the associated volatilities in the series have been quite profound, while in the case of logarithms, the volatilities appear in 1994 and immediately thereafter.

With regard to the annual differences in monthly international tourist arrivals to Maldives, which is illustrated in Figure 6.4, Italy, Germany, Japan and France have very similar patterns. The annual difference, which is the change in the number of monthly tourist arrivals from the four countries over a twelve-month period, has been quite stable from the beginning of the series through the first five-year period, after which it declined and then increased for the four countries. The associated volatilities in the four series depict clusterings at roughly the same point. For Switzerland, Austria and The Netherlands, the twelfth difference series have been changing throughout the sample period. For Switzerland, there is volatility clustering in the peak tourist seasons in 2000 and 2002, while for Austria it is evident in 1995 and 1999, and for The Netherlands volatility clusterings are evident in 1996 and 2001. Logarithmic differences in monthly international tourist arrivals denote the growth rate in monthly international tourist arrivals. As can be seen from Figure 6.5, the growth rates are somewhat similar and are clearly stationary, and the associated volatilities in all eight series show evidence of volatility clustering. From the annual difference series, the effect of 11 September, 2001 is quite profound in all series except for Austria, which suggests that this global shock has clearly increased uncertainty in tourist arrivals immediately after the event. Furthermore, in the case of the logarithmic difference series, the associated volatilities cluster around September 2001 for Germany, UK, Japan, Switzerland and The Netherlands. However, for the remaining countries, there is no significant evidence of volatility clustering.

Descriptive Statistics

In Tables 6.2–6.5, descriptive statistics for monthly international tourists in levels, logarithms, first differences and log-differences (or growth rates) are presented. It may be argued that the preferred series to model monthly international tourism demand to Maldives is one which has a distribution closest to a normal distribution. In order to examine the validity of the preferred series, we examine the descriptive statistics of monthly international tourist demand in levels, logarithms, twelfth differences, and log-differences.

The monthly international tourist arrivals series in levels depict very high standard deviations for the eight tourist source countries. For a series to be

Table 6.2   Descriptive Statistics of Monthly International Tourist Arrivals

Tourist Source	Mean	Median	Max.	Min.	Std. Dev.	Skewness	Kurtosis	J-B	Prob.
Italy	7 098	6 355	17 285	1 471	3 792	0.80	3.03	12.77	0.00
Germany	6 089	5 932	8 840	3 303	1 332	0.09	2.05	4.62	0.10
UK	5 029	4 827	10 782	1 340	1 911	0.37	2.74	3.12	0.21
Japan	3 178	3 211	5 433	982	978	0.10	2.55	1.22	0.54
France	1 990	1 765	5 925	271	1 219	1.14	3.88	29.80	0.00
Switzerland	1 977	1 836	3 722	715	703	0.58	2.63	7.53	0.02
Austria	986	889	2 272	262	453	0.72	2.96	10.38	0.01
The Nether.	500	444	1 140	91	249	0.49	2.34	6.98	0.03

Note: The number of observations is 120 for each country.

Table 6.3   Descriptive Statistics of Logarithm of Monthly International Tourist Arrivals

Tourist Source	Mean	Median	Max.	Min.	Std. Dev.	Skewness	Kurtosis	J-B	Prob.
Italy	8.72	8.76	9.76	7.29	0.58	−0.43	2.81	3.86	0.15
Germany	8.69	8.69	9.09	8.10	0.23	−0.29	2.27	4.29	0.12
UK	8.44	8.48	9.29	7.20	0.42	−0.57	3.02	6.57	0.04
Japan	8.01	8.07	8.60	6.89	0.34	−0.74	3.46	11.89	0.00
France	7.41	7.48	8.69	5.60	0.63	−0.26	2.84	1.45	0.48
Switzerland	7.53	7.52	8.22	6.57	0.36	−0.13	2.46	1.80	0.41
Austria	6.79	6.79	7.73	5.57	0.48	−0.28	2.64	2.25	0.32
The Nether.	6.08	6.10	7.04	4.51	0.55	−0.41	2.49	4.72	0.09

Note: The number of observations is 120 for each country.

Table 6.4   Descriptive Statistics of Annual Difference of Monthly
International Tourist Arrivals

Tourist Source	Mean	Median	Max.	Min.	Std. Dev.	Skewness	Kurtosis	J-B	Prob.
Italy	33	44	800	−749	243	−0.20	4.27	8.01	0.02
Germany	254	166	2372	−1145	513	0.88	6.62	72.97	0.00
UK	35	84	2779	−2533	970	−0.12	3.06	0.27	0.87
Japan	873	666	7827	−5036	1628	0.66	7.15	85.48	0.00
France	171	197	1678	−2033	651	−0.66	4.41	16.69	0.00
Switzerland	26	24	707	−583	221	0.36	3.84	5.52	0.06
Austria	626	670	2344	−1890	656	−0.35	4.15	8.12	0.02
The Nether.	141	142	1136	−762	327	0.29	3.59	3.09	0.21

Note: The number of observations is 108 for each country.

Table 6.5   Descriptive Statistics of Log-Difference of Monthly International
Tourist Arrivals

Tourist Source	Mean	Median	Max.	Min.	Std. Dev.	Skewness	Kurtosis	J-B	Prob.
Italy	0.007	−0.018	0.881	−1.240	0.410	−0.31	3.53	3.35	0.19
Germany	−0.001	0.022	0.361	−0.523	0.176	−0.65	3.07	8.39	0.02
UK	0.018	0.030	0.514	−0.484	0.199	−0.20	2.65	1.42	0.49
Japan	0.007	0.019	0.680	−0.767	0.291	−0.09	2.94	0.17	0.92
France	0.008	0.097	1.119	−1.226	0.483	−0.32	2.61	2.76	0.25
Switzerland	0.005	0.011	0.663	−0.833	0.311	−0.15	2.67	0.96	0.62
Austria	0.000	−0.015	1.051	−1.233	0.391	−0.16	3.64	2.49	0.29
The Nether.	0.008	−0.023	0.688	−0.611	0.255	0.15	3.03	0.43	0.81

Note: The number of observations is 119 for each country.

normally distributed, it is usually the case that the kurtosis, which measures the peakedness or flatness of a series, is close to 3. Skewness is a measure of asymmetry around its mean and is zero for a symmetric distribution, such as the normal distribution. There is considerable negative skewness in all the series, while Italy, Germany and Austria show kurtosis that is relatively close to 3. The null hypothesis that the series are normally distributed is tested at the 5 per cent level of significance, and the Jarque-

Bera test statistic rejects the null hypothesis of normality for all the series, apart from Japan and UK.

When the series are transformed to logarithms, an examination of the descriptive statistics gives a different perspective. The standard deviations of the series have become smaller relative to their counterparts in levels, while all the series are shown to be positively skewed, and with a smaller magnitude. The kurtosis of the eight transformed series is somewhat variable, with Italy, UK and France showing values that are close to 3. The null hypothesis of normality for the Jarque-Bera test is rejected only for UK and Japan.

Annual differences of the eight series were also analysed using the descriptive statistics. The standard deviations are very large and are somewhat similar to the series in levels. Half of the series in annual differences are positively skewed, while the other half is skewed to the left with similar magnitudes to those of the logarithmic series. As for kurtosis, there is significant variability, with the UK being the only series showing kurtosis that is close to 3, compared with the series in levels and logarithms. For Italy, Germany, Japan, France and Austria, the Jarque-Bera test rejects the null hypothesis of normality at the 5 per cent level of significance.

Finally, all of the eight series are transformed into log-differences, or growth rates, of international monthly tourist arrivals. The standard deviations are relatively small and are similar in magnitude to the series in logarithms. The log-differences of the time series are all positively skewed, with similar magnitudes. The Jarque-Bera statistic reveals that the null hypothesis of normality is rejected only for Germany.

The above examination of the descriptive statistics suggests that the transformed series in logarithms and log-differences are optimal as these two transformed series for the eight tourism source markets reveal that they are closest to the normal distribution.

Stationarity

Prior to estimating the mean of the univariate time series, it is sensible to test for unit roots in the series as there are adverse consequences for estimation and inference in the presence of unit roots. In the classical regression model, it is assumed that the variables are stationary and that the errors of the regression model are stationary, with zero mean and finite unconditional variance. In the case where the series are non-stationary, the judgment would be otherwise and may lead to spurious regression results (see Granger and Newbold, 1974). In this section, we model univariate time series data, where lagged dependent variables are included to capture dynamics. Furthermore, we will also model the conditional variance of the data generating process. If the series are non-stationary, then the variance of the data generating process will become infinitely large, so that statistical inference will be affected. In

242   *The Economics of Small Island Tourism*

this context, we conduct the Phillips-Perron (1990) (PP) test for stationarity, with truncated lags of order 5 for each of the eight series in levels, logarithms, annual differences and log-differences.

The Phillips-Perron test involves estimating the following auxiliary regression equation:

$$\Delta y_t = \alpha y_{t-1} + x_t' \delta + \varepsilon_t \qquad (6.1)$$

where $\alpha = \rho - 1$, in order to test the hull hypothesis $H_0 : \alpha = 0$ against the alternative hypothesis, namely $H_1 : \alpha < 0$. The test is evaluated using a modified t-ratio of the form:

$$\hat{t}_\alpha = t_\alpha \left(\frac{\gamma_0}{f_0} \right)^{1/2} - \frac{T(f_0 - \gamma_0)[se(\hat{\alpha})]}{2 f_0^{1/2} s} \qquad (6.2)$$

where $\hat{\alpha}$ is the estimate, t_α is the t-ratio of $\hat{\alpha}$, $se(\hat{\alpha})$ is the standard error of $\hat{\alpha}$, and s is the standard error of the regression. In addition, γ_0 is a consistent estimate of the error variance in the above regression. The remaining f_0 is an estimator of the residual spectrum at frequency zero. The above equation is also known as the non-augmented Dickey-Fuller test equation.

The results of the test for the null hypothesis that monthly international tourist arrivals have a unit root are given in Table 6.6. The critical values for

Table 6.6   Phillips-Perron Test for Stationarity with, Constant, Time Trend and Five Truncated Lags

Source	Levels	Logs	Annual Difference	Log-Difference
Italy	−3.480	−3.698	−4.422	−9.525
Germany	−4.560	−4.719	−5.860	−11.123
UK	**−2.002**	−2.892	−9.630	−15.753
Japan	−5.008	−4.904	−5.951	−12.454
France	−3.596	−4.395	−4.115	−9.051
Switzerland	−4.715	−5.111	−7.385	−14.548
Austria	−4.480	−4.877	−5.691	−9.537
The Netherlands	**−2.718**	**−2.598**	−3.297	−12.988

Notes:
The null hypothesis is that monthly international tourist arrivals have a unit root.
The critical values for the rejection of the null hypothesis of a unit root are −3.486 and −2.886 for 1% and 5%, respectively.
The three items in bold indicate non-rejection of the null hypothesis of a unit root.

the rejection of the null hypothesis of a unit root are –3.486 and –2.886 at the 1 per cent and 5 per cent levels of significance, respectively. For Italy, the test suggests that the series in levels has a unit root at the 1 per cent level of significance, but rejects the null hypothesis at the 5 per cent significance level. For the UK and The Netherlands, the test suggests there is a unit root at both the 1 per cent and 5 per cent significance levels for the series in levels. For the rest of the countries, the series in levels are stationary. The logarithm of monthly international tourist arrivals from the UK has a unit root at the 1 per cent significance level, whereas the null hypothesis is rejected at the 5 per cent level. In the Dutch tourist arrivals series to Maldives, the test suggests they are non-stationary at both the 1 per cent and 5 per cent significance levels. However, there is strong evidence against the presence of unit roots for each of the countries in both annual differences and log-differences.

These results are not surprising. Enders (2004, p. 76) argues that 'non-stationary variables may have pronounced trend or appear to meander without a long-run mean or variance'. This is precisely the case for Italy and UK, both of which have very strong linear trends, while The Netherlands shows a meandering series without a long-term mean or variance. These tests have been conducted using several different lags, but the results were robust to such changes. The choice in implementing the PP test over the widely-used augmented Dickey-Fuller (ADF) test is due mainly to the presence of GARCH errors. ADF tests incorporate techniques explicitly accommodating a serial correlation structure in the errors, but not heteroscedasticity. However, the PP test takes into account both serial correlation and heteroscedasticity using non-parametric techniques. As mentioned in Phillips and Perron (1990), the PP test generally has higher power as compared with the ADF test.

Seasonality

Monthly international tourist arrivals to Maldives show very strong seasonal patterns, so it is imperative that we identify and incorporate them into the conditional mean. The traditional and most frequently used technique is the ratio-to-moving average (multiplicative) method. The technique is computationally convenient and easy to use. In this approach, the fundamental assumption is that a moving average expresses the trend and cyclical component of the times series adequately. The original monthly international tourist arrivals series (TA_t) are divided by the respective moving average figure for each month (MA_t), and expressed as a percentage to produce the ratio-to-moving average. These ratios are averaged over months, which is intended to isolate the seasonal and cyclical components. Based on these ratios, monthly seasonal indices are calculated using EViews 4.1, as follows:

$$M_{Ratio} = \left(\frac{TA_t}{MA_t} \right) * 100 . \qquad (6.3)$$

Regardless of whether the monthly seasonal indices are calculated based on levels or on a transformed series such as logarithms, they are qualitatively similar. Seasons in tourism are determined in months and the allocated index for a given month is always 1. If the calculated index exceeds 1, then the monthly tourist arrivals exceed the trend and cyclical components due to underlying seasonal factors. The monthly seasonal indices estimated for international tourist arrivals in levels for the eight major source countries are given in Table 6.7, where the seasonal concentrations can be readily identified.

As seven of the eight major tourism source countries are from Western Europe, the seasonal concentrations of monthly international tourist arrivals occur during the European winter months, roughly from November to March. During 1994–2003, the peak month for Italian, German and Dutch tourists has been March; for UK, France and Austria it has been February; for Japan it has been May, and for Switzerland it has been November. The lowest months for these countries have been during their summer (warmer) months where they tend to choose domestic tourism to overseas travel. Nearly one-half of Italian and German tourists visit Maldives from December to March and from November to March, respectively. More than one-half of UK tourists visit during November to April, and one-fifth also visit during August and September, due to the popularity of Maldives as a

Table 6.7   Seasonal Indices for Monthly International Tourist Arrivals, 1994–2003

Month	Italy	Germany	UK	Japan	France	Switz.	Austria	The Nether.
January	1.596	1.156	1.000	0.951	1.751	1.201	1.739	0.862
February	1.579	1.232	1.125	1.054	2.009	1.180	1.889	1.008
March	1.606	1.253	1.108	1.044	1.845	1.135	1.570	0.951
April	1.252	1.104	1.099	0.961	1.465	1.302	1.056	0.815
May	0.534	0.901	0.774	0.652	0.621	0.738	0.560	0.838
June	0.488	0.682	0.747	0.680	0.358	0.616	0.499	1.000
July	0.679	0.799	0.954	1.110	0.738	0.928	0.861	1.156
August	1.327	0.859	1.053	1.448	1.071	0.663	0.829	1.112
September	0.951	0.902	1.101	1.374	0.586	0.883	0.663	1.318
October	0.897	0.995	0.989	0.945	0.701	1.269	0.849	1.290
November	0.782	1.202	1.090	0.964	1.115	1.307	1.291	0.963
December	1.261	1.115	1.058	1.115	1.308	1.165	1.266	0.842

family holiday destination during the British summers. Nearly 20 per cent of Japanese tourists visit during February and March, while most Japanese tourist influxes occur from July to September, peaking during August. Seventy per cent of French and Swiss tourist visitations occur during November to April. During the same period, 67 per cent of Austrian tourists arrived during November to April, while nearly one-half of Dutch tourists visited Maldives from June to October.

6.7   MODELS OF INTERNATIONAL TOURIST ARRIVALS

Univariate GARCH and GJR models are estimated for monthly international tourist arrivals, logarithm of monthly international tourist arrivals, annual differences of monthly international tourist arrivals, and log-differences (the growth rate) of monthly international tourist arrivals, from each of the eight major tourist source countries to Maldives. The univariate and multivariate empirical results from the estimated models enable validation of the regularity conditions underlying the model, highlight the importance of the uncertainty surrounding monthly international tourist arrivals from the eight major tourist sources to Maldives, and evaluate them for policy analysis. This chapter provides, for the first time, estimates of static conditional correlations between monthly international tourist arrivals from a pair of tourist source countries to a SITE, specifically Maldives. These results give an indication of the relationship between shocks to the number of monthly international tourist arrivals, logarithm of monthly international tourist arrivals, annual difference of monthly international tourist arrivals, and the growth rate of monthly international tourist arrivals. Furthermore, the direction of causality in these measures of monthly international tourist demand across the eight main international tourist source countries to Maldives is evaluated. For Maldives, it is vital to obtain an accurate estimate of the uncertainty surrounding monthly international tourist arrivals based on historical data.

The Conditional Mean

An important task is to model the conditional mean. In order to estimate the conditional variance, h_t, accurately, we need to obtain accurate estimates of the unconditional shocks, ε_t. Univariate time series data on monthly international tourist arrivals show a considerable degree of habit persistence. The literature on univariate time series analysis of international tourism demand has shown that the Box and Jenkins (1976) ARMA specifications typically fit the data reasonably well.

Before deciding on a specific ARMA(p,q) model, we examine the correlograms of the monthly international tourist arrivals from the eight main markets, in levels, logarithms, annual differences and log-differences. The sample autocorrelation functions (ACFs) and partial autocorrelation functions (PACFs), with the usual two standard error bounds for monthly international tourist arrivals in levels for Italy, UK and the Netherlands, illustrate very large autocorrelation coefficients up to the twelfth lag, indicating that the series are non-stationary. This result is consistent with the unit root test results given in Table 6.2. Hence, first differencing of the time series will be necessary in order to achieve stationarity. Furthermore, as can be seen from Figure 6.6, the ACFs of the same series for France, Germany, Switzerland and Austria depict similar patterns, showing a spiralling pattern of the ACFs, tapering off towards zero, and with highly significant autocorrelation coefficients exceeding the standard error bounds for at least two lags. For these four countries, this is convincing indication of either an ARMA(1,1) or an ARMA(2,1) process. In the case of Japan, the ACFs show a different pattern, with large, significant autocorrelation coefficients exceeding the two standard error bounds for lags 11, 12 and 13, indicating that seasonal differencing may be necessary.

The ACFs and PACFs of monthly international tourist arrivals in logarithms, which are illustrated in Figure 6.7, are almost identical to their levels counterparts. The only observable difference is in the case of Italy, where the ACFs show that the transformed series are still non-stationary, although the PP tests for a unit root in the monthly international tourist arrival series suggest otherwise. These results also indicate that the data generating process for all the series except The Netherlands is either ARMA(1,1) or ARMA(2,1). Since both the levels and the logarithmic series indicate large autocorrelation coefficients at the 11, 12 and 13 lags, seasonal differencing may be necessary since there is strong evidence of distinct seasonal patterns. The ACFs and PACFs for the annual differenced series are given in Figure 6.8. The autocorrelation coefficients for all series dampen out, except for The Netherlands. However, for Italy, Germany, Japan, France, Switzerland and Austria, the autocorrelation coefficients exceed the two standard error bands for at least the first three lags. The autocorrelation coefficients in the series for the UK do not overshoot the two standard error bands. Finally, we examine the correlograms of the series in log-differences, or the growth rate of the monthly international tourist arrivals, which are illustrated in Figure 6.9. In this case the autocorrelation coefficients dampen out for all eight series. Although the autocorrelation coefficients exceed the 2 standard error bounds, the most pronounced are given at lag 12 for each series.

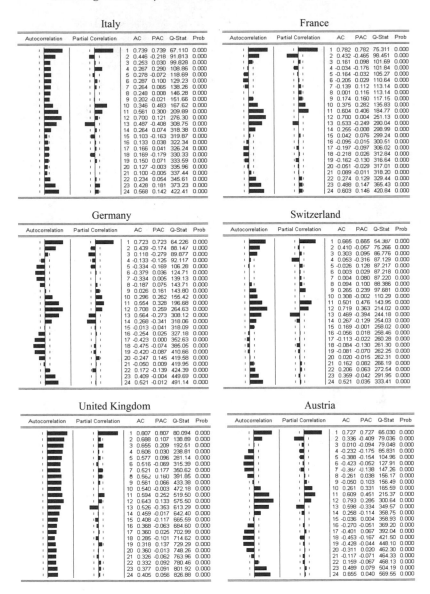

Figure 6.6   ACF and PACF of Monthly International Tourist Arrivals, 1994–2003

Japan

Autocorrelation	Partial Correlation		AC	PAC	Q-Stat	Prob
		1	0.613	0.613	46.236	0.000
		2	0.222	-0.246	52.369	0.000
		3	0.111	0.157	53.919	0.000
		4	0.185	0.142	58.260	0.000
		5	0.250	0.078	66.212	0.000
		6	0.226	0.034	72.743	0.000
		7	0.217	0.125	78.852	0.000
		8	0.127	-0.122	80.970	0.000
		9	-0.003	-0.089	80.971	0.000
		10	0.064	0.202	81.523	0.000
		11	0.379	0.401	100.87	0.000
		12	0.638	0.333	156.09	0.000
		13	0.382	-0.365	176.02	0.000
		14	0.038	-0.162	176.22	0.000
		15	-0.029	0.032	176.34	0.000
		16	0.065	-0.001	176.93	0.000
		17	0.157	0.046	180.43	0.000
		18	0.133	-0.081	182.97	0.000
		19	0.121	0.017	185.08	0.000
		20	0.044	0.011	185.36	0.000
		21	-0.085	0.002	186.44	0.000
		22	-0.042	-0.016	186.69	0.000
		23	0.265	0.145	197.29	0.000
		24	0.484	0.034	233.03	0.000

The Netherlands

Autocorrelation	Partial Correlation		AC	PAC	Q-Stat	Prob
		1	0.868	0.868	92.693	0.000
		2	0.771	0.071	166.43	0.000
		3	0.720	0.150	231.31	0.000
		4	0.651	-0.058	284.76	0.000
		5	0.599	0.055	330.51	0.000
		6	0.552	-0.012	369.63	0.000
		7	0.546	0.179	408.26	0.000
		8	0.552	0.092	448.12	0.000
		9	0.540	0.020	486.55	0.000
		10	0.527	0.002	523.53	0.000
		11	0.543	0.136	563.12	0.000
		12	0.545	0.016	603.40	0.000
		13	0.456	-0.320	631.86	0.000
		14	0.373	-0.127	651.08	0.000
		15	0.328	0.004	666.08	0.000
		16	0.287	0.033	677.67	0.000
		17	0.237	-0.065	685.65	0.000
		18	0.177	-0.129	690.17	0.000
		19	0.167	0.034	694.19	0.000
		20	0.157	-0.021	697.81	0.000
		21	0.113	-0.089	699.68	0.000
		22	0.093	0.026	700.98	0.000
		23	0.103	0.074	702.58	0.000
		24	0.096	0.008	703.97	0.000

Figure 6.6 ACF and PACF of Monthly International Tourist Arrivals, 1994–2003 (continued)

Italy

Autocorrelation	Partial Correlation		AC	PAC	Q-Stat	Prob
		1	0.739	0.739	67.110	0.000
		2	0.446	-0.218	91.813	0.000
		3	0.253	0.030	99.828	0.000
		4	0.267	0.290	108.86	0.000
		5	0.278	-0.072	118.69	0.000
		6	0.287	0.100	129.23	0.000
		7	0.264	0.065	138.26	0.000
		8	0.248	0.008	146.28	0.000
		9	0.202	-0.021	151.66	0.000
		10	0.346	0.483	167.62	0.000
		11	0.561	0.300	209.89	0.000
		12	0.700	0.121	276.30	0.000
		13	0.487	-0.408	308.75	0.000
		14	0.264	0.074	318.38	0.000
		15	0.103	-0.163	319.87	0.000
		16	0.133	0.038	322.34	0.000
		17	0.166	0.041	326.24	0.000
		18	0.169	-0.179	330.33	0.000
		19	0.150	0.071	333.59	0.000
		20	0.127	-0.003	335.96	0.000
		21	0.100	-0.005	337.44	0.000
		22	0.234	0.054	345.61	0.000
		23	0.428	0.181	373.23	0.000
		24	0.568	0.142	422.41	0.000

France

Autocorrelation	Partial Correlation		AC	PAC	Q-Stat	Prob
		1	0.694	0.694	59.337	0.000
		2	0.297	-0.359	70.260	0.000
		3	0.157	0.278	73.326	0.000
		4	0.027	-0.350	73.416	0.000
		5	-0.134	0.052	75.705	0.000
		6	-0.195	-0.106	80.599	0.000
		7	-0.135	0.138	82.949	0.000
		8	0.012	0.144	82.968	0.000
		9	0.122	-0.014	84.921	0.000
		10	0.231	0.292	92.029	0.000
		11	0.559	0.637	133.96	0.000
		12	0.782	0.026	216.86	0.000
		13	0.539	-0.264	256.58	0.000
		14	0.198	-0.109	261.99	0.000
		15	0.074	0.037	262.75	0.000
		16	-0.027	-0.014	262.85	0.000
		17	-0.175	-0.046	267.19	0.000
		18	-0.227	0.021	274.59	0.000
		19	-0.174	-0.131	278.96	0.000
		20	-0.051	-0.002	279.34	0.000
		21	0.049	0.021	279.70	0.000
		22	0.155	-0.022	283.28	0.000
		23	0.442	0.142	312.71	0.000
		24	0.655	0.069	378.09	0.000

Germany

Autocorrelation	Partial Correlation		AC	PAC	Q-Stat	Prob
		1	0.697	0.697	59.766	0.000
		2	0.412	-0.144	80.806	0.000
		3	0.100	-0.254	82.059	0.000
		4	-0.142	-0.138	84.599	0.000
		5	-0.327	-0.158	98.201	0.000
		6	-0.357	0.028	114.59	0.000
		7	-0.322	-0.039	128.00	0.000
		8	-0.191	0.052	132.78	0.000
		9	0.014	0.161	132.81	0.000
		10	0.267	0.231	142.31	0.000
		11	0.529	0.341	179.88	0.000
		12	0.697	0.295	245.68	0.000
		13	0.541	-0.272	285.67	0.000
		14	0.242	-0.327	293.79	0.000
		15	-0.034	-0.067	293.95	0.000
		16	-0.263	0.019	303.71	0.000
		17	-0.411	0.028	327.67	0.000
		18	-0.445	-0.064	356.03	0.000
		19	-0.404	-0.128	379.72	0.000
		20	-0.238	0.141	388.03	0.000
		21	-0.048	0.045	388.37	0.000
		22	0.162	-0.106	392.31	0.000
		23	0.398	-0.014	416.27	0.000
		24	0.520	-0.028	457.57	0.000

Switzerland

Autocorrelation	Partial Correlation		AC	PAC	Q-Stat	Prob
		1	0.624	0.624	47.964	0.000
		2	0.406	0.026	68.367	0.000
		3	0.312	0.081	80.562	0.000
		4	0.018	-0.350	80.605	0.000
		5	-0.067	0.058	81.181	0.000
		6	-0.034	0.074	81.332	0.000
		7	-0.056	0.057	81.733	0.000
		8	0.027	0.068	81.828	0.000
		9	0.247	0.295	89.895	0.000
		10	0.280	-0.008	100.32	0.000
		11	0.451	0.369	127.70	0.000
		12	0.710	0.443	196.09	0.000
		13	0.436	-0.392	222.06	0.000
		14	0.266	-0.142	231.79	0.000
		15	0.174	-0.057	236.04	0.000
		16	-0.087	0.036	237.11	0.000
		17	-0.143	0.024	240.02	0.000
		18	-0.123	-0.130	242.19	0.000
		19	-0.138	-0.049	244.97	0.000
		20	-0.046	-0.017	245.27	0.000
		21	0.133	0.047	247.87	0.000
		22	0.186	0.133	253.02	0.000
		23	0.332	-0.018	269.66	0.000
		24	0.554	0.115	316.55	0.000

Figure 6.7 ACF and PACF of Logarithmic Monthly International Tourist Arrivals, 1994–2003

United Kingdom

Autocorrelation	Partial Correlation		AC	PAC	Q-Stat	Prob
		1	0.830	0.830	84.826	0.000
		2	0.726	0.119	150.31	0.000
		3	0.678	0.157	207.88	0.000
		4	0.655	0.129	262.09	0.000
		5	0.632	0.072	312.91	0.000
		6	0.568	-0.082	354.39	0.000
		7	0.548	0.097	393.26	0.000
		8	0.557	0.115	433.74	0.000
		9	0.551	0.034	473.74	0.000
		10	0.544	0.060	513.08	0.000
		11	0.580	0.214	558.34	0.000
		12	0.610	0.093	608.77	0.000
		13	0.516	-0.335	645.21	0.000
		14	0.457	-0.029	674.09	0.000
		15	0.407	-0.097	697.15	0.000
		16	0.385	-0.052	718.03	0.000
		17	0.372	0.045	737.74	0.000
		18	0.301	-0.080	750.78	0.000
		19	0.317	0.163	765.37	0.000
		20	0.324	-0.032	780.75	0.000
		21	0.299	-0.079	793.98	0.000
		22	0.312	0.110	808.51	0.000
		23	0.356	0.132	827.67	0.000
		24	0.372	-0.020	848.82	0.000

Austria

Autocorrelation	Partial Correlation		AC	PAC	Q-Stat	Prob
		1	0.667	0.667	54.739	0.000
		2	0.257	-0.339	62.921	0.000
		3	0.038	0.071	63.105	0.000
		4	-0.175	-0.317	66.988	0.000
		5	-0.371	-0.154	84.510	0.000
		6	-0.423	-0.092	107.49	0.000
		7	-0.363	-0.075	124.55	0.000
		8	-0.202	0.093	129.87	0.000
		9	-0.009	0.011	129.88	0.000
		10	0.209	0.199	135.67	0.000
		11	0.564	0.542	178.37	0.000
		12	0.772	0.270	259.17	0.000
		13	0.519	-0.291	296.01	0.000
		14	0.187	-0.051	300.82	0.000
		15	-0.016	-0.089	300.86	0.000
		16	-0.221	-0.010	307.70	0.000
		17	-0.379	0.065	328.08	0.000
		18	-0.443	-0.160	356.27	0.000
		19	-0.393	0.001	378.65	0.000
		20	-0.250	-0.074	387.77	0.000
		21	-0.080	-0.055	388.71	0.000
		22	0.112	-0.106	390.57	0.000
		23	0.441	0.094	419.95	0.000
		24	0.614	0.013	477.40	0.000

Japan

Autocorrelation	Partial Correlation		AC	PAC	Q-Stat	Prob
		1	0.626	0.626	48.134	0.000
		2	0.255	-0.224	56.196	0.000
		3	0.125	0.121	58.158	0.000
		4	0.213	0.207	63.858	0.000
		5	0.292	0.076	74.700	0.000
		6	0.246	-0.005	82.503	0.000
		7	0.242	0.181	90.080	0.000
		8	0.154	-0.141	93.181	0.000
		9	0.026	-0.110	93.267	0.000
		10	0.094	0.254	94.433	0.000
		11	0.378	0.365	113.59	0.000
		12	0.593	0.212	161.25	0.000
		13	0.349	-0.334	177.91	0.000
		14	0.033	-0.120	178.07	0.000
		15	-0.028	0.053	178.18	0.000
		16	0.068	-0.065	178.83	0.000
		17	0.162	0.022	182.56	0.000
		18	0.131	-0.020	185.04	0.000
		19	0.132	0.051	187.58	0.000
		20	0.041	-0.085	187.83	0.000
		21	-0.080	0.005	188.77	0.000
		22	-0.029	0.014	188.89	0.000
		23	0.257	0.169	198.83	0.000
		24	0.444	0.045	228.94	0.000

The Netherlands

Autocorrelation	Partial Correlation		AC	PAC	Q-Stat	Prob
		1	0.881	0.881	95.589	0.000
		2	0.790	0.057	172.95	0.000
		3	0.730	0.106	239.65	0.000
		4	0.676	0.023	297.40	0.000
		5	0.618	-0.023	346.07	0.000
		6	0.571	0.022	387.87	0.000
		7	0.570	0.197	429.98	0.000
		8	0.564	0.037	471.63	0.000
		9	0.542	-0.017	510.34	0.000
		10	0.529	0.048	547.66	0.000
		11	0.526	0.043	584.81	0.000
		12	0.514	0.002	620.57	0.000
		13	0.434	-0.267	646.36	0.000
		14	0.365	-0.072	664.73	0.000
		15	0.325	0.015	679.47	0.000
		16	0.287	-0.006	691.04	0.000
		17	0.234	-0.075	698.84	0.000
		18	0.185	-0.080	703.73	0.000
		19	0.183	0.080	708.56	0.000
		20	0.161	-0.066	712.34	0.000
		21	0.127	-0.013	714.74	0.000
		22	0.095	-0.061	716.09	0.000
		23	0.092	0.084	717.36	0.000
		24	0.086	0.042	718.49	0.000

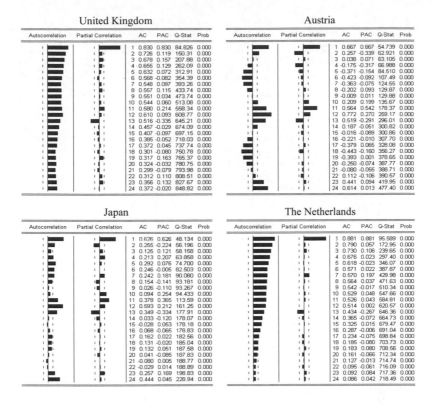

Figure 6.7 ACF and PACF of Logarithmic Monthly International Tourist Arrivals, 1994–2003 (continued)

Italy

Autocorrelation	Partial Correlation		AC	PAC	Q-Stat	Prob
		1	0.698	0.698	54.029	0.000
		2	0.559	0.141	89.048	0.000
		3	0.457	0.047	112.69	0.000
		4	0.263	-0.207	120.59	0.000
		5	0.138	-0.068	122.80	0.000
		6	0.063	0.002	123.26	0.000
		7	-0.025	-0.034	123.33	0.000
		8	-0.093	-0.059	124.35	0.000
		9	-0.220	-0.228	130.16	0.000
		10	-0.306	-0.121	141.53	0.000
		11	-0.319	0.025	153.98	0.000
		12	-0.423	-0.183	176.13	0.000
		13	-0.366	0.101	192.93	0.000
		14	-0.314	-0.016	205.36	0.000
		15	-0.311	-0.066	217.70	0.000
		16	-0.233	0.009	224.71	0.000
		17	-0.112	0.132	226.34	0.000
		18	-0.114	-0.123	228.07	0.000
		19	-0.068	-0.062	228.68	0.000
		20	-0.006	0.011	228.69	0.000
		21	0.007	-0.058	228.69	0.000
		22	0.062	0.027	229.22	0.000
		23	0.098	0.032	230.56	0.000
		24	0.125	-0.059	232.77	0.000

France

Autocorrelation	Partial Correlation		AC	PAC	Q-Stat	Prob
		1	0.716	0.716	56.990	0.000
		2	0.557	0.089	91.708	0.000
		3	0.378	-0.101	107.88	0.000
		4	0.173	-0.191	111.30	0.000
		5	0.074	0.034	111.93	0.000
		6	-0.070	-0.136	112.50	0.000
		7	-0.158	-0.059	115.43	0.000
		8	-0.146	0.101	117.98	0.000
		9	-0.162	-0.023	121.14	0.000
		10	-0.211	-0.191	126.55	0.000
		11	-0.209	-0.018	131.90	0.000
		12	-0.336	-0.284	145.85	0.000
		13	-0.230	0.275	152.45	0.000
		14	-0.176	0.017	156.35	0.000
		15	-0.152	-0.042	159.28	0.000
		16	-0.050	0.004	159.60	0.000
		17	-0.036	-0.052	159.77	0.000
		18	0.000	-0.083	159.77	0.000
		19	0.026	-0.014	159.86	0.000
		20	0.032	0.112	160.00	0.000
		21	0.017	-0.042	160.04	0.000
		22	0.077	0.074	160.85	0.000
		23	0.041	-0.095	161.09	0.000
		24	0.050	-0.145	161.44	0.000

Figure 6.8 ACF and PACF of Annual Difference of Monthly International Tourist Arrivals, 1994–2003

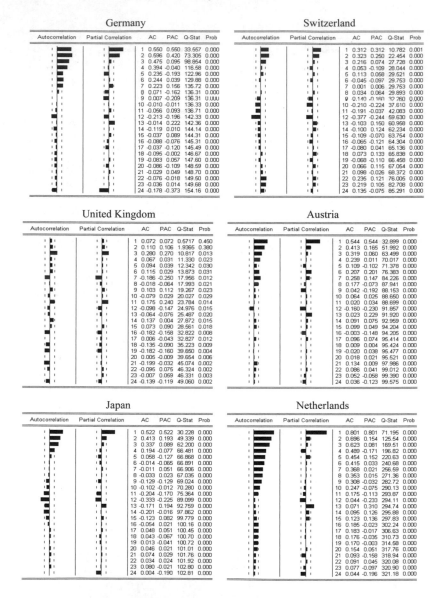

Figure 6.8   ACF and PACF of Annual Difference of Monthly International Tourist Arrivals, 1994–2003 (continued)

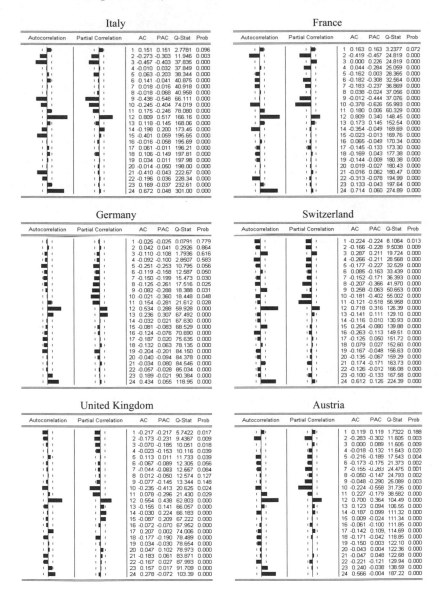

Figure 6.9   ACF and PACF of Log-difference of Monthly International Tourist Arrivals, 1994–2003

Japan

Autocorrelation	Partial Correlation		AC	PAC	Q-Stat	Prob
		1	0.008	0.008	0.0080	0.929
		2	-0.336	-0.336	13.877	0.001
		3	-0.318	-0.351	26.435	0.000
		4	-0.011	-0.198	26.451	0.000
		5	0.180	-0.097	30.529	0.000
		6	-0.016	-0.254	30.561	0.000
		7	0.137	0.094	32.980	0.000
		8	0.049	0.060	33.291	0.000
		9	-0.305	-0.327	45.493	0.000
		10	-0.299	-0.414	57.268	0.000
		11	0.106	-0.282	58.777	0.000
		12	0.626	0.260	111.51	0.000
		13	0.100	0.046	112.87	0.000
		14	-0.346	-0.102	129.24	0.000
		15	-0.236	-0.003	136.96	0.000
		16	-0.006	-0.059	136.97	0.000
		17	0.173	-0.006	141.21	0.000
		18	0.004	-0.063	141.22	0.000
		19	0.132	0.017	143.71	0.000
		20	0.033	-0.047	143.86	0.000
		21	-0.248	-0.003	152.88	0.000
		22	-0.321	-0.184	168.18	0.000
		23	0.155	-0.047	171.78	0.000
		24	0.504	0.040	210.25	0.000

The Netherlands

Autocorrelation	Partial Correlation		AC	PAC	Q-Stat	Prob
		1	-0.139	-0.139	2.3440	0.126
		2	-0.133	-0.155	4.5214	0.104
		3	-0.075	-0.123	5.2260	0.156
		4	-0.021	-0.080	5.2816	0.260
		5	0.037	-0.012	5.4514	0.363
		6	-0.196	-0.231	10.339	0.111
		7	0.062	-0.023	10.830	0.146
		8	0.057	-0.009	11.245	0.188
		9	-0.038	-0.076	11.437	0.247
		10	-0.116	-0.166	13.227	0.211
		11	0.026	-0.041	13.316	0.273
		12	0.333	0.269	28.203	0.005
		13	-0.010	0.092	28.218	0.008
		14	-0.135	-0.039	30.719	0.006
		15	-0.033	0.001	30.866	0.009
		16	0.061	0.064	31.386	0.012
		17	0.042	0.085	31.640	0.017
		18	-0.195	-0.082	37.059	0.005
		19	0.089	0.057	38.202	0.006
		20	0.075	0.044	39.030	0.007
		21	-0.023	0.029	39.105	0.010
		22	-0.179	-0.125	43.863	0.004
		23	-0.002	-0.062	43.864	0.005
		24	0.301	0.144	57.621	0.000

Figure 6.9   ACF and PACF of Log-difference of Monthly International Tourist Arrivals, 1994–2003 (continued)

Considering the analysis described above, ARMA(p,q) specifications of the following general form have been chosen:

$$TA_t = ARMA(p,q) + \sum_{i=1}^{12} \phi_i D_{it} + \sum_{i=1}^{12} \theta_i D_{it} t + \varepsilon_t , \qquad (6.4)$$
$$Vol(\varepsilon_t) = \varepsilon_t^2 ,$$

$$LogTA_t = ARMA(p,q) + \sum_{i=1}^{12} \phi_i D_{it} + \sum_{i=1}^{12} \theta_i Di_{it} t + \varepsilon_t , \qquad (6.5)$$
$$Vol(\varepsilon_t) = \varepsilon_t^2 ,$$

$$\Delta_{12} TA_t = ARMA(p,q) + \sum_{i=1}^{12} \phi_i D_{it} + \sum_{i=1}^{12} \theta_i D_{it} t + \varepsilon_t , \qquad (6.6)$$
$$Vol(\varepsilon_t) = \varepsilon_t^2 ,$$

$$\Delta \log TA_t = ARMA(p,q) + \sum_{i=1}^{12} \phi_i D_{it} + \sum_{i=1}^{12} \theta_i Di_{it} t + \varepsilon_t , \qquad (6.7)$$
$$Vol(\varepsilon_t) = \varepsilon_t^2 ,$$

where TA_t, $\log TA_t$, $\Delta_{12} TA_t$ and $\Delta \log TA_t$ are monthly international tourist arrivals, logarithm of monthly international tourist arrivals, the annual difference of monthly international tourist arrivals, and the log-difference (growth rate) of monthly tourist arrivals at time t. D_{it} (=1, 2, ..., 12 and is equal to zero elsewhere) denotes seasonal dummies; $t = 1$ to T, where $T = 120$ for all eight series. $D_{it} t$ is the seasonal dummy multiplied by the deterministic time trend to capture the trend effect of the seasonal dummies, particularly for Italy and Austria. Equations (6.4) to (6.7) are the empirical versions of the conditional mean equation (5.1) in Chapter 5.

Several models have been tested and fitted to determine the most appropriate ARMA process to describe monthly international tourist arrivals from the eight major tourist source countries to Maldives over the period 1994–2003. The choice of model that best explains monthly international tourists to Maldives is chosen on the basis of the statistical significance (at the 5 per cent level) of the AR and MA coefficients, the seasonal dummy variables, and the absence of serial correlation in the unconditional shocks. Furthermore, the empirical models are chosen according to the Box-Jenkins (1971) model selection criteria of the lowest values of AIC and SBC.

Conditional Variance

Univariate models
The univariate ARMA(p,q)-GARCH(1,1) and ARMA(p,q)-GJR(1,1) models are used to estimate the monthly international tourist arrivals, logarithm of monthly international tourist arrivals, annual difference of monthly international tourist arrivals, and the growth rate of monthly international tourist arrivals. Tables 6.8–6.20 present the empirical results for the different conditional means for the respective series and their conditional variances.

All the estimates in this chapter are obtained using EViews 4.1. The Berndt, Hall, Hall and Hausman (BHHH) (1974) algorithm has been used in most cases, but the Marquardt algorithm is used when the BHHH algorithm does not converge. Several different sets of initial values have been used in each case, but do not lead to substantial differences in the estimates. The asymptotic and robust t-ratios (see Bollerslev and Wooldridge, 1992) for the QMLE are reported in Tables 6.8–6.20. There are three entries for each estimate, namely the coefficient (in bold), the Bollerslev-Wooldridge (1992) robust *t*-ratio and the asymptotic *t*-ratio. In general, the robust *t*-ratios are smaller in absolute value than their asymptotic counterparts.

The estimates of the conditional mean for the ARMA(p,q)-GARCH(1,1) model for the monthly international tourist arrivals, logarithm of monthly international tourist arrivals, annual difference of monthly international tourist arrivals, and the growth rate of monthly international tourist arrivals for the eight main tourist source markets, are given in Tables 6.8, 6.12, 6.16 and 6.17, respectively. The conditional mean estimates for ARMA(p,q)-GJR(1,1) for the same series, except for annual differences, are given in Tables 6.10, 6.14 and 6.19. For annual differences, there was no evidence of asymmetry, so that the results have been omitted.

The conditional mean estimates are obtained through the general-to-

Table 6.8 Conditional Mean of Monthly International Tourist Arrivals, 1994–2003

	AR	MA(1)	D1	D2	D3	D4	D4T	D5	D6	D7	D8	D9	D10	D11	D12	D12T
Italy	0.952		2100.159		936.561		-43.080	-3062.293			3737.849	-1192.810				60.275
	34.949		4.579		2.523		-7.875	-8.177			14.373	-3.052				10.336
	68.503		11.307		4.311		-4.957	-15.110			11.945	-5.125				10.968
Germany	0.668	0.529	2353.688	3074.609	2743.739	1395.037				1466.837	2340.387	2216.435	2617.035	3763.686	2911.566	
	29.080	5.041	9.032	8.314	8.761	6.142				5.735	6.071	9.290	7.104	14.306	12.833	
	29.480	6.509	8.451	14.468	11.594	7.054				8.875	15.347	8.544	14.004	14.410	11.269	
UK	0.921	0.909						-421.157		1576.384	1588.114	1082.893		370.406	1016.941	
	32.820	16.321						-1.972		4.441	3.598	2.917		1.456	5.350	
	27.622	21.104						-2.394		6.746	5.845	4.987		1.072	3.025	
Japan	0.658	0.350	914.344	1083.526	1179.867	929.094				2045.894	3120.234	1810.620		534.577	1482.476	
	34.532	3.051	7.964	7.584	9.409	6.927				22.696	21.832	16.538		5.685	15.387	
	43.199	3.495	6.635	8.955	11.268	9.950				22.130	42.880	19.320		4.852	11.126	
France	0.740	0.934	1334.726	1424.698	666.153			-1006.755	-979.671	434.445	1118.271			1169.889	1171.733	
	21.477	18.773	11.621	10.802	5.580			-6.376	-4.768	2.125	7.419			18.035	10.147	
	25.833	24.752	9.633	12.361	8.137			-11.734	-10.711	6.577	20.385			10.583	10.290	

Note: AR column contains AR(1) for Italy and AR(2) for Germany, UK, Japan and France.

Table 6.8 Conditional Mean of Monthly International Tourist Arrivals, 1994–2003 (continued)

	AR(2)	MA(1)	D1	D2	D3	D4	D5	D6	D7	D8	D9	D10	D11	D12
Switzerland	0.685	0.684	484.760	680.786	470.506	791.588	.	-369.233	771.785	422.244	437.187	1526.140	1329.403	458.581
	15.901	8.817	3.615	5.362	3.198	7.246	.	-3.444	7.364	2.745	3.131	17.198	11.620	3.253
	16.416	8.049	3.493	5.845	4.432	8.928	.	-4.716	7.725	5.634	4.506	14.341	10.038	3.332
Austria	AR(2)		D1T	D2T		D4T	D5T	D6T	D7T		D9T		D11T	D12T
	0.907		6.270	7.224		-5.812	-7.547	-4.470	2.995		-1.410		5.951	4.061
	20.404		2.357	6.097		-4.085	-6.508	-2.335	1.120		-0.604		4.521	3.567
	21.847		9.288	5.800		-5.251	-6.417	-6.363	6.994		-2.472		8.372	4.941
Netherlands	AR(1)	MA(1)												
	0.992	-0.254												
	63.608	-2.029												
	49.514	-2.885												

Notes: The three entries associated with each parameter are their respective estimate, the asymptotic *t*-ratios and the Bollerslev-Wooldridge (1992) robust *t*-ratios.

Table 6.9   Conditional Variance of GARCH(1,1) Monthly International Tourist Arrivals, 1994–2003

Country	ω	α	β	Log-Moment	Second Moment
Italy	14 961.002	0.244	0.793	−0.015	1.037
	0.750	3.043	13.704		
	0.422	1.490	5.497		
Germany	11 994.683	0.101	0.876	−0.034	0.977
	0.349	1.130	5.468		
	0.658	1.545	9.159		
UK	10 447.938	0.124	0.875	−0.015	0.999
	0.513	1.402	10.627		
	0.456	1.788	10.062		
Japan	4 643.821	0.325	0.693	−0.046	1.018
	0.800	1.952	5.329		
	0.858	2.743	6.309		
France	3 021.869	0.288	0.737	−0.039	1.025
	0.858	2.264	7.342		
	0.762	2.455	7.139		
Switzerland	2 138.989	0.211	0.787	−0.038	0.998
	0.591	1.596	5.782		
	0.678	1.852	6.927		
Austria	561.733	0.092	0.894	−0.019	0.986
	0.254	1.600	13.596		
	0.265	1.794	16.605		
Netherlands	819.031	0.098	0.857	−0.060	0.955
	0.972	1.197	8.333		
	0.649	1.576	6.961		

Note: The three entries associated with each parameter are their respective estimate, the asymptotic *t*-ratios and the Bollerslev-Wooldridge (1992) robust *t*-ratio.

specific modelling procedure, in which insignificant variables are excluded until a parsimonious specification is achieved. It is evident from the results that there is a very strong degree of habit persistence in the monthly international tourist arrivals, with the AR(1) coefficients being very close to 1, and highly significant. This result is consistent with the findings in the literature. There is also strong evidence to suggest that tourism to Maldives is highly seasonal, with tourist arrivals being significantly concentrated in the peak tourist season, which coincides with the European winter months. This is consistent with the previously calculated seasonal indices given in Table 6.7. However, in the case of the Netherlands, there is no evidence of seasonality in the monthly international tourist arrivals, while there is support for seasonality in the logarithms and log-difference series. In the log-difference series, for Italy, Switzerland and Austria, the trended seasonal dummies are found to be more significant than their non-trended counterparts. The conditional mean estimates for the annual differences are deseasonalised estimates, as taking the twelfth difference eliminates the seasonal effects in the series. As monthly data are used, we are concerned with the significant partial autocorrelation function at lag 12.

The conditional variance estimates for GARCH(1,1) are given in Tables 6.9, 6.13, 6.16 and 6.18, and for GJR(1,1) in Tables 6.11, 6.15 and 6.20. In the case of conditional variance for the GARCH(1,1) model for monthly international arrivals series, the second moment conditions are satisfied only for Germany, UK, Switzerland, Austria and the Netherlands, while the log-moment condition is satisfied in all cases. Hence, the consistency and asymptomatic normality of the QMLE are guaranteed. The estimate of the GARCH coefficient, or β, is significant in all cases, while the estimated ARCH effect, or α, is only significant for Italy, Japan and France. These results imply that a shock to the tourist arrivals series has long-run persistence.

The GJR(1,1) estimates are illustrated in Table 6.11, and show satisfactory estimates of asymmetry for both Germany and the Netherlands. Both the log-moment and second moment conditions are satisfied for the Netherlands, while the log-moment condition is only satisfied for Germany, thereby guaranteeing the consistency and asymptotic normality of the QMLE. This implies that if German tourist arrivals are lower than expected, then the volatility surrounding their arrivals is highly uncertain in subsequent periods. Conversely, for Dutch tourists, the negative sign of the γ coefficient estimate implies that, if the anticipated arrivals are lower than expected, the uncertainty will be lower.

For the GARCH(1,1) estimates of the conditional variance of the logarithm of monthly international tourist arrivals, both the log-moment and second moment conditions are satisfied, so that the consistency and asymptotic normality of the QMLE are guaranteed. Interestingly, the results demonstrate that there is strong evidence of long-run persistence $(\alpha + \beta)$ as the GARCH(1) coefficients are relatively large and highly significant. The short-run persistence, or the ARCH effect, is only significant for Japan, Switzerland, Austria and the Netherlands. The GJR(1,1) estimates for the logarithm of monthly international tourist arrivals series show that both moment conditions are met only for Germany, Japan, France, Switzerland

Table 6.10   Conditional Mean of Monthly International Tourist Arrivals, 1994–2003

	AR(1)/AR(2)	MA(1)	D1	D2	D3	D4 / D4T	D5	D6	D7	D8	D9	D10	D11	D12 / D12T
Italy AR(1)	0.953		2119.107		893.537	−42.909	−2995.448			3778.016	−1195.295			60.986
	32.718		4.724		2.309	−8.015	−8.475			14.679	−2.767			10.045
	70.182		10.445		4.064	−4.869	−15.211			11.093	−5.389			11.747
Germany AR(2) MA(1)	0.652	0.442	2376.847	3288.713	2902.185	1545.710			1468.515	2488.295	2443.980	2815.475	3652.804	2579.422
	29.024	4.828	9.321	11.143	8.961	6.604			5.283	6.968	9.241	8.560	13.814	12.066
	87.814	4.880	11.438	20.106	20.945	7.568			11.517	22.561	11.981	18.822	22.369	12.126
UK AR(2) MA(1)	0.932	1.079					−395.389		1664.519	1798.615	1332.417		389.125	1079.941
	33.302	332.167					−2156.625		17.223	17.662	24.334		1.911	4.104
	1268.411	133.800					−7.087		7.064	5.503	5.561		1.539	5.818
Japan AR(2) MA(1)	0.659	0.460	973.058	1146.264	1194.895	969.690			2038.277	3094.621	1807.377		461.426	1462.621
	30.251	4.179	9.597	8.854	9.020	6.760			23.026	18.850	14.958		4.393	14.403
	42.023	5.245	5.995	7.713	9.666	10.258			18.571	36.414	21.303		4.520	10.650
France AR(2) MA(1)	0.770	0.911	1340.512	1442.781	672.786		−1008.836	−1019.062	429.727	1104.526			1154.417	1207.555
	22.449	17.158	13.872	10.056	5.498		−5.853	−4.768	2.465	8.654			17.077	13.080
	26.086	20.984	8.952	12.924	8.422		−11.900	−12.058	6.221	18.901			9.945	8.289

258

Table 6.10   Conditional Mean of Monthly International Tourist Arrivals, 1994–2003 (continued)

	AR(2)	MA(1)	D1	D2	D3	D4	D5	D6	D7	D8	D9	D10	D11	D12
Switzerland	0.661	0.545	564.694	846.889	585.597	904.156	.	−356.399	763.831	383.330	547.755	1593.750	1500.526	614.790
	22.237	6.921	4.673	8.399	6.614	12.076	.	−3.919	8.052	1.751	3.515	18.105	18.873	5.348
	18.231	5.214	4.958	7.410	5.811	11.769	.	−3.655	7.990	5.922	6.323	14.297	11.569	5.130
	AR(2)	.	D1T	D2T	.	D4T	D5T	D6T	D7T	.	D9T	.	D11T	D12T
Austria	0.927	.	7.095	8.538	.	−7.621	−8.909	−5.047	3.362	.	−1.590	.	6.852	5.035
	21.434	.	3.169	5.248	.	−4.277	−5.457	−2.049	1.063	.	−0.612	.	4.238	2.664
	24.045	.	6.153	5.864	.	−4.790	−5.857	−5.507	5.140	.	−2.125	.	6.940	5.332
	AR(1)	MA(1)	.	.	.	.	.	.	.	.	.	.	.	.
Netherlands	0.993	−0.148	.	.	.	.	.	.	.	.	.	.	.	.
	52.907	−1.385	.	.	.	.	.	.	.	.	.	.	.	.
	58.004	−1.902	.	.	.	.	.	.	.	.	.	.	.	.

Notes: The three entries associated with each parameter are their respective estimate   the asymptotic *t*-ratios and the Bollerslev-Wooldridge (1992) robust
t-ratio.

Table 6.11   *Conditional Variance of GJR(1,1) Monthly International Tourist Arrivals, 1994–2004*

Country	ω	α	γ	$\alpha+\gamma/2$	β	Log-Moment	Second Moment
Italy	15 525.900	0.306	−0.171	0.221	0.797	−0.017	1.018
	0.764	2.243	−0.738	·	14.353	·	·
	0.443	1.182	−0.515	·	5.858	·	·
Germany	19 977.019	−0.165	0.253	−0.039	0.986	−0.254	1.366
	3.566	−11.604	12.226	·	37.308	·	·
	2.890	−4.557	8.476	·	27.517	·	·
UK	196 745.090	0.442	−0.427	0.229	0.492	−0.945	−0.150
	1.144	1.025	−0.903	·	1.323	·	·
	1.305	2.265	−2.379	·	1.530	·	·
Japan	3 917.317	0.388	−0.274	0.250	0.757	−0.757	0.346
	0.773	1.682	−1.278	·	5.818	·	·
	0.672	2.355	−1.761	·	7.011	·	·
France	6 779.364	0.399	−0.460	0.169	0.772	−0.766	0.082
	1.562	1.934	−1.952	·	7.255	·	·
	2.326	2.694	−2.831	·	11.690	·	·
Switzerland	1 446.604	0.068	−0.196	−0.029	1.006	−0.397	0.712
	0.492	1.198	−6.266	·	14.738	·	·
	1.295	1.493	−2.915	·	17.303	·	·
Austria	68 900.038	0.041	0.298	0.190	0.125	−1.033	0.572
	1.358	0.223	0.855	·	0.224	·	·
	2.455	0.425	1.439	·	0.465	·	·
Netherlands	938.692	0.208	−0.322	0.048	0.873	−0.590	0.390
	0.993	1.573	−2.212	·	7.665	·	·
	1.189	2.557	−3.356	·	11.871	·	·

Note: The three entries associated with each parameter are their respective estimate, the asymptotic *t*-ratios and the Bollerslev-Wooldridge (1992) robust *t*-ratios.

and the Netherlands. For Italy, the UK and Austria, only the log-moment condition is satisfied, so that the QMLE are consistent and asymptotically normal. The asymmetric effects are somewhat mixed in the case of the logarithm of monthly international tourist arrivals for Italy, Germany, UK, Japan, France and Austria. For Italy, Germany, Japan and Austria, if there is

Table 6.12 Conditional Mean of Logarithmic Monthly International Tourist Arrivals, 1994–2003

Italy

AR(1)	.	.	D1T	.	.	D4T	D5T	.	D7T	D8T	D9T	.	.	D12T
0.998	.	.	0.002	.	.	−0.001	−0.010	.	0.005	0.005	−0.003	.	.	0.005
4.528	.	.	2.608	.	.	−1.565	−14.972	.	4.265	12.040	−3.235	.	.	11.466
3.515	.	.	3.233	.	.	−3.062	−16.002	.	14.778	7.615	−8.127	.	.	8.531

Germany

AR(1)	AR(2)	.	D1	D2	D3	D4	D5	D6	D7	D8	D9	D10	D11	D12
0.429	0.336	.	2.106	2.159	2.112	1.952	1.814	1.674	2.025	2.081	2.080	2.147	2.292	2.113
3.859	3.438	.	3.089	3.126	3.078	2.844	2.653	2.502	3.095	3.188	3.140	3.218	3.429	3.075
5.430	3.545	.	2.962	3.060	2.971	2.736	2.555	2.409	3.002	3.125	3.093	3.157	3.327	3.054

UK

AR(1)	AR(2)	MA(1)	D1	D2	D3	D4	D5	D6	D7	D8	D9	D10	D11	D12
0.644	−0.317	−0.318	0.248	0.444	0.387	0.336	.	0.185	0.541	0.512	0.446	0.247	0.447	0.373
3.181	1.563	−1.558	3.962	5.969	5.159	4.747	.	1.847	8.476	6.079	5.408	2.291	6.780	5.709
4.732	2.339	−2.437	4.044	8.395	6.865	4.906	.	2.525	10.507	7.880	8.401	5.526	5.972	5.596

Japan

AR(1)	AR(2)	MA(1)	D1	D2	D3	D4	D5	D6	D7	D8	D9	D10	D11	D12
0.606	0.337	−0.351	0.394	0.494	0.470	0.385	.	0.360	0.963	0.943	0.504	0.130	0.417	0.561
2.903	1.622	−1.966	6.503	8.901	6.909	6.325	.	3.742	11.821	8.208	5.052	2.373	5.516	10.572
4.092	2.297	−1.998	6.771	9.529	7.751	6.259	.	4.227	21.142	8.413	6.412	2.232	6.847	10.806

France

AR(1)	MA(1)	.	D1	D2	D3	D4	D5	D6	D7	D8	D9	D10	D11	D12
0.971	−0.416	.	0.526	0.358	0.134	.	−0.660	−0.324	0.937	0.568	−0.329	0.403	0.683	0.358
11.442	−4.563	.	5.237	3.559	1.251	.	−6.851	−4.399	13.718	7.905	−3.738	5.259	9.020	4.551
28.618	−4.567	.	13.100	9.557	2.809	.	−9.509	−6.166	17.570	9.177	−7.072	8.068	12.745	6.663

Table 6.12 Conditional Mean of Logarithmic Monthly International Tourist Arrivals, 1994–2003 (continued)

Switzerland

	AR(1)	AR(2)	MA(1)			D4T	D5T	D6T	D7T	D8T	D9T	D10T	D11T	D12T
	0.692	0.309	−0.363	.	.	0.001	−0.007	−0.005	0.004	−0.003	0.003	0.006	0.002	−0.001
	3.524	1.577	−1.885	.	.	0.795	−7.646	−3.876	4.087	−3.506	3.026	6.113	2.437	−2.088
	5.071	2.272	−2.821	.	.	2.009	−13.104	−4.511	5.005	−3.763	3.586	6.206	2.431	−1.862

Austria

	AR(1)			D1T	D2T	D4T	D5T	D6T	D7T	D8T	D9T	D10T	D11T	D12T
	0.986	.	.	0.005	0.002	−0.003	−0.004	−0.002	0.007	0.000	−0.002	0.004	0.004	0.001
	18.118	.	.	7.958	1.047	−2.939	−6.170	−2.000	8.450	0.679	−1.918	2.994	3.804	1.432
	15.554	.	.	4.336	2.691	−4.241	−5.519	−2.908	12.998	0.524	−5.050	9.719	11.600	2.481

Netherlands

	AR(1)	MA(1)		D1	D2	D3		D5	D6	D7	D8	D9	D10
	0.966	−0.296	.	0.249	0.364	0.210	.	0.211	0.448	0.356	0.140	0.429	0.187
	1.914	−2.523	.	2.972	5.526	2.600	.	2.545	7.585	4.645	1.965	5.521	2.731
	2.007	−3.278	.	3.837	5.440	3.540	.	3.536	6.396	6.039	2.284	7.196	2.447

Notes: The three entries associated with each parameter are their respective estimate, the asymptotic *t*-ratios and the Bollerslev-Wooldridge (1992) robust *t*-ratios.

262

Table 6.13   Conditional Variance of GARCH(1,1) of Logarithmic Monthly International Tourist Arrivals, 1994–2003

Country	ω	α	β	Log-Moment	Second Moment
Italy	−1.5E–04	0.069	0.918	−0.013	0.988
	−0.308	1.766	21.274		
	−0.367	1.452	19.147		
Germany	2.2E–04	0.117	0.878	−0.018	0.995
	0.452	1.494	9.091		
	0.619	1.555	8.390		
UK	0.001	0.050	0.864	−0.092	0.915
	0.650	1.570	8.477		
	0.500	0.765	4.031		
Japan	0.001	0.266	0.697	−0.101	0.963
	0.897	1.851	4.911		
	1.320	1.826	5.591		
France	0.001	0.068	0.895	−0.041	0.964
	0.460	0.798	5.770		
	0.552	1.558	8.765		
Switzerland	0.001	0.072	0.883	−0.050	0.955
	0.499	2.020	15.044		
	0.739	1.240	8.734		
Austria	−0.001	0.047	0.949	−0.003	0.996
	−4.165	7.330	4.249		
	−4.188	1.100	3.437		
Netherlands	0.007	0.177	0.634	−0.244	0.811
	0.754	1.116	1.821		
	1.454	2.156	3.562		

Note: The three entries associated with each parameter are their respective estimate, the asymptotic *t*-ratios and the Bollerslev-Wooldridge (1992) robust *t*-ratios.

a shock to the logarithm of international tourist arrivals, the uncertainty becomes greater, while it is lower for the UK and France. This interpretation is plausible for Germany, Austria and the UK, because Germany and Austria seem to show no clear trend or pattern, while the UK shows a more consistent pattern with a strong linear trend in the arrivals over the sample period.

Table 6.14 *Conditional Mean of Logarithmic Monthly International Tourist Arrivals, 1994–2003*

	AR(1)	AR(2)	MA(1)	D1	D2	D3	D4	D5	D6	D7	D8	D9	D10	D11
Italy	0.996			0.002			−0.001	−0.010		0.005	0.005	−0.003		
	546.998			1.884			−1.715	−23.242		4.791	7.308	−3.255		
	546.846			9.436			−3.132	−23.382		15.729	15.961	−8.085		
Germany	0.433	0.343	−0.326	2.024	2.075	2.020	1.865	1.733	1.581	1.913	2.024	2.014	2.057	2.140
	4.805	4.507	−2.282	3.742	3.876	3.751	3.454	3.221	2.979	3.714	3.958	3.826	3.942	4.075
	5.497	4.545	−2.817	5.505	5.652	5.457	5.105	4.713	4.355	5.510	5.750	5.647	5.702	6.076
UK	0.577	0.384	−0.253	0.266	0.451	0.400	0.330		0.179	0.543	0.518	0.446	0.279	0.475
	4.090	2.732	−1.783	4.856	6.917	6.124	5.757		2.638	9.881	6.796	7.372	3.876	9.038
	4.928	3.287	−1.683	4.582	10.433	7.997	5.856		2.562	11.322	9.651	9.497	6.455	9.707
Japan	0.510	0.428		0.405	0.509	0.509	0.397		0.365	0.997	0.988	0.593	0.172	0.438
	3.466	2.940		6.268	10.346	8.212	7.567		4.699	15.743	10.781	7.234	3.013	6.680
	3.858	3.293		7.173	9.257	9.293	6.359		5.067	20.455	9.341	7.875	3.210	8.082
France	0.970		−0.255	0.528	0.376	0.172		−0.651	−0.317	0.971	0.532	−0.327	0.444	0.697
	141.186		−2.567	5.917	3.441	1.744		−8.900	−5.339	19.926	7.815	−5.072	6.534	10.864
	273.834		−3.563	13.432	10.826	3.862		−11.068	−7.282	18.988	14.146	−5.786	8.548	14.457

For Italy the seasonal dummy columns are the transformed versions (D1T, D4T, D5T, D7T, D8T, D9T).

Table 6.14 Conditional Mean of Logarithmic Monthly International Tourist Arrivals, 1994–2003 (continued)

Switzerland

	AR(1)	AR(2)	MA(1)			D4T	D5T	D6T	D7T	D8T	D9T	D10T	D11T
	0.721	0.279	-0.408			0.002	-0.007	-0.005	0.004	-0.003	0.003	0.006	0.002
	4.240	1.648	-2.464			1.786	-8.883	-3.724	5.073	-2.990	3.598	6.388	2.225
	4.965	1.931	-3.259			3.115	-11.429	-4.195	4.555	-3.262	3.201	5.615	2.310

Austria

	AR(1)			D1T	D2T		D4T	D5T	D6T	D7T	D8T	D9T	D10T	D11T
	0.991			0.005	0.003		-0.006	-0.008	-0.002	0.005	-0.001	-0.003	0.003	0.004
	174.508			4.173	1.766		-6.187	-7.630	-2.231	6.069	-0.395	-2.658	1.760	3.086
	226.371			6.849	4.309		-4.583	-11.904	-4.646	10.687	-1.098	-5.608	8.111	9.420

Netherlands

	AR(1)	MA(1)		D1	D2	D3		D5	D6	D7	D8	D9	D10
	0.965	0.257		0.359	0.216	0.217		0.446	0.355	0.146	0.432	0.184	-0.301
	190.554	3.157		5.102	2.704	2.514		7.569	4.743	1.994	5.481	2.667	-2.594
	200.778	3.894		5.556	3.631	3.752		6.385	5.961	2.445	7.488	2.399	-3.328

Notes: The three entries associated with each parameter are their respective estimate, the asymptotic *t*-ratios and the Bollerslev–Wooldridge (1992) robust *t*-ratios.

Table 6.15   Conditional Variance of GJR(1,1) Logarithmic Monthly International Tourist Arrivals, 1994–2003

Country	ω	α	γ	β	$\alpha + \gamma/2$	Log-Moment	Second Moment
Italy	1.1E–03	–0.153	0.647	0.870	0.171	–0.097	1.041
	0.316	–1.301	2.321	22.274			
	3.718	–2.565	3.455	17.136			
Germany	1.1E–03	–0.240	0.334	0.948	–0.073	–0.234	0.875
	1.953	–3.486	3.425	10.796			
	2.291	–2.208	2.902	16.651			
UK	1.8E–04	0.111	–0.233	1.008	–0.005	–0.016	1.003
	0.430	1.408	–1.989	17.874			
	0.417	1.828	–2.050	11.892			
Japan	1.9E–03	–0.118	0.464	0.793	0.114	–0.177	0.907
	2.593	–1.561	2.690	7.696			
	2.314	–2.144	1.970	9.047			
France	0.012	0.127	–0.282	0.380	–0.014	–1.055	0.365
	1.103	0.903	–1.599	0.668			
	2.211	1.105	–2.123	1.155			
Switzerland	0.001	–0.048	0.208	0.919	0.056	–0.040	0.974
	1.191	–0.959	1.707	14.861			
	0.473	–0.620	1.718	7.123			
Austria	0.010	–0.207	0.940	0.789	0.264	–0.253	1.052
	3.602	–3.076	3.009	17.844			
	2.473	–4.593	2.796	7.122			
Netherlands	0.006	0.139	0.088	0.663	0.183	–0.201	0.846
	0.736	0.889	0.398	2.123			
	1.462	1.491	0.580	4.432			

Note: The three entries associated with each parameter are their respective estimate, the asymptotic *t*-ratios and the Bollerslev-Wooldridge (1992) robust *t*-ratios.

The conditional variance estimates for GARCH(1,1) for annual differences are given in Table 6.16. In the case of Switzerland, only ARCH(1) is considered because it is significant and the GARCH estimate is negative, which is theoretically implausible. Likewise, although the GARCH estimate for the UK is positive, it is nevertheless insignificant. For the rest of the countries, both the second moment and log-moment conditions are met for

Table 6.16 *Conditional Mean and Variance of Annual Differences of Monthly International Tourist Arrivals, 1994–2003*

Country	Conditional Mean		Conditional Variance				
	AR	MA	ω	α	β	Log-Moment	Second Moment
Italy	AR(2)	MA(2)	123 171.100	0.687	0.400	−0.187	1.086
	0.871	−0.507	1.672	3.099	3.216	.	.
	22.204	−5.430	1.796	3.260	4.463	.	.
	14.835	−3.939	.	.	.	.	.
Germany	AR(1)	MA(1)	25 213.492	0.074	0.881	−0.051	0.955
	0.874	−0.488	0.592	0.907	6.758	.	.
	15.509	−4.019	0.480	1.348	6.197	.	.
	9.783	−3.236	.	.	.	.	.
UK	AR(1)	MA(2)	367 382.860	0.269	0.012	−2.103	0.281
	0.344	0.414	1.230	1.655	0.020	.	.
	3.140	4.168	2.484	1.691	0.041	.	.
	3.660	4.489	.	.	.	.	.
Japan	AR(1)	MA(1)	12 090.387	0.107	0.859	−0.045	0.965
	0.877	−0.528	0.600	1.288	6.085	.	.
	11.180	−3.966	0.526	1.573	7.523	.	.
	9.495	−3.102	.	.	.	.	.
France	AR(2)	.	45 820.845	0.414	0.379	−0.447	0.794
	0.498	.	1.847	1.755	1.403	.	.
	5.477	.	1.572	2.645	1.984	.	.
	5.673	.	.	.	.	.	.
Switzerland	AR(1)	MA(2)	59 871.590	0.429	.	.	.
	0.359	0.326	3.768	2.153	.	.	.
	3.037	2.644	5.295	2.002	.	.	.
	5.113	3.106	.	.	.	.	.
Austria	AR(1)	MA(1)	27 286.588	0.646	−0.113	−1.749	0.533
	0.886	−0.656	3.728	2.733	−1.123	.	.
	23.471	−9.494	4.462	12.259	−3.409	.	.
	45.726	−15.755	.	.	.	.	.
Netherlands	AR(1)	.	1 250.571	−0.016	0.954	−0.065	0.938
	0.816	.	1.490	−0.645	14.865	.	.
	13.360	.	1.744	−0.488	21.203	.	.
	13.702	.	.	.	.	.	.

Note: The three entries associated with each parameter are their respective estimate, the asymptotic *t*-ratios and the Bollerslev-Wooldridge (1992) robust *t*-ratios.

Table 6.17 Conditional Mean of Log-differences of Monthly International Tourist Arrivals, 1994–2003

	AR(1)	AR(2)/MA(1)	D1T	D2T	.	D4T	D5T	D6T	D7T	D8T	D9T	D10T	D11T	D12T
Italy	-0.201	.	0.003	0.001	.	-0.002	-0.010	-0.003	0.005	0.006	-0.002	-0.001	.	0.005
	-1.935	.	3.408	2.027	.	-1.672	-20.607	-2.267	7.308	9.461	-2.215	-3.059	.	18.145
	-2.065	.	3.711	1.477	.	-5.103	-21.465	-2.615	16.470	9.105	-4.327	-3.352	.	12.134
Germany	-0.495	.	.	0.055	.	-0.118	-0.289	-0.379	.	0.093	0.103	0.151	0.264	0.068
	-5.714	.	.	0.924	.	-6.174	-8.323	-12.983	.	3.440	3.827	3.181	12.463	2.342
	-9.578	.	.	3.810	.	-4.997	-14.602	-13.821	.	2.104	3.493	9.847	10.382	2.633
UK	-0.538	-0.393	.	.	.	.	-0.414	-0.310	.	0.001	0.152	-0.096	0.071	.
	-7.782	-5.803	.	.	.	.	-6.608	-6.076	.	5.363	3.373	-0.083	4.679	.
	-6.707	-5.882	.	.	.	.	-9.513	-6.365	.	4.287	3.778	-3.533	1.463	.
Japan	-0.217	-0.454	.	.	.	.	-0.495	.	0.511	0.407	.	-0.349	.	0.059
	-3.049	-3.429	.	.	.	.	-15.229	.	7.491	7.227	.	-9.433	.	2.235
	-4.422	-4.574	.	.	.	.	-14.402	.	23.881	7.241	.	-8.656	.	1.579
France	-0.424	.	0.006	0.003	.	-0.002	-0.010	-0.008	0.004	.	-0.002	0.005	0.003	0.003
	-5.148	.	7.136	1.875	.	-1.220	-21.929	-7.335	2.692	.	-2.269	3.695	3.399	2.930
	-7.085	.	5.205	5.072	.	-4.648	-6.334	-10.930	4.418	.	-2.481	7.847	4.171	5.794

Table 6.17 Conditional Mean of Log-differences of Monthly International Tourist Arrivals, 1994–2003 (continued)

Switzerland

AR(1)				D4T	D5T	D6T	D7T	D8T	D9T	D10T	D11T	.
-0.460				0.001	-0.007	-0.006	0.003	-0.002	0.002	0.006	0.003	.
-5.020				1.560	-10.054	-8.102	5.760	-2.962	3.615	8.668	5.440	.
-5.487				3.291	-13.049	-7.085	4.160	-3.649	2.960	9.825	3.848	.

Austria

AR(1)	MA(2)	D1T	D2T	D4T	D5T	D6T	D7T	D8T	D9T	D10T	D11T	D12T
-0.144	-0.220	0.003	0.002	-0.004	-0.006	-0.003	0.006	.	-0.003	0.003	0.004	0.001
-1.265	-2.299	3.995	3.512	-4.545	-8.486	-3.450	6.081	.	-3.251	5.447	4.175	1.019
-3.381	-2.298	5.452	2.426	-6.036	-7.660	-6.947	13.287	.	-13.560	8.940	23.911	3.183

Netherlands

AR(1)	MA(1)	D2T	D3T	D7T	D8T	D9T	D10T	D11T
0.517	-0.727	0.003	-0.003	0.002	-0.004	0.004	.	-0.003
3.164	-5.052	3.347	-4.007	1.480	-2.602	3.813	.	-4.597
3.118	-5.412	2.474	-2.481	3.169	-3.885	4.366	.	-4.088

Notes: The three entries associated with each parameter are their respective estimate, the asymptotic *t*-ratios and the Bollerslev-Wooldridge (1992) robust *t*-ratios.

Table 6.18   Conditional Variance of GARCH(1,1) Log-differences of Monthly International Tourist Arrivals, 1994–2003

Country	ω	α	β	Log-Moment	Second Moment
Italy	−3.328E–04	0.080	0.910	−0.011	0.990
	−1.061	2.039	24.057		
	−1.717	1.387	18.701		
Germany	3.253E–04	0.370	0.680	−0.040	1.050
	0.488	1.899	4.397		
	1.239	1.622	4.532		
UK	2.368E–04	0.050	0.927	−0.023	0.977
	0.828	1.165	7.200		
	0.498	1.106	16.497		
Japan	0.001	0.208	0.762	−0.069	0.970
	1.118	2.082	9.182		
	1.060	1.459	5.847		
France	0.002	0.064	0.893	−0.044	0.957
	1.129	1.325	13.717		
	0.658	1.468	10.916		
Switzerland	0.001	0.078	0.884	−0.039	0.963
	0.860	1.511	13.718		
	0.714	1.497	10.566		
Austria	−0.001	0.079	0.922	−0.001	1.000
	−4.100	2.259	31.370		
	−3.171	1.493	16.574		
Netherlands	0.001	0.020	0.939	−0.040	0.959
	0.378	0.409	6.685		
	0.436	0.591	9.165		

Note: The three entries associated with each parameter are their respective estimate, the asymptotic *t*-ratios and the Bollerslev-Wooldridge (1992) robust *t*-ratios.

Germany, Japan, France, Austria and the Netherlands, while only the log-moment condition is met for Italy. Hence, the QMLE for these six countries are consistent and asymptotically normal. The GARCH effect is still relatively strong in these six countries, while the ARCH effect is significant only for Italy, France, Switzerland and Austria. Overall, the results are

Table 6.19   Conditional Mean of Log-differences of International Monthly Tourist Arrivals, 1994–2003

Italy

AR(1)		D1T	D2T		D4T	D5T	D6T	D7T	D8T	D9T	D10T		D12T
-0.333	.	0.003	0.001	.	-0.001	-0.011	-0.004	0.005	0.006	-0.001	-0.002	.	0.004
-2.939	.	3.282	0.891	.	-2.258	-38.413	-3.132	15.620	8.601	-1.600	-4.811	.	12.703
-3.746	.	5.290	2.372	.	-9.561	-55.678	-4.399	35.673	12.424	-3.281	-6.655	.	55.434

Germany

AR(1)			D2		D4	D5	D6		D8	D9	D10	D11	D12
-0.510	.	.	0.088	.	-0.145	-0.275	-0.401	.	0.148	0.098	0.148	0.238	-0.006
-10.021	.	.	1.608	.	-6.601	-9.117	-18.036	.	3.612	3.309	2.318	8.388	-2.334
-8.766	.	.	5.535	.	-4.471	-10.144	-11.162	.	6.915	3.295	9.287	7.274	-1.954

UK

AR(1)	AR(1)					D5	D6		D8	D9	D10	D11	
-0.485	-0.315	.	.	.	.	-0.426	-0.258	.	0.001	0.126	-0.116	0.054	.
-7.847	-5.823	.	.	.	.	-6.501	-5.914	.	5.108	3.692	-0.085	4.579	.
-6.920	-4.738	.	.	.	.	-11.758	-5.082	.	5.881	3.873	-4.732	1.319	.

Japan

AR(1)	MA(1)					D5		D7	D8		D10		D12
-0.271	-0.524	.	.	.	.	-0.547	.	0.516	0.429	.	-0.336	.	0.054
-4.291	-6.135	.	.	.	.	-15.772	.	9.864	8.403	.	-11.021	.	1.851
-5.323	-8.139	.	.	.	.	-15.505	.	22.125	8.249	.	-9.087	.	1.803

France

AR(2)		D1T	D2T		D4T	D5T	D6T	D7T		D9T	D10T	D11T	D12T
-0.445	.	0.006	0.003	.	-0.001	-0.011	-0.008	0.003	.	-0.004	0.005	0.003	0.003
-6.120	.	4.473	1.818	.	-0.861	-19.546	-13.366	1.590	.	-2.888	2.831	2.080	1.998
-6.837	.	6.478	5.037	.	-1.748	-27.288	-14.559	3.464	.	-3.924	9.554	4.404	6.508

271

Table 6.19 Conditional Mean of Log-differences of Monthly International Tourist Arrivals, 1994–2003 (continued)

Switzerland

	AR(1)				D4T	D5T	D6T	D7T	D8T	D9T	D10T	D11T	D12T
estimate	-0.438	.	.	.	0.002	-0.007	-0.006	0.003	-0.003	0.002	0.006	0.003	.
asymptotic t	-6.409				1.635	-9.281	-7.505	4.398	-2.915	4.513	8.817	5.016	
robust t	-5.460				2.983	-11.561	-7.118	3.087	-3.785	2.333	10.258	3.473	

Austria

	AR(1)	MA(2)	D1T	D2T		D4T	D5T	D6T	D7T		D9T	D10T	D11T	D12T
estimate	-0.208	0.154	0.004	0.003	.	-0.006	-0.008	-0.004	0.004	.	-0.004	0.002	0.004	0.021
asymptotic t	-4.301	0.786	2.406	1.009		-6.380	-10.182	-2.906	2.918		-2.286	0.834	3.236	0.325
robust t	-4.256	2.953	7.225	3.880		-4.598	-12.336	-10.045	10.125		-7.398	4.529	7.987	0.532

Netherlands

	AR(1)	MA(1)	D2T	D3T	D5T		D7T	D8T	D9T		D11T
estimate	0.473	-0.681	0.003	-0.003	0.001	.	0.002	-0.003	0.004	.	-0.003
asymptotic t	3.278	-6.025	2.815	-3.366	0.806		1.733	-2.905	4.143		-4.226
robust t	2.827	-4.577	2.799	-2.535	1.622		2.954	-3.524	4.496		-3.722

Notes: The three entries associated with each parameter are their respective estimate, the asymptotic t-ratios and the Bollerslev-Wooldridge (1992) robust t-ratios.

Table 6.20   Conditional Variance of GJR(1,1) Log-differences of Monthly International Tourist Arrivals, 1994–2003

Country	ω	α	γ	β	$\alpha+\gamma/2$	Log-Moment	Second Moment
Italy	−6.3E−05	−0.136	0.500	0.906	0.114	−0.040	1.020
	−0.515	−2.107	2.948	30.794	.	.	.
	−0.662	−3.833	3.352	24.701	.	.	.
Germany	−3.2E−05	−0.123	0.200	1.046	−0.023	−0.243	1.345
	−0.099	−2.372	4.350	16.493	.	.	.
	−3.466	−2.574	3.366	27.037	.	.	.
UK	9.8E−04	0.076	−0.231	0.992	−0.040	−0.382	0.645
	0.824	1.202	−0.933	7.371	.	.	.
	1.701	1.333	−2.722	16.077	.	.	.
Japan	1.6E−03	−0.176	0.456	0.836	0.052	−0.150	0.888
	2.629	−2.546	4.197	10.449	.	.	.
	2.542	−2.616	2.667	15.518	.	.	.
France	3.1E−02	−0.143	0.850	0.285	0.283	−1.061	0.568
	3.406	−2.555	2.931	1.765	.	.	.
	2.850	−3.656	1.900	1.487	.	.	.
Switzerland	−3.7E−04	−0.114	0.244	1.014	0.008	−0.019	1.022
	−0.518	−6.561	5.309	12.997	.	.	.
	−0.123	−0.681	1.595	3.270	.	.	.
Austria	9.2E−03	−0.173	0.700	0.718	0.177	−0.271	0.895
	2.717	−1.171	2.750	3.109	.	.	.
	1.844	−2.966	2.027	3.598	.	.	.
Netherlands	−1.6E 03	0.026	0.088	1.026	0.018	−0.038	1.044
	−1.478	−7.255	2.290	38.902	.	.	.
	−0.271	−0.282	0.735	4.941	.	.	.

Note: The three entries associated with each parameter are their respective estimate, the asymptotic *t*-ratios and the Bollerslev-Wooldridge (1992) robust *t*-ratios.

relatively poor compared with the log-arrivals series discussed above, possibly due to a loss of 12 observations through differencing.

For the log-difference series, or the growth rate in monthly international tourist arrivals, the estimates for GARCH(1,1) and GJR(1,1) are displayed in Tables 6.18 and 6.20, respectively. Except for Germany and Austria, both the second moment and log-moment conditions are satisfied, guaranteeing that the QMLE are consistent and asymptotically normal. These estimates also show that there are significant and strong GARCH effects, while there is evidence of ARCH effects only in the case of Italy, Germany, Japan and Austria. These results are quite similar to the results for the log-arrivals series. The estimates for GJR(1,1) are significant for all countries, except for the UK, where there is a negative coefficient estimate. These results show that, if there is a decline in the anticipated growth rate in monthly international tourist arrivals from the eight major markets, apart from the UK, there will be significant uncertainty about the growth rate in the long run, while for the UK the reverse is true.

From the empirical results obtained for the ARMA(p,q)-GARCH(1,1) and ARMA(p,q)-GJR(1,1) models in Tables 6.8–6.20, it can be observed from the conditional mean estimates that, on average, there is very strong habit persistence and seasonality in monthly tourist arrivals to Maldives from the eight major tourist source countries. From the conditional variance estimates, it is observed that there is a very strong and significant GARCH effect and a relatively low ARCH effect. This implies that, in general, given any unanticipated shocks to monthly international tourist arrivals to Maldives from the eight main tourist source countries, the effect of that shock will last for a considerable period of time. It can also be observed from the empirical results that, across the series modelled, asymmetric effects are not very profound, and hence no empirically useful information can be obtained from the ARMA(p,q)-GJR(1,1) model. The preferred specification is the ARMA(p,q)-GARCH(1,1) model, and the empirical results are relatively weak compared with the estimates obtained for the other three series. The empirical results for the log-series are the best, followed by the log-differenced series and finally the series in levels.

Multivariate models
The monthly standardised residuals obtained from the univariate ARMA(p,q)-GARCH(1,1) and ARMA(p,q)-GJR(1,1) models can be used to calculate the corresponding static conditional correlations for the monthly international tourist arrivals, logarithm of monthly international tourist arrivals, twelfth difference in monthly international tourist arrivals, and the log-difference in monthly international tourist arrivals.

From the estimates of the univariate ARMA(p,q)-GARCH(1,1) and ARMA(p,q)-GJR(1,1) models, the former are to be preferred because the evidence regarding asymmetric effects in the latter models is not strong. Hence, we shall consider the static conditional correlations of the standardised residuals from the ARMA(p,q)-GARCH(1,1) model. Tables 6.21–6.24 provide the conditional correlation matrices for the four series across the eight main tourist source countries.

In Tables 6.21–6.24, there are a total of 28 conditional correlations for each of the series among the eight main tourist source countries. Of the

Table 6.21   *Conditional Correlations of Uncertainty in Monthly International Tourist Arrivals, 1994–2003*

Country	Italy	Germany	UK	Japan	France	Switzerland	Austria	The Nether.
Italy	1	.	.	.	.	.	.	.
Germany	0.158	1	.	.	.	.	.	.
UK	0.306	−0.018	1	.	.	.	.	.
Japan	0.040	0.162	0.244	1	.	.	.	.
France	0.167	−0.091	0.345	0.127	1	.	.	.
Switzerland	0.247	0.080	0.426	0.285	0.465	1	.	.
Austria	0.068	0.224	−0.050	0.077	−0.115	−0.160	1	.
The Nether.	0.079	−0.076	−0.038	0.144	0.068	0.125	−0.074	1

Table 6.22   *Conditional Correlations of Uncertainty in Logarithmic Monthly International Tourist Arrivals, 1994–2003*

Country	Italy	Germany	UK	Japan	France	Switzerland	Austria	The Nether.
Italy	1	.	.	.	.	.	.	.
Germany	0.058	1	.	.	.	.	.	.
UK	0.136	−0.143	1	.	.	.	.	.
Japan	0.195	0.081	0.158	1	.	.	.	.
France	0.250	0.025	0.166	0.335	1	.	.	.
Switzerland	0.166	0.090	0.032	0.367	0.196	1	.	.
Austria	0.398	0.157	−0.084	0.051	0.129	0.439	1	.
The Nether.	0.327	−0.008	0.067	0.176	0.271	0.020	0.112	1

Table 6.23   *Conditional Correlations of Uncertainty in Annual Differences of Monthly International Tourist Arrivals, 1994–2003*

Country	Italy	Germany	UK	Japan	France	Switzerland	Austria	The Nether.
Italy	1	.	.	.	.	.	.	.
Germany	0.181	1	.	.	.	.	.	.
UK	0.316	0.052	1	.	.	.	.	.
Japan	0.184	0.138	0.322	1	.	.	.	.
France	0.437	0.184	0.193	0.346	1	.	.	.
Switzerland	0.263	0.182	0.254	0.295	0.213	1	.	.
Austria	0.226	0.277	0.124	0.181	0.127	0.174	1	.
The Nether.	0.123	0.057	0.129	0.146	0.036	0.193	0.204	1

*Table 6.24   Conditional Correlations of Uncertainty in the Log-Difference
               of Monthly International Tourist Arrivals, 1994–2003*

Country	Italy	Germany	UK	Japan	France	Switzerland	Austria	TheNether.
Italy	1	.	.	.	.	.	.	.
Germany	0.034	1	.	.	.	.	.	.
UK	0.080	−0.197	1	.	.	.	.	.
Japan	0.216	0.034	0.163	1	.	.	.	.
France	0.472	0.193	−0.104	0.211	1	.	.	.
Switzerland	0.101	0.087	0.094	0.288	0.273	1	.	.
Austria	0.381	0.232	−0.223	0.059	0.495	0.376	1	.
The Nether.	0.254	−0.014	0.098	0.162	0.156	0.037	0.097	1

global total of 112 pairs of conditional correlation coefficients, the overall mean is 0.145, ranging from a maximum of 0.495 between Austria and France, to a minimum of −0.223 between Austria and the UK. These countries also appear in the conditional correlations in the log-difference series.

There are altogether 16 negative conditional correlations, of which nine, three and four conditional correlation coefficients appear in monthly international tourist arrivals, logarithms of monthly international tourist arrivals and log-difference of monthly international tourist arrivals, respectively. There are no negative correlation coefficients in annual differences of monthly international tourist arrivals.

For the monthly international tourist arrivals series, the conditional correlations of standardised shocks are given in Table 6.21. Of the 28 feasible correlation coefficients, nine are negative coefficients. The ten highest conditional correlations appear among the following pairs of countries, in descending order: (France, Switzerland), (Switzerland, UK), (UK, France), (UK, Italy), (Switzerland, Japan), (Switzerland, Italy), (UK, Japan), (Austria, Germany), (France, Italy) and (Germany, Japan). The maximum conditional correlation is 0.465 and the minimum is 0.162. Of the ten highest conditional correlation coefficients, the UK and Switzerland are paired with four countries, while Italy and France are paired with three countries.

The conditional correlation coefficients which are displayed in Table 6.22 for the logarithm of monthly international tourist arrivals show there are three negative conditional correlations from 28 possible pairs. In ascending order, the ten highest conditional correlations of the standardised shocks are between the following countries: (Austria, Switzerland), (Austria, Italy), (Japan, Switzerland), (France, Japan), (Italy, The Netherlands), (France, The Netherlands), (France, Italy), (France, Switzerland), (Italy, Japan) and (Japan,

The Netherlands). The highest conditional correlation among these ten countries is 0.439 and the lowest is 0.176.

Table 6.23 presents the conditional correlations of the standardised shocks in the annual difference series, where no conditional correlations appear as the series are deseasonalised. The ten highest pairs of correlation coefficients are, in descending order: (France, Italy), (France, Japan), (Japan, UK), (Italy, UK), (Japan, Switzerland), (Austria, Germany), (Italy, Switzerland), (Switzerland, UK), (Austria, Italy) and (France, Switzerland). The highest conditional correlation among these ten pairs of countries is 0.437, while the lowest conditional correlation is 0.213.

Finally, the conditional correlation matrix of the standardised shocks for the log-difference in monthly international tourist arrivals is given in Table 6.24, with four negative correlation coefficients registering from 28 possible pairs. The following pairs of countries record the highest correlation coefficients and are, in descending order: (Austria, France), (Italy, France), (Austria, Italy), (Austria, Switzerland), (Japan, Switzerland), (France, Switzerland), (Italy, The Netherlands), (Austria, Germany), (Italy, Japan) and (Japan, France). Of these ten pairs of countries, the highest conditional correlation is 0.495 for (Austria, France), and the lowest is 0.221 for (France, Japan), with these extreme figures applying to the entire sample of 112 conditional correlation coefficients calculated.

The estimated constant conditional correlations given in Tables 6.21–6.24 are somewhat lower than expected. It is surprising that Germany, which is one of the dominant tourist source countries, produces relatively low conditional correlations, compared with its European counterparts, which have similar tastes in holiday tourism abroad and identical seasons. Germany produced the greatest number of negative conditional correlations. The interpretation is that the environmental effect of El Nino (shock) adversely affected German tourist arrivals to Maldives, relative to the other major tourist source countries. Hence, the shock is more diversified on the alternative tourist sources.

It is perfectly plausible for Japan to have produced lower conditional correlations because the remaining tourist source countries are from Europe, with moderately different tastes for holiday tourism, and are also in the northern hemisphere. The effect of a shock to Japanese monthly tourist arrivals to Maldives is segmented from the shocks to tourist arrivals from the alternative markets. Furthermore, the low conditional correlations indicate that, in general, the shocks from alternative tourist markets are independent or segmented. Therefore, the government of Maldives and the major tour operators need to concentrate their promotional efforts independently of a specific tourist source.

6.8 CONCLUSION

In this chapter the uncertainty of monthly international tourist arrivals from the eight major tourist source countries to Maldives have been modelled based on historical time series data. The empirical results provided a gauge to compare the conditional means and the conditional volatilities associated with monthly international tourist arrivals, logarithm of monthly international tourist arrivals, annual difference of monthly international tourist arrivals, and the log-difference of monthly international tourist arrivals. They also enabled validation of the regularity conditions underlying the model, and highlighted the importance of evaluating the uncertainties surrounding monthly international tourist arrivals. The results for the univariate ARMA(p,q)-GARCH(1,1) and ARMA(p,q)-GJR(1,1) models showed that the sufficient parametric conditions for the estimated uncertainties (specifically, that they should be positive) are satisfied, as were the moment and log-moment conditions for the QMLE to be consistent and asymptotically normal.

The estimated empirical results for the estimates for the ARMA(p,q)-GARCH(1,1) and ARMA(p,q)-GJR(1,1) models showed that there was a considerable degree of habit persistence and seasonality, particularly for the peak tourist season, which coincides with the European winter months. Moreover, the conditional variance estimates showed that there was a strong GARCH effect for all four series and a moderate ARCH effect for a selected number of series across the eight tourist source countries. There were no significant asymmetric effects in the monthly international tourist arrivals.

The estimated static conditional correlations for monthly international tourist arrivals, as well as for the respective transformed series, were found to be significantly different from zero, but nevertheless relatively low. This indicated that the government of Maldives and the major tour operators that organise tourist vacations should emphasise their marketing efforts independently of each tourist source country.

REFERENCES

Berndt, E.K., B.H. Hall, R.E. Hall and J.A. Hausman (1974), 'Estimation and inference in nonlinear structural models', *Annals of Economic and Social Measurement*, **3**, 653–65.

Bollerslev, T. and J.M. Wooldridge (1992), 'Quasi-maximum likelihood estimation and inference in dynamic models with time-varying covariances', *Econometric Reviews*, **11**, 143–73.

Box, G.E.P. and G.M. Jenkins (1976), *Time Series Analysis: Forecasting and Control*, Second Edition, San Francisco: Holden Day.

Domroes, M. (1985), 'Tourism resources and their development in Maldives islands', *GeoJournal*, **10**(1), 119–26.

Domroes, M. (1989), 'Tourism in the Maldives: The potential of its natural attraction and its exploitation', *Applied Geography and Development*, **36**, 61–77.

Domroes, M. (1993), 'Maldivian tourist resorts and their environmental impact', in P.P. Wong (ed.), *Tourism vs Environment: The Case for Coastal Areas*, Dordrecht: Kluwer Academic Publishers, pp. 69–82.

Domroes, M. (1999), 'Tourism in the Maldives: The resort concept and tourist related services', *Insula: International Journal of Island Affairs*, **8**, 7–14.

Enders, W (2004), *Applied Time Series Econometrics*, New York: Wiley.

Granger, C.W.J and P. Newbold (1974), 'Spurious regressions in econometrics', *Journal of Econometrics*, **2**, 111–20.

Phillips, P.C.B. and P. Perron (1990), 'Testing for a unit root in time series regressions', *Biometrika*, **75**(2), 335–46.

Shareef, R. and M. McAleer (2007), 'Modelling the uncertainty in monthly international tourist arrivals to the Maldives', *Tourism Management*, **28**, 23–45.

7. Modelling Country Risk and Volatility in Small Island Tourism Economies

7.1 INTRODUCTION

Country risk refers broadly to the likelihood that a sovereign state or borrower from a particular country may be unable and/or unwilling to fulfil their obligations towards one or more foreign lenders and/or investors (Krayenbuehl, 1985). The Third World debt crisis in the early 1980s, political changes resulting from the end of the Cold War, the implementation of market-oriented economic and financial reforms in Eastern Europe, the East Asian and Latin American crises that have occurred since 1997, and the tumultuous events flowing from 11 September, 2001 indicate that the risks associated with engaging in international relations have increased substantially. Such risks have become more difficult to analyse and predict for decision makers in the economic, financial and political sectors (for further details, see Hoti and McAleer, 2005a).

A primary function of country risk assessment is to anticipate the possibility of debt repudiation, default or delays in payment by sovereign borrowers (Burton and Inoue, 1985). There are three major components of country risk, namely economic, financial and political risk. The country risk literature holds that economic, financial and political risks affect each other. Country risk assessment evaluates economic, financial and political factors, and their interactions in determining the risk associated with a particular country. Perceptions of the determinants of country risk are important because they affect both the supply and cost of international capital flows (Brewer and Rivoli, 1990).

The importance of country risk analysis is underscored by the existence of several prominent country risk rating agencies. Over the last two decades, commercial agencies such as Moody's, Standard and Poor's, Fitch IBCA, Euromoney, Institutional Investor, Economist Intelligence Unit, International Country Risk Guide, and Political Risk Services, have compiled country risk indexes or ratings as measures of credit risk associated with lending and/or investing in a country (for a critical survey of the country risk rating systems, see Hoti and McAleer, 2004). Country risk ratings are crucial for countries seeking foreign investment and selling government bonds on the international financial market, and for lending and investment decisions by large corporations and international financial institutions. These agencies provide qualitative and quantitative country risk ratings, combining information about arbitrary measures of economic, financial and political risk ratings to obtain a composite risk rating.

The country risk literature has recently been reviewed in Hoti and McAleer (2004), in which 50 empirical papers published in the last two decades were evaluated according to established statistical and econometric criteria used in estimation, evaluation and forecasting. Such an evaluation permitted a critical assessment of the relevance and practicality of the economic, financial and political theories pertaining to country risk in general. However, to date there has been no discussion of country risk in Small Island Tourism Economies (SITEs). As SITEs share a number of common characteristics, it is important to examine risk ratings and risk returns for such countries.

Risk ratings and risk returns of six SITEs are examined in this chapter, these being the only SITEs for which monthly International Country Risk Guide (ICRG) risk ratings and risk returns are available. Following the ICRG classification, the six SITEs represent two geographic regions, namely North and Central America (the Bahamas, Dominican Republic, Haiti and Jamaica) and West Europe (Cyprus and Malta). These island economies have delicate ecosystems, and are consistently threatened by natural disasters as well as the effects of environmental damage. Careful planning is required to maintain sustainability of tourism and to limit its environmental damage. Although tourism has contributed significantly to economic development in many SITEs, they need to be managed responsibly to secure long-term sustainability.

The plan of this chapter is as follows. Section 7.2 discusses aspects of country risk assessment, with particular emphasis on the ICRG rating system regarding economic, financial, political and composite risk ratings. The analysis of the relationship between economic growth and the four ICRG risk ratings for the six SITEs in Section 7.3 follows from Shareef and Hoti (2005). A detailed analysis and comparison of the risk ratings, risk returns and associated volatility for the Bahamas, Cyprus, Dominican Republic, Haiti, Jamaica and Malta, for which monthly ICRG data are available, is presented in Section 7.4. In this chapter the symmetric and asymmetric models of univariate conditional volatility for country risk returns that were presented in Chapter 5 are evaluated in Section 7.5. Sections 7.4 and 7.5 follow closely from Hoti et al. (2005). Some concluding remarks are given in Section 7.6.

7.2   COUNTRY RISK ASSESSMENT

In the finance and financial econometrics literature, conditional volatility has been used to evaluate risk, asymmetric shocks and leverage effects. The volatility present in risk ratings also reflects risk considerations in risk ratings. As risk ratings are effectively indexes, their rate of change (or returns) merits attention in the same manner as financial returns (for further details, see McAleer et al., 2008). This chapter provides a comparison of country risk ratings, risk returns and associated volatilities for the six SITEs. The ratings were compiled by the ICRG, which is the only risk rating agency to provide detailed and consistent monthly data over an extended period for a large number of countries.

The ICRG has provided economic, financial, political and composite risk ratings for 93 countries on a monthly basis since January 1984. As of June 2006, the four risk ratings were available for a total of 140 countries. The ICRG rating system comprises 22 variables representing three major components of country risk, namely economic, financial and political. There are five variables (GDP per capita, GDP growth, inflation rate, budget balance as a percentage of GDP, and current account balance as a percentage of GDP) representing the economic risk component, five variables (foreign debt as a percentage of GDP, foreign debt service as a percentage of export in goods and services, current account as a percentage of export in goods and services, net liquidity as months of import cover, and exchange rate stability) representing the financial risk component, and 12 variables (government stability, socio-economic conditions, investment profile, internal and external conflicts, corruption, military in politics, religious and ethic tensions, law and order, democratic accountability, and bureaucracy quality) representing the political risk component. Using each set of variables, a separate risk rating is created for the three components, on a scale of 0–100. The three component risk ratings are then combined to derive a composite risk rating, as an overall measure of country risk. Each of the five economic and financial components account for 25 per cent, while the twelve political component accounts for 50 per cent of the composite risk rating. The lower (higher) is a given risk rating, the higher (lower) is the associated risk. In essence, the country risk rating is a measure of country creditworthiness.

The ICRG rating system does not take into account the interdependencies between economic, financial and political risk ratings, which are very important in determining a composite country risk rating. Hoti and McAleer (2005b) found significant multivariate spillover effects in the rate of change of country risk ratings (or risk returns) across economic, financial, political and composite risk returns. Similarly, the ICRG rating system does not accommodate country spillover effects in economic, financial, political and composite risk returns. However, Hoti (2005) found significant spillover effects for risk returns across different countries using monthly risk ratings data for six Balkan countries.

7.3 ECONOMIC GROWTH AND ICRG RATINGS FOR SIX SITES

This section provides an analysis of the relationship between economic growth and the four ICRG risk ratings, namely economic, financial, political and composite, for the six SITEs. Annual data are used for both economic growth rates and the four risk ratings. The data are available from 1985–2000, apart from Malta for which the data are available from 1986–2000. Annual risk ratings correspond to the arithmetic mean of the 12 monthly risk ratings for each year. The geometric mean was also used to construct the annual ratings and gave virtually identical results.

Table 7.1 presents the correlation coefficients between economic growth rates and the four risk ratings for the common period 1986–2000. The correlation coefficients between the economic growth rate and the four risk ratings vary across the six SITEs, ranging from –0.722 for economic growth rate, economic risk rating for Jamaica to 0.30 for economic growth rate, political risk rating for the Bahamas. For the Bahamas and Cyprus, the highest correlation coefficient is for economic growth rate, political risk rating. The second highest correlation for the Bahamas is for economic growth rate, composite risk rating, while for Cyprus it is economic growth rate, economic risk rating. Dominican Republic, Jamaica and Malta have the highest correlation coefficient for economic growth rate, economic risk rating. The second highest correlations are observed for economic growth rate, composite risk rating for both the Dominican Republic and Jamaica, and economic growth rate, political risk rating for Malta. Haiti's two highest correlations are for economic growth rate, composite risk rating and economic growth rate, political risk rating.

There is no general pattern in the direction of the relationship between economic growth rate and the four risk ratings for the six SITEs. Of the 24 correlation coefficients, 13 are positive and the remaining 11 negative. The economic growth rate is positively correlated with all four risk ratings for the Bahamas, Dominican Republic and Haiti, the exception being the financial risk rating for the Bahamas. There is a negative correlation between the economic growth rate and the four risk ratings for Cyprus, Jamaica and Malta, apart from the economic risk ratings for Cyprus and Malta. These are surprising results since the country risk literature asserts that increases in risk ratings are noticeably influenced by higher economic growth rates, and vice-versa.

Table 7.1   Correlation Coefficients for Risk Ratings and Economic Growth Rates for Six SITEs

Risk Ratings	GR_BHS	GR_CYP	GR_DOM	GR_HTI	GR_JAM	GR_MLT
ECO-R_BHS	0.139	.	.	.	.	.
ECO-R_CYP	.	0.298	.	.	.	.
ECO-R_DOM	.	.	0.58	.	.	.
ECO-R_HTI	.	.	.	0.39	.	.
ECO-R_JAM	.	.	.	.	−0.722	.
ECO-R_MLT	.	.	.	.	.	0.584
FIN-R_BHS	−0.375	.	.	.	.	.
FIN-R_CYP	.	−0.222	.	.	.	.
FIN-R_DOM	.	.	0.422	.	.	.
FIN-R_HTI	.	.	.	0.375	.	.
FIN-R_JAM	.	.	.	.	−0.58	.
FIN-R_MLT	.	.	.	.	.	−0.20
POL-R_BHS	0.30	.	.	.	.	.
POL-R_CYP	.	−0.313	.	.	.	.
POL-R_DOM	.	.	0.444	.	.	.
POL-R_HTI	.	.	.	0.43	.	.
POL-R_JAM	.	.	.	.	−0.7	.
POL-R_MLT	.	.	.	.	.	−0.552
COM-R_BHS	0.41	.	.	.	.	.
COM-R_CYP	.	−0.27	.	.	.	.
COM-R_DOM	.	.	0.479	.	.	.
COM-R_HTI	.	.	.	0.42	.	.
COM-R_JAM	.	.	.	.	−0.700	.
COM-R_MLT	.	.	.	.	.	−0.425

Notes:
Economic, Financial, Political, Composite Risk Ratings and Economic Growth Rates are denoted as ECO-R, FIN-R, POL-R, COM-R and GR, respectively.
The Bahamas, Cyprus, Dominican Republic, Haiti, Jamaica and Malta are denoted as BHS, CYP, DOM, HTI, JAM and MLT, respectively.

Further to the results reported in Table 7.1, Figure 7.1 presents snapshots of composite risk ratings, denoted COM-R, and economic growth rates, denoted GR, for the six SITEs. As a weighted sum of the three component risk ratings, the composite risk rating is an overall measure of country creditworthiness. The higher is the creditworthiness of a country, the lower is

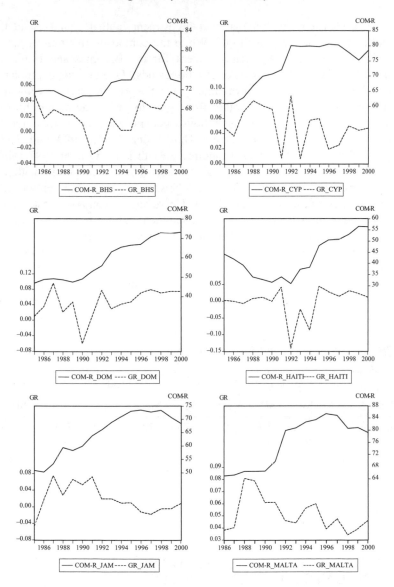

Notes:
Economic, Financial, Political, Composite Risk Ratings and Economic Growth Rates are denoted as ECO-R, FIN-R, POL-R, COM-R and GR, respectively.
The Bahamas, Cyprus, Dominican Republic and Jamaica are denoted as BHS, CYP, DOM and JAM, respectively.

Figure 7.1   Composite Risk Ratings and Economic Growth Rates for Six SITEs

the risk associated with international investment in that country, and the higher is the economic growth rate. While the composite risk ratings for all six SITEs have increasing trends, except for the Bahamas and Haiti, the economic growth rates have no general trends. Overall, there are large fluctuations in economic growth rates over the sample period, while the composite ratings change smoothly from year to year. The composite risk ratings and economic growth rates follow a generally increasing trend for the Bahamas, Dominican Republic and Haiti after 1991, 1990 and 1992, respectively. For the Bahamas, economic growth is rising after 1997, while the composite risk rating is falling steadily. This is consistent with the general positive correlation in Table 7.1 between the economic growth rate and the four risk ratings for these SITEs. However, the composite risk ratings and economic growth rates for Cyprus, Jamaica and Malta tend to move in opposite directions after 1991. This supports the results in Table 7.1 which show a generally negative correlation between the economic growth rate and the four risk ratings for these SITEs. Overall, the results in Table 7.1 and Figure 7.1 indicate that the economic characteristics of SITEs, particularly their structural base, should be examined more carefully in the country risk literature.

Table 7.2   Descriptive Statistics for Risk Ratings

	Economic		Financial		Political		Composite	
SITE	Mean	SD	Mean	SD	Mean	SD	Mean	SD
Bahamas	74.2	3.8	75.9	7.5	72.8	7.0	73.9	3.3
Cyprus	79.0	3.0	83.3	7.1	9.0	9.0	75.1	0.3
Dominican Rep.	7.5	8.7	5.0	1.3	0.7	8.1	1.4	10.0
Haiti	58.0	4.3	40.2	19.2	38.0	10.8	43.7	9.9
Jamaica	59.1	5.9	8.9	12.3	8.5	0.8	0.3	7.1
Malta	81.4	8.0	7.3	9.1	73.5	13.1	7.2	7.5

7.4   RISK RATINGS, RISK RETURNS AND VOLATILITIES FOR SIX SITES

ICRG risk ratings, risk returns and the associated volatilities for the six SITEs are given in Figures 7.2 to 7.7 for the period January 1984 to April 2005 for the Dominican Republic, Haiti and Jamaica, December 1984 to April 2005 for the Bahamas and Cyprus, and April 1986 to April 2005 for Malta. Risk returns are defined as the monthly percentage change in the respective risk ratings. For each country, the risk ratings and risk returns are

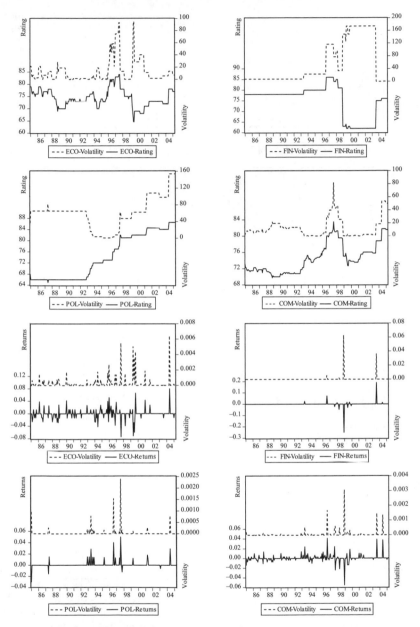

Note: ECO, FIN, POL and COM refer to economic, financial, political and composite risk
          ratings (or risk returns), respectively.

Figure 7.2   Risk Ratings, Risk Returns and Volatilities for the Bahamas

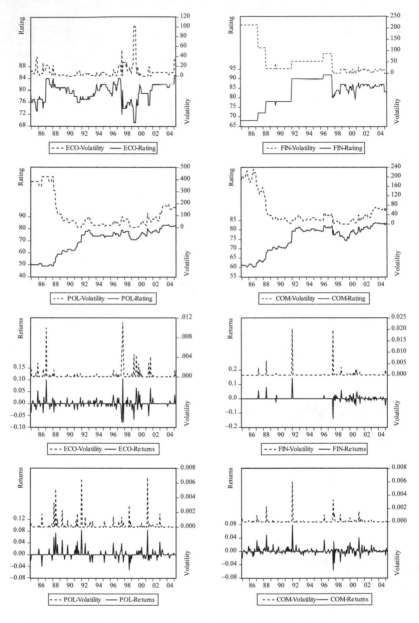

Note: ECO, FIN, POL and COM refer to economic, financial, political and composite risk
          ratings (or risk returns), respectively.

Figure 7.3   Risk Ratings, Risk Returns and Volatilities for Cyprus

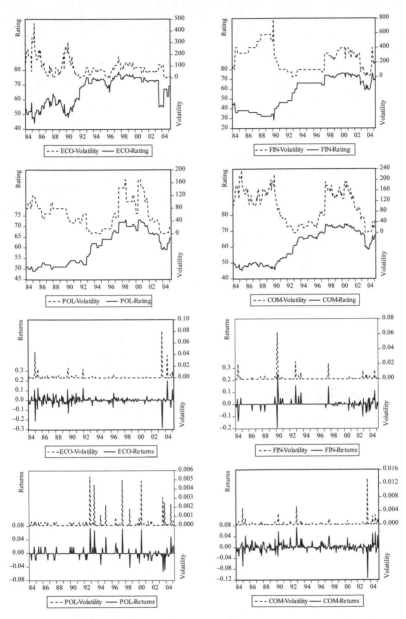

Note: ECO, FIN, POL and COM refer to economic, financial, political and composite risk
ratings (or risk returns), respectively.

*Figure 7.4   Risk Ratings, Risk Returns and Volatilities for the Dominican
Republic*

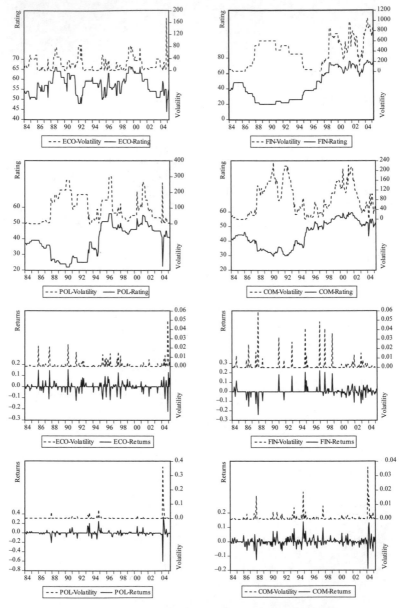

Note: ECO, FIN, POL and COM refer to economic, financial, political and composite risk
          ratings (or risk returns), respectively.

Figure 7.5   Risk Ratings, Risk Returns and Volatilities for Haiti

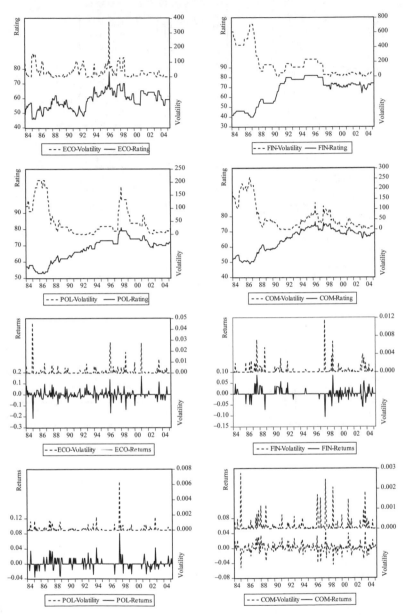

Note: ECO, FIN, POL and COM refer to economic, financial, political and composite risk
          ratings (or risk returns), respectively.

Figure 7.6   Risk Ratings, Risk Returns and Volatilities for Jamaica

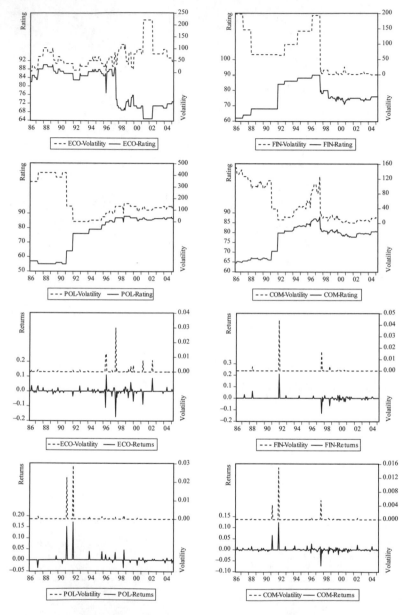

Note: ECO, FIN, POL and COM refer to economic, financial, political and composite risk
ratings (or risk returns), respectively.

Figure 7.7   Risk Ratings, Risk Returns and Volatilities for Malta

denoted ECO-R, FIN-R, POL-R and COM-R for the economic, financial, political and composite risk ratings and risk returns, respectively. Defining volatility as the squared deviations of each observation from the respective sample mean risk ratings or risk returns, the four volatilities are denoted ECO-V, FIN-V, POL-V and COM-V. The descriptive statistics for the country risk ratings used in the analysis are presented in Table 7.2

As there are significant differences among the economic, financial, political and composite risk ratings, risk returns and their associated volatility across different SITEs, a careful analysis of each of these components of country risk would be of great interest to private tourism operators and foreign direct investors in the tourism and hospitality industry, tourism commissions and governments.

As argued in Hoti et al. (2007), although the ICRG rating system does not include a specific measure of tourism earnings for countries, the importance of tourism earnings and tourism growth can still be traced through the ICRG economic and financial risk components. As tourism is a service export, tourism earnings are accommodated in the current account balance, one of the 22 variables in the ICRG rating system. Therefore, higher tourism earnings lead to a higher current account balance, higher economic and financial risk ratings, and hence composite risk rating. The higher the composite risk rating, the higher is the likelihood that a country will repay its obligations to its foreign lenders/investors, and the higher the creditworthiness of a country. Overall, the creditworthiness of a country with an increasing risk rating results in higher inflows of foreign capital and investment which, in turn, will assist the country's economic development. In SITEs, such as the Maldives, the development of tourism infrastructure, namely airports to accommodate wide-bodied aircrafts, is facilitated through capital raised in international financial markets. Moreover, foreign debt obligations are predominantly serviced by tourism earnings. Any unfavourable shocks to tourism earnings, such the 2004 Boxing Day Tsunami, lead to considerable difficulty in servicing the debt. Hence, it is important to examine the time series properties of country risk ratings and risk returns for SITEs.

Information regarding the economic, financial and political environments for the six selected SITEs has been collected and extended from four widely-used international sources, namely the US Department of State (2004), BBC News (2004), *The Economist* (2004), and Central Intelligence Agency (2004). Figure 7.2 presents the four risk ratings, risk returns and their associated volatility for the Bahamas. Comprising 700 islands and islets, the Bahamas attracts more than five times its population in tourists, the majority coming from the USA. With a high per capita income and a concentration of wealth in the main commercial and tourist centres, the Bahamas has experienced remarkable growth in the services sector, namely tourism and financial services. Economic performance has been mixed over the sample period, with the economic risk rating having a slightly declining trend. The economic risk rating fell to 1988, had a rising trend to 1997, a sharp decreasing trend to 1999, and a rising trend to 2005. Strong growth in the tourism sector and a boom in the construction of new hotels, resorts and residences led to a solid GDP growth after 1999. However, the slowdown in the US economy and the events of 11 September, 2001 hampered economic growth in 2002, resulting in a flat economic risk rating. The economic risk rating increased after mid 2004 due to improved economic conditions. In general, the volatility associated with the economic risk rating increased substantially after 1995. Surprisingly, the financial risk rating was flat for much of the sample period, with mild volatility after 1996 and a peak in 1998. Financial risk rose significantly after the sharp fall in the risk rating in 1998 and 2003. The rating remained flat in the low 60s until 2002 but increased to the high 70s after 2003. With few domestic resources and a small industry, the Bahamas is heavily reliant on imports of food and manufactured goods. The domestic resistance to foreign investment due to local concerns about foreign competition has resulted in stagnant growth in many sectors, which clearly need diversification. Prior to 1992, the political risk rating was rather flat in the high 0s, with little or no volatility. Under the leadership of the late Sir Lynden Pindling, the Progressive Liberal Party (PLP), which led the Bahamas to independence in 1973, was dominant until 1992. Political risk fell considerably after 1992 when the Free National Movement (FNM) won the general elections against the PLP, which faced accusations of corruption and drug trafficking. There was greater volatility after 1992, as the rating increased, reaching the mid 80s by 2005. The FNM lost to PLP in 2002 after ten years in power. Overall, the composite risk rating reflects the trends in the three component risk ratings, and is generally less volatile than the economic risk rating.

In Figure 7.3 are the four risk ratings, risk returns and their associated volatility for Cyprus, a country with an open economy based on the service sector. Over the last two decades, the economy has shifted from agriculture to light manufacturing and services, with tourism contributing 70 per cent of GDP. There was robust growth in the 1980s, especially after 1987, when the economic index increased by almost 10 points. However, the performance from 1988 to 2005 has been mixed, as the index decreased and then increased before falling by more than 10 points in 1997 as the trade deficit increased substantially. This pattern reflected the economic vulnerability to swings in tourism arrivals and the need to restructure the economy. Declining competitiveness in tourism and manufacturing has led to economic reforms. The index recovered in 1997, only to fall again to the low 70s due to the high trade deficit. Negotiations for accession to the EU in 1998 led to an increasing trend until early 1999. From mid-2001 to 2005, the economic risk index followed an increasing trend as the economic performance improved, especially after the 2004 EU membership. The financial risk index generally increased, with big jumps to 1997, reaching the low 90s. Financial risk increased in 1997 and the index fell by more than 10 points. However, the index started a rising trend in the same year as Cyprus revised its policy on foreign investment and passed modern banking laws, incorporating all the EU provisions for the prudential supervision of credit institutions. Political risk in Cyprus decreased over the sample period, with the index following a generally increasing trend and associated high volatility. Such risk was very high in the 1980s as the tension between Turkish and Greek Cypriots increased. In 1983, Turkish Cypriots declared an independent Turkish Republic of Northern Cyprus, which has been recognized only by Turkey. From 1988 to 1992, the index had an increasing trend, which was followed by an absence of trend. Increasing tensions between the two groups has led to a vulnerable political scene. After the initiation of negotiations for EU accession in 1998, the index started an increasing trend as both groups pursued EU membership aspirations. Political risk seems to have a significant impact on the perceptions of country risk for Cyprus, as the composite risk rating index closely reflects the trends and volatility in the political risk index.

The four risk ratings, risk returns and their associated volatility for the Dominican Republic are given in Figure 7.4. Sharing the Island of Hispaniola with Haiti, the country has become the most popular tourist destination in the Caribbean, with tourism and free-trade zones as key sources of foreign exchange. While still one of the poorest countries in the Caribbean, with a large wealth gap between the rich and poor, the Dominican economy has experienced a very fast growth rate over the past decade. As a result, the economic risk rating had a rising trend over the sample period, with higher associated volatility prior to 1992 and peaks in 1985, 2003 and 2004. The rating reached a level of 80 in 1997, after which it followed a slightly declining trend, with a big drop in 2003 followed by an increasing trend to 2005. Unlike the Bahamas, the financial risk rating for the Dominican Republic had a generally rising trend throughout the sample period, with little associated volatility, apart from a peak in 1990 and few extreme observations. The rating rose by almost 10 points in 1997, after which it remained flat in the low-mid 70s. Large tourism earnings and remittances have helped to build foreign exchange reserves. However, the government faces several economic policy challenges, given the widening merchandise trade deficit, large foreign debt payment arrears, high real interest rates, low tax collection, and lower demand for exports due to the world economic slowdown. The political risk rating was below the mid 50s until early 1993, after which the rating increased steadily until 1998 and followed a generally decreasing trend until late 2003, followed by an increasing trend to 2005. From 1993, there was a discernable increase in the associated volatility, with a number of peaks and extreme observations. Joaquin Balaguer, elected president in 1966 and leader of the Christian Social Reform Party, dominated politics for much of the following 30 years. He was re-elected in 1994, but agreed to serve only a two-year term after being accused of fraud. Since 1996, regular competitive elections have been held, in which opposition candidates have won the presidency. A serious concern for the Dominican Republic remains the growing immigration from, and political instability in, Haiti. In response, the government has re-evaluated its relations with its neighbour at both the country and international levels. In general, the composite risk rating reflects the trends and volatility in the economic, financial and political risk ratings.

Figure 7.5 presents the risk ratings, risk returns and their associated volatility for Haiti, one of the poorest countries in the Americas. Haiti has been plagued by political instability, violence, poverty, unemployment, migration, and environmental degradation for much of its history since independence in 1804. Especially since the 1980s, these factors have led to economic stagnation and damaged Haiti's image as a major tourist destination. The country's infrastructure has deteriorated, and drug trafficking has corrupted both the judicial system and police force. There was a slight upward trend in the economic risk rating over the sample period, with discernable clusterings of volatility and volatility peaks. A military coup in 1991 led to a sharp fall in the economic risk rating, which rose in 1992. However, after 1999, the rating fell consistently, reaching the low 40s by late 2004, but rose to the low 50s by 2005. Following serious irregularities in the 2000 legislative elections, international donors such as the USA and EU suspended almost all aid to Haiti, leading to a significant contraction in the economy. Surprisingly, despite inadequate economic and financial reforms and slow economic progress after 1991, the financial risk rating had a rising trend after 1990, reaching the mid 60s in 2005. There was a noticeable associated volatility throughout the sample period. As with the financial risk rating, the political risk rating had an increasing trend after 1990, with discernable volatility after 1987 and peaks in 1987, 1993, 1994 and 2004. The index fell to the low 20s by early 2004 but rose to the high 30s by 2005, reflecting a high associated political risk. More than three decades of dictatorship, followed by a military regime, ended in 1990 when Jean-Bertrand Aristide was elected president. Aristide was ousted in a 1991 military coup, which triggered sanctions by the USA and the Organisation of American States. He returned to office in 1994, after the military regime had relinquished power and US troops landed peacefully to oversee the transition to civilian government. Aristide won a second term as president in 2000, and took office early in 2001. However, a political crisis stemming from fraudulent legislative elections in 2000 remained unresolved by the end of the sample period. In general, the composite risk rating reflects the trends and volatility in the financial and political risk ratings.

The four risk ratings, risk returns and associated volatility for Jamaica are given in Figure 7.6. Although a politically stable country, Jamaica does not enjoy social and economic harmony, with both luxurious tourist resorts and densely populated and impoverished ghettos. Deteriorating economic conditions during the 1970s led to recurrent violence and a fall in tourism. The Jamaican economy depends heavily on tourism and bauxite, and has the potential for growth and modernization despite widespread crime and poverty. There was a general rising trend in the economic risk rating, with discernable volatility and peaks throughout the sample period. The rating fell considerably during 1988–1992 and 1996–2000, after which it rose by almost 10 points, remained low in the mid 60s to 2003, and fell to the mid 50s by 2005. After five years of recession, the economic performance improved in 2000, but the global economic slowdown and the events of 11 September, 2001 hampered the economic recovery. The financial risk rating had a generally rising trend to 1996, after which the index fell by more than 10 points and remained flat in the low 70s. There was a discernable clustering of volatility and peaks after 1997. High interest rates, increased foreign competition, an unstable exchange rate, and an increasing merchandise trade deficit still remain unresolved. Government bailouts to various ailing sectors of the economy, particularly the financial sector, have resulted in a growing internal debt. Economic progress depends upon encouraging investment and tourism, maintaining a competitive exchange rate, selling off reacquired firms, and implementing proper fiscal and monetary policies. Jamaica gained full independence within the British Commonwealth in 1962. The political risk rating fell until 1986, rose to the low 80s in 1998, and fell to the high 60s in 2005, with a noticeable clustering of volatility and an associated peak in 1997. Since the 1980s, subsequent governments have supported open market reforms, but political violence marred elections during the 1990s. The government has occasionally deployed army units to suppress violent crime, with more than 1000 murders reported in 2002. Moreover, there have been accusations of extrajudicial killings by law enforcers. Overall, the composite risk rating closely reflects the trends and volatility associated with the financial and political risk ratings.

Figure 7.7 presents the four risk ratings, risk returns and their associated volatilities for Malta. With a small domestic market, Malta's economic development is based on tourism promotion and exports of manufactured goods. Malta's population is tripled by tourist arrivals every year. Since the early 1990s, expansion in these two sectors has been the main engine for strong economic growth. Malta is privatizing state-controlled firms and liberalising markets in order to prepare for membership of the European Union in 2004. However, the island remains politically divided over the question of joining the EU. Moreover, the slowdown in the global economy is holding back exports and tourism. Prior to 1997, the economic risk ratings varied around the mid 80s, with little associated volatility. The rating fell by almost 20 points after 1997, with a volatility peak, increased until early 2000, followed a generally falling trend to the mid 60s in 2002, but rose substantially by 2005, especially due to the 2004 EU membership. Unlike the economic risk rating, the financial risk rating had a generally rising trend to 1997, after which the index fell by almost 15 points, followed a slight declining trend to the mid 60s in 2002, and increased slightly after 2004. There was little or no volatility throughout the sample period, with two peaks in 1991 and 1997. The fiscal situation remains difficult despite some progress in consolidating public finances. In 1998 the budget deficit reached a level of 10 per cent of GDP. The deficit decreased in 2002, primarily through higher tax rates and improved tax collection. Current expenditures, which were reduced in the late 1990s, increased in 2002 due to the public sector wage bill and subsidies to public enterprises. Formally acquired by Great Britain in 1814, the island strongly supported the UK through both World Wars and remained in the Commonwealth until independence in 1964. Malta became a republic one decade later. Prior to 1991, the political risk rating was flat in the low 50s, after which the index followed a generally increasing trend reaching the high 80s in 2005. There was little or no volatility throughout the sample period, with two peaks in 1991. Two parties dominate Malta's politics, namely the Nationalist Party and the Malta Labour Party. Eddie Fenech Adami's Nationalist Party returned to power in 1998 and revived the application to enter the EU. Overall, the composite risk rating closely reflects the trends and volatility in the financial and political risk ratings.

7.5   EMPIRICAL EVALUATION

This section discusses empirical results obtained from estimating alternative models of volatility, namely the GARCH and GJR models, of the logarithmic difference in country risk ratings, or risk returns. These models have been extensively discussed in Chapter 5. All the estimates in this chapter are obtained using EViews 5.0. The Berndt, Hall, Hall and Hausman (BHHH) (Berndt et al., 1974) algorithm has been used in most cases, but the Marquardt algorithm is used when the BHHH algorithm does not converge.

Risk returns and volatilities for the six SITEs are estimated using the univariate AR(1)-GARCH(1,1) and AR(1)-GJR(1,1) models. The monthly ICRG data for the Bahamas and Cyprus are available from December 1984 to April 2005, Dominican Republic, Haiti and Jamaica from January 1984 to April 2005, and Malta from April 1986 to April 2005.

Univariate GARCH(1,1) and GJR(1,1) estimates for the six SITEs are presented in Tables 7.3 to 7.14, and are summarised in Table 7.15. The second moment conditions for the AR(1)-GARCH(1,1) and AR(1)-GJR(1,1) models in Tables 7.3 to 7.15 are the empirical versions of (5.5) and (5.11), respectively, while the log-moment conditions are the empirical versions of (5.6) and (5.12), respectively. Asymptotic and robust *t*-ratios are reported for the QMLE in Tables 7.3 to 7.14 (see Bollerslev and Wooldridge, 1992).

As reported in Table 7.15, the short-run persistence, α_i, and the contribution of the shocks to the long-run persistence, β_i, are positive fractions in 12 and 17 cases, respectively, for the GARCH(1,1) model. There are nine cases, namely the Bahamas, Cyprus, Dominican Republic, Haiti and Malta for economic risk returns, Jamaica for financial risk returns, the Bahamas and Malta for political risk returns, and Haiti for composite risk return, where both the α_i and β_i estimates are positive fractions. In these cases, the short-run persistence of previous shocks on risk returns is smaller than the contribution of these shocks to the long-run persistence. The log-moment condition is satisfied in 23 of 24 cases, while the second moment condition is satisfied 20 times. Only in the case of Dominican Republic for political risk returns are both the second and long-moment conditions not satisfied. Except for this case, the consistency and asymptotic normality of the QMLE are guaranteed, even in the presence of infinite second moments. Generally, the log-moment condition is satisfied when the second moment condition is not, and the second moment condition is satisfied for all cases when the log-moment condition could not be computed.

For the GJR(1,1) model, only of the 24 γ_i estimates are significant. The average short-run persistence $\alpha_i + (\gamma_i / 2)$ and the contribution of shocks to long-run persistence β_i estimates are positive fractions in 13 and 21 cases, respectively. Specifically, the $\alpha_i + (\gamma_i / 2)$ and β_i estimates are both positive fractions in 11 cases, namely the Bahamas for economic and political risk returns, Haiti for all four risk returns, and Jamaica for economic, financial and composite risk returns. In general, the short-run persistence of the shocks in these risk returns is lower than the contribution of the shocks to long-run persistence. Of the six significant γ_i estimates, those for the Bahamas for composite risk returns, Cyprus for economic risk returns, Haiti for political and composite risk returns are positive, while the estimates for the Dominican Republic for political risk returns and for Malta for economic risk returns are negative. This implies that the short-run and long-run effects of a

Table 7.3   Univariate GARCH(1,1) Estimates of Risk Returns for Bahamas

Risk Return	ω	α	β	Moment	
				Log	Second
Economic	1.3E–04	0.099	0.371	–0.845	0.470
	2.790	1.720	1.390		
	0.757	1.428	0.541		
Financial	2.9E–04	–0.011	0.570	–0.585	0.559
	–2.519	–4.375	1.240		
	–0.014	–0.081	1.879		
Political	1.3E–05	0.911	0.350	–0.794	1.210
	7.730	3.373	5.357		
	1.490	1.212	2.555		
Composite	2.7E–05	–0.021	0.583	–0.582	0.520
	1.042	–1.489	1.429		
	24.270	–0.878	4.105		

Table 7.4   Univariate GJR(1,1) Estimates of Risk Returns for Bahamas

Risk Return	ω	α	γ	β	$\alpha+\gamma/2$	Moment	
						Log	Second
Economic	9.3E–05	–0.037	0.122	0.020	0.024	–0.491	0.2
	1.980	–1.090	1.500	2.030			
	77.314	–0.779	0.943	5.490			
Financial	3.0E–04	0.000	–0.011	0.572	–0.00	–0.51	0.5
	0.707	–0.004	–0.347	0.940			
	9.819	–0.005	–0.042	2.930			
Political	–8.0E–08	0.044	0.291	0.094	0.189	0.010	0.283
	–0.000	0.847	1.797	3.945			
	–0.013	1.900	1.850	1.020			
Composite	2.9E–05	–0.041	0.020	0.579	–0.031	–0.581	0.548
	1.144	–4.515	0.574	1.540			
	148.200	–2.130	1.932	4.940			

Note: The three entries for each parameter are their respective estimate, the asymptotic *t*-ratio and the Bollerslev-Wooldridge (1992) robust *t*-ratio.

Table 7.5 Univariate GARCH(1,1) Estimates of Risk Returns for Cyprus

Risk Return	ω	α	β	Moment Log	Second
Economic	1.1E–05	0.140	0.843	–0.00	0.989
	4.339	0.510	51.371		
	1.099	1.832	11.508		
Financial	5.9E–0	–0.019	1.000	–0.049	0.987
	13.973	–29.724	473.90		
	7.484	–0.978	31.341		
Political	1.4E–05	–0.020	0.920	–0.04	0.942
	5.007	–4.879	87.355		
	1.850	–1.555	31.230		
Composite	8.1E–07	–0.021	1.013	–0.010	0.992
	1.982	–7.883	777.95		
	0.872	–1.12	5.004		

Table 7.6 Univariate GJR(1,1) Estimates of Risk Returns for Cyprus

Risk Return	ω	α	γ	β	$\alpha + \gamma/2$	Moment Log	Second
Economic	4.8E–05	–0.042	0.411	0.805	0.130	–0.14	0.980
	2.890	–9.817	2.788	12.539			
	4.800	–1.380	2.091	22.732			
Financial	1.1E–05	–0.021	0.010	0.981	–0.013	–0.048	0.970
	10.913	–15.823	4.752	27.517			
	2.472	–0.305	0.324	1.480			
Political	7.9E–05	0.001	–0.093	0.715	–0.040	–0.372	0.700
	4.383	0.041	–5.171	9.744			
	11.738	0.024	–1.200	9.921			
Composite	5.7E–05	–0.021	0.058	0.540	0.008	–0.15	0.549
	0.31	–0.558	0.810	0.739			
	4.739	–0.502	0.572	5.440			

Note: The three entries for each parameter are their respective estimate, the asymptotic *t*-ratio and the Bollerslev-Wooldridge (1992) robust *t*-ratio.

Table 7.7   Univariate GARCH(1,1) Estimates of Risk Returns for Dominican Republic

Risk Return	ω	α	β	Moment	
				Log	Second
Economic	9.8E–05	0.020	0.90	–0.075	0.932
	1.222	1.455	12.130		
	0.314	0.917	4.155		
Financial	1.4E–03	0.233	–0.210	–1.537	0.023
	11.053	2.790	–2.704		
	3.912	2.071	–1.85		
Political	–.2E–07	–0.007	1.008	0.002	1.002
	–2.171	–3.373	59.011		
	–0.402	–0.431	7.73		
Composite	1.1E–04	–0.022	0.23	–0.500	0.01
	0.725	–0.734	1.180		
	10.459	–0.705	7.347		

Table 7.8   Univariate GJR(1,1) Estimates of Risk Returns for Dominican Republic

Risk Return	ω	α	γ	β	$\alpha + \gamma/2$	Moment	
						Log	Second
Economic	1.8E–03	0.219	–0.188	–0.191	0.125	–1.780	–0.0
	8.975	2.215	–1.982	–1.580			
	2.255	0.725	–0.480	–0.743			
Financial	1.1E–03	0.223	0.119	–0.181	0.283	–1.13	0.102
	13.102	4.190	0.922	–2.590			
	13.438	1.730	0.454	–1.874			
Political	9.5E–05	–0.041	–0.031	0.578	–0.057	–0.1	0.521
	9.189	–10.073	–5.170	11.57			
	2.080	–8.245	–11.75	12.15			
Composite	8.1E–05	–0.052	0.030	0.738	–0.037	–0.37	0.700
	2.003	–2.912	1.950	5.339			
	29.125	–2.805	0.220	9.530			

Note: The three entries for each parameter are their respective estimate, the asymptotic t-ratio and the Bollerslev-Wooldridge (1992) robust t-ratio.

Table 7.9   Univariate GARCH(1,1) Estimates of Risk Returns for Haiti

Risk Return	ω	α	β	Moment	
				Log	Second
Economic	2.7E–04	0.133	0.714	–0.219	0.847
	3.22	3.232	10.310		
	0.750	1.4	2.444		
Financial	5.2E–03	–0.051	–0.733	–0.271	–0.784
	9.030	–8.597	–5.028		
	5.582	–5.571	–4.15		
Political	3.5E–03	0.2	–0.195	–1.704	0.070
	10.942	3.003	–2.008		
	1.520	1.581	–1.135		
Composite	3.7E–04	0.20	0.377	–0.5	0.37
	2.882	2.837	1.994		
	1.939	1.871	2.302		

Table 7.10   Univariate GJR(1,1) Estimates of Risk Returns for Haiti

Risk Return	ω	α	γ	β	$\alpha+\gamma/2$	Moment	
						Log	Second
Economic	1.8E–04	–0.051	0.250	0.839	0.074	–0.134	0.913
	3.15	–27.707	5.002	17.143			
	13.991	–0.948	1.474	21.32			
Financial	0.001	0.055	0.19	0.528	0.029	–0.40	0.557
	3.073	–21.989	2.290	3.327			
	1.414	–4.93	1.01	1.528			
Political	0.002	–0.093	0.275	0.542	0.044	–0.0	0.58
	2.534	–2.84	2.14	3.023			
	2.370	–3.513	2.482	2.499			
Composite	4.8E–04	–0.058	0.423	0.488	0.154	–0.43	0.42
	4.075	–8.750	2.429	4.008			
	3.180	–1.07	2.354	4.789			

Note: The three entries for each parameter are their respective estimate, the asymptotic *t*-ratio and the Bollerslev-Wooldridge (1992) robust *t*-ratio.

Table 7.11　Univariate GARCH(1,1) Estimates of Risk Returns for Jamaica

Risk Return	ω	α	β	Moment	
				Log	Second
Economic	1.2E–04	–0.030	0.947	–0.099	0.917
	5.054	–7.575	4.438		
	2.112	–2.312	43.49		
Financial	0.2E–05	0.081	0.78	–0.187	0.849
	3.059	2.739	10.741		
	0.723	1.188	3.33		
Political	1.4E–04	–0.025	0.138	–2.148	0.113
	1.53	–0.80	0.2		
	0.39	–4.357	0.01		
Composite	2.9E–04	0.07	–0.924	–0.183	–0.857
	17.82	5.052	–45.28		
	5.994	4.014	–23.981		

Table 7.12　Univariate GJR(1,1) Estimates of Risk Returns for Jamaica

Risk Return	ω	α	γ	β	$\alpha+\gamma/2$	Moment	
						Log	Second
Economic	1.7E–03	0.093	–0.135	0.194	0.025	–1.150	0.219
	0.917	0.92	–.249	0.223			
	1.792	0.500	–0.738	0.424			
Financial	5.5E–05	0.08	0.015	0.790	0.075	–0.15	0.8
	2.821	2.042	0.480	11.318			
	0.711	0.987	0.150	3.779			
Political	2.2E–07	–0.010	–0.012	1.015	–0.01	–0.005	0.999
	0.483	–5.14	–1.849	34.772			
	0.235	–0.205	–0.332	15.471			
Composite	0.3E–05	0.118	–0.178	0.300	0.029	–0.455	0.590
	1.739	3.47	–2.109	3.127			
	1.039	0.955	–1.140	1.815			

Note:　The three entries for each parameter are their respective estimate, the asymptotic *t*-ratio and the Bollerslev-Wooldridge (1992) robust *t*-ratio.

Table 7.13   Univariate GARCH(1,1) Estimates of Risk Returns for Malta

Risk Return	ω	α	β	Moment	
				Log	Second
Economic	1.1E–05	0.048	0.932	–0.03	0.980
	0.139	7.500	10.842		
	0.490	0.880	10.509		
Financial	2.0E–05	–0.013	0.990	–0.053	0.95
	7.794	–12.397	17.10		
	2.57	–0.255	14.90		
Political	2.0E–05	0.048	0.891	–0.088	0.939
	3.375	2.540	2.093		
	1.025	0.582	25.104		
Composite	4.3E–0	–0.011	0.989	–0.027	0.979
	15.870	–9.950	3.541		
	1.11	–0.793	42.03		

Table 7.14   Univariate GJR(1,1) Estimates of Risk Returns for Malta

Risk Return	ω	α	γ	β	$\alpha+\gamma/2$	Moment	
						Log	Second
Economic	1.2E–04	3.877	–3.812	0.272	1.971	–0.840	2.243
	10.759	4.877	–4.934	5.091			
	1.918	1.881	–1.852	2.04			
Financial	2.2E–04	–0.011	–0.013	0.552	–0.018	–0.05	0.534
	0.77	–0.503	–0.344	0.943			
	1.491	–2.08	–1.598	1.17			
Political	1.5E–04	–0.014	–0.020	0.28	–0.024	–0.479	0.05
	1.590	–2.171	–0.139	2.571			
	337.174	–1.520	–0.050	3.577			
Composite	7.8E–05	–0.011	–0.022	0.579	–0.022	–0.50	0.557
	0.39	–0.05	–0.73	0.87			
	4.858	–1.717	–0.051	1.959			

Note: The three entries for each parameter are their respective estimate, the asymptotic *t*-ratio and the Bollerslev-Wooldridge (1992) robust *t*-ratio.

Table 7.15   Summary of Univariate GARCH(1,1) and GJR(1,1) Estimates for six SITEs

Regularity conditions	GARCH(1,1)	GJR(1,1)
$\alpha > 0$	12	.
$\alpha + \gamma/2 > 0$	.	13
$\beta > 0$	17	21
$\gamma \neq 0$	.	6
Log-moment satisfied	23	23
Second moment satisfied	20	22

Notes:
The figures relate to four risk returns for six SITEs, giving a total of 24 combinations.
Although the second moment condition implies the log-moment condition, the latter could not be computed in 14 and 15 cases for GARCH(1,1) and GJR(1,1), respectively.

Table 7.16   Preferred Models for 6 SITEs by Risk Returns

SITE	Risk Return			
	Economic	Financial	Political	Composite
The Bahamas	GARCH	GARCH	GARCH	GARCH*
Cyprus	GJR	X	GARCH	GJR*
Dominican Republic	GARCH	X	X	GARCH
Haiti	GARCH	GJR*	GJR	GJR
Jamaica	GJR*	GARCH	X	GJR*
Malta	GARCH*	GARCH	GARCH	GARCH

Notes:
GJR* refers to cases when the γ estimate of asymmetry for a particular risk return was insignificant, but the GJR(1,1) estimates were superior to their GARCH(1,1) counterparts.
X refers to cases when neither model was preferred.

negative shock in the political (economic) risk returns will result in less uncertainty in subsequent periods for the Dominican Republic (Malta). For the GJR(1,1) model, the log-moment condition is satisfied 23 times and the second moment condition is satisfied 22 times. In all cases either one of the two regularity conditions is satisfied, which implied that the consistency and asymptotic normality of the QMLE are guaranteed in all cases, even in the presence of infinite second moments.

Table 7.17 reports the preferred model for the six SITEs by risk return. For economic risk returns, GARCH(1,1) is superior to GJR(1,1) for the Bahamas, Dominican Republic, Haiti and Malta, even though the γ estimate for the

Table 7.17   GARCH(1,1) Conditional Correlations for six SITEs by Risk Returns

Economic Risk Returns	Bahamas	Dominican Republic	Cyprus	Haiti	Jamaica	Malta
Bahamas	1					
Dominican Rep.	**0.251**	1				
Cyprus	−0.008	0.113	1			
Haiti	−0.129	−0.025	0.011	1		
Jamaica	0.110	0.047	**−0.211**	0.116	1	
Malta	**0.305**	0.196	0.102	−0.164	−0.075	1

Financial Risk Returns	Bahamas	Dominican Republic	Cyprus	Haiti	Jamaica	Malta
Bahamas	1					
Dominican Rep.	0.016	1				
Cyprus	−0.113	−0.072	1			
Haiti	−0.083	−0.081	**0.321**	1		
Jamaica	0.109	**0.262**	−0.155	−0.086	1	
Malta	0.045	**0.665**	−0.085	−0.159	**0.216**	1

Political Risk Returns	Bahamas	Dominican Republic	Cyprus	Haiti	Jamaica	Malta
Bahamas	1					
Dominican Rep.	0.104	1				
Cyprus	**0.236**	0.070	1			
Haiti	−0.076	−0.021	0.126	1		
Jamaica	0.133	0.186	**0.201**	0.082	1	
Malta	0.085	**0.227**	0.071	0.040	0.107	1

Composite Risk Returns	Bahamas	Dominican Republic	Cyprus	Haiti	Jamaica	Malta
Bahamas	1					
Dominican Rep.	0.097	1				
Cyprus	−0.088	0.053	1			
Haiti	−0.040	−0.048	**0.240**	1		
Jamaica	0.174	0.122	0.014	0.112	1	
Malta	0.179	**0.424**	0.118	−0.122	0.123	1

Bahamas is significant. GJR(1,1) model is preferred for Cyprus and Jamaica, even though the γ estimate for the Jamaica is insignificant.

For financial risk returns, the GARCH(1,1) model is preferred only for Jamaica, and neither model is favoured for Malta. Overall, the GARCH(1,1) model is superior to GJR(1,1) model for the Bahamas, Jamaica and Malta, while neither model is preferred for Cyprus and Dominican Republic. For Haiti, GJR(1,1) is preferred even though the γ estimate is insignificant.

Similarly, GARCH(1,1) is the preferred model for political risk returns for the Bahamas, Cyprus and Malta, while neither model is appropriate for Dominican Republic and Jamaica. GJR(1,1) is preferred only for Haiti.

The two models are equally preferred for composite risk returns. GARCH(1,1) is preferred in three cases, namely the Bahamas, Dominican Republic and Malta, even though the γ_i estimate for the Bahamas is significant. For the other three cases, namely Cyprus, Haiti and Jamaica, GJR(1,1) is the preferred model although the γ_i estimates for Cyprus and Jamaica are insignificant.

Overall, for the six SITEs, the GARCH(1,1) model is suitable in 13 cases (even though the γ_i estimates in two cases were significant), the GJR(1,1) model is suitable in seven cases, and neither model is preferred in four cases.

In summary, the empirical results show that the univariate GARCH(1,1) and GJR(1,1) estimates are statistically adequate for the six SITEs. The regularity conditions are typically satisfied, with the conditions regarding β_i (the contribution to long-run persistence) and second moments satisfied in a high proportion of cases. Either GARCH(1,1) or GJR(1,1) is found to be statistically adequate in 20 of 24 cases. One of the two volatility models is determined as being adequate for all six SITEs for economic and composite risk returns, and in four of six cases for financial and political risk returns.

Overall, the empirical results reported in Tables 7.3–7.16 permitted a distinction to be made between the short- and long-run persistence of shocks to economic, financial, political and composite risk returns for the six SITEs. These results imply that shocks to the economic, financial, political and composite risk returns for the six SITEs have only long-run persistence, with shock effects that accumulate over time without an immediate impact. This is an important finding for policy makers in the economic, financial and political sectors of the countries. In drawing up policy prescriptions, emphasis should be given to the long-run aspects of the economic, financial and political components of country risk for the six SITEs.

Moreover, shocks to country risk returns in one SITE can affect country risk returns in another SITE. The magnitude of such an affect can be quantified by the degree of correlation of such shocks to country risk returns across SITEs. This permits a classification of SITEs according to volatility in economic, financial, political and composite risk returns.

Using the estimated standardised shocks to the four risk returns for the six SITEs obtained from the preferred GARCH(1,1) model, the conditional correlations for these series are calculated and reported in Table 7.17. It is clear that the conditional correlations between the six SITEs for the four risk returns are generally very low, indicating independence of risk return shocks across SITEs. They can be positive or negative and range from –0.211 to 0.305 for economic risk returns, –0.159 to 0.665 for financial risk returns, –0.076 to 0.236 for political risk returns, and –0.122 to 0.424 for composite risk returns.

Of the correlation coefficients that are higher than 0.200 in absolute value for economic risk returns, the highest correlation holds for Bahamas, Malta at 0.305, followed by Bahamas, Dominican Republic at 0.251, and Cyprus, Jamaica at –0.211. There are four country pairs with conditional correlations higher than 0.200 for financial risk returns, namely Dominican Republic, Malta at 0.665, Cyprus, Haiti at 0.321, Dominican Republic, Jamaica at 0.262, and Jamaica, Malta at 0.216. For political risk returns, Bahamas, Cyprus have the highest correlation at 0.236, followed by Dominican Republic, Malta at 0.227 and Cyprus, Malta at 0.201. Only two conditional correlation pairs are higher than 0.200 for the composite risk returns, namely Dominican Republic, Malta at 0.424 and Cyprus, Haiti at 0.240. This suggests that the degree of relationship between country risk return shocks across the six SITEs is highly independent. Such issues have not been previously examined in the country risk literature for SITEs.

7.6 CONCLUSION

This chapter provided a comparison of country risk ratings, risk returns and associated volatilities for six Small Island Tourism Economies (SITEs) for which monthly ICRG data were available. Aspects of country risk assessment, with particular emphasis on the ICRG rating system regarding economic, financial, political and composite risk ratings, were discussed in detail. For each of the six SITEs, the trends and associated volatility of the four country risk ratings and risk returns were analysed according to economic, financial and political environments in the country. There were substantial differences in the trends of the risk ratings, risk returns and their associated volatilities.

Monthly ICRG risk returns were used to estimate symmetric and asymmetric models of univariate conditional volatility. The empirical results showed that the univariate GARCH(1,1) and GJR(1,1) models are statistically adequate for the six SITEs. The regularity conditions were typically satisfied, with the conditions regarding the contribution to long-run persistence and second moments satisfied in a high proportion of cases. Either GARCH(1,1) or GJR(1,1) was found to be statistically adequate in 20 of 24 cases. This was a particularly strong empirical finding, especially as these models of volatility have not been customized for any particular SITE, but have been applied generically to all six SITEs.

The empirical results implied that shocks to the economic, financial, political and composite risk returns for the six SITEs have only long-run persistence, with shock effects that accumulate over time without an immediate impact. This is an important finding for policy makers in the economic, financial and political sectors of the countries. In drawing up policy prescriptions, emphasis should be given to the long-run aspects of the economic, financial and political components of country risk for the six SITEs.

In general, conditional correlation coefficients for the four risk returns across the six SITEs were found to be very low, indicating independence of risk return shocks across the SITEs. In cases where the correlation coefficients were above 0.200, the degree of relationship between country risk return shocks varied substantially across the six SITEs. Such issues have not been previously examined in the country risk literature for SITEs.

REFERENCES

BBC News (2004), *Country Profiles and Timeline*, http://news.bbc.co.uk/1/shared/bsp/hi/country_profiles/html/default.stm [last accessed: May 2007].

Berndt, E.K., B.H. Hall, R.E. Hall and J.A. Hausman (1974), 'Estimation and inference in nonlinear structural models', *Annals of Economic and Social Measurement*, **3**, 53–56.

Bollerslev, T. and J.M. Wooldridge (1992), 'Quasi-maximum likelihood estimation and inference in dynamic models with time-varying covariances', *Econometric Reviews*, **11**, 143–73.

Brewer, T.L. and P. Rivoli (1990), 'Politics and perceived country creditworthiness in international banking', *Journal of Money, Credit and Banking*, **22**, 357–96.

Burton, F.N. and H. Inoue (1985), 'An appraisal of the early-warning indicators of sovereign loan default in country risk evaluation systems', *Management International Review*, **25**, 45–56.

Central Intelligence Agency (2004), *The World Factbook 2004*, http://www.odci.gov/cia/publications/factbook/index.html [last accessed: May 2007].

Hoti, S. (2005), 'Modelling country spillover effects in country risk ratings', *Emerging Markets Review*, **6**, 324–45.

Hoti, S. and M. McAleer (2004), 'An empirical assessment of country risk ratings and associated models', *Journal of Economic Surveys*, **18**(4), 539–88.

Hoti, S. and M. McAleer (2005a), *Modelling the Riskiness in Country Risk Ratings*, Contributions to Economic Analysis Series, Volume 273, Amsterdam: Elsevier.

Hoti, S. and M. McAleer (2005b), 'Modelling spillover effects for country risk ratings and returns', *Risk Letters*, **1**, 11–17.

Hoti, S., M. McAleer and R. Shareef (2005), 'Modelling country risk and uncertainty in small island tourism economies', *Tourism Economics*, **11**(2), 159–83.

Hoti, S., M. McAleer and R. Shareef (2007), 'Modelling international tourism and country risk spillovers for Cyprus and Malta', to appear in *Tourism Management*.

Krayenbuehl, T.E. (1985), *Country Risk: Assessment and Monitoring*, Toronto: Lexington Books.

McAleer, M., S. Hoti and F. Chan (2008), 'Structure and asymptotic theory for multivariate asymmetric conditional volatility', to appear in *Econometric Reviews*.

Shareef, R. and S. Hoti (2005), 'Small island tourism economies and country risk ratings', *Mathematics and Computers in Simulation*, **68**, 557–70.

The Economist (2004), *Country Briefings*, http://www.economist.com/countries/ [last accessed: May 2007].

US Department of State (2004), Countries and Regions, http://www.state.gov/countries/ [last accessed: May 2007].

8. Conclusion

8.1 SUMMARY OF THE MONOGRAPH

The aim of this monograph was to analyse the conditional volatility of monthly international tourist arrivals to SITEs in a univariate and multivariate framework. The most important characteristics of SITEs were examined in Chapter 2, while taking account of the implications for economic development. The common size measures given in Table 2.1 clearly showed that the most prominent feature of these economies is that they are small. SITEs are well known for having a limited productive base and small domestic markets. Many of these SITEs are necessarily and relatively undiversified in their production of exports. SITEs face difficulties when they need to respond to any changing external circumstances because there is a capacity constraint in the private sector. To address this problem, SITEs have to rely considerably on international trade and FDI. This is beneficial in terms of gaining access to international competition and to new ideas.

SITEs do not have developed capital markets domestically, and so they need to gain access to international capital markets to hedge against adverse external shocks and the profound volatility of GDP growth. SITEs are considered risky entities, so that it can become very costly and difficult for them to gain access to private international capital markets.

The efforts of SITEs to exploit economies of scale and to diversify their productive base within their small domestic markets does not necessarily imply that these SITEs have smaller per capita GDP, or an exceptionally low record on economic growth. SITEs may be better off relative to larger developing countries because of their per capita natural resource abundance, with the best example being the development of tourism. In this regard, the disadvantage of being small is offset by the higher per capita natural resource abundance. In SITEs, social indicators tend to be higher relative to larger developing countries. They tend to have higher formal education attainment, better health care facilities, and access to safe drinking water, as well as other advantages. This is a clear reflection of sound domestic social policies.

Being former colonies of some of the Group of 7 countries, the most noticeable advantage for these economies has been in the post-colonial era, where they benefited from relatively high inflows of official development assistance. These were mostly in the form of grants-in-kind, where SITEs did not have any obligation to repay funding. This inflow of aid has been relatively high in per capita terms, and has been skewed primarily towards the advancement of social infrastructure, such as schools and hospitals. This inflow of official assistance also explains their economic development records.

If we compare the economic well-being of SITEs with larger developing countries, there are substantially qualitative differences in the per capita incomes and economic growth rates between SITEs and other relatively large developing countries. One possible explanation for this outcome is that SITEs have relatively large natural resource abundance, which fosters tourism and offsets the inherent disadvantages of being small.

Chapter 3 evaluated published empirical research with reference to the frequency of data used, choice of both dependent and explanatory variables, use of proxy variables, type of model chosen, economic hypotheses tested, methods of estimation and calculation of standard errors for inference, reported descriptive statistics, use of diagnostic tests of auxiliary assumptions, use of information criteria and empirical implications for tourism demand.

Compared with recent surveys of empirical examination in tourism analysis, particularly Lim (1997), there is evidence to show that substantial changes have occurred in reporting empirical results. Of the 53 papers examined in Chapter 3, nine and three papers failed to report diagnostic tests and descriptive statistics, respectively. Lim (1997) highlighted concern over the 100 papers surveyed of failing to report diagnostic tests and descriptive statistics, such that inferences regarding those results should be made with caution. From the findings in Chapter 3, the assertion made in Lim (1997) seems to have been well received in the tourism research community.

In Chapter 3, relatively high frequency of applications of recently innovated techniques such as cointegration, ECM and Artificial Neural Networks, is observed. Furthermore, the traditional empirical tourism analysis of single destination and single tourism source country only appeared in two papers. The most widely used analytical setting is single destination and multiple tourism source countries, and such analyses are enabled through the availability of comprehensive data sets maintained by destination countries. This indicates the importance of empirical tourism analysis for individual economies since greater emphasis has been given to the tourism industry than ever before. There has been substantial empirical research in tourism analysis over the period 1995–2003, and significant progress has been achieved in application and presentation of empirical results, as compared with the recent surveys conducted.

Detailed country economic profiles of 20 SITEs were presented Chapter 4. It was evident from the descriptions given that the large proportion of these SITEs was dependent on agriculture, now they have diversified their economies to more service-oriented and tourism-dependent economies. Tourism development requires substantial financial capital, but only requires unskilled or semi-skilled labour. Therefore, in these SITEs it is relatively easy to expand tourism development if it is well managed. Hence, in most of these SITEs tourism is the predominant economic activity. The composition of tourist arrivals in these SITEs is mainly from the world's richest nations that are geographically located in the temperate zone. The most widely travelled tourists are from the UK, visiting all of the 20 SITEs. The relative cross-correlation coefficients of monthly international tourist arrivals showed that the six SITEs, namely Barbados, Cyprus, Dominica, Fiji, Maldives and Seychelles, are complementary destinations as far as total monthly international tourist arrivals are concerned. However, when the monthly arrivals from eleven different tourist source markets to these six economies are examined separately, some markets consider these SITEs as substitutes as well as complements. Furthermore, when international tourism receipts for the 20 SITEs are considered together, all SITEs except Haiti are complements.

The most recent theoretical results for the univariate GARCH models of conditional volatility developed by Engle (1982), subsequent developments by Bollerslev (1990), and the recently developed constant conditional correlation VARMA-GARCH model of Ling and McAleer (2003) and VARMA-AGARCH model of McAleer et al. (2008), were presented in Chapter 5.

The associated volatilities of the logarithms of monthly international tourist arrivals, and the growth rate of monthly tourist arrivals, for seven SITEs, namely Barbados, Cyprus, Dominica, Fiji, Maldives, Malta and Seychelles, were also examined in Chapter 5. The conditional means of the logarithms of monthly international tourist arrivals and the growth rate of monthly international tourist arrivals were specified for each SITE as ARMA(p,q) models, with 12 monthly seasonal dummy variables in each case, and a combination of linear and quadratic time trends for the monthly tourism arrivals. Two models, namely GARCH(1,1) and GJR(1,1), were used to estimate the conditional volatility of the shocks to monthly international tourist arrivals to each of these SITEs. The constant conditional correlations for were estimated for the univariate GARCH(1,1) and GJR(1,1). Furthermore, the constant conditional correlation VARMA-GARCH(1,1) and VARMA-AGARCH(1,1) models were estimated for four separate samples, with two, three, four and five SITEs in each sample.

The estimates for the univariate analysis presented in Chapter 5 showed satisfactory results, particularly the GARCH(1,1) results for the logarithms and log-differences of monthly international tourist arrivals. Asymmetric models for Cyprus and Malta for the logarithms, and Dominica and Maldives for the log-differences, of monthly international tourist arrivals were preferable. For the rest, GARCH(1,1) was the preferred model. The empirical results presented in Tables 5.15–5.22 showed strong country effects as well as significant asymmetric behaviour that are worth noting. The results were mixed for the different sample periods. However, the empirical results that were presented in Tables 5.16 and 5.20, and estimated for the second longest sample for the 3 SITEs, namely Fiji, Malta and Seychelles, were preferred.

In Chapter 6, the uncertainty of monthly international tourist arrivals from the eight major tourist source countries to the Maldives was modelled using historical data. The empirical results provided a gauge to compare the conditional means and the conditional volatilities associated with monthly international tourist arrivals, logarithm of monthly international tourist arrivals, annual difference of monthly international tourist arrivals, and the log-difference of monthly international tourist arrivals. They also enabled validation of the regularity conditions underlying the model, and highlighted the importance of evaluating the uncertainties surrounding monthly international tourist arrivals. The results for the univariate ARMA(p,q)-GARCH(1,1) and ARMA(p,q)-GJR(1,1) models showed that the sufficient parametric conditions for the estimated uncertainties (specifically, that they should be positive) were satisfied, as were the moment conditions for the QML estimates to be consistent and asymptotically normal.

The estimated empirical results for the estimates of the ARMA(p,q)-GARCH(1,1) and ARMA(p,q)-GJR(1,1) models showed that there was a considerable degree of habit persistence and seasonality, particularly for the peak tourist season, which coincides with the European winter months. Moreover, the conditional variance estimates showed that there was a strong GARCH effect for all four series and a moderate ARCH effect for a selected number of series across the eight tourist source countries. There were no significant asymmetric effects in the monthly international tourist arrivals. The estimated static conditional correlations for monthly international tourist arrivals, as well as for the respective transformed series, were found to be significantly different from 0, but nevertheless relatively low. This indicates that the government of the Maldives and the major tour operators that organise tourist vacations have to emphasise their marketing efforts independently of each tourist source country.

A comparison of country risk ratings, risk returns and associated volatilities for six SITEs for which monthly ICRG data were available were presented in Chapter 7. Aspects of country risk assessment, with particular emphasis on the ICRG rating system regarding economic, financial, political and composite risk ratings, were discussed in detail. For each of the six SITEs, the trends and associated volatility of the four country risk ratings and risk returns were analysed according to economic, financial and political environments in the country. There were substantial differences in the trends of the risk ratings, risk returns and their associated volatilities.

Monthly ICRG risk returns were used to estimate symmetric and asymmetric models of univariate conditional volatility. The empirical results showed that the univariate GARCH(1,1) and GJR(1,1) models are statistically adequate for the six SITEs. The regularity conditions were typically satisfied, with the conditions regarding the contribution to long-run persistence and second moments satisfied in a high proportion of cases. In general, shocks to the economic, financial, political and composite risk returns for the six SITEs had only long-run persistence, with shock effects that accumulate over time without an immediate impact. This is an important finding for policy makers in the economic, financial and political sectors of the countries. In drawing up policy prescriptions, emphasis should be given to the long-run aspects of the economic, financial and political components of country risk for the six SITEs.

Moreover, conditional correlation coefficients for the four risk returns across the six SITEs were very low, indicating independence of risk return shocks across the SITEs. In cases where the correlation coefficients exceeded 0.200, the degree of relationship between country risk return shocks varied substantially across the six SITEs. Such issues have not been previously examined in the country risk literature for SITEs.

8.2   FURTHER RESEARCH

The research undertaken in this monograph can be extended in terms of the models presented in Chapter 5, as well as in new directions for research.

Extensions of Models

(i)   Estimation of univariate symmetric and asymmetric conditional volatility models using rolling and recursive estimations.
(ii) Estimation of multivariate symmetric and asymmetric conditional volatility models using rolling and recursive estimations.
(iii) Estimation of univariate and multivariate models of conditional volatility with complementary or alternative distributional assumptions regarding the standardised residuals.

New Directions for Research

(i)   Estimating the spillover effects between country risk and monthly international tourist arrivals for a number of SITEs.
(ii) Estimating conditional volatility simultaneously with incorporating an economic model of the conditional mean.

REFERENCES

Bollerslev, T. (1990) 'Modelling the coherence in short-run nominal exchange rate: A multivariate generalized ARCH approach', *Review of Economics and Statistics*, **72**, 498–505.

Engle, R.F. (1982) 'Autoregressive conditional heteroscedasticity with estimates of the variance of United Kingdom inflation', *Econometrica*, **50**, 987–1007.

Lim, C. (1997) 'Review of international tourism demand models', *Annals of Tourism Research*, **24**(4), 835–49.

Ling, S. and M. McAleer (2003) 'Asymptotic theory for a vector ARMA-GARCH model', *Econometric Theory*, **19**, 278–308.

McAleer, M., S. Hoti and F. Chan (2008) 'Structure and asymptotic theory for multivariate asymmetric conditional volatility', *Econometric Reviews*, forthcoming.

Index